THE NATURE AND ORIGINS OF MASS OPINION

THE NATURE AND ORIGINS
OF MASS OPINION

JOHN R. ZALLER

University of California, Los Angeles

CAMBRIDGE
UNIVERSITY PRESS

Published by the Press Syndicate of the University of Cambridge
The Pitt Building, Trumpington Street, Cambridge CB2 1RP
40 West 20th Street, New York, NY 10011-4211, USA
10 Stamford Road, Oakleigh, Melbourne 3166, Australia

© Cambridge University Press 1992

First published 1992
Reprinted 1993, 1995

Printed in the United States of America

Library of Congress Cataloging-in-Publication Data is available.

A catalogue record for this book is available from the British Library.

ISBN 0-521-40449-5 hardback
ISBN 0-521-40786-9 paperback

To my parents,
Raymond and Lucy Zaller

Contents

Tables and figures

TABLES

FIGURES

Preface

Philosophers of the late Middle Ages felt that they understood certain things better than the Greeks, who had dealt with the same questions in earlier centuries. Yet their reverence for the ancient philosophers was such that they never considered themselves to be as talented or insightful as those who had come before. Rather, they said, they were pygmies on the shoulders of giants, and only because of this could they see just a bit farther.

In much the same way, I am so immodest as to believe that this book does advance certain important questions, but, like the medieval philosophers, I understand that my work is advancing questions that were framed by my predecessors, and that, with only minor deviations, I am plodding down the center of a path that was clearly marked out by them. Which is to say that my intellectual debt to my predecessors in the political behavior field is very great. Three of these debts stand out. One is to William McGuire, a social psychologist whose masterly synthesis of research on attitude change has provided the starting point for all of my work in this area. The greater part of the second half of the book is simply an elaboration of the model he originally proposed in the late 1960s.

The second debt is to Philip Converse, whose work has dominated the political behavior field for more than two decades and dominates my own as well. What I take to be Converse's most important insight – that differences among citizens in their levels of political conceptualization and awareness are as consequential as differences in values and interests – is reflected in every important argument I make. This book, in fact, might be considered essentially a synthesis and extension of two of Converse's classic papers, "The nature of belief systems in mass publics" and "Information flow and the stability of partisan attitudes."

During the period of their greatest influence on me, I knew McGuire and Converse only through their published work. Not so the third of the formative influences, Herbert McClosky. As teacher, mentor, and friend, he introduced me to the great works of political behavior and showed me how to think about them. I was, of course, deeply and permanently impressed by his published work, especially his theory of social learning, but, as I suspect is often the case with great thinkers, McClosky knows and has taught his students much more than he has been able to publish, and I was one of the fortunate recipients of this wisdom.

Outside the political behavior field, my greatest debts are to Chris Achen and Nelson Polsby. Achen taught me to adapt statistical models to substantive theories rather than the other way around. A more important lesson is hard to imagine, and I am most grateful. I would also like to note that much of the first part of this book is, in effect, an argument with one of Achen's most important and influential papers. Far from discouraging me from criticism, Achen has done everything he could to support me.

My debts to Polsby are more diffuse but not less important. It was he who showed me that I ought to be a political scientist when I still thought I wanted to return to journalism. And it was he who told me that graduate school is more about taste and judgment than about facts and theories, and who was for nine years at Berkeley a constant influence on my taste and judgment.

About half of this book is concerned with political attitude formation and change, the other half with the nature of attitudes. The core of the attitude-change work derives from my dissertation at the University of California at Berkeley, which was filed in January 1984 (Zaller 1984a); the core of the work on the nature of attitudes was added in a convention paper done the following summer (Zaller, 1984b). Since that time, many people have read pieces of the writing that has gone into this book and I am grateful for their critical remarks. Among these are Henry Brady, Patricia Connoly, Jim DeNardo, Shanto Iyengar, Gary Jacobson, Stanley Kelley, Robert Luskin, Kathleen McGraw, Michael MacKuen, John Mueller, Vincent Price, Paul Sniderman, and Timothy Wilson. Among those who have read the whole manuscript in one or another of its iterations, and to whom I am especially grateful, are Stephen Ansolabehere, Larry Bartels, Jack Citrin, Donald Kinder, Jon Krosnick, Milton Lodge, Rus Neuman, Sam Popkin, George Tsebelis, Tom Schwartz, Pam Singh, and James Q. Wilson. Although limiting his attention to certain technical issues, Doug Rivers made several invaluable suggestions. Several individuals deserve special thanks. Larry Bartels influenced the project at many steps from 1984 onward – advising on the general structure of my argument, reading and meticulously criticizing the first draft of the book, and remaining always available to talk about whatever problems I had. Don Kinder also read the initial draft, as well as many of the papers that fed into it, with extraordinary care, making a bushel of trouble for me but also helping me to turn out a better product. I am in Steve Ansolabehere's debt for many things, but most of all for pointing out, just at the moment that I thought I had finally finished the book, that I still had one whole chapter left to write. Chapter 12 exists because of his urging. Kinder also caused trouble on this chapter: After I had finished what I thought was a pretty wild and woolly version of it, Kinder urged me to spend a weekend in the woods with it, a bottle of vodka, and a laptop – which, perhaps foolishly, I did. Whether Kinder deserves credit or blame for this bit of advice must be decided by the reader. Finally, Mark Hunt and Pam Singh read the entire manuscript with great care as it neared completion, saving me from numerous errors.

Another intellectual debt deserves lavish acknowledgment – to the Center for Political Studies and National Election Studies at the University of Michigan, which, over the years and under a variety of leaders (but mainly Warren Miller) and by means of many different funding sources (but mainly the Ford Foundation and the National Science Foundation), have collected the data on which this book depends. In all, I used 23 different CPS/NES studies. Without these studies, all carrying excellent standard complements of both explanatory and topical variables, the type of integrative effort made in this book could never have been achieved and perhaps not even conceived. One hears grousing about how much of the discipline's resources are consumed by CPS/NES; but the return on those resources to individual researchers, who would never otherwise be able to study such a broad range of topics over so long a span of time, is enormous. The Michigan studies are an invaluable national asset and I am extremely grateful to the people who brought them into existence and made them publicly available.

I would also like to express my gratitude to the professionals I worked with at Cambridge University Press, Cynthia Benn, Katharita Lamoza, and Emily Loose, all of whom did all they could to help me through the difficult process of completing a book.

I turn now to the delicate task of thanking wives. The project owes much to Debra Lavender Zaller, to whom I was married when I began it. In fact, although she never articulated it in so many words, the theory of the survey response, which takes up much of the book, derives from her insights. Without her, the book in its present form would simply not exist. I thank her most sincerely.

My debt to my present wife is even more profound. Barbara Geddes has read and helped me to improve upon everything I have written since I have known her. Her capacity for seeing what I am trying to say no matter how badly I have expressed it never ceases to amaze me. And she never gets headaches. For this and Demetria and much more, I do my best to thank her every day.

Having benefited from so much sage and helpful advice, the reader may wonder what is left for me to claim as my contribution. Well, for what it is worth, I am the one who put it all together, and for this I certainly deserve, if nothing else, full credit for all errors of fact, judgment, omission, and commission.

1

Introduction: The fragmented state of opinion research

This book is an extended argument about how people form political preferences. It seeks to show how news and political arguments diffuse through large populations, how individuals evaluate this information in light of their political values and other predispositions, and how they convert their reactions into attitude reports on mass surveys and vote decisions in elections.

The argument of the book applies to a very wide range of problems in mass political behavior – among them, racial and political tolerance, support for American involvement in overseas wars, voting in presidential and congressional elections and in presidential primaries, presidential popularity, trust in government, and judgments about the economy.

The dynamic element in the argument – the moving part, so to speak – is coverage of public affairs information in the mass media. This coverage may consist of ostensibly objective news reports, partisan argumentation, televised news conferences, or even paid advertisements, as in election campaigns. What matters for the formation of mass opinion is the relative balance and overall amount of media attention to contending political positions.

Although the book deals with the formation of political preferences in numerous cases, it maintains a high level of generality. The aim is to integrate as much as possible of the dynamics of public opinion within a cohesive theoretical system.

The ideas necessary to accomplish this integration are few and surprisingly simple. The first is that citizens vary in their habitual attention to politics and hence in their exposure to political information and argumentation in the media. The second is that people are able to react critically to the arguments they encounter only to the extent that they are knowledgeable about political affairs. The third is that citizens do not typically carry around in their heads fixed attitudes on every issue on which a pollster may happen to inquire; rather, they construct "opinion statements" on the fly as they confront each new issue. The fourth is that, in constructing their opinion statements, people make greatest use of ideas that are, for one reason or another, most immediately salient to them – at the "top of the head," to use the phrase of Taylor and Fiske (1978).

Once these basic notions have been appropriately organized and to a limited extent formalized, the need for numerous domain-specific theories and conventional distinctions in the political behavior field disappears, even distinctions between vote choices and choices between opposing response options on questionnaires. Each "domain" can be treated as simply another context in which citizens formulate responses on the basis of the ideas that have reached them and been found acceptable. Several major methodological issues, as well as discussions concerning the nature of mass belief systems, can also be fruitfully accommodated within the model.

Efforts at integration of research findings are uncommon in the public opinion field. With only a handful of exceptions, the trend is in the other direction – toward the multiplication of domain-specific concepts and distinctions. Thus, analysts largely explain voting in presidential elections separately from voting in congressional elections, racial tolerance separately from political tolerance, foreign policy attitudes separately from all other attitudes, and so on. Certain general topics, such as political attitude change, are typically addressed only in the context of particular substantive topics, such as "agenda setting" or presidential popularity, so that there is presently little general literature on attitude change within the public opinion field. But other general topics, such as the nature of political attitudes, are typically addressed only in specialized literatures.

The result of all this specialization is that the public opinion field has devolved into a collection of insular subliteratures that rarely communicate with one another. Hence, we know much more about the details of particular dependent variables than we do about theoretical mechanisms that span multiple research domains.

Despite this, the potential for theoretical integration is great. Two types of individual-level variables, political awareness and political values, are important across a wide range of situations and, as I seek to show in this book, have essentially the same effects across domains. Mass opinion change, as will become apparent, seems to conform to the same principles in whatever context it occurs. The sketchy evidence that exists suggests that elite discourse has much the same effects on public opinion across a broad range of topics. And finally, the process by which people choose between opposing policy prescriptions appears quite similar to how they choose between candidates. There seems, thus, to be no strong justification for the current practice of organizing nearly all public opinion research around particular dependent variables, and this book is a deliberate attempt to break with this practice.

All scientific theories, as William James observed, tend to leak about the joints. Mine will be no exception. In particular, the breadth and generality for which I aim in this book have been achieved at the expense of strong assumptions and some important simplifications. There has been little choice about this. Any study of public opinion, or any other large-scale social phenomenon, that took seriously every plausible avenue of influence and every proposed conceptual distinction would be able to provide little more than descriptive accounts of the phenomena of interest. Broad social theory and strong results require strong assumptions and significant simplifications, and it is foolish to pretend otherwise.

This methodological posture will suit the tastes of some readers, but it will make others uneasy. To those who find my approach dubious, I can say two things: First, that the public opinion field is long overdue for an attempt to sketch a unified theory of its major empirical regularities, and without some license to make assumptions and simplifications, no such theory is possible. And second, that I will not disguise my simplifications but will, on the contrary, both highlight them by bald statement and make clear why they may be questioned. To avoid confusion and the appearance of constant waffling, I will not always criticize my argument in the same paragraphs in which I make it, but will instead save most of my self-criticism for a later chapter. But the self-criticism will be there. The skeptical reader, having weighed it, can then decide whether my results have been worth their price.

In attempting to state my arguments as clearly and generally as possible, I make limited use of formal and statistical modeling. Despite this, the book is no more technical than many studies of public opinion and much less technical than some. The taste and limited technical abilities of the author are the main reason for this. In only one chapter (Chapter 9) is it important for the reader to follow extensive mathematical arguments, and even there it is possible to skip the math without missing the central points of the chapter.

A preliminary word on the disciplinary orientation of the book will perhaps also be useful to readers. The book, as indicated, is primarily concerned with how individuals convert political information and argumentation into political opinions. As such, it is essentially a study in political psychology. As will become apparent, the book also draws heavily on ideas and evidence that have been developed by psychologists. Nevertheless, the book is closer to the discipline of political science than to psychology. A superficial indication of this is that the book avoids technical psychological terms and tends instead to favor terms from the language of everyday politics. Thus, the primitive term in my model of how citizens organize political information in their minds will not be "schema" but "consideration." A more important indication of disciplinary orientation is that, in contrast to some psychological studies of politics, this book pays vastly more attention to the social sources of mass attitudes – in particular, the availability of information in elite discourse – than to the largely autonomous operation of people's minds and psyches on the world as they perceive it. Finally, and most importantly, the book limits itself to ideas that can be readily tested in typical public opinion surveys. I leave those phenomena that can be effectively demonstrated only in psychological laboratories – even those phenomena that undeniably exist and have consequences outside the laboratory – to researchers in other disciplines.[1] Thus, experimental psychologists, in particular, should be warned that my arguments may be simpler, even

---

1 This orientation does not rule out the conduct of experiments, provided they can be conducted in a typical survey setting. Nor does it rule out ideas that originate in psychological laboratories and do have testable implications for mass surveys, such as McGuire's (1969) theory of attitude change.

radically simpler, than they may feel is warranted by the type of data available
to them.

To put the matter somewhat differently, I, as an analyst of public opinion, am
not concerned with developing models that approximate as closely as possible
the intricacies of human information processing. Rather, I am concerned with
capturing, with as little extraneous theoretical apparatus as possible, those aspects of information processing that have demonstrable relevance for understanding the dynamics of public opinion on major issues, as public opinion on
major issues is typically measured.

Inasmuch as the book is centrally concerned with how citizens use information from the mass media to form political preferences, it also substantially over-
laps core concerns of the field of mass communication. If mass communications
is broadly defined, as it often is, to include concern with the nature of public
opinion, the overlap is even greater. I am not, however, aware of any important
difference between my general approach to these concerns and the approaches
taken in the communication field.

One consequence of the stress on generality in this book is that its organization is somewhat unusual. Rather than having a chapter on each of several
substantive domains – foreign policy attitudes, domestic policy attitudes, presidential elections, congressional elections, and so forth – the book is organized
around more general theoretical matters: how people answer survey questions,
how attitude change occurs, the effects of opposing mass communications of unequal intensities, and so forth.

This mode of organization turns out to have an enormous practical advantage.
Quite different kinds of data have been collected in different substantive domains, some of which provide leverage on questions that are unanswerable from
data that are, or are likely to be, available from other domains. Data from the
1978 congressional election are particularly valuable to this book because they
contain identical and highly detailed measures of attitudes that have been formed
across several dozen separate political campaigns. Once it has become clear how
choosing between candidates on a ballot is like choosing between response options on a typical attitude survey, these congressional data become extremely
useful for illustrating the dynamics of preference formation in general.

The argument of the book develops as follows: Chapters 2 and 3 introduce the
principal theoretical concepts of the book and a simple model based on them.
The remainder of the book is then concerned with drawing out the deductive
implications of this model and testing them against the available data.

Chapters 4 and 5 deal with the nature of political attitudes – or more precisely, how individuals convert the ideas in their heads to answers to closed-
ended survey questions. Chapter 6 turns to the substantive content of people's
attitudes, showing how elite opinion leadership, individuals' level of attentiveness to elite cues, and differences in individual political values interact to affect
opinion statements. Chapter 6, however, deals only with static distributions of
opinion, such as can be observed in typical, one-shot opinion surveys. Chapters

7 through 10 shift the focus to attitude change by developing a dynamic formulation of the argument used in Chapter 6. A source of possible difficulty in these chapters is that they conduct tests in many different issue domains, skipping from one topic to another (from race to presidential popularity to judgments of the performance of the national economy to support for the Korean War) in order to take full advantage of the limited amount of pertinent data. In consequence, this part of the book may seem somewhat disjointed. However, the chapters have, I hope, a compensating theoretical unity, as they test increasingly complex ideas on how the public responds to competing communications of unequal intensities or "loudness." The fullest tests of the model appear in Chapters 9 and 10. Chapter 9 analyzes the evolution of mass attitudes on the Vietnam War over the period 1964 to 1970, and Chapter 10 examines the formation of candidate preferences in contested elections (presidential, Senate, House, and presidential primary). Although the two types of cases seem quite different, the dynamics of attitude formation and change in each seem to be exactly the same.

Following the presentation of the core arguments of the book in Chapters 2 through 10, I present what are, in effect, two concluding chapters. The first evaluates the strengths and weaknesses of the model developed in the body of the book, suggests some corrections and extensions, and illustrates the form that future theorizing might take. The second of the concluding chapters is an epilogue that stands somewhat apart from the rest of the book. It shows how elements of the system of political information in the United States are linked to the model of attitude formation sketched in the earlier part of the book.

Finally, I should add a word about my data sources. All of the original empirical analyses in this book are based on data that are available through the Interuniversity Consortium for Social and Political Research (ICPSR) at the University of Michigan. In presenting my results, I have done my best to make clear how I have used these data so that interested scholars can double-check them.

The most commonly used datasets are the election studies conducted under the auspices of the Center for Political Studies (CPS) at the University of Michigan and, within the last several years, the Board of Overseers of the National Election Studies (NES). I have made particularly heavy use of the 1986 NES election survey and the 1987 NES pilot study, which reinterviewed some 450 of the 1986 respondents. By luck, the 1986–7 study captured two of the most interesting cases of attitude change I have been able to find; by design, it also carried an extensive investigation of the microfoundations of political attitudes, including one, evaluations of President Reagan's job performance, that was undergoing rapid change. Without the 1987 pilot study, this book would have had significantly weaker empirical foundations. Altogether, I make use of twenty-three CPS/NES datasets, plus a twenty-fourth (concerning attitudes in Brazil) that is archived with ICPSR.

2

Information, predispositions, and opinion

Every opinion is a marriage of information and predisposition: information to form a mental picture of the given issue, and predisposition to motivate some conclusion about it. The central aim of this book is to show how, across a very wide range of issues, variations in the information carried in elite discourse, individual differences in attention to this information, and individual differences in political values and other predispositions jointly determine the contours of public opinion. The book, thus, is most crucially about the relationship among information, predispositions, and opinion.

The present chapter introduces and defines these key terms, examines some critical problems associated with their study, and shows in a preliminary way how they relate to one another. In so doing, it develops the intuitions behind the more technical core of the book, which begins in Chapter 3.

INFORMATION AND ELITE DISCOURSE

To an extent that few like but none can avoid, citizens in large societies are dependent on unseen and usually unknown others for most of their information about the larger world in which they live. As Walter Lippmann wrote in his classic treatise, *Public Opinion* (1922/1946),

Each of us lives and works on a small part of the earth's surface, moves in a small circle, and of these acquaintances knows only a few intimately. Of any public event that has wide effects we see at best only a phase and an aspect. . . . Inevitably our opinions cover a bigger space, a longer reach of time, a greater number of things, than we can directly observe. They have, therefore, to be pieced together out of what others have reported and what we can imagine. (p. 59)

The "others" on whom we depend, directly or indirectly, for information about the world are, for the most part, persons who devote themselves full time to some aspect of politics or public affairs – which is to say, political elites. These elites include politicians, higher-level government officials, journalists, some activists, and many kinds of experts and policy specialists. Even when we learn from friends or family members about some aspect of public affairs, often we may still be secondhand consumers of ideas that originated more distantly among some type of elite.

The information that reaches the public is never a full record of important events and developments in the world. It is, rather, a highly selective and stereotyped view of what has taken place. It could hardly be otherwise. But even if it could, the public would have little desire to be kept closely informed about the vast world beyond its personal experience. It requires news presentations that are short, simple, and highly thematic – in a word, stereotyped. Thus, Doris Graber (1984), in a close study of how a sample of citizens monitored the news, found that her subjects "grumbled frequently about the oversimplified treatment of [television] news . . . " Yet when

special news programs and newspaper features presented a small opportunity for more extensive exposure to issues, they were unwilling to seize it. For the most part, [citizens] would not read and study carefully the more extensive versions of election and other news in newspapers and news magazines. Masses of specific facts and statistics were uniformly characterized as dull, confusing, and unduly detailed. . . . (p. 105)

Lippmann, who remains perhaps the most insightful analyst of the process by which the public comes to form an understanding of complex and distant events, devoted a large section of *Public Opinion* to news stereotypes, or what today are more often called frames of reference. In one lucid passage, he described World War I as it would probably have been perceived by a character in Sinclair Lewis's *Main Street:*

Miss Sherwin of Gopher Prairie is aware that a war is raging in France and tries to conceive it. She has never been to France, and certainly she has never been along what is now the battlefront. Pictures of France and German soldiers she has seen, but it is impossible for her to imagine three million men. No one, in fact, can imagine them, and professionals do not try. They think of them as, say, two hundred divisions. But Miss Sherwin has no access to the order of battle maps, and if she is to think about the war, she fastens upon Joffre and the Kaiser as if they were engaged in a personal duel. Perhaps if you could see what she sees with her mind's eye, the image in its composition might be not unlike an Eighteenth Century engraving of a great soldier. He stands there boldly unruffled and more than life size, with a shadowy army of tiny little figures winding off into the landscape behind. (p. 8)

As suggested by Miss Sherwin's reliance on an eighteenth-century engraving, Lippmann doubted that individuals can personally create the stereotypes and other symbolic representations – "the pictures in our heads" – by which remote and even proximate events are understood. Rather,

[i]n the great blooming, buzzing confusion of the outer world we pick out what our culture has already defined for us, and we tend to perceive that which we have picked out in the form stereotyped for us by our culture. (p. 61)

Many of the stereotypes to which Lippmann refers are permanent features of the culture – the corrupt politician, the labor strike, the election contest, the yeoman farmer. But because society is always churning up new issues and problems, many stereotypes are recent creations. For example, research has shown how, in the debate over the Equal Rights Amendment, stereotypes of unisex toilets and women combat troops came into being as a reflection of the organizational and ideological needs of the contending activists (Mansbridge, 1986). Luker has done similar research on the origins of the Pro-Choice and Pro-Life labels in the contrasting world views of abortion activists (Luker, 1984). A powerful stereotype that has emerged in recent years is that of "the homeless." Stereotypes and frames like these are important to the process by which the public keeps informed because they determine what the public thinks it is becoming informed about, which in turn often determines how people take sides on political issues (Edelman, 1964; Bennett, 1980; Gamson and Modigliani, 1987; Kinder and Sanders, 1990).

Although culturally given and elite-supplied stereotypes may be most powerful in shaping public understanding of events that are "out of reach, out of sight, out of mind" (Lippmann, 1922/1946, p. 21), they can be important even for matters within people's powers of direct observation. For example, Iyengar (1991) has used experimental evidence to argue that whether television news focuses on "episodic" cases of individual poverty, or the societywide conditions that cause poverty, affects the public's attribution of blame for poverty and thereby its willingness to support programs aimed at alleviating it.

Perhaps the most fundamental question about news stereotypes, or frames of reference, is whether the public is given any choice about them – whether, that is, it is permitted to choose between alternative visions of what the issue is. For in the absence of such choice, the public can do little more than follow the elite consensus on what should be done. For example, in the early phase of American involvement in the Vietnam War, the public was offered only one way to think about the war, namely as a struggle to preserve freedom by "containing Communism." Even news stories that criticized government policy did so within a framework that assumed the paramount importance of winning the war and defeating communism (Halberstam, 1979; Hallin, 1986). During this period, public support for American involvement in the war was very strong, and those members of the public most heavily exposed to the mass media supported the "official line" most strongly.

In the later phase of the war, however, journalists began to present information in ways suggesting that it was essentially a civil war among contending Vietnamese factions and hence both inessential to U.S. security interests and also perhaps unwinnable. Coverage implicitly supportive of the war continued, but it no longer had near-monopoly status. Owing, as I show in Chapter 9, to this change in media coverage, public support for the war weakened greatly. Also, heavy exposure to the mass media was no longer associated with support for the war, but with a polarization of opinion that reflected the division in political discourse. Politically attentive liberals within the general public tended to adopt the position taken by elites conventionally recognized as liberal, while politically attentive conservatives in the general public moved toward the position of conservative opinion leaders.

So, when elites uphold a clear picture of what should be done, the public tends to see events from that point of view, with the most politically attentive members of the public most likely to adopt the elite position. When elites divide, members of the public tend to follow the elites sharing their general ideological or partisan predisposition, with the most politically attentive members of the public mirroring most sharply the ideological divisions among the elite.

These claims about the effects of elite discourse, which are an important part of what this book will attempt to demonstrate, are obviously quite strong ones. By way of further preliminary examination, I would like to give an overview of the evolution of American racial attitudes in the twentieth century. I strongly emphasize that my purpose in reviewing this sensitive subject is not to convince anyone of the final correctness of my view, but only to illustrate as clearly as possible the general vision that underlies the more specific arguments of later chapters.

Elite discourse and racial attitudes

At the turn of the century, the United States was a deeply racist society – not only in the caste structure of the southern states and in the widespread practice of discrimination, but in the political ideas that informed elite and mass thinking about race. Although there was some mainstream elite disagreement on the subject of race, it was confined to a very narrow range. Virtually all white elites accepted some notion of the inferiority of other racial groups (Fredrickson, 1971). It is both distasteful and unnecessary to recount these ideas, but one point is important to the argument I wish to make. It is that racist ideas about blacks – and, indeed, about most non–Anglo-Saxon groups, including Asians, southern and eastern Europeans, and Jews – had the support of the biological and psychological science of that period. Racist ideas, thus, were not confined to an extremist or backwater fringe; they were as common among the nation's white intellectual leaders as among other types of whites. Given this pattern of elite attitudes, any attempts to mobilize white support for black equality, whether by blacks themselves or sympathetic whites, were bound to fail.

By 1930, however, the attitudes of political elites seemed to be changing. In that year, President Hoover's nomination of John Parker of North Carolina to the Supreme Court was rejected in large part because of a ten-year-old speech in which Parker had said that "The Negro as a class does not desire to enter politics" and that the "participation of the Negro in politics is a source of evil and danger to both races" (cited in Kluger, 1975: p. 142). That a single racist speech, of a type that was entirely conventional throughout the nineteenth and early twentieth centuries, could become a basis for the rejection of a Supreme Court nominee by the Senate was an indication that attitudes toward race were undergoing a historic shift.

Despite this, race was apparently not a major public issue in the 1930s (Sheatsley 1966: p. 217). Moreover, Gunnar Myrdal (1944), in his massive investigation of American race relations, found that neither the material condition of blacks nor the amount of discrimination they faced were much different in

1940 than they had been in the immediate aftermath of the Civil War. To the extent that there had been any improvement at all, it was only because some blacks had migrated to the North, where conditions had always been somewhat better. Nonetheless, Myrdal maintained that a period of great racial progress lay just ahead. White Americans believed deeply in their creed of equality and had come to realize that black demands for equality were justified. He therefore thought the days of white resistance to racial equality were near their end.

Thus, by Myrdal's account, which proved extraordinarily prescient, a change in white attitudes preceded any change in the actual conditions of blacks. What, then, brought about the attitude change?

One can imagine many possibilities, but Myrdal found the explanation in purely intellectual developments. Scientists, who as recently as 1920 had over-whelmingly endorsed the notion that some racial groups were superior to others, had by their subsequent research discredited it. The magnitude of the change in scientific thinking is captured by the following two passages from the work of Carl Brigham, who was for a time a leading authority on race. In 1923 Brigham concluded his *Study of American Intelligence* by claiming flatly that "the intellectual superiority of our Nordic group over the Alpine, Mediterranean, and negro groups has been demonstrated" (p. 192). However, in a review of subsequent research that was published just seven years later, Brigham felt compelled to withdraw this conclusion. As he wrote in the final sentence of his paper,

This review has summarized some of the more recent test findings which show that comparative studies of various national and racial groups may not be made with existing tests, and which show, in particular, that one of the most pretentious of these comparative racial studies – the author's own – was without foundation. (Brigham, 1930: p. 165)

Reviewing this and other research, Myrdal wrote that "A handful of social and biological scientists over the past fifty years have gradually forced informed people to give up some of the more blatant of our biological errors" (p. 92). As Degler (1991) has recently shown, changing scientific theories of race in the 1920s were part of a much larger scientific movement away from biological explanations of human behavior.[1]

With the intellectual defeat of early theories of racial inferiority, psychologists shifted their research to the stigmatizing effects on blacks of what was now taken to be white prejudice, and to the origins of racial prejudice in various kinds of mental disorders and educational deficiencies (Allport, 1954).[2]

In consequence of all this, the stereotypes used to explain racial differences in material conditions underwent a major change. Until about 1930 these stereotypes stressed racial inferiority as the reason for inequality. Since then the

1 Degler (1991) has also made the interesting argument that the new research was ideologically motivated in the sense that its practitioners were nonrationally committed to the defeat of racist theories. This may or may not be true. But Degler makes no argument that fraud or dishonesty was present in the research, nor does he present any evidence that the large number of scientists who decided to accept the research were motivated by anything other than their own judgments of the facts of the matter.
2 The possibility that white prejudice might have been due, at least in part, to the racist elite discourse of previous decades was not, so far as I can tell, given serious consideration.

dominant tendency of elite discourse has been to blame inequality either on a failure of *individual* effort or, in its common liberal variant, on the effects of white discrimination against blacks. A more profound shift in elite discourse can scarcely be imagined.

Owing to the lack of opinion data until the late 1930s, the effects on public opinion of this revolution in elite discourse cannot be fully documented. But three points about public opinion are reasonably clear. First, there has been a massive shift toward greater public support by whites for the principle of racial equality. The shift has not extended as far as many would like – most notably, whites have resisted many government efforts to combat discrimination and have been even more opposed to most efforts to make up for the effects of past discrimination. Nor is the sincerity of some people's professions of belief in equality beyond question. But evidence of great change is hard to deny (Schuman, Steeh, and Bobo, 1985). For example, only 45 percent of whites in a 1944 survey said blacks "should have as good a chance as white people to get any kind of job," whereas in 1972, this figure had risen to 97 percent. Similarly, the percentage saying that "white students and black students should go to the same schools" rather than separate ones rose from 32 percent in 1942 to 90 percent in 1982. These changes may have begun to occur at the time of the first mass opinion polls on race in the early 1940s, or the changes may have been already under way at that time. In either case, the shift in mass attitudes roughly coincides with the shift in elite attitudes.

Second, the people most heavily exposed to the new elite discourse on race, namely the better educated, have been most likely to support those ideas that constitute the modern elite consensus on race. Thus, the better educated are not especially likely to support affirmative action or the more controversial efforts to combat inequality, such as school busing, which tend not to have consensual elite support; but they do exhibit disproportionate support for the principle of equality and for those efforts to combat discrimination, such as federal laws against segregated restaurants and transportation systems, that do enjoy mainstream elite support (Allport, 1954; Schuman et al., 1985). Thus, exactly as in the Vietnam case described earlier, exposure to elite discourse appears to promote support for the ideas carried in it. (I present further evidence on the racially liberalizing effects of exposure to elite discourse in Chapter 8.)

Finally, the public has been responsive to partisan elite cues on the subject of race. The evidence on this point, much of which comes from the recent work of Carmines and Stimson (1989), is worth examining in some detail.

Throughout the 1950s and early 1960s, elite Democrats and Republicans exhibited no consistent partisan differences on racial issues. The Democratic Party was home to many prominent racial liberals, most notably Hubert H. Humphrey, and had, under the leadership of President Harry S Truman, pressed to achieve a measure of equality for blacks, especially in the military. Yet racially conservative Southerners remained a major power within the Democratic party. Meanwhile, the Republican President Dwight Eisenhower, though no crusader on race, appointed the racially liberal Earl Warren to be chief justice of the

a. Voting trends on racial issues among U.S. Senators

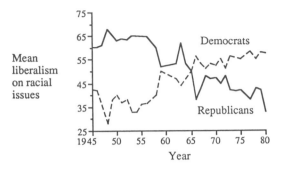

b. Racial attitudes among rank-and-file party identifiers

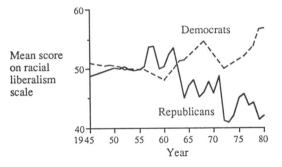

Figure 2.1. Racial liberalism scores of Democrats and Republicans, 1945–1980. *Source:* Carmines and Stimson (1989).

Supreme Court, and used federal troops to enforce its landmark school deseg-regation decisions. Finally, despite the impression created by such prominent Democratic liberals as Humphrey, Republican congressmen were more liberal than Democrats on race, as shown in Figure 2.1. As a result of this lack of clearly differentiated leadership cues, as Carmines and Stimson argue, Demo-crats and Republicans in the general public did not differ on racial issues.

Beginning in late 1963, however, the Democratic Party, overcoming the re-sistance of its Southern wing, stepped out as the party of racial liberalism, while the Republican party became the more racially conservative party. Thus, Pres-ident Lyndon Johnson, as titular leader of his party, pressed for and won major civil rights bills in Congress, while Senator Barry Goldwater, the Republican presidential nominee in 1964, became the most prominent opponent of this leg-islation. Also, congressional voting on racial issues began to follow closely Democratic–Republican party lines (see upper portion of Figure 2.1).

The effect of this change in party leadership cues is apparent in the lower portion of Figure 2.1. Rank-and-file Democrats and Republicans began in 1964 to exhibit substantial amounts of party polarization on racial issues – the result, it would seem, of the sudden change in the structure of party leadership cues.[3]

There is, however, an ambiguity in these results. Mass polarization along party lines could have come about from a reshuffling of party loyalties, with racial liberals flocking to the Democratic Party and racial conservatives moving over to the Republican side. This is the *party conversion* thesis. Or polarization could have come about from opinion conversion, that is, existing Democrats becoming more racially liberal and existing Republicans becoming more racially conservative. This is the *opinion leadership* thesis. Although Carmines and Stimson make no attempt to sort out these competing possibilities, it appears that both processes were at work. Petrocik (1989) has shown that, beginning in 1964, the Democratic Party lost Southern whites and gained blacks, which indicates a reshuffling of party loyalties along lines of preexisting racial opinions. And Gerber and Jackson (1990) have shown that many existing Democrats and Republicans also changed their racial opinions to accord with the new party leadership cues, which indicates a mass response to elite opinion leadership.[4]

For purposes of this book, the latter phenomenon is the more important. If elite cues can change racial opinions, which appear to be among the most deeply felt of mass opinions (Carmines and Stimson, 1982; Converse, 1964; Converse and Markus, 1979), they can probably affect most other types of opinions as well.

Conceptualizing and measuring elite discourse

The political information carried in elite discourse is, as we have seen, never pure. It is, rather, an attempt by various types of elite actors to create a depiction of reality that is sufficiently simple and vivid that ordinary people can grasp it. This "information" is genuinely information in the sense that it consists of what may be assumed to be sincere attempts to capture what is most important about what is happening in the world and to convey it in its proper perspective. But it is never "just information," because it is unavoidably selective and unavoidably enmeshed in stereotypical frames of reference that highlight only a portion of what is going on.

In consequence, the public opinion that exists on a given issue can rarely be considered a straightforward response to "the facts" of a situation. Even topics that are within the direct experience of some citizens, such as poverty, homosexuality, and racial inequality, are susceptible to widely different understandings, depending on how facts about them are framed or stereotyped, and on

3 Actually, Carmines and Stimson (1989) find the first evidence of mass-level partisan polarization on race in a Harris poll taken in November 1963, which was just after President John Kennedy declared his support for a major civil rights bill.

4 Gerber and Jackson (1990) report comparable evidence of opinion leadership on Vietnam. Franklin and Kosaki (1989) show that a heightened mass polarization on abortion attitudes followed the 1973 Supreme Court decision in *Roe v. Wade*.

which partisan elites are associated with which positions. In view of this, it is difficult to disagree with Lippmann's observation that while the

orthodox theory holds that public opinion constitutes a moral judgment of a group of facts . . . [it is more reasonable to hold that] . . . public opinion is primarily a moralized and codified version of the facts (1922/1946: p. 93).

Thus, when I refer in the course of this book to the "information carried in elite discourse about politics," as I often will, I will be referring to the stereotypes, frames of reference, and elite leadership cues that enable citizens to form conceptions of and, more importantly, opinions about events that are beyond their full personal understanding. The aim of the book is to show how variations in this elite discourse affect both the direction and organization of mass opinion.

This conception of elite discourse, however, is more elaborate than can be fully measured and tested in this book. I have sketched it in order to indicate the larger picture into which my argument fits, and to acknowledge that elite discourse is a more complex phenomenon than my simple measures will make it out to be. For my measures really are quite simple and concrete. Often, I will make only a dichotomous measurement – whether there is a monolithic elite point of view on what a given issue is and how it should be handled, or whether there are important elite disagreements over the issue (see especially Chapter 6). In a few other cases, I will determine the relative intensity of opposing elite communications and how relative intensity changes over time. In these cases, I will be counting the number of media reports on a given issue, and the direction in which each report would tend to push opinion.

Yet, as much research has shown, even simple story counts are sufficient to show a close relationship between elite discourse and mass opinion (Erbring, Goldenberg, and Miller, 1980; MacKuen, 1984; Page, Shapiro, and Dempsey, 1987; Fan, 1988; Page and Shapiro, in press; Brody, 1991). And, as the reader will see, they suffice equally well for the purposes of this book.

By way of illustration, let me briefly describe changes in news reports on the issue of U.S. defense spending in the late 1970s and early 1980s, along with the associated changes in public opinion that they appear to have produced.

On the cover of the October 27, 1980, issue of *Newsweek* was the headline, "Is America strong enough?" The inside story began as follows:

Seldom in time of peace has the United States been so troubled by talk of war – and so much concerned that the country is incapable of waging it. The Army Chief of Staff, General Edward C. Meyer, complains publicly that he presides over a "hollow army," undermanned, undertrained, and underfunded. General Lew Allen, the Air Force Chief of Staff, warns that his planes lack the spare parts necessary to command the skies in any sustained fight. The Chief of Naval Operations, Admiral Thomas B. Hayward, protests that he has a three-ocean mission and a "one-and-a-half ocean Navy." And for the first time since the missile-gap scare of the 1960 presidential campaign, a feeling is building that American defenses have slipped – so badly that the nation may no longer be capable of protecting its interests abroad, or containing Soviet expansionism.

After what the magazine bluntly characterizes as inadequate responses to this situation by President Jimmy Carter and Ronald Reagan, his Republican opponent in the fall election, the story continues:

There is little question that America's defense posture is not what it could be – or should be. Much of the military's equipment has aged to the point of obsolescence – and even the critical Minutemen ICBM's and B-52 bombers need continuing and expensive maintenance to stay competitive. Skyrocketing operating costs have ravaged the services and hamstrung their training efforts. Low pay scales and increasingly long stretches of sea duty for sailors and overseas tours for soldiers and airmen have prompted a mass exodus of the experienced noncoms who are at the heart of any fighting force. These problems all raise legitimate questions about the ability of the U.S. military to react to crisis and perform in combat.

Stories of this type were not unusual in the late 1970s and early 1980s. By my count, in the 24 months prior to the 1980 election, *Newsweek* carried 57 stories that bore more or less directly on defense spending, 46 of which wholly or predominantly favored greater spending.

A pro-spending posture was not, however, a permanent feature of *Newsweek* coverage of defense issues. As the new Reagan administration began to increase the level of defense spending, elite discussions of the issue – most notably in the form of objections by many congressional representatives that defense spending was squeezing out social spending – changed dramatically, and as this occurred, *Newsweek* coverage of the issue assumed a radically different character. Now the magazine filled its columns with information about multimillion dollar cost overruns, $600 air force screwdrivers, and other indications of Pentagon mismanagement. Instead of images of a decrepit U.S. fighting force, the public was given pictures of a bloated and wasteful military. Thus, in the 24 months following the 1980 election, there were 60 stories on defense spending, 40 of which assumed a posture opposed to defense spending. So, over a short period of time, coverage swung from about four-to-one in favor of greater defense spending, to two-to-one in favor of reduced expenditures.

Public opinion on defense spending moved in tandem with these shifts in media coverage. At the end of the Vietnam War, most Americans wanted to cut defense spending, and as late as 1975, only about 10 percent felt too little money was being spent on defense. But, in response to a steady stream of pro-defense images of the type just described, support for such spending rose steadily in the late 1970s, so that by early 1981, a slight majority of Americans felt that "too little" was being spent on defense. Then, as the news media began carrying a preponderance of information against defense spending, support for greater spending fell by more than 30 percentage points within a single year, leaving public opinion lopsidedly against increased defense spending. Such changes in public opinion, linked to clear shifts in the information carried in elite discourse, are a central topic of analysis of this book, especially the latter half of it.

This section has suggested why and how elite discourse affects mass opinion. The next section will consider more carefully which members of the public are most susceptible to elite influence.

MASS ATTENTION TO ELITE DISCOURSE

Although most Americans are, to use Downs's (1957) apt phrase, rationally ignorant about politics, they differ greatly in the degree of their ignorance. There is a small but important minority of the public that pays great attention to politics and is well informed about it. Members of this minority can recognize important U.S. senators on sight, accurately recount each day's leading news stories, and keep track of the major events in Washington and other world capitals. They are, thus, heavily exposed to elite discourse about politics.

Any attempt to gauge the absolute size of this highly informed minority is essentially arbitrary (though see Bennett, 1989; Smith, 1989; Delli Carpini and Keeter, in press). Nonetheless, one indication of size is that when respondents to a National Election Study were asked to name as many members of the U.S. Supreme Court as they could remember, about 1.9 percent of the public could mention as many as half of the members, and a disproportionate number of those who could do so were lawyers or educators.[5] Few Americans, it appears, are deeply familiar with the operation of their government. (By way of comparison, it is interesting to speculate what percentage of adults can name five or more starters on their city's major league baseball team; almost certainly, the figure is above 1.9 percent.)

At the other end of the attentiveness spectrum is a larger group of people who possess almost no current information about politics. In late 1986, for example, when George Bush was halfway into his second term as vice-president of the United States, 24 percent of the general public either failed to recognize his name or could not say what office he held.[6] People at this level of inattentiveness can have only the haziest idea of the policy alternatives about which pollsters regularly ask them to state opinions, and such ideas as they do have must often be relatively innocent of the effects of exposure to elite discourse.

Most citizens, of course, fall between these extremes.[7] Probably from some combination of civic obligation and the entertainment value of politics, a majority pays enough attention to public affairs to learn something about it. But even so, it is easy to underestimate how little typical Americans know about even the most prominent political events – and also how quickly they forget what for a time they do understand. For example, in the spring of 1989, the speaker of the House of Representatives, James Wright, resigned the speaker-

5 No person among the 1,500 respondents to the 1966 National Election Study survey named all nine justices.
6 1986 National Election Study.
7 Neuman (1986) attempts to be more precise than I am about the distribution of awareness in the general public. (See more generally Tichenor, Donohue, and Olien, 1970; Delli Carpini and Keeter, in press; Bennett, 1989; Just, Neuman, and Crigler, 1989.)

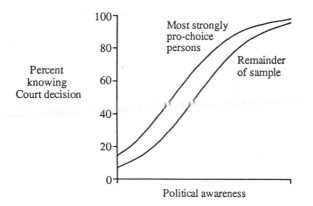

Figure 2.2. Estimated diffusion of news about Supreme Court decision on Webster. Estimates are for respondents interviewed three days after the Supreme Court's decision in the Webster case, as calculated from model and coefficients in Price and Zaller, 1990. Political awareness is measured by means of simple factual questions about politics, as described in the Measures Appendix. The awareness measure in this figure runs ±2 SD. *Source:* 1989 NES pilot survey.

ship amid allegations of scandal, the first time in American history that this had happened. The story was heavily covered in the media over a period of several months. Yet when, about three weeks after Wright's resignation, a national sample was asked about his resignation, only 45 percent could supply any reason for the resignation – even so much as a bare mention of scandal or wrongdoing. Or to take one other example: In the early summer of 1989, the U.S. Supreme Court announced a major decision on women's right to abortion, *Webster v. Reproductive Services.* Because pro- and antiabortion activists held large-scale demonstrations in an attempt to lobby the Court, there was extensive news coverage of the impending decision in the weeks before it was taken, and very heavy coverage when the decision was finally announced. Yet, in a survey done just after the decision, only about 50 percent of the public could say anything at all about how the Court had ruled, and, as the survey continued over the next several weeks, this percentage fell gradually to about 35 percent (Zaller and Price, 1990).

Those who did learn about the abortion decision were obviously not a random 50 percent of the population: Citizens who paid regular attention to politics were far more likely to learn about the abortion decision than those who didn't. Figure 2.2 makes this point. Respondents to the survey were rated according to their general background levels of "political awareness." Persons scored high on political awareness if they were able to correctly answer a variety of simple factual information tests (such as which political party controls the House of Representatives), whereas persons scored low on awareness if they could answer none of these questions. As can be seen in the figure, almost all of the most highly informed persons – upward of 95 percent of those interviewed within the first three days of the Court's decision – could, when asked, supply the rudiments of the Court's ruling in the abortion case; but almost none of the persons at the low end of the awareness spectrum had absorbed any information about the decision.

Data such as these on differential attentiveness to political news have immense implications for the impact of elite discourse on mass opinion, and taking systematic account of them will be a central task of this book.

Figure 2.2 also shows that the people most strongly committed to women's right to abortion – in particular, the minority who said women should have an absolute right to decide for themselves whether to get abortions – were more likely to find out about the court decision than other persons. Yet their informational advantage was rather modest. There was, moreover, no difference at all between men and women in awareness of the decision. Even women of childbearing age did not differ from the rest of the public in their awareness of this issue (Price and Zaller, 1990). I mention this in order to give pause to readers who may suspect that, although citizens are often poorly informed about politics in general, they still manage to learn about matters that are especially important to them. Although there is some tendency for this to occur, as emphasized in Converse (1964), Iyengar (1990), Delli Carpini and Keeter (1990), McGraw and Pinney (1990), and some other studies, the tendency appears not to be very great or very widespread (Price and Zaller, 1990).

The two main points about political awareness, then, are (1) that people vary greatly in their general attentiveness to politics, regardless of particular issues; and (2) that average overall levels of information are quite low. More succinctly, there is high variance in political awareness around a generally low mean.

These points are widely familiar to professional students of public opinion (Converse, 1975; Kinder and Sears, 1985; Luskin, 1987; Bennett, 1989). Yet familiarity is often as far as it goes. Most of the time, when scholars attempt to explain public opinion and voting behavior, they build models that implicitly assume all citizens to be adequately and about equally informed about politics, and hence to differ mainly in their preferences and interests. In other words, they build models that ignore the effects of political awareness.[8] One aim of this book is to provide a corrective for this dominant research practice.

It may be useful to give an example of why a corrective is needed. The example concerns the effects of campaigns on voting behavior in congressional elections, but the issues it raises parallel those concerning the effect of elite discourse on public opinion generally.

One of the most heavily researched problems in the congressional elections literature in recent years has been the advantage enjoyed by incumbents in the House of Representatives in their reelection bids. The average winning margin

8 Among the exceptions are Stimson (1975), Nie, Verba, and Petrocik (1976), and their assorted critics. Studies done by psychologists and psychologically oriented political scientists pay somewhat more attention to political awareness, often referring to it as "political expertise" (see Sniderman, Brody, and Tetlock, 1991; Kinder and Sanders, 1990; and the 1990 volume of essays edited by Krosnick).

has increased dramatically in the past three decades, with the result that most House seats appear safe for the incumbent. House members have been able, by dint of their own efforts, to build a "personal vote" that is loyal to them regardless of partisan considerations. Thus it sometimes happens that a seat will be safe for a particular incumbent for a decade or more, but that when the incumbent retires, the seat will quickly become safe for a person of the opposite party. This development has given House members an independent standing that is almost unique among legislators in Western democracies and that seems to have vitally affected the performance of the American Congress (Cain, Ferejohn, and Fiorina, 1987; Jacobson, 1991).

The reason for the rise of the personal vote, however, remains somewhat unclear. Less than half of the eligible electorate can recall the name of their congressional representative, and this figure has not changed in the period in which incumbents have become safer. But although most people cannot *recall* their incumbent's name, about 80 percent can *recognize* it. This discovery has become the basis for a claim that much of an incumbent's advantage occurs in the voting booth where voters are asked only to recognize rather than to recall who is serving as their member of Congress (Mann and Wolfinger, 1980).

The typical congressional election, thus, takes place in a low-information environment in which a few people know the name of the incumbent and perhaps something about his or her record; many others can, with a prompt, recognize the incumbent's name and perhaps hazily recall one or two facts about the person's record or background; and still others know nothing at all about the incumbent.

These differences in political awareness greatly affect the capacity of incumbents to develop a "personal vote" among their constituents – and yet they are typically ignored in research on the subject. In consequence, the dynamics of the personal vote have remained murky. To preview arguments that are more fully developed in Chapter 10, the people who know most about politics in general are also most heavily exposed to the incumbent's self-promotional efforts. Yet, as political sophisticates, they are also better able to evaluate and critically scrutinize the new information they encounter. So in the end, highly aware persons tend to be little affected by incumbent campaigns. If they share the party and values of the incumbent, they will support the incumbent whether he or she campaigns vigorously or not; if they do not share the incumbent's values, they will refuse to support him or her no matter how hard he campaigns. Meanwhile, at the low end of the awareness spectrum, those who pay little attention to politics tend to get little or no information about congressional politics. Hence they are also relatively unaffected by the efforts of the incumbent to build a personal following. This leaves the moderately aware most susceptible to influence: They pay enough attention to be exposed to the blandishments of the incumbent but lack the resources to resist.

Evidence on this point is shown in Figure 2.3, which depicts the relationship between political awareness and the chances that people will desert their own party to vote for an incumbent member of Congress rather than their own

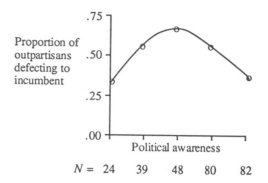

Figure 2.3. Defections to House incumbent among partisans of outparty. See the Measures Appendix for a description of the measure of political awareness. *Source:* 1978 NES survey.

party's candidate. The data involve contested seats in the 1978 general election. As can be seen, defection rates to the incumbent are markedly higher among moderately aware persons than among persons at the extremes of either high or low awareness.[9]

Note that if, as some researchers have done, one checks for a linear relationship in these data, one will discover little of interest. Awareness has strong effects, but its relationship with vote defection is nonmonotonic. (A relationship is said to be nonmonotonic when the association between variables is positive over part of the range of the independent variable and negative over the other part, as in Figure 2.3.)

What is true of congressional elections is true of numerous other cases: Political awareness has important effects on many aspects of public opinion and voting behavior, but these effects are often strongly nonlinear. This makes them difficult to detect and model.

Nonlinearity is, however, far from the only complication in detecting the effects of political awareness. In the example just discussed, we were concerned with the effects of a single political campaign, that of the congressional incumbent. Obviously, this is a highly simplified account of electoral politics. In most congressional elections, there are two main campaigns, each having some capacity to reach and mobilize sympathetic persons (though that of the incumbent nearly always has more).

The same holds true in other mass persuasion situations. Public opinion is sometimes formed by streams of a monolithically one-sided elite discourse, but, more often, it is shaped by multiple and typically conflicting information flows, some of which are more intense, or easier to learn about, than others. Under-

---

9 There are three reasons for the small number of cases in Figure 2.3: First, the voting rate in off-year congressional elections is relatively low, even among NES respondents; second, the figure involves only members of the party not holding the given congressional seat; and third, uncontested and open seat races have been eliminated.

standing the effects of elite discourse on preference formation requires modeling the effects of awareness in mediating exposure to each of the major campaign messages in the environment, a task that presents serious complications.

A final complication, as has already been suggested, is that opinion formation is a multistage process, and awareness may affect different parts of the process differently: Political awareness is associated with increased exposure to current communications that might change one's opinion, but it is also associated with heightened capacity to react critically to new information. These two effects may be cross cutting, as in the case of congressional elections, where the most aware persons are most heavily exposed to the incumbent's campaign but also most resistant. But this needn't be the case. There are, as we shall see, cases in which the most aware persons are the easiest segment of the public to reach and persuade, and other cases in which very inattentive persons are most susceptible to persuasion. Systematically explaining these and other ways in which political awareness affects public opinion and voting behavior will be the most important single contribution of this book.

In view of the central importance of political awareness, it is worthwhile to digress briefly to consider how best to conceptualize and measure it. *Political awareness,* as used in this study, refers to the extent to which an individual pays attention to politics *and* understands what he or she has encountered. Attention alone is not enough, since people who, for example, watch the TV news while lying on the couch after dinner and a couple of glasses of wine will typically fail to enhance their political awareness.

The key to political awareness, then, is the absorption of political communications. Political awareness denotes intellectual or cognitive engagement with public affairs as against emotional or affective engagement or no engagement at all. Scholars have used a wide variety of concepts and measures to capture what is here being called political awareness. The concepts in the research literature include political expertise, cognitive complexity, political involvement, attentiveness, sophistication, and political acuity. Although choice of labels is perhaps mainly a matter of personal or disciplinary taste, my reason for preferring political awareness is that this term, better than the others, seems to capture the key processes in the model to be introduced here, namely an individual's reception and comprehension of communications from the political environment.

Scholars have also used several different types of questions to operationalize what I am calling political awareness. These include media exposure, political participation, education, and self-described interest in politics. As I argue in the Measurement Appendix, political awareness is, for both theoretical and empirical reasons, best measured by simple tests of neutral factual information about politics. The reason, in brief, is that tests of political information, more directly than any of the alternative measures, capture what has actually gotten into people's minds, which, in turn, is critical for intellectual engagement with politics. Typical information questions, as suggested earlier, ask which political party controls the House of Representatives, or whether Mainland China is a member of the United Nations.

Thus the information tests used to assess political awareness in this book are strictly *neutral* or *factual*. This point is stressed because, as indicated earlier, much of the information carried in elite discourse is neither neutral nor strictly factual. A news report implying that the Pentagon is awash in scandal and mismanagement, or a presidential remark to the effect that most unemployed persons could get jobs if they tried hard enough, constitute factual information in that they may contain some simple facts, and that they convey sincerely held beliefs about factual states of affairs. Yet they are not neutral, since they have been framed for partisan purposes and can be reasonably disputed by fairminded people. Some kinds of assertions, such as the claim that the spread of abortion signifies a degradation of American morals, are not even fully susceptible to empirical verification; yet the broadcast of this claim in the media would constitute a broadcast of information, since it would involve an assertion about the actual state of the nation.

Nonneutral and not necessarily factual information, thus, is indistinguishable from political argumentation. Neutral factual information, such as which party controls Congress, is important in this book insofar as it measures a person's likely level of exposure to this other, nonneutral and not exclusively factual information.

To avoid confusion between information of the neutral and nonneutral types, I will from this point onward use information exclusively in its *nonneutral* sense, as in "information about the deterioration of American morals." Instead of referring to tests of neutral factual information, as used in measuring political awareness, I will simply refer to tests of political awareness or political knowledge.

In order to remind the reader that information is normally used in its nonneutral sense, I will occasionally place the term in quotes. Also, for aesthetic reasons, I will sometimes substitute cognates of attentiveness for awareness, as in "politically inattentive" for "politically unaware."

POLITICAL PREDISPOSITIONS

Citizens differ greatly in their levels of exposure to elite discourse, but these exposure differences can, by themselves, explain only a part of the variance in individual opinions. For citizens are more than passive receivers of whatever media communications they encounter. They possess a variety of interests, values, and experiences that may greatly affect their willingness to accept – or alternatively, their resolve to resist – persuasive influences.

In this book, I refer to all of these factors as *political predispositions,* by which I mean stable, individual-level traits that regulate the acceptance or non-acceptance of the political communications the person receives. Because the totality of the communications that one accepts determines one's opinions (by means that I will specify), predispositions are the critical intervening variable between the communications people encounter in the mass media, on one side, and their statements of political preferences, on the other.

The sources of variability in individuals' political predispositions are beyond the scope of this book. My assumption, however, is that predispositions are at least in part a distillation of a person's lifetime experiences, including childhood socialization and direct involvement with the raw ingredients of policy issues, such as earning a living, paying taxes, racial discrimination, and so forth. Predispositions also partly depend on social and economic location and, probably at least as strongly, on inherited or acquired personality factors and tastes.[10]

Since this book emphasizes the role of elite-supplied information in shaping mass opinions, I wish to stress that elites are *not* assumed to have an important role in shaping individuals' political predispositions. In my argument, predispositions mediate people's responses to elite information in the manner just indicated, but predispositions are not in the short run influenced by elites.

It is likely that, over the long run, the elite ideas that one internalizes have some effect on one's values and other predispositions. But however this may be, this book is a study of opinion formation and change in particular short-term situations, and for this purpose, the long-term influence of elites on predispositions, to the extent that it exists, may be safely neglected.[11]

Of the various different types of predispositions, political values will receive the most sustained attention in this book. This is because they seem to have a stronger and more pervasive effect on mass opinions than any of the other predispositional factors.[12] But some of the other factors, especially race and party attachment, are also very important and will receive significant attention.

Values refer to "general and enduring standards" that hold a "more central position than attitudes" in individuals' belief systems (Kinder and Sears, 1985: p. 674) and that "lead us to take particular positions on social issues" (Rokeach, 1973: p. 13). Thus, for example, a person strongly attached to the value of economic individualism would, all else equal, be more likely to reject an argument for higher taxes to pay for social welfare spending than would someone less attached to this value.

Political values, understood in this way, have recently become objects of serious scholarly study (for a review, see Kinder and Sears, 1985). Although this research has been quite useful in invigorating a previously moribund debate on the structure of mass opinions, it appears to have two important weaknesses.

10 Although the academic literature on personality and opinion is problematic, individual differences in political attitudes appear to reflect more than just differences in economic and social location, and it seems reasonable to describe these underlying differences in terms of personality. (See Adorno et al., 1950; Smith, Bruner, and White, 1956; McClosky, 1958; Altemeyer, 1981; Costantini and Craik, 1980; Wilson, 1983.)

11 Elite ideas, having been internalized, can have important effects on susceptibility to subsequent elite influence, but, as I show in my discussion of "inertial resistance" to persuasion in later chapters, they are able to do so without having any intervening effect on political values.

12 Except perhaps race. But there is too little variance in race – that is, the population is too one-sidedly white – to permit making race a central predispositional factor in this study.

One of these weaknesses will be centrally addressed in this book, but the second must be provisionally resolved by assumption.

The first limitation is that, like most public opinion research, the current literature on values largely fails to take systematic account of the vast differences in political awareness that exist among citizens. This failure is unfortunate because a frequent claim of the values literature has been that citizens who are, as most scholars agree, too unsophisticated to possess "ideologies" nonetheless possess sufficient awareness to make reliable use of "values" to structure their policy preferences. Thus, in a leading example of this research, Hurwitz and Peffley (1987) propose a hierarchical model of foreign policy opinions in which "core values" determine individuals' "general postures," which in turn determine opinions on particular foreign policy issues. The fact that many Americans are quite ignorant of foreign affairs is, according to Hurwitz and Peffley, precisely the reason that individuals must often fall back on core values and general postures to instruct their policy preferences:

we see individuals as attempting to cope with an extraordinarily confusing world . . . by structuring views about specific foreign policies according to their more general and abstract beliefs. (p. 1114)

Although this point is an excellent one, citizens must still possess some minimal degree of information in order to recognize the relevance of their values for a given issue, and, as I have been arguing, it is quite easy to underestimate how often even minimal political information may be absent for some citizens.

By way of illustration, we may examine opinions toward the U.S. policy of aid to the Contra rebels in Nicaragua. Figure 2.4 shows how citizens who differed in both their political awareness and in their predisposition toward use of military force responded in 1987 to a question on this topic. The persons classified as "hawks" in the figure are ones who said, over a set of general questions, that they strongly value military strength, an aggressive posture toward potential adversaries, and uncompromising opposition to communism. "Doves" are persons who rejected these positions, preferring to emphasize negotiations and accommodation with communism. Political awareness in the figure is measured by simple tests of factual knowledge about politics. (Items used in scale construction may be found in the Measures Appendix.)

The left side of the figure shows that politically aware hawks and doves differ greatly on the question of whether U.S. "aid to the Contras in Nicaragua" should be increased, decreased, or kept the same: Forty-two percent of the most aware hawks, but only 3 percent of the most aware doves, favored increased Contra aid. However, among persons in the middle third of the awareness scale, hawks and doves differed only modestly, and among persons at the bottom of the scale, there were no value-based differences at all – a result that raises doubts whether the hawk–dove value dimension has any utility for understanding the views of poorly informed persons.

However, the right-hand side of Figure 2.4 supports the conventional view of the importance of values. It shows responses to a question about whether the

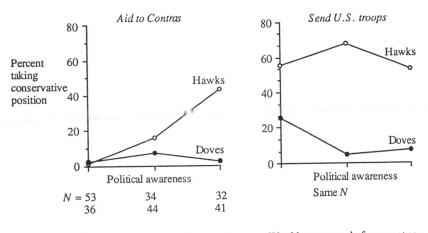

Percent taking conservative position

Figure 2.4. Two questions about Central America policy. *Source:* 1987 NES pilot survey.

United States should send troops "to stop the spread of communism" in Central America. Here we find sharp differences between hawks and doves at all levels of awareness.

Why the difference in response pattern to the two items, especially among less politically aware persons? The likely explanation is the contextual information carried in the two questions: The first, although scarcely lacking in clarity, requires respondents to know who the Contras are and what they stand for. This requirement will often go unmet among persons who are, in general, poorly informed about politics. (Commercial surveys taken in 1985 indicated that only about half of the American public knew which side the United States was supporting in the fighting in Nicaragua.) The second question in Figure 2.4, by mentioning communism, makes clear what the value implications of the issue are, thereby enabling people inclined toward hawkish foreign policies to recognize and support them.

Thus, the impact of people's value predispositions always depends on whether citizens possess the contextual information needed to translate their values into support for particular policies or candidates, and the possession of such information can, as shown earlier, never be taken for granted. This contingency in the relationship between values and support for particular policies or candidates underlies this entire study, whose purpose, as I have indicated, is to show

how individuals use information from the political environment to translate their values and other predispositions into more specific opinion statements.

A second shortcoming of the values literature arises from its failure, so far, to specify the nature of the theoretical relationship of different value continua to one another and to political ideology. The problem arises from the fact that, although there are numerous "value dimensions" between which there is no obvious logical connection, many people nonetheless respond to different value dimensions *as if* they were organized by a common left–right dimension. There is, in other words, a tendency for people to be fairly consistently "left" or "right" or "centrist" on such disparate value dimensions as economic individualism, opinions toward communists, tolerance of nonconformists, racial issues, sexual freedom, and religious authority. The correlations among these different value dimensions are never so strong as to suggest that there is one and only one basic value dimension, but they are always at least moderately strong, and among highly aware persons, the correlations are sometimes quite strong.[13] And, of course, there are also moderately strong correlations between people's self-descriptions as liberal or conservative and their scores on the various values measures.

What, then, is the nature of the relationship between "values," as examined in recent research, and "ideology," which an older generation of researchers took so seriously? In view of the empirical covariation among measures of the two concepts, the question seems an obvious and important one.

Let "values" be defined, as they normally are, as domain-specific organizing principles, such as economic individualism, where each value dimension lends structure to public opinions within a particular domain. "Ideology" may then be defined as a more general left–right scheme capable of organizing a wide range of fairly disparate concerns, where the concerns being organized include various value or issue dimensions or both.

These definitions closely link the two concepts without, as far as I can see, violating the conventional meaning of either term. There are, however, two significant novelties. First, the various value dimensions are no longer conceptually independent; rather, each is one among several correlated dimensions of a master concept, ideology. Second, ideology is no longer the strictly unidimensional concept that many discussions have considered it to be, but a constellation of related value dimensions.

The dimensionality of ideology may be analogous, in a certain respect, to the dimensionality of human intelligence. As a large psychological literature has shown and as common experience confirms, it is mistaken to say that there is a single dimension of intelligence. Thus, we all know people who are better at some kinds of tasks than others – mathematical reasoning rather than verbal expression, to take the most obvious case. Yet it is rare to find someone who is very high on one dimension and very low on another – a brilliant writer who

13 For evidence of the breadth of attitudes apparently organized by the left–right dimension, see Monroe, 1990; McClosky and Zaller, 1984: chap. 7.

cannot do simple addition and multiplication, or a great mathematician who cannot also generate fluent written prose. A person who is extraordinarily high on one dimension of intelligence tends to be at least fairly high on others. A similar thing appears to be true for ideology. It is unusual to encounter a person who is very liberal on one dimension of ideology and extremely conservative on another.[14] There is a tendency, which is clear but not overpowering, for people to stake out roughly comparable positions on a series of seemingly unrelated left–right value dimensions.

There are two practical implications of this view for the measurement of predispositions in this study. First, one should, whenever possible, use appropriate domain-specific measures of political values, rather than a general measure of ideology, as the operational measure of citizens' predispositions to accept or reject the political communications they receive. The reason is that ideology, as the more general measure of people's left–right tendencies, is more likely to miss reactions to a particular issue than is an indicator that has been tailored to that issue.

The second implication of this analysis is that, since values are, to a significant extent, organized by a person's general ideological orientation, one can, if necessary, use general or omnibus ideology measures to capture people's left–right tendencies. And often it is necessary. Much of this book focuses on cases of opinion change, but there are relatively few cases of mass opinion change that have been captured by high-quality, publicly available surveys. Hence I must make full use of what little good data on opinion change are available. In some of these datasets, there are excellent measures of political values that capture exactly the value dimensions that regulate the opinion change. But in other cases, a survey may have only a very general measure of value orientation, such as liberal–conservative self-identification, or measures of value orientations that are not particularly close to the opinion that is undergoing change. In cases of this kind, I develop the best measure of general left–right tendency that I can and go ahead, hoping that one such measure may be, in practice, almost as good as another. (The measures employed are always generally described in the text of the book and exactly described in the Measures Appendix.) The justification for this practice, beyond sheer necessity, is the notion that there is a general left–right organizing principle that runs through many different value dimensions.

This practice is obviously a conservative one. To the extent that general measures of value orientation fail to capture a predisposition that is related to the opinion undergoing change, I will tend to get weak or nonexistent relationships with values. And indeed, some of the relationships I have found appear weaker than I believe they would be if stronger value measures were available.

Finally, a note on terminology. At some points in this study I will describe individuals as "liberal" or "conservative." In so doing, I will *never* mean to

---

14 The obvious exceptions here are libertarians, who tend to be conservative on economic issues and liberal on life-style issues. But libertarians are sufficiently uncommon in the United States that studies of ideology routinely and apparently safely ignore them.

imply that the people so designated are necessarily full-fledged, doctrinaire ideologues of the left or right. I will mean only that the people tend to be closer to the left or right pole of some particular value dimension, or closer to one or the other pole of the constellation of associated liberal–conservative values. Thus, rather than say that a person is high on a measure of equalitarianism or high on a measure of hawkishness, I may say that the person is liberal or conservative. But whichever term I use, the important point to remember is that, for purposes of this book, values and ideology have exactly the same theoretical status: They are indicators of *predispositions* to accept or reject particular political communications.

WHAT IS AN OPINION?

John Mueller begins his study of *War, Presidents, and Public Opinion* (1973) with a series of caveats that ought to appear on the opening pages of every book on public opinion, but which rarely do. He writes:

The interview situation is an odd social experience. The respondent, on his doorstep or in his living room, is barraged with a set of questions on a wide variety of subjects by a stranger, usually a rather well-educated woman over 30, who carefully notes each response on a sheet of paper. Few people are accustomed to having their every utterance faithfully recorded and many find the experience flattering. And, aware that their views are being preserved for the ages, they do not wish to appear unprepared at that moment. Under these circumstances it is not surprising to find respondents pontificating in a seemingly authoritative, if basically "truthful," manner on subjects about which they know nothing or to which they have never given any thought whatsoever. . . . (p. 1)

The consequences of asking uninformed people to state opinions on topics to which they have given little if any previous thought are quite predictable: Their opinion statements give every indication of being rough and superficial. The opinion statements vacillate randomly across repeated interviews of the same people (see Table 2.1; also see Converse, 1964; Achen, 1975; Dean and Moran, 1977; Erickson, 1979; Feldman, 1989; Zaller, 1990); entirely trivial changes in questionnaire construction, such as switching the order in which questions are asked or response options are listed, can easily produce 5 to 10 percentage point shifts in aggregate opinion, and occasionally double that (Schuman and Presser, 1981; Bishop, Oldendick, and Tuchfarber, 1984; Tourangeau et al., 1989); and different ways of phrasing questions regularly have large effects on measured levels of public support for an issue. For example, Rasinski (1989) reports that, over several surveys, 68 percent of Americans felt too little money was being spent on "halting the rising crime rate," but that only 55 percent felt too little was being spent on "law enforcement." Similarly, 68 percent felt that too little was being spent on "protecting social security," but only 53 percent felt this way about spending on "social security." Or, in another type of case, 45 percent of Americans would "not allow" a communist to give a speech, whereas only 20 percent of Americans would "forbid" the same behavior (Schuman and

Table 2.1. *Response stability in repeated interviews: Two examples*

Opinion on cooperation with Russia[a] January 1980				Opinion on level of government services[b] January 1980			
	Coop.	Mid.	Tough	DK		Cut	Middle	Same	DK
June 1980					*June 1980*				
Cooperate	52%	25	13	19	Cut	54%	38	19	34
Middle	14	24	17	16	Middle	18	24	10	10
Tougher	23	41	60	18	Keep same	11	25	59	15
Don't know	11	11	10	47	Don't know	17	14	13	41
	100%	100	100	100		100%	100	100	100
N	266	153	238	74		362	122	208	138

[a] The question was: "Some people feel it is important for us to try very hard to get along with Russia. Others feel it is a big mistake to try too hard to get along with Russia . . ." People were asked to place themselves on a 7-point scale. Points 1, 2, and 3 have been counted as "cooperate"; 4 as middle; 5, 6, and 7 as "tougher."

[b] The question was: "Some people think the government should provide fewer services, even in areas such as health and education, in order to reduce spending. Other people feel it is important for the government to continue the services it now provides even if it means no reduction in spending . . ."

Source: 1980 NES panel survey.

Presser, 1981: p. 277). A record instance of the effects of changes in question wording may be a *New York Times* poll in 1983 which found that public support for a "freeze" on nuclear weapons production, at that moment a topic of heated interest, varied between 18 percent and 83 percent, depending on how the issue was framed.[15]

It is easy to think of reasons why few analysts of public opinion follow Mueller's example in exhibiting this catalogue of horrors in their opening pages. The most obvious is that they fear being dismissed out of hand, losing their audience before any argument has been made, if they too candidly reveal the dubious nature of the data on which their study depends.

But a more important reason, I believe, is that no one knows quite what to make of the multiple vagaries of mass opinion. Most analysts truly believe that public opinion is a more substantial entity than is indicated by the evidence just cited – and yet the gloomy indications are all too real. Being unable to square all the facts with what one believes is true, one simply puts aside the troubling evidence for the time being, leaving it to survey methodologists to work out, and writes about those aspects of public opinion one does understand.

An obvious problem with this approach is that it conceals information from the reader. Another is that it relinquishes the opportunity of making realistic statements about how mass opinion, in all of its elusiveness, forms and changes.

15 Judith Miller, 30 May 1982, p. A1.

In view of these considerations, the present study will make no effort to hide or underplay the types of problems with opinion data that have just been described. Indeed, it will make a theory of why the problems exist an integral part of its analysis. The theory is more simplistic than I would like, but it will at least address the problems head on.

This approach is a gamble. Placing at the center of the book a theory of the nature of public opinion – a subject that neither I nor anyone else fully understands – ties its entire argument to some weak reeds, giving critics an opportunity to complain, correctly, that its foundations are uncertain. Whether the returns on this risky strategy, the opportunity to sketch a unified and realistic treatment of the dynamics of public opinion, have been worth their cost will be up to the reader to decide.

Let me begin this part of my argument by recounting in more detail the vagaries of mass political opinion to which I have alluded; the relatively narrow-gauge theories by which scholars have sought to explain some of these phenomena; and the more general theory that I will use to explain these findings and to integrate them into a model of the effect of elite discourse on mass opinions.

Problems with mass opinion reports: Over time instability

Table 2.1 gives two typical examples of response instability over time. The first question, from a sample of respondents who were interviewed in January and again in June of 1980, asks whether the United States should try harder to cooperate with the Soviet Union, our Cold War adversary, or whether we should get tougher. As can be seen, 60 percent of those who favored a tougher stand in January still took this position in June; the rest were scattered across the other three options (greater cooperation with Russia, a middle position, or "no opinion"). Of those who took a neutral middle position in January, only 24 percent still did so in June, with most of the rest now favoring either more cooperation or less. Altogether, only 50 percent of the respondents took the same position in June that they had taken in January. (If everyone were simply guessing each time he were asked the question, roughly 32 percent would be expected by chance alone to state the same opinion on successive interviews, given my recoding of the item.) The same tendencies are apparent in the second question, which concerns the proper level of government services. Here, some 55 percent of the survey respondents managed to state the same opinion on successive interviews.

One obvious interpretation of these flip-flops is that many people undergo genuine opinion change between interviews. The evidence, however, fails to support this interpretation. When the same respondents are asked the same question on three different occasions, one can typically predict their opinion on the third interview as well from the first interview as the second. If changes between the first and second interviews represented systematic opinion change, this would not be possible. The generally accepted conclusion, therefore, has been that response instability of the type shown in Table 2.1 predominantly represents some sort of chance variation. But what sort of chance variation, and why so much of it?

In his famous paper on "The nature of belief systems in mass publics," Converse (1964) argued that opinion instability is due mainly to individuals who lack strong feelings on the given issue but nevertheless indulge interviewers by politely choosing as best they can between the response options put in front of them – but often choosing in an essentially random fashion. [Large portions] of an electorate," he suggested, "simply do not have meaningful beliefs, even on issues that have formed the basis for intense political controversy among elites for substantial periods of time" (1964: p. 245).

This conclusion has been strongly challenged by scholars who contend that, although people's "survey responses" fluctuate greatly, citizens have underlying "true attitudes" that are overwhelmingly stable (Achen, 1975, 1983; Dean and Moran, 1977; Erikson, 1979; Judd and Milburn, 1980; Judd, Milburn, and Krosnick, 1981; Feldman, 1989; Zaller, 1990; an exception is Krosnick, 1988; for general reviews, see Kinder and Sears, 1985 and Smith, 1984). The fluctuations that appear in people's overt opinion statements are attributed to "measurement error," where such error is said to stem from the inherent difficulty of mapping one's preexisting opinions onto the unavoidably vague language of survey questions.

The theory of measurement error has an especially attractive implication. If one believes that attitudinal variables have been measured with large amounts of random error, it follows that their correlations with other variables will be artificially deflated. And if this is so, it is legitimate to reinflate these depressed correlations by means of standard psychometric techniques, which researchers routinely do. Thus, attitudinal variables which, in fact, exhibit high instability over time and low correlations with other variables are made, by means of correction procedures, to appear almost perfectly stable and highly correlated with other variables. In this way, the problem of response instability is rendered not only innocuous but invisible.

Both the Converse and measurement error approaches to response instability appear to have deficiencies. Converse's thesis, which takes any instability as evidence of a "nonattitude," was an extreme claim intended to characterize opinions only on certain highly abstract issues. On more typical issues, as Converse and Markus (1979) argue, people's opinions may be more or less "crystallized" and are, as a result of this, more or less stable. But this only raises the question of what exactly crystallization consists of. Since no one has ever said, opinion crystallization remains more a metaphor than a testable theory of opinion stability (Krosnick and Schuman, 1988).

The newer "measurement error" theory of response instability seems equally underspecified at its theoretical core. When, as all estimates agree, *measurement "error" normally constitutes one-half to three-quarters of the variance of opinion items,* one naturally wonders what this chance "error" consists of and how it has been generated. Yet researchers have been remarkably uncurious about this problem. In a large majority of cases in which it is acknowledged, analysts make a statistical correction for it and move quickly on to whatever their study is mainly about. As a result, "measurement error" is closer to being a euphemism for "unexplained variance" than it is to being a well-understood phenomenon (see, however, Schuman and Presser, 1981; Krosnick and Berent, 1992).

Problems with mass opinion reports: "Response effects"

A second embarrassment to the conventional view of opinions has been the discovery of substantial amounts of nonrandom or "systematic error" in people's opinion reports. Many respondents react to the context in which a question is asked, to the order in which alternative responses are presented, and to wholly nonsubstantive and trivial alterations in questions. The systematic effects of such seemingly irrelevant features of the interview process are known as "response effects."

Consider a well-known experiment during the 1970s on Americans' opinions toward Soviet journalists. In a split-half sample, 37 percent of respondents were willing to allow Communist reporters in the United States. Yet when, in the other half-sample, respondents were first asked whether U.S. reporters should be allowed in Russia (which most favored), the percentage agreeing to allow Russian reporters into the United States nearly doubled to 73 percent. The explanation for this huge difference, as Schuman and Presser (1981) suggest, is that when people are asked the Communist reporters item alone, they respond on the basis of anti-Communist opinions. When, however, the question is preceded by one about American reporters working in Russia,

a norm of reciprocity is immediately made salient and a substantial number of respondents feel bound to provide an answer that is consistent with their previous response. . . . The crux of the matter seems to be that the reporter questions have two meanings, one involving an attitude toward an object and another involving an attitude toward a norm. (p. 28)

Note that this explanation implicitly abandons the notion that individuals possess a single, fixed opinion toward the rights of Communist reporters. Rather, individuals are assumed to have at least two considerations, one involving Communists and the other involving the norm of fair play, and to answer the question according to whichever consideration has been made salient by the questionnaire.

There are numerous other findings of this type: People are less likely to describe themselves as interested in politics just after they have been asked about obscure issues (Bishop et al., 1984); people's opinions toward abortion are affected by the kinds of items (concerning, for example, religion or women's rights) that precede it (Tourangeau and Rasinski, 1988; Tourangeau et al. 1989);

people give quite different answers to open-ended questions than to questions that ask them to choose among a series of prespecified options (Schuman and Scott, 1987).

Question-wording effects

It is uncommon for a change in question order to shift public opinion by more than 10 or 15 percentage points, and many shift opinion by smaller amounts or not at all. Changes in the substantive wording of questions can, on the other hand, produce much larger effects on political opinions and can do so much more reliably. Yet these changes are not normally considered either worrisome or even especially interesting. The feeling seems to be that differently worded questions *should* get different answers, since they change either the emotional loading of the issue or, in some cases, what the respondent is being asked about.

It is not clear, however, that this complaisance is warranted. It is, for example, well established that adding the endorsement of a prominent politician to a policy question – as in, "Do you favor or oppose President X's policy of . . . ?" – is likely to change the public's response to that issue, depending on the popular view of President X. But if, as conventional opinion models assume, citizens have preexisting "true attitudes" that they merely reveal to the inquiring pollster, such "endorsement effects" should not occur. The fact that they do occur, and quite reliably, indicates that many respondents are making up their opinions – or at least editing and modifying them – as they go through the questionnaire.

Consider another type of question wording effect. In his study of support for the Korean War, Mueller (1973) found that people were more likely to express support for the war if the antiwar option required them to confess that their country had made a mistake by entering the war. Similarly, support for the war was consistently 15 to 20 percentage points greater if the war was described as necessary to stop communism. When both factors were at work, their joint impact on opinion was considerable. Thus, in one poll taken in the fall of 1953, only about 38 percent of the public said that "the Korean War has been worth fighting"; but in another poll taken at about the same time, 64 percent said that the United States "did the right thing in sending troops to stop the Communist invasion" (Mueller: table 3.1). As Mueller remarked,

These data suggest somewhat conflicting observations. On the one hand, support for the war was clearly tied to the anti-Communist spirit in America at the time. To generate a kind of war fever, one merely had to toss the words, "Communist invasion," into the discussion. On the other hand, the Communist element was not entirely built into the response to the war because Americans had to be reminded of it before their anti-Communism was fully activated. . . . (Mueller 1973, pp. 46–8)

So, we again find out that a sizable fraction of survey respondents appear to form their opinions during the interview on the basis of the ideas made salient to them by the question, rather than simply revealing preexisting "true attitudes."

The counterargument to this conclusion – that different questions were involved and should therefore be expected to produce different answers even if people did have preexisting opinions – does not seem to me credible. The issue that people were addressing – the appropriateness of the U.S. response to an invasion of South Korea by the Communist government of North Korea – was the same whether or not the survey question used the critical phrase, "Communist invasion." Thus, anyone who had a fixed opinion on the war should have been able to express it whether communism was mentioned or not.

A clear demonstration that changes in question wording can change people's responses *even when the underlying issue remains exactly the same* may be found in Tversky and Kahneman's (1982) case of the rare Asian disease. These two psychologists put the following questions to a sample of college students:

Imagine the U.S. is preparing for the outbreak of an unusual Asian disease, which is expected to kill 600 people. Two alternative programs have been proposed. Assume that the exact scientific estimates of the consequences of the programs are as follows:

If program A is adopted, 200 people will be saved.

If program B is adopted, there is a one-third probability that 600 people will be saved, and a two-thirds probability that no people will be saved.

Which of these two programs do you favor?

This problem requires respondents to choose between a certain fixed loss and a gamble having an identical expected loss. In this case, 72 percent chose the certain loss, that is, saving 200 persons via program A. Yet when a comparable sample was asked in a differently worded question to respond to precisely the same dilemma, the results were radically different. In the second sample, the alternatives were described as follows:

If program C is adopted, 400 people will die.

If program D is adopted, there is a one-third probability that nobody will die, and a two-thirds probability that 600 people will die.

In this situation, only 22 percent chose the certain loss of 400 lives – a reduction of 50 percentage points. The conclusion to be drawn from this example, as from earlier ones, is that differences in the wording of questions can determine how people think about and hence respond to issues even when, as here, the denotative meanings of the competing wordings are exactly the same.

The need for a model of the survey response

There are, to reiterate, two types of evidence that weigh against the conventional notion that individuals have preexisting attitudes that they simply reveal in response to survey questions. The first is the widely replicated finding that 50 to 75 percent of the variance in typical opinion items is *random* "error" – an amount that is too large to be comfortably ascribed to the effects of vaguely worded questions. The second is the evidence of large amounts of *systematic* "error" arising from the effects of question order and question wording.

These findings are more than methodological curiosities. They seriously undermine the conventional view that surveys are passive measures of "what the public really believes." More ominously, they raise the fear that a large fraction of what opinion researchers measure is either random or systematic "noise."

In the last fifteen years, survey methodologists and social psychologists have recognized this problem and sought to deal with it. They have tended to abandon the conventional notion that people possess fixed opinions that they simply *reveal* in surveys, and have begun to concentrate instead on the "question-answering process" by which individuals *construct* opinion reports in response to the particular stimulus that confronts them.

In a recent example of this research, Wilson and Hodges (1991) describe the traditional view of attitudes as being essentially a "file drawer" model of attitudes:

When people are asked how they feel about something, such as legalized abortion, their Uncle Harry, or anchovies on a pizza, presumably they consult a mental file containing their evaluation. They look for the file marked "abortion," or "Uncle Harry," or "anchovies," and report the evaluation it contains.

But Wilson and Hodges (1991) reject the general validity of this model. "People often construct their attitudes, rather than simply reporting the contents of a mental file." Their attitude reports are based on the ideas in a large but internally conflicted "database," so that the "attitude" that is reported at a given time is a "temporary construction" which depends on peculiarities of the process by which a person has constructed it.

Wilson and Hodges are not the only researchers to entertain such radical notions. In a prominent 1988 paper, Tourangeau and Rasinski also abandoned the traditional view of political attitudes and proposed to replace it with a general model of the "question-answering" process by which people construct attitude statements. (I will deal further with their model later on.) Similar though more modest steps have been taken by Schuman and Presser (1981), Bishop et al. (1984), Iyengar and Kinder (1987), Bartels (1988), Kinder and Sanders (1990), and Popkin (1991).

Unfortunately, most research on the new "question-answering models" has tended to focus on response effects, and has had nothing to say about either random response instability or the larger process by which people form their opinions in response to information gleaned from the political environment. What is therefore needed is a broader question-answering model.

This is what I attempt to provide in this book. Like a fair number of survey methodologists and psychologists, I abandon the conventional but implausible view that citizens typically possess "true attitudes" on every issue about which a pollster may happen to inquire, and instead propose a model of how individuals construct opinion reports in response to the particular stimuli that confront them. This model unites in one theory an account of how people acquire information about politics, as sketched in the first part of this chapter, with an account of how they use that information to formulate responses to typical survey items. The model is consistent with – indeed, it seeks to provide explanations for – the vagaries of the mass survey response, as outlined in these pages.

The argument, first made in a 1984 convention paper (Zaller, 1984b), is roughly as follows: People are continuously exposed to a stream of political news and information, much of it valenced so as to push public opinion in one direction or the other. But, owing to the generally low levels of attention to politics in this country, most people on most issues are relatively uncritical about the ideas they internalize. In consequence, they fill up their minds with large stores of only partially consistent ideas, arguments, and considerations. When asked a survey question, they call to mind as many of these ideas as are immediately accessible in memory and use them to make choices among the options offered to them. But they make these choices in great haste – typically on the basis of the one or perhaps two considerations that happen to be at the "top of the head"[16] at the moment of response.

The basic claim of the model, thus, is that survey responses are a function of immediately accessible "considerations," where the flow of information in elite discourse determines which considerations are salient. The reason for response instability, on this view, is that different considerations happen to be salient at different times, which causes people's survey responses to differ over repeated interviews. Changes in question order or question wording can bring about systematic changes in the considerations immediately salient to people, and hence systematic changes in their survey responses.

By way of illustrating the operation of the model, consider how typical citizens might have responded to a question about the proper level of U.S. defense spending during the cold war. Most would have heard a fair amount about the issue without ever having had the occasion to answer a survey question about it. They might have been upset about reports of Pentagon waste and mismanagement, but they might also have worried about the Soviet threat and America's capacity to contain it – all without thinking about or even recognizing the trade-offs between these competing concerns. When unexpectedly asked on a survey for their opinion on defense spending, they must have, in just a second or two, somehow pulled these and other thoughts together into a "survey response" on defense spending. In doing so, they did not fully canvass their minds for all relevant thoughts. Rather, if they had happened the night before to see a news program on a major defense procurement scandal, they might answer the question on the basis of that consideration. But if, on the other hand, they had been reminded by an earlier question about the threat of Soviet aggression they might instead answer that defense spending should remain high. And if, in a follow-up survey sometime later, the survey questions were asked in a different order, or if they had seen a different TV program the night before, they might have had different ideas at the tops of their heads and hence made different survey responses.

16 This useful description, which will recur many times in this book, is owed to Taylor and Fiske (1978).

An important feature of the model is that people who are more politically aware are more selective about the "information" that they internalize – which is to say, they will be more likely to reject ideas that are inconsistent with their values. As a result of this selectivity, the ideas they internalize are more internally consistent and more consistent with their values. Responses to closed-ended survey questions reflect this by exhibiting greater over time stability and greater ideological consistency with one another.

Background of the question-answering model

Although the suggestion of a question-answering approach to understanding mass opinions is still novel within the public opinion field, it is approaching the status of orthodoxy in some psychological circles. It is instructive to review some of the research on which this emerging orthodoxy rests.

One strand of this research, conducted by mathematical psychologists and focusing on problem solving, regards the mind as a sort of bin filled with multiple interpretive constructs. Confronted with a set of "stimulus elements" (raw sensory impressions) in a problem, individuals stochastically search their minds for constructs that enable them to make sense of the stimuli (Atkinson, Bower, and Crothers, 1965). An interpretive construct, once chosen, determines one's understanding of the stimuli and hence one's response to it. A person's judgments, thus, depend quite directly on the ideas that happen to come to the top of the mind at critical points in the problem-solving exercise.

Another research tradition, common among social psychologists and mainly concerned with social cognition, focuses on the organization of ideas in the mind. A central concept in this research is "schema," a term that has been adapted from cognitive psychology. A schema is a cognitive structure that organizes prior information and experience around a central value or idea, and guides the interpretation of new information and experience.

A critical point about schemata is that people typically have several of them available for understanding any given phenomenon. For example, an individual being introduced to a "forty-year-old professor" would react quite differently if the same person were instead introduced as "a forty-year-old mother of three." That is, different associations would come to mind, different qualities of the person would be noticed, different conclusions would be drawn from the person's mannerisms, and so forth. In short, the perceiver's "attitude" toward the person would be different. Thus Tesser (1978), in statements that nicely capture a central feature of the model being suggested, writes:

An attitude at a particular point in time is the result of a constructive process. . . . And, *there is not a single attitude toward an object* but, rather, any number of attitudes depending on the number of schemas available for thinking about the objects.

[P]ersons do not have a *single* feeling or evaluation of an object. Feelings vary depending upon the particular cognitive schema we "tune in." (pp. 297–8, 307, emphasis in the original)

The key idea in these studies is that individuals do not typically possess "just one opinion" toward issues, but multiple potential opinions. The logical next question is then how, in the face of this, people manage to come to decisions at all.

This turns out to be an immensely complicated issue, involving the encoding of incoming information, perception or interpretations of information, efficiency of memory search, and degree of motivation, among other things. Thus, psychologists attempting to come to grips with these various issues have proposed models that are fearfully complicated (e.g., Wyer and Srull, 1989).

One point that does, however, appear reasonably clear is that, in the course of making decisions, including those involving political matters, individuals rarely take the time to canvass their minds for all relevant thoughts. Life is too short and the human mind too fallible. Rather, they appear to make decisions "off the top of the head" on the basis of whatever ideas are immediately accessible in memory. Thus, as Taylor and Fiske (1978) note, numerous studies have shown that the introduction or emphasis of a single piece of information – such as the fact that a particular person is a woman or a lawyer – can greatly affect subsequent expressions of opinion. Reviewing a variety of such evidence, Taylor and Fiske maintain, in an argument quite novel for its time, that many people make social judgments by seizing on

a single, sufficient and salient explanation . . . often the first satisfactory one that comes along. . . . [I]nstead of employing base rate or consensus information logically, people are more often influenced by a single, colorful piece of case history evidence. . . . Instead of reviewing all the evidence that bears upon a particular problem, people frequently use the information which is most salient or available to them, that is, that which is most easily brought to mind. (p. 251)

On the basis of a much larger volume of evidence, Wyer and Srull (1989) maintain that people are

unlikely to conduct an exhaustive search of memory for all of the knowledge they have accumulated that is relevant to a particular decision. Rather they retrieve and use only a small subset of this knowledge, apparently assuming that its implications are representative of all the knowledge they have acquired. (p. 81)

Yet, at the same time, much data in political science (Kelley, 1983), political psychology (Lodge, McGraw, and Stroh, 1989), and cognitive psychology (Anderson, 1974) make it clear that individuals may often utilize many diverse pieces of information in their decision making. For example, Kelley (1983) shows that voters decide between presidential candidates as if they were summing up numerous "likes" and "dislikes" about each party and candidate and choosing the one with the highest net total. Anderson's information-averaging models, which have achieved wide recognition in psychology, likewise show that individuals make use of a wide set of relevant cognitions in formulating opinion statements.

The model I propose tries to accommodate both top-of-the-head decision making, as suggested by Taylor and Fiske, and averaging across potentially large amounts of disparate information, as suggested by Kelley and by Anderson. It does so by assuming that individuals make decisions by averaging over a non-random but stochastic sample of relevant considerations, where the size of the sample of considerations may vary between 1 and large. The size and composition of this sample depend on a variety of contextual and individual motivational factors, such as what ideas have been made salient by the questionnaire and how much attention a person generally pays to the subject at hand.

SUMMARY

This study focuses on interactions among three broad classes of variables: Aggregate-level variation in the information carried in elite discourse, including elite cues about how new information should be evaluated, individual-level differences in attention to this discourse, and individual-level differences in political values. Interactions among these variables determine the mix of ''considerations'' that gets into people's heads. Which of these considerations is available at the top of the head at the moment of confronting survey questions determines responses to the questions. A model based on these ideas is presented in the next chapter.

3

How citizens acquire information
and convert it into public opinion

The comprehensive analysis of public opinion requires attention to two phenomena: how citizens learn about matters that are for the most part beyond their immediate experience, and how they convert the information they acquire into opinions.

This chapter proposes a model of both phenomena. The model does not provide a fully accurate account of how people process information and form attitude statements. No model that is both parsimonious and testable on typical mass opinion data – the two most important constraints on my enterprise – could possibly do so. But the proposed model, as I hope to persuade the reader, does a plausible job of approximating what must actually occur, and a quite excellent job of accounting for the available survey evidence across a wide range of phenomena.

Having stated a model of the opinionation process in this chapter, I proceed in the rest of the book to test a series of propositions derived from the model. Some additional ideas will be needed to accomplish this, but they are few and incidental. All of the important features of my analysis derive from the model that is presented here.

SOME DEFINITIONS

I begin the statement of the model with definitions of primitive terms. The first is *consideration,* which is defined as any reason that might induce an individual to decide a political issue one way or the other.[1] Considerations, thus, are a compound of cognition and affect – that is, a belief concerning an object and an evaluation of the belief. "President Bush's plan to balance the federal budget is fair to all competing interests" is an example of a consideration that might impel an individual to say, in response to a survey question, that she approves of the way President Bush is handling his job as president. The cognitive element in

---

1 This term is a borrowing from Kelley (1983), who showed that individuals appear to make vote decisions in presidential elections on the basis of a net score across numerous competing "likes" and "dislikes" about the candidates, which he called "considerations."

this consideration is information about Bush's tax plan, and the affect is the favorable evaluation of it.[2]

Suppose that someone sees on the TV news the image of a "bum on the street," reacts with hostility, and makes this hostility the basis of an opinion statement opposing increased government spending on the homeless. It might initially seem that this hypothetical opinion statement is based on a purely affective response rather than a blend of cognition and affect. Yet a cognitive component is clearly present: The person on the street has been seen as a "bum" rather than "a person like myself who has unfortunately lost his job." Thus, the negative evaluation depends on a particular cognitive representation of what one has seen, which is to say, a combination of cognitive and affective elements.

Although much more could be said about considerations, particularly their possible role in guiding perception, the concept in its present spare form suffices for a great many purposes, as will become apparent.[3]

Second, I define two types of political messages: persuasive messages and cueing messages. Persuasive messages are arguments or images providing a reason for taking a position or point of view; if accepted by an individual, they become considerations, as the term was just defined. A speech by a Democratic politician charging that "President Bush's budget plan is a sham and a delusion" is an example of a persuasive message.

Note that there is nothing in this account that implies that either political messages or the considerations that result from them must be coldly rational. On the contrary, messages may involve subtle or even subliminal images, and considerations may involve feelings or emotions. Thus, a president may seek to project a "message" of competence in his public presentations, in the hope that it will make the public feel warm or secure. If the president is cognized in this way, and if this cognitive representation generates feelings of security that positively influence how citizens evaluate the president's job performance, the feelings of security must be counted as reasons for favorably evaluating the president – that is, as considerations. I wish to underscore these points because, although the model I propose has a cognitive flavor, it is, in principle, as capable of dealing with nonrational appeals and inarticulate feelings as with other kinds of political discourse.

2 In many cases the evaluation associated with a consideration is implicit rather than explicit, as in "The Pentagon wastes a lot of money," a piece of "information" that almost everyone would accept as reflecting unfavorably on the need for more defense spending.

3 There is a temptation simply to borrow the psychological concept of a schema and use it in place of the term "consideration." Yet "schema" is not quite right for my argument. For one thing, the concept stresses cognition rather than affect. However suitable this may be in other domains of life, it is not suitable in politics, where people appear to make decisions on the basis of ideas that are affectively charged. Consideration, defined as a reason for favoring a position, is perhaps idiosyncratic, but the term has the critical advantage of combining cognition and affect. Also, consideration has an everyday meaning that is more compatible with the *political* analysis of public opinion than terms such as schema.

Cueing messages, which are the second type of message carried in elite discourse, consist of "contextual information" about the ideological or partisan implications of a persuasive message. The importance of cueing messages is that, as suggested by Converse (1964), they enable citizens to perceive relationships between the persuasive messages they receive and their political predispositions, which in turn permits them to respond critically to the persuasive messages. Thus, a Republican voter will be more likely to reject criticism of President Bush's budget plan if she recognizes that the person making the criticism is a Democrat.

We saw a clear illustration of the importance of cueing information in the last chapter, where politically unaware hawks and doves were unable to make a partisan response to a question about aid to the Contra guerrillas in Nicaragua because they apparently lacked contextual information about who the Contras were. These same hawks and doves could, however, respond in partisan fashion to a question about combating communism in Central America because communism was a cue they understood.

THE MODEL

The model itself consists of four assertions, or axioms, about how individuals respond to political information they may encounter. Each is stated first as a general theoretical position and then elaborated and justified in more precise terms.

As will become apparent, none of the axioms is individually original, nor can it be said that any of the four axioms is a perfect representation of what occurs in the world. I hope, however, to show that the axioms, taken as a group, have some highly novel and empirically correct implications, and also that, even though not perhaps perfectly true, the axioms are quite plausible approximations of the processes that must actually occur as individuals acquire information about politics and use it to formulate statements of their political preferences.

A1. *RECEPTION AXIOM. The greater a person's level of cognitive engagement with an issue, the more likely he or she is to be exposed to and comprehend – in a word, to receive – political messages concerning that issue.*[4]

The messages people may receive include all types: that is, persuasive messages and cueing messages.

In specifying the reception axiom in terms of cognitive engagement rather than, say, strength of feeling about an issue, the model obviously stresses the cognitive aspect of exposure to political communications. There are two reasons for this. The first is that, as indicated, the model is most centrally concerned with how individuals acquire information from the environment and convert it into opinion statements. These are essentially cognitive processes, so that affective engagement is likely to be able to affect them only insofar as it leads to

4 These terms derive from McGuire, 1969.

intellectual – which is to say, cognitive – engagement. Hence it is appropriate to define the model in terms of cognitive engagement.

The second reason is that, as an empirical matter, survey measures that capture cognitive engagement with politics outperform measures of affective engagement in explaining most aspects of public opinion. For example, people who score higher on tests of political knowledge are substantially more stable in their attitude reports than people who score low on political awareness (Feldman, 1989, Zaller, 1990); however, people who describe themselves as highly interested in politics, which I take as a form of affective involvement, are not significantly more stable than persons who express little political interest (Zaller, 1990: table 2).

It is interesting to note that political interest, despite its limited effect on response stability, is a strong correlate of voter turnout – slightly stronger, in fact, than political knowledge (Zaller, 1990: table 1). So, affective engagement can be important, but unless coupled with intellectual engagement, it appears to have only limited effects on opinion per se.

Although cognitive engagement is the right specification for my model, it is a cumbersome and somewhat precious phrase. Therefore, I will, through most of the analysis that follows, use a simpler phrase, namely *political attentiveness* or *political awareness*. But cognitive engagement, political attentiveness, and political awareness are meant to convey the same meaning.

In the analysis that follows, political awareness is operationally measured mainly by means of a general measure of political knowledge – that is, a person's summary score across a series of neutral, factual tests of public affairs knowledge, as discussed in the previous chapter.

Political awareness, measured in this way, is a measure of *general, chronic awareness*. As such, it does not directly test individuals' information about or attention to a particular issue at a particular time. In using this sort of measure, I will be assuming that persons who are knowledgeable about politics in general are habitually attentive to communications on most particular issues as well.

This measurement strategy is less than ideal. More narrowly focused measures of awareness – devoted exclusively, say, to intellectual engagement with foreign policy issues or race policy issues, and used exclusively in connection with reception of information concerning foreign or race policy issues – would be preferable to general awareness measures. However, such domain-specific awareness measures are rarely carried on opinion surveys and none are available for the cases I examine in this study. As a practical matter, thus, I must make do with general measures. Yet, as far as I have been able to tell from investigation of similar problems, the loss from using general rather than domain-specific awareness measures to capture exposure to elite discourse is minimal (Zaller, 1986; Price and Zaller, 1990; though see also Iyengar, 1990; see Chapter 2 and the Measures Appendix for further discussion.)

The reader should note that the Reception Axiom, A1, indicates nothing about the sources of the political communications that shape mass opinion. As far as that axiom is concerned, political communications may originate in elite discourse, in purely personal exchanges among friends and neighbors, or in other ways. All that is claimed in A1 is that reception of politically relevant communications, whatever their origin, is positively associated with intellectual engagement with a given issue. By extension, political awareness is assumed to capture propensity for reception of political communications generally, regardless of their point of origin.

It would obviously be desirable to be able to measure exposure to interpersonal influence independently of exposure to elite discourse in the mass media. However, it is not possible to do so from the available data. Some surveys do carry measures of people's self-reported frequency of personal discussion of politics, but there is, as with measures of political awareness, no guarantee that they would capture exposure to only one type of communication.[5]

Thus, the reader should bear in mind that the assumption that it is the information carried in elite discourse, rather than personal influence or something else, which shapes mass opinion is not a part of the formal model that I am laying out in this chapter. It is, rather, an auxiliary assumption that requires independent justification, as I have sought to provide in the first part of Chapter 2 and will provide in parts of the analysis reported below. I extensively discuss this point in my closing evaluation of the book's argument in Chapters 11 and 12.

A2. *RESISTANCE AXIOM. People tend to resist arguments that are inconsistent with their political predispositions, but they do so only to the extent that they possess the contextual information necessary to perceive a relationship between the message and their predispositions.*

The key to resistance, in this formulation, is *information* concerning the relationship between arguments and predispositions, where the requisite information is carried in cueing messages. According to the Reception Axiom, the probability of individuals acquiring cueing information depends on their levels of awareness of each given issue. Thus, A1 and A2 together imply that the likelihood of resisting persuasive communications that are inconsistent with one's political predispositions rises with a person's level of political attentiveness. Or, to put it the other way, politically inattentive persons will often be unaware of

5 Price and I (1990) have found that, although frequency of political discussions with one's peers has a moderate bivariate relationship with the likelihood of reception of particular current news items, discussion has no impact once habitual political awareness is controlled. Even self-reported media use has little impact on measured news reception once general awareness is controlled. Neither of these findings, however, indicates anything about the sources of the news that individuals have received.

It might be suggested that if media use and frequency of political discussion were used *instead of* rather than *in addition to* general political awareness, it would be possible to distinguish their relative importance. The difficulty with this idea is that media exposure is extremely unreliably measured in typical surveys – much less reliably than the generally high alpha reliability statistics of indices of media exposure would indicate. In consequence, substitution of media use for political awareness results in dreadfully anemic results even when strong media effects are clearly present, as Price and I (1990) show. I suspect that the actual reliability of self-reported frequencies of political discussion would, if carefully investigated, prove low as well.

the implications of the persuasive communications they encounter, and so often end up "mistakenly" accepting them.

This postulate makes no allowance for citizens to think, reason, or deliberate about politics: If citizens are well informed, they react mechanically to political ideas on the basis of external cues about their partisan implications, and if they are too poorly informed to be aware of these cues, they tend to uncritically accept whatever ideas they encounter.[6]

As normatively unappealing as this implication of the model may be, it is consistent with a large body of theory and research concerning political persuasion. Philip Converse, the leading theorist of mass opinion, maintains that few people reason for themselves about how political ideas relate to one another. Rather, to the extent that individuals respond critically to the political ideas they encounter, they rely on contextual information from elites about how different ideas "go together" and thereby "constrain" one another (Converse, 1964). Although he does not say so, the contextual information that Converse describes would surely include the particular groups or leaders who favor or oppose an idea.

A central point in Converse's analysis is that awareness of contextual information is likely to depend on general levels of political awareness. Hence, only people attaining fairly high levels of awareness are likely to respond to communications in a manner that is "constrained" by their values.

The psychological literature on opinion change lends great support to the notion that individuals typically fail to reason for themselves about the persuasive communications they encounter. Instead, people rely on cues about the "source" of a message in deciding what to think of it. Reviewing this evidence in an influential 1969 article, William McGuire wrote:

> The given message is judged as fairer, more factual, more thoroughly documented, its conclusion following more validly from its premises, and even more grammatical, when it is ascribed to a high- as opposed to a low-credibility source. (p. 198)

Although the studies McGuire cites do not necessarily involve political sources that are Democrat or Republican, or liberal or conservative, they ought to generalize to these kinds of sources (see, for example, Belknap and Campbell, 1951–2; Mueller, 1973; Price, 1989).

McGuire goes on to note that people do not seem to *learn* more from credible sources; they simply tend to accept their opinion leadership more readily. This pattern, he continues,

> suggests again that the receiver can be regarded as a lazy organism who tries to master the message contents only when it is absolutely necessary to make a decision. When the purported source is clearly positively or negatively valenced, he uses this information as a cue to accept or reject the message's conclusions without really absorbing the arguments used.

6 As operationalized below, the model will not require that inattentive citizens accept *all* ideas they encounter; it requires only that they be more accepting than highly aware persons, and that they not be able to respond selectively to issues on the basis of their predispositions. However, the empirically estimated acceptance rates (given exposure) of uninformed people turn out to be very high; see Figures 7.4 and 10.1.

Recent research has sketched a somewhat more encouraging picture of the critical capabilities of the "receiver." For example, Rhine and Severance (1970) have found that college students pay no attention at all to credibility of the source when the topic of the message is one that engages their interest, which in this case was whether college tuition should be raised. Source effects, these researchers found, were limited to non–"ego-involving" issues, such as how much land should be set aside for parks in a distant community.

Most recently, the work of Chaiken (1980) and Petty and Cacioppo (1986) has provided clear support for the view that individuals will, under certain circumstances, entirely ignore such factors as "source credibility" and instead base their attitudes on the quality of the persuasive information they have been given. A typical Petty and Cacioppo experiment runs like this: Underclass college students are presented with persuasive arguments on a topic of potentially great interest to them – whether senior comprehensive exams should be a requirement for graduation. This is an idea that, needless to say, undergraduates are predisposed to resist. Half the students are exposed to "strong" arguments for comprehensive exams, such as the example of a university that instituted such exams and then found that the starting salaries of its graduates rose $4,000 over a two-year period, and the argument that law schools give preference to students from schools having the senior exam requirement. The other half of the students are given "weak" arguments, such as the arguments that many colleges are considering the exams, so the school could be at the forefront of a national trend, and that graduate students, who must take comprehensive exams, feel it is only fair that undergraduates should have to take them too. In each of these conditions, half the students are told that the proposal is to institute the new requirement the following year, so that it would apply to them ("high-involvement" condition) and half are told that the requirement is being considered for possible adoption in ten years ("low-involvement" condition). Finally, half the students are told that the source of the arguments they are getting is a Princeton professor (a "high-credibility" source) and half are told that the arguments have been taken from the report of a local high school class (a "low-credibility" source). The experimental design, thus, is two message types × two involvement conditions × two source types.

The results are as follows: Low-involvement students pay some attention to the quality of the arguments but are most strongly affected by the credibility of the sources advocating them; hence they are favorable toward comprehensive exams only when the source advocating them is a Princeton professor. High-involvement students, by contrast, pay no attention to source credentials, but are powerfully influenced by the strength of the arguments. Thus, they are very favorable to senior comprehensive exams when the arguments for them have been good and strongly negative otherwise. Petty and Cacioppo are able to show, in addition, that the different reactions of the high- and low-involvement students are due precisely to the fact that the former have thought more extensively about the arguments being made.

One wishes one could be confident that the general public were as good at detecting weak arguments as were Petty and Cacioppo's "high-involvement" college students. But the reasons for doubt are great.

First, the weak arguments used in Petty and Cacioppo's experiments were extremely weak, sometimes comically so. It took systematic effort to develop such weak but still coherent arguments, and political persuaders in real life cannot be expected to take similar pains. Bad as the arguments of many politicians may be, politicians (and their media consultants) try to be persuasive. In cases of real-life political controversy, citizens are likely to face two sets of opposing arguments that, when compared to those of a typical Petty and Cacioppo experiment, will all be "strong."

Second, most politics, at least in the contemporary United States, is notoriously low key and uninvolving. The stakes are theoretically high, but people find it hard to stay interested. (The evidence on this point was reviewed in Chapter 2.) In such "low-involvement" conditions, Petty and Cacioppo's work indicates that most people engage in "peripheral" message processing, that is, processing that ignores the intrinsic quality of arguments and uses superficial cues such as source credibility as the basis for accepting or rejecting messages.

Third, the students in the Petty and Cacioppo experiments were judging issues that were rooted in their everyday experiences. (Other issues Petty and Cacioppo use are tuition increases and liberalization of dormitory visiting hours.) With respect to issues like these, virtually all students are fully capable, without any particular past attention to the issues, of responding in the manner of informed experts. This condition does not even remotely hold for most political issues, where the information and judgment necessary to reach reliable conclusions is beyond the direct experience of even the most attentive persons.

Thus, the conditions that make possible Petty and Cacioppo's encouraging findings – weak arguments, and "receivers" who are both involved in and well-informed about the issue at hand – are simply not present in typical situations of mass persuasion. On the contrary, real-world conditions, according to the work of Petty and Cacioppo and that of others, encourage reliance on peripheral cues, such as whether the person advocating a position is liberal or conservative, a union leader or a priest, or whatever (Belknap and Campbell, 1951–2; Campbell et al., 1960; Key, 1961; Mueller, 1973; Price, 1989; Gerber and Jackson, 1990; Pollock, Lisle, and Vittes, 1991; Page and Shapiro, in press).

There is, then, solid empirical support for the assumption that citizens normally respond to new information on the basis of external cues concerning the implications of that information for their values and other predispositions, provided that, as Converse emphasizes, they are sufficiently attentive to politics to have learned the cues.

Having stated a strong argument for why political awareness should be associated with resistance to persuasion, let me now state an equally strong caveat: The argument applies only to cases in which the contextual information necessary to evaluate an issue in light of one's predispositions is, for one reason or another, obscure. Thus, as we saw in Chapter 2, steadfast anticommunists were quite able to state opinions consistent with their predispositions when they were asked about "stopping communism" in Central America. It was only when they were asked about "aid to the Contras," an obscure reference, that they had trouble. To take another example, one would expect strong age-related differences, independent of political awareness, in responses to a question about taxing social security benefits. The reason is that virtually everyone, even the least politically aware, would possess the contextual information necessary to answer this question in relation to their predispositions, in this case, nearness to retirement age.

The extent to which contextual information is obscure may depend either on the nature of the issue – race, as Converse pointed out, is one area in which most people can understand what is at stake – or on the way a question is phrased, as in the example of aid to the Contras.

Generally speaking, the more abstract the link between a predisposition and a related policy issue, the greater the amount or obscurity of knowledge necessary to perceive the linkage, or the more complicated the chain of reasoning involved, the more important political awareness is likely to be in regulating individual responses to political communications on that issue. Conversely, the more simple and direct the link between a predisposition and an issue, the less important awareness is likely to be in regulating responses to political communications on that issue.

Although it is important to note that awareness can be expected to enhance resistance to persuasion only when the full significance of the issue or survey question is to some degree obscure, this qualification by no means robs the resistance axiom of its bite. Obscurity, in the sense I have indicated, is extremely common in politics.

A3. *ACCESSIBILITY AXIOM. The more recently a consideration has been called to mind or thought about, the less time it takes to retrieve that consideration or related considerations from memory and bring them to the top of the head for use.*

Conversely, the longer it has been since a consideration or related idea has been activated, the less likely it is to be accessible at the top of the head; in the limit, a long unused set of considerations may be completely inaccessible, which is to say, forgotten.

This axiom appropriates for use in the model one of the best-established empirical regularities in cognitive psychology. General support for the basic idea is overwhelming and, as far as I can tell, undisputed. When an idea or concept has been recently used, seen, heard, or indirectly referenced, it is significantly more likely to be available for reuse than if it has not been recently activated (for reviews, see Higgins and King, 1981; Wyer and Srull, 1989).

Note, however, an element of ambiguity in this axiom. Although specifying that use of one consideration can increase the accessibility of related considerations, it says nothing about what it means for different considerations to be related. I am therefore implicitly relying on common understanding to determine when considerations are related to one another.

A4. *RESPONSE AXIOM. Individuals answer survey questions by averaging across the considerations that are immediately salient or accessible to them.*

This axiom, which completes the statement of my proposed model, implies that persons who have been asked a survey question do not normally canvass their minds for all considerations relevant to the given issue; rather, they answer the question on the basis of whatever considerations are accessible "at the top of the head." In some cases, only a single consideration may be readily accessible, in which case individuals answer on the basis of that consideration; in other cases, two or more considerations may come quickly to mind, in which case people answer by averaging across accessible considerations.

An important feature of the Response Axiom is that it permits different people to respond to issue questions on the basis of different considerations – one, for example, emphasizing ideological concerns, another gut-level likes and dislikes, and yet another self-interest. This renders the model consistent with a growing literature indicating that such interpersonal heterogeneity is quite common (Graber, 1984; Rivers, 1988; Sniderman, Brody, and Tetlock, 1991; Hollis, 1991).

Many readers will suspect that the top-of-the-head Response Axiom is too simple – as, indeed, it surely is. Psychologists working with data from laboratory studies and from experimentally controlled surveys have developed more complex and hence presumably more realistic models of how individuals process information and reach decisions.

For example, Tourangeau and Rasinski (1988) have proposed a four-stage model in which individuals (1) interpret the question to determine what the issue before them really is, (2) canvass their minds for relevant thoughts, (3) integrate their thoughts into a coherent opinion, and (4) map that opinion onto the response options available in the question. Because features of the questionnaire can affect each of these steps, the questionnaire also affects what gets reported as public opinion.

Although the Tourangeau and Rasinski model is still fairly simple, it may nonetheless be too complex for use in the context of mass opinion survey data. I say this because it is quite consistent with the evidence that Tourangeau and Rasinski cite that their four-stage process has only one important step: the retrieval from memory of a dominant consideration. So, for example, a conservative who happens to think about a government services question in terms of "welfare cheats" may already have done all he needs to do in the way of canvassing his mind for beliefs, integrating them into a coherent opinion, and mapping the opinion onto the given response options. Tourangeau and Rasinski are aware of their limited ability to distinguish empirically the steps in their model with survey data and do what they can to combat it. But my point remains that complex models may have only limited utility for general analyses of public opinion.

Models that are still more complex, such as the forty-three-postulate information-processing model proposed by Wyer and Srull (1989), are even more dubious in the context of public opinion data. Analysts of mass opinion can profitably use such models for heuristic guidance in devising their models, but, in the end, it is necessary to make radical simplifications if the purpose is to engage in the rigorous analysis of typical public opinion data.

If there is a threat to my simplified top-of-the-head Response Axiom, it comes from recent psychological studies of "on-line" information processing. The argument here is that people do not form their attitude statements from ideas accessible at the moment of response but instead use a "judgment operator" to continuously update their attitudes as they acquire new information; people are said to store these updated attitudes in memory and retrieve them as required by a given situation, including interview situations (Hastie and Park, 1986; Lodge, McGraw, and Stroh, 1989).

Although a fair amount of evidence supports the on-line model, there are strong reasons for doubting that it holds generally within the domain of political attitudes. These reasons are best discussed after the evidence supporting my model has been presented. For the moment, however, I briefly note two of the most important. The first is that it is wildly unrealistic to expect citizens to use each piece of incoming information to update all of the "attitudes" to which it might be relevant. Thus, for example, a news story about the suffering of homeless people would, in the idealized world of on-line processing, require updates of attitudes toward the welfare system, the value of big government, the efficiency of capitalism, the president's attempts to trim welfare spending, voluntary charity, the American way of life, among others – which is to say, many more subjects that a person could possibly rethink at the moment of encountering each new piece of political information. The second reason for doubting the applicability of the on-line model to political attitudes is that this model, with its notion that attitudes are simply "retrieved" from memory and reported to the inquiring interviewer, is quite obviously just a restatement of the conventional "true attitude" model, a model that, as I have been at pains to show, is simply not capable of accommodating the available evidence on the nature of mass political attitudes.

The survey responses that people make within the proposed model may reasonably be described as attitudes or opinions, in that they represent people's true feelings at the moment of answering a given survey question; they could not, however, be described as "true attitudes," in the technical sense of the term, because survey responses are not assumed to represent anything more than a single aspect of people's feelings toward a given attitude object.

Perhaps the most apt description of a survey response within the proposed model is "opinion statement." This term implies that the expression of opinion is genuine without also implying that it either represents prior reflection or is destined for a long half-life. The phrase "attitude report" has similar virtues.

Opinion statements, as conceived in my four-axiom model, are the outcome of a process in which people *receive* new information, decide whether to *accept* it, and then *sample* at the moment of answering questions. For convenience, therefore, I will refer to this process as the Receive-Accept-Sample, or RAS, Model.

HOW THE MODEL IS USED IN THIS BOOK

The model I have outlined consists of four very general claims about how people acquire information from the political environment (in the form of persuasive arguments and cues) and transform that information into survey responses. In the remainder of the book, I use these axioms to explore and explain numerous aspects of mass opinion. In particular, I will use the axioms to explain the distributions of mass opinion that may be expected to occur in various kinds of political environments – for example, a political environment in which people are exposed to two equally intense streams of competing liberal and conservative messages on a given issue; a political environment in which most of the messages one-sidedly favor a given issue; and an environment in which the proportions of liberal and conservative messages are changing, thereby producing attitude change in the mass public. The four axioms, standing by themselves, have limited analytical utility; but they come to life under these various configurations of the flow of political information.

The method of the book, then, is to develop the deductive implications of the four basic axioms for a given, highly specific set of conditions; review evidence indicating whether or not these implications are empirically correct; and present new evidence as necessary and possible to resolve outstanding empirical questions.

At a few points in the analysis, it will be necessary to supplement the four axioms in nonfundamental ways. For example, I will need in Chapter 7 to stipulate a functional form for the relationship between political awareness and reception of political messages. More and less complicated operational models will also be built from the axioms at various points in the book, depending on the strength of the data available to test the models. But no significant new substantive claims about public opinion will be introduced. The burden of the book will be to show how various aspects of public opinion, some well-established and some novel, can be deduced from the four axioms, given particular information flows – that is, particular streams of liberal and conservative communications – in the political environment.

The argument to be made from the RAS model may be previewed as follows. It follows from the Response Axiom that the probability that a person will support or oppose a given policy depends on the mix of positive and negative considerations available in the person's mind at the moment of answering a question about it. If, for the moment, we overlook the probability of nonresponse (which occurs when no considerations are immediately salient in memory), and assume also that every consideration a person has internalized is as likely to be sampled as any other, then the probability of a liberal response by a given person is

$$Prob(Liberal\ response)\ =\ \frac{L}{L + C}$$

where L and C refer to the number of liberal and conservative considerations available in the person's mind. (I reiterate that here, as elsewhere in this book, liberal and conservative are simply *labels* for the directional thrust of ideas; a person may use a liberal consideration as the basis for a liberal response even though she is not, in any deeper sense, "a liberal.")

The balance of liberal and conservative considerations in people's minds depends on both society-level and individual-level variables. The key societal variables are the intensities of liberal and conservative information flows in the political environment with respect to a given issue. The key individual variables are political awareness and political predispositions. More aware persons will be exposed to more political communications (via the Reception Axiom) but will be more selective in deciding which communications to internalize as considerations (via the Resistance Axiom). Thus, politically aware citizens will tend to fill their minds with large numbers of considerations, and these considerations will tend to be relatively consistent with one another and with the citizens' predispositions. Less aware persons will internalize fewer considerations and will be less consistent in doing so. As a result, more aware people will be more likely to be able to state opinions, and more likely to state opinions that are ideologically consistent with their predispositions.

Changes in the relative intensity of liberal and conservative communications on an issue will produce changes in the kinds of considerations people form, which will in turn produce changes in the opinion statements they make. One of the things that gives the RAS model its strength is its ability to forecast that different segments of the public will change their attitudes in different amounts and even different directions, depending on their political awareness, their political values, and the particular changes in information flow that have occurred.

Thus, the four basic postulates of the sampling model, unprepossessing as they are, entail quite definite claims about how public opinion forms and changes, as we will now begin to see.

4

Coming to terms with response instability

Respondents to the 1987 NES pilot study were asked to answer what academic analysts of public opinion will recognize as an entirely standard question:

Some people think the government in Washington should cut government services, even in areas such as education and health care, in order to reduce the deficit. Others think government services should be increased.

In an unusual twist, however, respondents to this survey were not permitted to give an immediate answer to the question. Instead, the interviewer continued:

Before telling me how you feel about this, could you tell me what kinds of things come to mind when you think about *cutting government services?* (Any others?)

The interviewer wrote down respondents' remarks verbatim, and then asked:

Now, what comes to mind when you think about increases in government services? (Any others?)

At this point, the original question was repeated and the respondents were, at last, permitted to render a simple dichotomous judgment on the matter of government services. But in the meantime, each individual had revealed what the issue of government services meant to him or her at the moment of answering a standard closed-ended question about it. Because every respondent was asked the same questions again four weeks later, these probes make it possible to see how their thinking on the issue might have changed over time. The open-ended comments elicited by these probes constitute some of the best evidence currently available on what citizens' survey responses mean and why they are so beset by vagaries.

As it happened, I was at the University of Michigan's Survey Research Center when completed interviews from this study began to arrive from the field office.[1] The first pair of these interviews involved a person who described himself — or herself, I have no way of knowing — as a teacher, and who spoke quite emphatically in favor of higher levels of services and spending. The country was

Parts of the analysis in this and the next chapter are from my and Stanley Feldman's report of results from the 1987 NES pilot study, as published in Zaller and Feldman (in press). The theory underlying this analysis is from Zaller (1984b).

1 Because I had helped to design these unusual questions, I was present to help supervise their administration and to watch for problems.

facing an educational crisis, the respondent said, and, as a teacher, he or she knew that more education expenditures were drastically needed. Any cuts in federal services or spending would inevitably reduce the already inadequate amounts of money available for education, and that would be a disaster.

What was striking about this interview was that it seemed to exemplify the kind of highly crystallized "true attitude" that many opinion researchers implicitly take to be the norm. Yet, in responding to the same questions several weeks later in the second wave of the survey, the teacher favored *reductions* in government services. And in open-ended remarks, the same respondent now spoke just as emphatically as in the earlier interview, except taking the opposite line. Government was too big, he or she asserted, and something had to be done to prune it back or it would take over everything. There was no reference to the educational crisis that had preoccupied the respondent a few weeks earlier.[2]

I read over these remarks with a member of the NES staff, who immediately concluded that a mistake had been made. "Those turkeys downstairs got the case ID's on the interviews scrambled," the person declared. "These are different respondents."

It turned out, however, that the case ID's were correct. Although perfectly stable in remarks about two other questions, even using sometimes identical language to discuss them, the teacher-respondent had changed his or her response on the services item, though without indication of having done so knowingly. The respondent appeared simply to think about the issue differently in the second interview, and so to reach a different conclusion about it.

This respondent turned out to be representative of many others. Like that first respondent, most citizens appeared not to have "just one attitude" toward political issues, and like him or her, they appeared to base their survey responses on whichever of their multiple and sometimes conflicting attitudes was most immediately salient to them.

The model I have proposed is an attempt to be faithful to this and similar evidence. It abandons the notion that individuals typically possess preformed attitudes that they simply reveal when asked by a pollster to do so. It instead adopts the view that people possess numerous, frequently inconsistent "considerations" relating to each issue, and that they base their survey responses on whichever of them are at the top of the head at the moment of response.

I should add that nothing in the model I have proposed prevents individuals who pay great attention to an issue from developing a perfectly homogeneous set of considerations with respect to every aspect of that issue, so that every consideration that comes to mind impels them toward the same opinion statement. In fact, in the limiting case of very great attention to an issue, this is exactly

2 This general characterization of the teacher's views is based on my unaided recall of the transcript of the interview. I would like to present verbatim transcriptions of what this and other respondents said, but, unfortunately, the Board of Overseers of the NES prohibits such use of the protocols. In conformity with the rules of the Human Subjects Protection Committee at the University of Michigan, the NES has determined that any publication of the raw protocols would be an invasion of the respondents' right to privacy. Obviously, this policy detracts from the ability to communicate the findings of the pilot study to the research community in a fully credible manner.

what, according to the RAS model, should happen. Persons who are highly engaged with an issue may thus develop the crystallized attitudes that most opinion researchers take to be the norm. But for the majority of persons on the majority of issues, inconsistencies in their considerations concerning different aspects of a given issue remain unresolved and probably unrecognized. Their responses to typical survey questions then depend on which aspect of the issue is most salient to them, where saliency depends partly on purely chance factors, such as what appeared on television the night before or what happened to them that morning at the office, and partly on systematic factors, such as how the question has been framed or what related questions have been asked in immediate proximity to it.

This model, as I show in this and the next chapter, can account for a wide range of evidence concerning the nature of political attitudes. Much of the evidence presented in this chapter will be familiar to professional students of public opinion, but some of the most important of it – that involving attempts to make direct measurements of the considerations that people bring to bear in answering survey questions – comes from the 1987 NES pilot study, which is not widely familiar. It is therefore necessary to pause to describe that study.

THE 1987 PILOT STUDY

In recent years, the National Election Studies at the University of Michigan has regularly conducted small surveys in nonelection years for the purpose of testing new survey questions and ideas. Space on the survey is allocated by the NES Board of Overseers, which solicits proposals from the community of public opinion specialists and allocates survey time to the proposals it judges most promising. The data described below were collected on the 1987 pilot study of the NES under a proposal submitted by Stanley Feldman of the State University of New York (SUNY) Stony Brook and me, and are, of course, publicly available through the Inter-university Consortium for Political and Social Research at the University of Michigan.

The 1987 pilot study was a two-wave telephone survey of respondents who had earlier participated in the 1986 National Election Study. The first wave interviewed 450 persons in early summer, the second wave reinterviewed 357 of these people a month later.

In this survey, respondents were asked a series of standard issue questions on federal job guarantees, the proper level of government services, and aid to blacks. Immediately afterward, a random half of respondents were asked:

Still thinking about the question you just answered, I'd like you to tell me what ideas came to mind as you were answering that question. Exactly what things went through your mind?

This probe was designed to reveal the considerations that were most important in determining respondents' answers. In the other half of the survey, interviewers read the items in the usual way, but, without waiting for the respondent to answer, they asked the respondent to discuss particular phrases and ideas in the question, as indicated in the opening paragraph of this chapter. After administration of the "stop-and-think" probes, as they have been labeled,[3] the interviewer reread the entire question and recorded the person's reply to it.

Feldman and I designed the two types of open-ended questions for different purposes. The "retrospective" probes, which were posed after people had already answered the question in the normal way, were designed to elicit a sort of "memory dump" of what was on people's mind at the moment of response. The stop-and-think, prospective probes were asked *before* respondents could answer the question and were designed to induce people to think more carefully about their opinions than they ordinarily would; the expectation was that the extra thought might make people's responses more reliable. The stop-and-think probes were also intended to elicit, as nondirectively as possible, the range of considerations that a person considered relevant to the issue at hand.

Interviewers wrote down as faithfully as possible all responses to the open-ended probes.[4] The transcribed comments were subjected to an elaborate classification scheme, with as many as four comments coded in connection with each probe. Respondents averaged about four codable comments per policy item, with almost all respondents offering at least one codable comment.[5]

Each comment or remark was rated on several variables by staff coders at the Institute for Social Research (ISR) at the University of Michigan. Because the coding project was considered a difficult one, only experienced coders were used. The most important and simplest variable was "directional thrust of comment," which indicated which side of the issue, if any, the remark tended to support. Although coders were instructed to note ambivalence, confusion, and nonsubstantive concerns, three-quarters of all comments were assigned a clear directional thrust. About 8 percent of remarks were uncodable because, although a directional thrust may have been intended by respondents, coders could not discern what it was. The other key coding classification was the "frame of reference" code, a variable that included more than 140 categories and tried to capture the substantive content of each remark.[6]

About one-tenth of all interviews were double-coded. Although exact reliability data are not available, the coding supervisor reported a "difference" between coders on 10 to 15 percent of all cases. This difference rate was regarded as reasonable for difficult open-ended material.[7]

3 Kathleen Knight of the University of Houston invented the label.
4 I listened to about fifteen interviews and checked afterward to see how well interviewers had captured the open-ended material. I felt that interviewers did an excellent job with respondents who had little to say, but could capture only key ideas and phrases in the perhaps 40 percent of cases in which respondents spoke at paragraph length.
5 For the Aid to Blacks item, there were up to six probes – three questions, each followed by the query "Any others?" As many as four remarks were coded in connection with each of the six probes. On the other items, there were up to two initial probes, two follow-up probes, and four coded remarks per probe.
6 The coding scheme was derived empirically from pretests and modified as the need arose during the coding of the pilot data.
7 Personal communication from Steve Pinney, the coding supervisor at ISR.

These data, although collected for the specific purposes to which they are put below, are not without limitations. The most obvious is the difference rate between coders. Although within the normal range, it is high enough to seriously undermine the ability to make precise tests of certain hypotheses, as will become apparent.

Less obvious but probably more important is the difficulty in sharply distinguishing one "consideration" from another. When two remarks have opposing thrusts – one favoring a policy and the other opposing it – this is no problem. But in some cases, people made several consecutive remarks on the same side of the question. Do these remarks represent separate considerations, or simply elaborations on a single consideration? Even a person listening to the interviews as they were taking place, as I did, would sometimes have difficulty being certain; for coders working from an imperfect transcript, the problem is more serious. Hence, although the following analysis sometimes attempts to count the number of pro- and con- considerations that individuals raise, the reader should bear in mind that the data on which these counts depend are, at best, approximate.

Three other, more common data problems also merit notice. One is small sample size. After normal rates of attrition across waves and "no opinion" responses, there were just over a hundred complete cases on the retrospective side. This led to a second difficulty. Less politically aware respondents drop out of surveys at disproportionately high rates; anticipating this problem, the pilot study oversampled less aware respondents (by using their scores on an information test in the regular 1986 study). But even so, the low-information respondents who survived three interviews *and* who answered the target items on both waves of the pilot are a highly selected and hence unrepresentative group of politically unaware persons. In particular, they are likely to be more interested in the issue, all else equal, than persons who had equal scores on the awareness scale but either dropped out of the study or failed to answer the question both times. Finally, the unusually short time between interviews, one month, resulted in less than the usual amount of response instability. All three of these problems reduce statistical power to observe and understand over time response instability, the key dependent variable in this analysis.

Notwithstanding these limitations, the first two of which are inherent in any attempt to gather data on considerations from a nationally representative sample, the measures of considerations available in this study constitute the best data of which I am aware – in fact, the only available data – for testing certain of the expectations derived from the RAS model. Despite their limits, they provide some revealing glimpses of the microfoundations of political attitudes.

FIRST DEDUCTIONS FROM THE MODEL

In the remainder of this chapter, I use the axioms of the Receive-Accept-Sample (RAS) model, as outlined in the previous chapter, to make testable deductions

Table 4.1. *Axioms of Receive-Accept-Sample (RAS) model*

A1. Reception Axiom. *The greater a person's level of cognitive engagement with an issue, the more likely he or she is to be exposed to and comprehend – in a word, to receive – political messages concerning that issue.*

A2. Resistance Axiom . *People tend to resist arguments that are inconsistent with their political predispositions, but they do so only to the extent that they possess the contextual information necessary to perceive a relationship between the message and their predispositions.*

A3. Accessibility Axiom. *The more recently a consideration has been called to mind or thought about, the less time it takes to retrieve that consideration or related considerations from memory and bring them to the top of the head for use.*

A4. Response Axiom. *Individuals answer survey questions by averaging across the considerations that are immediately salient or accessible to them.*

concerning the nature of citizens' responses to survey questions. I then proceed to test empirically these deductions. (For easy reference, the axioms of the RAS model are restated here as Table 4.1.)

The Receive-Accept-Sample Model is, as explained, a set of claims about how citizens acquire ''information'' and convert it into attitude statements, which is to say, it is a type of information-processing model. Attitude statements on particular issues therefore depend fundamentally on the amount and direction of information available to the public on each issue.

Given this, one cannot test the model without making definite assumptions about the information environment that sustains citizens' attitudes on a given issue. For purposes of this chapter, I make the following simple assumption about this environment: that it consists of moderately intense, temporally stable information flows favoring both the liberal and the conservative side of each issue. By *moderately intense,* I refer to information flows that involve neither dominating headline stories (for example, the Iran–Contra scandal of 1987 or the Persian Gulf War) nor obscure and esoteric stories (such as congressional debates over the organizational structure of the Commerce Department). Thus, in the case of a survey item about the proper level of government services, my assumption will be that there is a steady but not overwhelming stream of messages that give individuals reasons both to favor increased government services (news stories about children living in poverty, for instance) and to favor decreased government services (news stories about the federal budget deficit). By *temporally stable* information flows, I mean that the intensities of the opposing messages are stable over the period prior to the survey. (When information flows change over time, they produce attitude change, which is the topic of investigation in later chapters.)

Under the assumption, then, of stable, moderately intense information flows on both sides of a given issue, what follows from the RAS model about the nature of citizens' attitude reports on this issue?

My first deduction concerns what I see as a fundamental claim concerning most people's attitudes on most issues, namely a tendency toward some degree of ambivalence.

From A2, the Resistance Axiom, we know that individuals can reliably resist the arguments to which they are exposed only to the extent that they possess "information" about the implications of those arguments for their predispositions. We also know from Chapter 2 that, as a matter of fact, most Americans do not rate very highly on political awareness. From these two points it follows that citizens will be unlikely to exhibit high levels of resistance to arguments that are inconsistent with their values, interests, or other predispositions. This implies that, in an environment that carries roughly evenly balanced communications on both sides of issues, people are likely to internalize many contradictory arguments, which is to say, they are likely to form considerations that induce them both to favor and to oppose the same issues. This deduction from the model, *D1*, will be referred to as the Ambivalence Deduction. (Subsequent deductions from the model are labeled by means of the deduction number in parentheses immediately following the inference.)

The anecdote of the teacher-respondent who, at different times, both favored and opposed increases in government services has already given us a hint that the ambivalence deduction is correct. The question we must now ask is: How common is the internally conflicted attitude pattern exhibited by the vacillating teacher?

Hochschild's (1981) study of citizens' attitudes toward equality, which was based on lengthy open-ended interviews with twenty-eight persons, strongly suggests that it is quite common. Consider her account of the attitudes of one of her subjects toward government income guarantees:

Vincent Sartori cannot decide whether or not the government should guarantee incomes, because he cannot decide how much weight to give to the value of productivity. He believes that the rich are mostly undeserving and . . . yet he is angry at "welfare cheats" who refuse to work. . . . Caught between his desire for equality and his knowledge of existing injustice, on the one hand, and his fear that a guaranteed income will benefit even shirkers, on the other, he remains ambivalent about policies toward the poor. (p. 252)

One of Hochschild's principal conclusions in her study was that most individuals' political beliefs are characterized by similarly high levels of "ambivalence." People would, Hochschild found, readily provide answers to fixed-choice questions, but given the opportunity to talk,

people do not make simple statements; they shade, modulate, deny, retract, or just grind to a halt in frustration. These manifestations of uncertainty are just as meaningful and interesting as the definitive statements of a belief system. (p. 238)

Depth interviews such as Hochschild's are, of course, susceptible to many criticisms, including the possibility that aggressive probing might have induced some people to say things they didn't actually feel very strongly. It would be useful, therefore, to corroborate Hochschild's conclusions from survey data.

Open-ended interview data from the 1987 NES pilot study, in which people describe their thoughts as they answer survey questions, afford several ways of doing so. Although these data do not, in their aggregate form, have the richness and human feel of Hochschild's depth-interview data, they have the advantage of having been derived from a nationally representative sample by means of standardized, nonreactive, and relatively nonintrusive probe techniques.

Perhaps the most straightforward test for the existence of ambivalence is simply to make a count of the number of opposing remarks by a person that can be paired against each other. If, for example, a respondent makes two open-ended comments favoring higher levels of government services and two that indicate a desire to cut government services, his score on the conflict measure would be 2. If he makes three (or more) on one side of the issue and only two on the other, the conflict score is still 2 because the number of opposing comments that can be paired remains two. Any conflict score above zero indicates that the person experiences some degree of internal conflict on the given issue.

It is also possible to make a count of the number of times people spontaneously express ambivalence or difficulty in making up their minds. Such remarks indicate that the person is caught between opposing ideas. Coders were instructed to be alert for such conflict, and were given a special code for use in capturing it, as follows:

Mention indicates ambivalence, conflict (e.g., "I see merit in both sides"; "that's a tough question"; "depends"; "both are valid points").

Finally, the frame of reference codes included special codes, designated "star codes," that indicate a directional thrust to the comment, but also some ambivalence with respect to that direction. Star codes were intended to cover cases in which respondents had a preference but were clearly paying some attention to the other side of the issue. Instructions to coders for use of star codes are as follows:

A STAR CODE is used only for cases in which there is a single thought or comment that encompasses two opposing elements, e.g., "Although I think X, I nevertheless favor Y." Star codes are used for comments in which R[espondent] sees two sides to an issue.[8]

Examples of star codes are "People should try to get ahead on their own, but government should help when necessary" and respondent "admits problem(s) with any program or type of program, but insists it is worthwhile anyway."[9] A count of the star-coded remarks may thus be considered an indicator of degree of a person's internal conflict on an issue.

8 ICPSR codebook.
9 These are codes 120 and 313 from the ICPSR codebook.

Table 4.2. *Expressions of ambivalence on political issues*

	Retrospective probes			Stop-and-think probes		
	Guarantee jobs	Gov't services	Aid blacks	Guarantee jobs	Gov't services	Aid blacks
Conflicting considerations						
Count						
0	74%	58	73	37%	31	29
1	23	34	23	27	29	22
2	4	5	4	22	22	25
3+	0	3	0	13	19	24
Spontaneous statements of ambivalence or conflict						
Count						
0	77	84	79	63	72	71
1+	23	16	21	37	27	29
Two–sided remarks (star codes)						
Count						
0	75	92	81	65	85	72
1+	25	8	19	35	15	28
Total indications						
Count						
0	60	51	64	26	24	25
1+	40	49	36	74	76	75
N	108	109	118	174	169	166

Source: 1987 NES pilot survey.

From these three measures one can create a fourth: a count of the ambivalence indices on which a person scored + 1 or higher.

Because internal conflict and ambivalence are equally consequential whether they occur within the course of one interview or across separate interviews, and because we wish to capture as many as possible of the conflicting considerations that are in people's minds, all four of these count indices have been calculated across responses from both waves of the survey.

Distributions of respondents' scores on these four measures of ambivalence are shown in Table 4.2. As can be seen, respondents exhibited substantial amounts of internal conflict on all measures, a result that corroborates Hochschild's contention and thereby offers additional, clear support for the Ambivalence Deduction, D1. Even on the more conservative evidence of the retrospective probes, which involve only one query in each wave,[10] the summary measure indicates that 36 to 49 percent of respondents are to some degree ambivalent on these three issues. And this is surely an understatement. What the retrospective probes capture, as indicated, is the reason the person has answered the item as he just has; they cannot capture anything like the full range of ideas

10 More probes were made, but since they were directive, I make no use of them.

in a person's head. However, the stop-and-think probes were designed to tap a wider range of the ideas in people's minds; on evidence from them, roughly 75 percent of respondents are at least somewhat conflicted on the three issues. And this is still probably an understatement, since further probes and more reliable coding of open-ended remarks would almost certainly disclose further indications of conflict.

Granted, then, most people are to some degree ambivalent about the political issues they confront. What else follows from the model?

Let us consider next the relationship between the responses people make to closed-ended policy questions and the ideas that are at the top of their heads as they do so. The model leads us to expect a strong relationship between these two attitude measures because A4, the Response Axiom, claims that people answer survey questions on the basis of the ideas that are most salient to them at the moment of response. Thus if, for example, a person makes two open-ended remarks favoring the liberal side of the issue and one favoring the conservative side, we would expect, on average, that the person will take the liberal side of the issue on the closed-ended item. Similarly, a person who raises mostly conservative considerations would be expected to choose the conservative option on the closed-ended item. This is D2, the second deduction from the model. This deduction is important because, if it turned out that there was no relationship between people's open-ended remarks and their choices on closed-ended items, the ambivalence embodied in the open-ended remarks would be inconsequential.

Although D2 is so straightforward that it may seem hardly worth testing, it is not obvious that it can be confirmed. Social psychologists, working in the domain of personality evaluation, have turned up many cases in which people's open-ended thoughts are completely uncorrelated, or occasionally even negatively correlated, with their responses to closed-ended questions about the same subject (Hastie and Park, 1986).[11] The explanation given is as follows: People form personality evaluations "on-line" as they encounter each new bit of relevant information. These evaluations are then stored as long-term attitudes and used as the basis of attitude reports, when such attitude reports are subsequently requested. There is, therefore, no necessary relationship between the information that is immediately accessible in memory and the attitude reports that people make (see also Lodge, McGraw, and Stroh, 1989).

All of this is, of course, contrary to the RAS model. For reasons outlined in Chapter 2, the RAS model assumes that, at least in the domain of political issues, people do not possess preformed, long-term attitudes on most of the issues on which pollsters query them, and so base their attitude reports on the considerations that are immediately salient to them. Thus, in the RAS model, there should be a close relationship between considerations and opinion.

Data from the 1987 pilot study, in which people described their thoughts as they answered survey questions, have been used to test these competing expec-

11 A noncorrelation would indicate no relationship between people's attitude reports on closed-ended items and the thrust of their open-ended remarks concerning the same subject.

Table 4.3. *Relationship between direction of open-ended remarks and direction of opinion statement*

	Correlation between opinion statement and open-ended remarks		
	Wave 1	Wave 2	Combined
Retrospective condition			
Guaranteed job	.79	.70	.79
N	(126)	(123)	(105)
Government services	.80	.70	.78
	(137)	(105)	(106)
Aid to blacks	.67	.83	.83
	(144)	(114)	(112)
Stop-and-think condition			
Guaranteed job	.39	.39	.50
	(212)	(161)	(173)
Government services	.31	.36	.41
	(187)	(153)	(165)
Aid to blacks	.57	.48	.63
	(220)	(165)	(166)

Source: 1987 NES pilot survey.

tations. An additive index was created to summarize the directional thrust of each person's open-ended remarks on each issue. This index was then correlated with responses to the closed-ended policy questions, with results that are shown in Table 4.3. In the stop-and-think condition, in which people talked about the meaning of the question before answering it, Pearson correlations between the index and its associated item in each wave of the survey average .42 over the three items. When an index of all remarks over both waves of the survey is correlated with an index consisting of the sum of the two closed-ended policy items, the correlations average about .51.[12] Given that the closed-ended items in these tests are essentially dichotomies – a few people volunteered responses of "both" and "in between" – these are sizable correlations.

When, in the retrospective condition, respondents were asked, just *after* answering the question, to say what they were thinking about as they answered it, the correlations between their remarks and their closed-ended responses averaged .75. When remarks and items were summed and correlated across both waves of the survey, the correlations averaged .80.

Although correlations from the retrospective data are higher, those from the stop-and-think data are the stronger evidence for D2. For in this case individuals cannot be covertly justifying a response just given; they are simply explaining

12 The measure of directional thrust of considerations is (liberal remarks − conservative remarks)/ (liberal remarks + conservative remarks + ambivalent remarks). Respondents who did not make at least one directionally codable remark are treated as missing data.

in their own words "what comes to mind" when they think about the issue. Yet despite this, and contrary to the evidence from the domain of personality evaluation (Hastie and Park, 1986), people's political attitude statements are significantly correlated with "top-of-the-head" ideas. Thus, although I do not claim that the confirmation of D2 is either deeply surprising or definitive evidence for the RAS model, it is a confirmation that could not have been taken for granted and is therefore useful evidence on behalf of the model.[13]

RESPONSE INSTABILITY

As I have indicated, instability in people's attitude reports over time is one of the most deeply worrisome, if not routinely emphasized, empirical findings of modern survey research. The existence of widespread ambivalence, in conjunction with the Response Axiom, provides a ready explanation for it.

If people form conflicting considerations on most issues, and if they base their survey responses on whichever of these considerations happen to be at the top of the head at the moment of response, one should expect a fair amount of variability in people's responses to survey questions (*D3*). This deduction has been strongly confirmed on numerous occasions, as illustrated in Table 2.1 and in various publications (Converse, 1964; Achen, 1975; Dean and Moran, 1977; Erikson, 1979; Judd and Milburn, 1980; Judd, Milburn, and Krosnick, 1981; Feldman, 1989; Zaller, 1990).

The model also has strong implications for the structure of this response instability *so long as the flow of information in the political environment remains steady.* The qualifying phrase is extremely important. If people are exposed to a shifting balance of liberal and conservative communications, the balance of considerations in their minds will shift in the direction of the more recent communications, and this will bring about systematic attitude change. But if the flow of communications remains steady, the balance of positive and negative considerations in each person's mind should be, on average for each given issue, roughly the same at one point in time as at another. What will then vary, according to the model, is the particular consideration that happens to be at the top of the head at a given interview. If this is true, we should expect to find a fair amount of purely chance variation around a stable central tendency (*D4*).

There is wide agreement among researchers who have investigated this matter that deduction D4 is correct. In applications of models designed to separate

13 In a recent paper, McGraw, Lodge, and Stroh (1990) argue that the finding of correlations between top-of-the-head thoughts and attitude statements could come about in many ways, including post hoc rationalization of attitudes previously developed. The objection is well founded. However, D2 is only one of some thirty deductions from the RAS model. Although there may be alternative explanations for some of the individual findings to which these thirty deductions refer, there are no obvious alternative explanations for anything like the range of findings covered by the RAS model.

See Chapter 11 for further discussion of the "on-line" model of attitude formation, which McGraw et al. prefer.

chance variability in attitude statements from long-term change, it has repeatedly been found that response instability consists almost exclusively of chance variation around a largely stable central tendency (Converse, 1964; Achen, 1975; Dean and Moran, 1977; Erikson, 1979; Judd and Milburn, 1980; Judd, Milburn, and Krosnick, 1981; Feldman, 1989; Zaller, 1990; see, however, Krosnick, 1988). Thus a person's long-term average score on a seven-point scale may be 5, but the score may fluctuate considerably around that long-term average – say, between 3 and 7 – over repeated interviews.

An additional deduction from the RAS model is that more politically aware persons will exhibit less chance variability in their survey responses. This deduction may be reasoned as follows: More aware persons are more likely (from axiom A1) to possess the cueing messages necessary to respond to incoming information in a critical manner. As a result, they are more likely than less informed persons to reject information that conflicts with their values and to accept only information that is consistent. This will tend to increase the homogeneity of the considerations from which politically aware persons sample, which will tend to increase response stability.

We have, then, three deductions: Better informed persons are more likely to possess the cueing information necessary to reject communications inconsistent with their values (*D5*); this will make it more likely that they will form considerations that are homogeneously consistent with their values (*D6*), and this homogeneity will lead, inter alia, to greater response stability over time (*D7*).

Deduction D5 is easy to test, as shown in Table 4.4. The data in the top panel of this table were generated from a series of questions in the 1988 National Election Study, the first of which asserted:

Some people feel the government in Washington should see to it that everyone has a job and a good standard of living. Others think the government should let each person get ahead on his own.

Respondents were next asked to state their position on a seven-point scale anchored by the two polar positions, and then, in a final stage, they were asked to indicate the position of several prominent political figures or groups on this scale, including Ronald Reagan, George Bush, Michael Dukakis, Jesse Jackson, and each of the political parties.

As can be seen, highly aware persons were, as expected, much more likely than unaware ones to know that support for job guarantees is the position of the Democratic Party and its leading figures, and to know also that Republicans do not normally endorse this idea. For many Democrats and Republicans, this is knowledge that may affect their response to communications touching on the general issue of job guarantees. As Table 4.4 also shows, a similar pattern held for the issue of defense spending.

To test D6, I created a measure of ideological consistency at the level of considerations. I began by classifying each person's considerations as "consistent" with their underlying ideology or "inconsistent." For example, if a person who

Table 4.4. *Effect of political awareness on reception of leadership cues*

	Level of political awareness									
	Low				Middle					High
Percent who say cue-giver believes government should guarantee . . . a job and a good standard of living										
Ronald Reagan	9%	14	14	12	9	7	5	5	4	4
George Bush	10	16	14	11	8	11	6	6	4	0
Michael Dukakis	25	19	28	31	41	47	49	61	76	89
Jesse Jackson	30	31	36	45	51	54	60	72	82	100
Democratic Party	20	17	19	30	31	42	48	57	64	81
Republican Party	7	7	8	10	10	6	5	7	5	0
Percent who say cue-giver believes U.S. spending on defense should be increased										
Ronald Reagan	42%	48	57	66	65	73	82	84	89	85
George Bush	36	36	49	62	64	72	74	80	77	70
Michael Dukakis	15	18	17	15	13	10	11	10	4	7
Jesse Jackson	12	15	17	10	11	10	7	5	4	7
Democratic Party	19	25	25	18	20	20	18	16	15	19
Republican Party	37	42	51	62	58	69	74	80	76	81
N	486	147	178	195	197	230	238	219	123	27

Source: 1988 NES survey.

scored liberal on a social egalitarianism scale (described in Measures Appendix) said that ''blacks need special aid to make up for the effects of past discrimination,'' it would be counted as a consistent consideration; but if a conservative made the same remark, it would be an inconsistent consideration, since it runs against the grain of conservative ideology. A measure of consistency was then constructed as follows:

$$\frac{\sum (\text{Consistent remarks})}{\sum (\text{Consistent remarks}) + \sum (\text{Inconsistent remarks})}$$

This consistency measure, which runs from 0 to 1, gives the proportion of a person's remarks that are consistent with his underlying ideology. Figure 4.1 shows the relationship of these consistency scores to political awareness. As expected, respondents who are low on political awareness exhibit little ideological consistency in their underlying considerations; in fact, they are about as likely to mention ideologically inconsistent considerations as consistent ones. Highly aware respondents, by contrast, exhibit a fair degree of consistency, though not

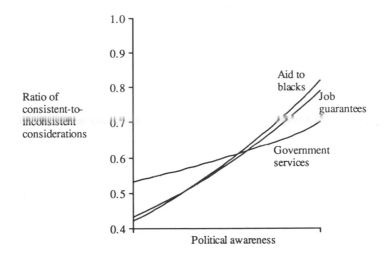

Figure 4.1. Political awareness and ideological consistency of considerations. *Source:* 1987 NES pilot survey.

so much as to violate the ambivalence deduction.[14] Lusk and Judd (1988) have reported other confirming evidence for D6.

Existing literature also provides clear support for D7. Although some research failed to find any relationships between political awareness and response stability (Achen, 1975; Erikson, 1979), three studies, each using a different dataset, have now found statistically reliable evidence that more politically aware persons exhibit less random instability in their closed-ended attitude reports, thus supporting D7 (Dean and Moran, 1977; Feldman, 1989; Zaller, 1991).

The chain of reasoning that led to D7 has some additional testable implications. If, as was argued, more aware persons are more stable in part because they are more likely to possess the cueing messages necessary to develop homogeneous pools of considerations, then the population as a whole should be able to develop more stable attitudes for issues on which partisan elites divide sharply and clearly, thereby providing clearer message cues for everyone. Conversely, attitude stability should be weaker for issues on which partisan divisions are hazy or nonexistent, because in such cases the public gets few message cues (*D8*). Using two-wave panel data from the United States and Sweden, Niemi and Westholm (1984) confirm that response instability is greater for issues on which partisan cues are weaker.[15] Thus, the extent to which ordinary citizens

14 Two of the awareness relationships in Figure 4.1 are significant at the .01 level; the third is significant at the .10 level.
15 Niemi and Westholm (1984) measure the clarity of party cues by the strength of relationship between party attachment and issue position within their samples. A more direct measure of party clarity would obviously be desirable.

    There is some additional evidence that clarity of party cues induces attitude stability; namely, overall stability rates appear higher in Sweden, where party cues are generally regarded as

develop stable attitude reports does, as inferred from the model, partly depend on the cues conveyed to the public by elite discourse.

In the argument for D7, political awareness is simply a proxy for attention to an issue. Thus, any factor that is also associated with greater attention to an issue should produce the same effects as greater political awareness. One such factor is the extent to which an issue is relatively "close-to-home," in the sense that almost everyone in the public follows it and thinks about it a fair amount. When the degree of public attentiveness to an issue is generally high, it follows that attitude statements on this issue will, in the public as a whole, exhibit less variability, all else equal, than will attitude statements on a more remote or abstract issue (D9). The tendency of attitude statements on race, abortion, and drugs to be more reliable than other types of attitude statements may be taken as supporting evidence for this deduction (Converse, 1964; Converse and Markus, 1979; Feldman, 1989).

By parallel logic, the model also implies that individuals who care more strongly about issues, or who are members of what Converse has called "issue publics," will pay more attention to issues and hence exhibit less chance variability in their attitude statements about these issues (D10).

Initial evidence from Converse (1964) and Schuman and Presser (1981) seemed to support this expectation. However, Krosnick's (1988) more sophisticated probing of the question, which distinguishes random response variation from actual attitude change, produced disconfirming evidence. His analysis of data from the three-wave 1980 NES panel study, as well as other data, concluded that people who care more about an issue exhibit more rather than, as the RAS model anticipates, less random variability in their attitude reports.

To find the reason for Krosnick's unexpected findings, I examined the 1980 panel data. What I discovered was that people who rated issues as extremely important were hardly more knowledgeable about them than people who said they were unimportant. For example, someone who rated toughness with Russia at 100 (the top rating) on the importance scale was only about 13 percentage points more likely to know that Ronald Reagan was to the right of Jimmy Carter on this issue than was a person who rated it at 25 on the importance scale (25 was the lowest importance rating given by any significant number of respondents). On one item, government services, there was no relationship at all between importance and knowledge of where Carter and Reagan stood on the issue.[16]

The reason for Krosnick's unexpected finding on response stability now seems clear: In arguing that people who regard an issue as important should be more stable in their response to it, I was assuming that they would also be more cog-

clearer than in the United States. Moreover, differences in the magnitude of cross-national differences appear to follow differences in party emphasis in the two countries.

16 In a 1992 paper, Krosnick et al. have confirmed this finding, showing with much better evidence than is available in the 1980 NES study that people who rate issues as highly important are only "modestly" more knowledgeable about these issues than people who do not rate them as important.

nitively engaged with that issue. If this intervening condition is not met, the RAS model provides no expectation that these people will be more stable in their attitude reports.[17]

These findings on the noneffects of issue importance on response stability underscore an important point about the RAS model: It is cognitive engagement with an issue, rather than concern or feeling about it, that drives the processes captured by the model.

To this point, my analysis of response instability has focused on the effect of awareness and issue concern on random response fluctuation. But if less aware persons exhibit greater chance fluctuation, shouldn't they also exhibit greater susceptibility to enduring or systematic attitude change?[18] Perhaps surprisingly, the answer to this question is no, or more precisely: No, not over the long run in a stable informational environment. For if, as the analysis of this chapter has explicitly assumed, information flows are stable over time, then all individuals, who are idealized in the model simply as "information processors," must remain near their equilibrium points. People's responses to particular questions may, for the reasons just given, vary stochastically around their equilibrium points, but the equilibrium points themselves should remain constant as long as the environment remains stable (*D11*).

The qualifying phrase "over the long run" is important here. In practice, the flow of communications will always have some short-term lumpiness and minor unevenness. (If the unevenness is great, it produces aggregate changes in mass attitudes, a topic analyzed in later chapters of this book.) Thus, if a person becomes unemployed, or sees a compelling news program, it may raise the salience of a particular consideration for a few days or perhaps a few months. But

---

17 Krosnick's (1988) finding that people who rate an issue as highly important exhibit more random response variation with respect to that issue than people who rate it as completely unimportant does not make sense from any theoretical perspective. What seems to be happening, as Krosnick suggests in the paper and as my analysis confirms, is that people who rate an issue as unimportant place themselves in the neutral middle of the seven-point scale and do not vary from this location over time. Many of these people are, it seems, using the middle position on the scale to make what is, in effect, a "no opinion" statement. By contrast, people who regard the issue as important rarely locate themselves at the neutral midpoint, but instead attempt to state an actual opinion, which introduces the possibility of some measurement error. Thus Krosnick's findings may rest on an artifact in the way that different kinds of people use seven-point scales.

I attempted to control for this artifact by recoding the seven-point issue scales to three-point scales (left, neutral, and right), thereby counting only gross changes in directional thrust as evidence of response instability. In this analysis, importance was slightly *negatively* associated with random response error, as would be expected. However, this approach makes it easier for people at the neutral center of the scale to appear unstable than for people near the endpoints, which introduces a bias in the opposite direction of the original problem.

Krosnick's (1988) analysis, as indicated earlier, is the only one of eight studies investigating response instability over time to find that a significant portion of the instability is due to true attitude change rather than random fluctuation. Owing to his central concern with the effects of issue importance, however, Krosnick does not remark on this aspect of his findings, nor have other researchers appeared to notice it.

18 In the language of the measurement models: Should not less aware persons exhibit lower stability coefficients as well as higher error variance scores?

in the long run, the person should encounter countervailing communications that raise other considerations and restore opinion to its long-term mean.

As a result of this lumpiness in the flow of communications, the average of salient considerations in people's minds will normally be near but not quite at its theoretically expected equilibrium. The regression of this average to its equilibrium point, which would take some time to occur, could give a misleading impression of gradual true attitude change, if attitude measurements were spaced closely enough to capture it. Thus, the expectation that susceptibility to real attitude change not vary by level of awareness or issue involvement would hold only for measurements that were fairly widely spaced.

My investigation of attitude stability in the 1972–74–76 NES panel, in which attitude measurements were spaced at two-year intervals, supports this argument: Awareness had no effect on susceptibility to systematic attitude change – which is to say, the stability coefficients in Wiley–Wiley estimates were near 1.0 and did not vary by respondents' level of political awareness (Zaller, 1986).

There is, then, a fair amount of evidence that is consistent with the notion that response instability over time arises from a tendency of people to base attitude reports on a quick and incomplete sampling from a pool of internally conflicted considerations. So far, however, we have seen no *direct* evidence that people's attitudes are unstable for this reason – no evidence, that is, showing that instability occurs *because* people call to mind different considerations when thinking about a given issue at different times.

One way to check this claim is to see whether changes in the directional thrust of people's open-ended remarks are associated with changes in the direction of their closed-ended remarks (D12). Thus, a person who makes mostly liberal comments when discussing a policy issue at the first interview and mostly conservative remarks at the second interview would be expected to change her closed-ended response from liberal to conservative as well. To test this expectation, I use the following model:

$$\text{Attitude}_2 = b_0 + b_1 \, \text{Attitude}_1 + b_2 \, \text{Considerations}_1 + b_3 \, \text{Considerations}_2,$$

where considerations are measured at time 1 and time 2.

A large coefficient on b_3, in conjunction with a moderate estimate for b_2, would indicate an important role for immediately salient considerations in explaining departures from the closed-ended survey responses made in the initial interview. As can be seen in Table 4.5, the data tend to fit this pattern.[19]

Another test of the mechanism that, as I claim, is responsible for response instability is to check whether people who exhibit higher levels of internal conflict in their open-ended remarks are more likely to be unstable in their closed-ended survey responses. To create a measure of consistency of open-ended

19 If unstandardized coefficients are used in this test instead of easy-to-interpret Beta coefficients, the substantive results remain the same.

Table 4.5. *The effect of considerations from second interview on response stability*

	Jobs	Services	Blacks
Retrospective considerations			
Policy attitude$_1$	0.51*	0.40*	0.55*
Considerations$_1$	−0.04	0.03	0.04
Considerations$_2$	0.38*	0.36*	0.35*
N	107	108	117
Stop-and-think considerations			
Policy attitude$_1$	0.36*	0.41*	0.48*
Considerations$_1$	0.12	0.03	0.15**
Considerations$_2$	0.16*	0.24*	0.15*
N	177	168	165

Note: Cell entries are standardized coefficients.
Dependent variable is policy item in second survey.
* p < .05   ** p < .10
Source: 1987 NES Pilot survey.

remarks, the following calculation was made for each respondent who answered the open-ended questions on both waves of the survey.

$$\frac{\left| \sum (\text{Liberal remarks}) - \sum (\text{Conservative remarks}) \right|}{\sum (\text{Liberal}) + \sum (\text{Conservative}) + \sum (\text{Ambivalent})}$$

A score of 1.0 on this measure would indicate that the person's remarks were either all liberal in their thrust or all conservative, while a score of 0 would indicate that the person had made an equal number of liberal and conservative remarks. Persons achieving the score of 1.0 should be *perfectly* stable in their responses to the closed-ended items. People who mention an equal number of opposing considerations should be stable only as often as could be expected by chance alone, which is 50 percent of the time (*D13*).

The data for this test are shown in Table 4.6. In five of six tests, the measure of internal consistency is associated with a statistically significant increase in response stability; in the sixth case, the relationship achieves marginal statistical significance ($p = .07$). These results, however, fall short of expectations. Particularly on the stop-and-think side, response stability does not vary, as expected, between a floor of 0.50 and a ceiling of 1.0. Why do we observe a shortfall from expectations, and why is it greater when questions are asked in the stop-and-think format?

The most likely explanation is a mundane type of measurement error. As earlier reported, coders disagreed on the coding of 10 to 15 percent of all open-ended remarks. Such error obviously impairs our ability to determine which

Table 4.6. *The effect of consistent considerations on response stability*

Consistency of considerations[a]	Job Guarantees		Government Services		Aid to Blacks	
Retrospective considerations						
		N		N		N
.00	.50	(7)	.59	(11)	.57	(7)
.01 to .50	.80	(20)	.70	(25)	.71	(19)
.51 to .99	.77	(15)	.78	(16)	.80	(15)
1.00	.90	(63)	.87	(54)	.96	(71)
	(p < .01)		(p < .02)		(p <.01)	
Stop–and–think considerations						
.00	.63	(16)	.54	(14)	.57	(14)
.01 to .50	.68	(74)	.77	(63)	.83	(66)
.51 to .99	.73	(37)	.80	(50)	.84	(44)
1.00	.88	(45)	.73	(37)	.88	(41)
	(p < .02)		(p < .07)		(p .<01)	

Note: Cell entries are proportion who are stable in their closed-ended responses from wave one to wave two. P-values are based on uncollapsed measure.

[a] Measure, which is described in text, runs from evenly balanced considerations (.00) to perfectly consistent considerations (1.00).

Source: 1987 NES Pilot survey.

respondents should be perfectly stable and which not. It would, therefore, strengthen our confidence in D13 if it could be shown that the items having the highest level of coding error also produced the largest shortfall from theoretical expectations in Table 4.6.

Although direct data on coding errors are not available at the level of individual items, there is a way of estimating item-level error rates indirectly. In cases in which coders were unable to assign a directional thrust to remarks even though one was presumably intended, they declared the remark directionally uncodable. The rate of such uncodable remarks varied from a low of 2 percent for one item to a high of 16 percent for another. These item-level rates of uncodable responses may be taken as a general indicator of the difficulty of assigning accurate codes to other remarks associated with each given item.

We should expect, then, that the shortfall from theoretical expectations in Table 4.6 is greatest for those items with the highest levels of directionally uncodable remarks. Figure 4.2 confirms that this is the case. The independent variable in that figure consists of the item-level rates of uncodable remarks. The dependent variable consists of the slopes (one for each item) obtained from regressing item stability on the consistency of the person's considerations; thus, regression coefficients have been used to summarize the relationships between stability and consistency in Table 4.6. As can be seen, these consistency-

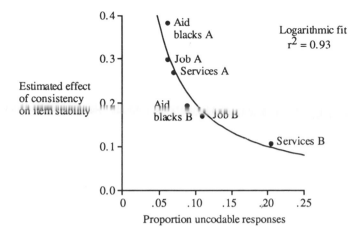

Figure 4.2. How measurement error weakens the effect of consistency on stability. Form A items are from retrospective side, form B from stop-and-think side. *Source:* 1987 NES pilot survey.

stability relationships are greatly stronger for items that had lower percentages of uncodable remarks ($r^2 = 0.93$, $p < .05$),[20] thereby confirming the suspicion that coding error has contributed significantly to the weaker than expected relationships depicted in Table 4.6.

Inspection of Figure 4.2 provides one additional bit of information. There were many more uncodable remarks associated with the stop-and-think probes (lower right) than with the retrospective probes.[21] This would seem the most likely reason why the consistency effects from the stop-and-think probes are so much weaker in Table 4.6 than the effects from the retrospective probes.[22]

Within the limits inherent in this type of data, then, the results in Table 4.6 are probably about as strong as can be expected. They involve sizable consistency effects at conventional levels of statistical significance in five of six trials, as well as an effect close to significance on the sixth – despite a significant amount of measurement error, a small sample, and abnormally low base rates of instability owing to the short time between reinterviews.

These data can be used to make one other point. The measure of consistency of open-ended remarks in Table 4.6 has been calculated over both waves of the survey in order to capture consistency both within and across interviews. The

20 A simple linear relationship between these two variables is also statistically significant at the .05 level.
21 The difference in the percentage of uncodable remarks across question form achieved statistical significance at the .01 level for each of the three items.
22 It is not surprising that error rates are higher on the stop-and-think side. It would seem easier, a priori, to determine the directional thrust of a remark if the remark has been made in justification of an opinion just rendered, as on the retrospective side, than if it has been given as part of a discussion of what a given phrase means to the respondent, as on the stop-and-think side.

measure can, however, be calculated within a single interview and used to predict response stability on the closed-ended item at the second interview. When this is done, we come up with a strong, clear finding: The one-wave measure has almost no capacity to predict response instability across waves. This suggests that the internal conflict most responsible for response instability is conflict of which respondents themselves are unaware because it occurs across rather than within interviews. Thus, for example, once the vacillating teacher from the introduction to this chapter began to view the government services issue through the prism of "bloated government," she (or he) may have put herself in a mindset that prevented her from thinking about the "education crisis" that had so agitated her in the first interview.[23] This suggestion fits nicely with A4, the Response Axiom, which holds that people tend to answer survey questions hastily and on the basis of incomplete memory searches.

By virtue of the importance of the phenomenon they purport to explain, the nine deductions concerning the existence and nature of response instability are among the most significant in the book. Most of the empirical findings to which the section refers are well-established; what is new is the explanation given for them.

At present, the most widely accepted explanation for response instability is that of Achen (1975). He maintains, as discussed in Chapter 2, that it is due primarily to measurement error. The everyday language used in survey questions is inevitably somewhat vague, and this makes it difficult for people to reliably map the attitudes in their heads into the appropriate response categories.

It must be emphasized that nothing in the RAS model is strictly inconsistent with this view. One reason that, as the RAS model claims, individuals so often bring different considerations to the evaluation of the same question may be, exactly as Achen contends, that most questions are open to multiple interpretations.[24] In other words, both the measurement error and the RAS models agree that response instability occurs because ordinary language is rarely precise enough to force individuals to think about an issue in the same way every time they confront it.

Two examples may serve both to underscore and clarify this point. Consider a person who vacillates on whether the government should "guarantee each person a job and a good standard of living." It is easy to imagine that, as the RAS model would suggest, this vacillation depends on whether the person thinks about the issue in terms of the government's responsibility to maintain a "full-employment economy" (which most people favor), or in terms of a Swedish-style welfare state (which most oppose). But it would certainly also be

23 Tourangeau and Rasinski (1988) distinguish between "interpretation" of a question and "retrieval" of information relevant to answering it. In terms of this distinction, these results indicate that intepretation is the more important source of response instability.
24 Alternatively, one might say that most issues are inherently multidimensional, and that individuals respond to different dimensions at different times.

reasonable to attribute such vacillation to question vagueness, since the question can readily be criticized as both double-barreled and unclear. Now consider this example: A person vacillates over whether "defense spending" should be increased or decreased. One might, in the spirit of the RAS model, imagine that the respondent is ambivalent between fear of foreign enemies, on one hand, and anger at Pentagon waste, on the other. In the measurement error tradition, one would instead contend that the stimulus is vague (what exactly is meant by "defense spending"?). Thus, both theoretical approaches can, at least in a technical sense, handle quite different cases of response instability, one of which involves a question that is easily criticized as vague and the other of which involves a question that is, by the standards of survey research, quite clear and direct.

There is, however, a fundamental difference between the two models. In the measurement error tradition, response error is simply so much noise. It has no substance and signifies nothing of interest about the nature of mass opinion. Insofar as we learn anything of theoretical significance from it, we learn about the vagueness of natural language rather than the nature of public opinion. In the RAS model, by contrast, response variation is rooted in an important substantive phenomenon, namely the common existence of ambivalence in people's reactions to issues. This ambivalence has numerous implications, as we shall see as the book progresses, for such matters as the priming effect of the mass media, the effects of survey question order, and attitude change. The RAS model's account of response instability, thus, is an integral part of a much more comprehensive way of thinking about public opinion.

5

Making it up as you go along

In a simple but inspired experiment, George Bishop and his colleagues at the University of Cincinnati began a survey with questions about the local congressman. This was bound to prove embarrassing to respondents, since fewer than half typically know the name of their representative, and even fewer have any real information beyond this. One of the questions read:

Is there any legislative bill that has come up in the House of Representatives, on which you remember how your congressman has voted in the last couple of years? (IF YES) What was that?

Only 12 percent could think of anything. Following this, respondents were asked to describe their level of interest in politics. Altogether, 45 percent said they follow politics "only now and then" or "hardly at all," which was one of the lowest reported levels of political interest ever recorded in a general population survey in the United States.

Meanwhile, another group of respondents to the poll was asked their level of interest in politics without first having to suffer through the difficult questions about their congressman. In this group, only half as many – 22 percent – indicated low levels of interest in politics. The lesson in this experiment is wonderfully capsulized in the title to the article describing the experiment: "What must my interest in politics be if I just told you 'I don't know'?" (Bishop, Oldendick, and Tuchfarber, 1984).

To state the matter more generally, most people really aren't sure what their opinions are on most political matters, including even such completely personal matters as their level of interest in politics. They're not sure because there are few occasions, outside of a standard interview situation, in which they are called upon to formulate and express political opinions. So, when confronted by rapid-fire questions in a public opinion survey, they make up attitude reports as best they can as they go along. But because they are hurrying, they are heavily influenced by whatever ideas happen to be at the top of their minds. Thus, what was most salient to many of the respondents in the Bishop experiment, who had just had an opportunity to observe how little they knew about politics, was that they were apparently not very interested in politics.

This sort of dependence on immediately salient ideas is ubiquitous in public opinion polling and, as I argue in this chapter, leads to a large number of empirical regularities – from race-of-interviewer effects to question-order effects to the priming effects of TV news – which can be usefully grouped together as salience effects. Most of these regularities are well established in the research literature, but their common dependence on a salience mechanism has not been widely appreciated.

RESPONSE EFFECTS

Let me begin with "response effects," a term that refers to cases in which seemingly irrelevant features of questionnaire design affect the responses given. One of the most important of these has been the oft-repeated finding that the order in which questions are asked can affect the responses given (Schuman and Presser, 1981; Tourangeau and Rasinski, 1988). Thus, as described in Chapter 2, 37 percent of Americans would have permitted communist reporters to operate in the United States when the question was asked alone, but 73 percent would have done so when the communism question was preceded by a question about the rights of U.S. reporters in Russia.

This type of occurrence is perhaps the simplest and most direct evidence that many respondents are making up their survey responses as they confront each question in the survey. Note, however, that my claim is not that people have no thoughts at all on public issues: In the case of communist reporters, for example, most Americans were obviously wary of anything described as communist; many no doubt also cared about freedom of expression and reciprocal freedom for U.S. reporters in Russia. But which of these considerations controlled their response to a question about communist reporters in the United States – a matter about which few people had probably ever thought before being surveyed – was by no means predetermined. Rather, it depended on which of the concerns was made salient by the questionnaire.

Response effects of this type may be readily explained by axiom A3, which implies that the more recently a consideration has been activated, the more accessible it is for use in answering questions. It is as if ideas, once used, remain at the top of a heap of ideas in one's memory, readily available for use. Different question orders may then bring different considerations to the tops of people's memory heaps, thereby increasing chances that they will affect responses to subsequent questions (*D14*). Thus, in the case of the communist reporters items, asking first about the rights of U.S. reporters in Russia raised a consideration that many people would not ordinarily have thought of.

The intrusion of unexpected or novel considerations into the question-answering process would not, however, be expected to affect all respondents equally. Some people may possess considerations that are so consistent in support of one side of an issue that the admission of additional considerations should have no effect. Others, however, may be deeply ambivalent on the issue – that is, may possess a roughly even balance of considerations for and against the issue. These are the persons who should be most strongly affected by artificial changes in question order (*D15*).

Tourangeau et al. (1989) have reported support for this expectation. People who reported that they had mixed feelings about an issue (and who also said the issue was very important to them) were quite susceptible to question-order effects, or what the authors call "carryover effects," while others were not susceptible at all. The carryover effects in the vulnerable groups (which varied from issue to issue) ranged from lows of 4 and 8 percentage points on abortion and welfare, to highs of 34 and 36 percentage points on aid to the Contra rebels and defense spending, with an average carryover of 19 percentage points.

Until recently, response effects like these were widely considered to be "methodological artifacts" that indicated nothing of theoretical significance about the nature of mass political attitudes. Some, however, have always been given substantive interpretations. Consider these three:

Race of interviewer. Shortly after a 1986 *New York Times* poll found that President Reagan's approval rate among blacks was 37 percent, a *Washington Post* poll estimated that black approval of Reagan was only 23 percent. The difference, too large to be due to sampling error, was traced to the fact that, while the *Times* followed normal interview procedures, the *Post* used black interviewers who informed their black respondents that they would be participating in a study of the attitudes of black Americans. As Sussman (1986) persuasively argues, the likely effect of this was to induce black respondents to "think black" in their evaluations of Reagan's performance, the first item on the survey. (For additional evidence on race of interviewer effects, see Anderson, Silver, and Abramson, 1988.)

Reference groups. In a classic social psychology experiment, Charters and Newcomb (1958) found that Catholics were more likely to state attitudes that were consistent with Church doctrine (on birth control, for example) if, just prior to questioning, their religion was made salient to them. Salience was achieved by having a priest make a brief appearance in the room near the time at which the questionnaire was administered. The effect of this manipulation has been taken as evidence of the importance of "reference groups" on attitudes.

"Priming effects" of television news. Iyengar (1991) has shown that TV news often functions to make ideas more accessible for use in answering questions about the attribution of social and political responsibility. In this way, TV news is said to affect attitude reports without permanently changing individuals' underlying attitudes. For example, people are more likely to say, in response to a survey question, that the poor are predominantly to blame for their poverty if they have just watched a news story that deals with an individual or "episodic" case of poverty, than if they have seen a newscast that deals with poverty as a societal phenomenon.

The mechanism responsible for each of these effects is the tendency for people to respond to questions at least partly on the basis of whatever ideas are immediately salient to them.[1] Accordingly, they may be counted as additional empirical regularities for which the RAS model, in particular A3 and A4, gives an explanation (*D16–D18*).

Some readers may suspect that salience effects are limited to the domain of attitude measurement, where people's preferences may be less firm than they are when real choices are involved, as in election campaigns. This is not the case, however. A striking case of a salience effect in an electoral context occurred during the 1984 presidential election. Throughout the summer campaign, polls attempting to gauge the race between Walter Mondale and Ronald Reagan differed substantially. Some polls estimated Reagan to be as much as 20 points ahead of Mondale, while others saw the race as dead even. This high margin of difference across polls cannot be explained by chance sampling variation alone.

These persistent differences were not only disturbing to pollsters, but also puzzling. The best explanation for the phenomenon appeared in an August article in the *New York Times,* as follows:

Professor [Seymour Martin] Lipset [of Stanford University] observed that President Reagan seemed to do better in polls that asked the [candidate preference] question at the beginning [before any policy questions had been asked] rather than the end. He likened this to mixed feelings about Reagan, theorizing that many turned against him after being questioned about his policies. (Robert Reinhold, *New York Times,* 15 August 1984, p. 1)

Pollsters cited in the article felt that the discrepancies between polling organizations would disappear later in the campaign, after people's preferences crystallized. However, the discrepancies continued well into the fall campaign, with Reagan doing consistently better when the preference question was asked prior to issue questions (Michael Oreskes, *New York Times,* 20 October 1984, p. 8).

Although one cannot be certain that Lipset's explanation is correct, it has the aura of plausibility. Throughout the Reagan presidency, polls showed that citizens felt better about "Reagan the man" than they did about his political program. This makes it plausible that they would rate him more highly before being reminded of that program. Lipset's hypothesis, moreover, mirrors the campaign itself: Reagan's strategy was to avoid divisive issues and to capitalize instead on his personal charm; Mondale, recognizing that charm was not his long suit, instead attempted to run a more issue-oriented campaign. Thus, without necessarily meaning to do so, surveys that asked early in the questionnaire about presidential preference were playing to Reagan's strength; surveys that asked later were playing to Mondale's strength.

This example drives home a central theoretical point: Question order effects should not be classified as methodological artifacts; they should be seen, rather, as revealing a fundamental property of mass political preferences – a tendency for people to be ambivalent (even though perhaps unconsciously so) and to deal

1 Memory research indicates that the temporary effects of activating an idea may last from a few seconds to a few weeks (Higgins and King, 1981).

with this ambivalence by making decisions on the basis of the ideas that are most immediately salient.

"PRIMING" AS A TYPE OF SALIENCE EFFECT

Salience effects are actually quite a lot more complicated and interesting than has been indicated in my treatment of them so far. They can involve not only changes in the marginal distribution of responses, as when more people indicated a vote for Reagan when asked about their vote intention early in the questionnaire, but also changes in the types of people who make a given response, which then manifest themselves as changes in the *correlates* of attitude reports. For example, experimental evidence shows that people's evaluation of a president will be more strongly correlated with their attitudes on defense spending if they have just viewed a series of news programs dealing with defense than if they have not (Iyengar, Peters, and Kinder, 1982; Iyengar et al., 1984; Iyengar and Kinder, 1987).

A similar sort of priming effect has also been observed in a naturalistic setting. Krosnick and Kinder (1990) have shown that people's attitudes toward U.S. policy in Central America were apparently "primed" by the Iran–Contra scandal so as to become more strongly correlated with their evaluation of President Reagan's job performance. In other words, attitudes toward Central American intervention were a strong determinant of Reagan's job evaluations in the aftermath of Iran–Contra, even though they had not previously been engaged as correlates of presidential evaluation.

The RAS model is well suited to explaining such priming effects. Let us dissect a concrete example, the case of the effects of the Iran–Contra controversy on ratings of Reagan's job performance. To simplify matters, we assume that, prior to Iran–Contra, most media messages on Reagan focused on his performance in the domain of social welfare policy, and that people's general feelings about social welfare determined their responses to these messages. One could say that, in this situation, people's social welfare predispositions functioned as the "gatekeepers" that regulated (via A2) which considerations were admitted to the set of considerations on which Reagan's job performance ratings were based. Thus persons having conservative social welfare predispositions filled their minds with arguments that led them to evaluate Reagan positively, while people having liberal predispositions on this policy dimension filled their minds with arguments that induced them toward a negative evaluation of Reagan. If, at this point, citizens were asked to evaluate Reagan's job performance, their social welfare predispositions, as the gatekeeper for considerations entering their heads with respect to Reagan's job performance, would be strongly correlated with their evaluations of job performance.

But now suppose that the Iran–Contra scandal had brought about a situation in which arguments relating to Reagan's social welfare performance were almost entirely absent from the media, and in which the media were instead filled with messages indicating that Reagan was so strongly anticommunist that he flirted with illegalities in order to fund the Contra guerrillas in Central America. In this situation, people's social welfare predispositions would no longer have functioned as the gatekeepers determining which pro- and anti-Reagan arguments were accepted. People's predispositions on the issue of anticommunism would instead have played this gatekeeper role. Thus, strong anticommunists would have begun to fill their heads with pro-Reagan considerations, and people who were not so strongly anticommunist would have filled their heads with anti-Reagan considerations, such as the use of arguably illegal means to aid the Contras. As a result, people's anticommunism predispositions would have become more strongly engaged as determinants of evaluations of Reagan's job performance.

This is, as noted previously, exactly the effect that Krosnick and Kinder (1990) observed during the course of the Iran–Contra scandal. Thus, we may say that the considerations that citizens use in evaluating presidential performance – and presumably in making other types of attitude reports – are significantly affected by the way the topic has been framed in elite discourse.

Yet it is not only elite discourse, whether in the form of particular TV news stories or months-long episodes such as Iran–Contra, that can prime the considerations that citizens use in making attitude reports. How a question is framed in a survey can accomplish the same thing.

To see this, suppose that, with respect to a given issue, citizens' heads are filled with two types of considerations – considerations for which social welfare or anticommunist predispositions played the gatekeeper role of determining acceptance or rejection. If, then, a survey question is framed in such a way as to elevate the salience of social welfare considerations, people will decide the issue on the basis of considerations for which their social welfare predispositions were gatekeeper. As a result, their responses to that issue will be strongly correlated with their social welfare predispositions. But if the issue is instead framed in terms of anticommunism, people's anticommunist predispositions will become engaged, thereby inducing a correlation between anticommunist predispositions and the given issue.

There have been several recent demonstrations of cases in which, as this argument suggests, question frames have primed one type of response rather than another. Kinder and Sanders (1990) examine the effects of two types of questions, both from the 1987 NES pilot study, on affirmative action:

AFFIRMATIVE ACTION – UNFAIR ADVANTAGE FRAME

Some people say that because of past discrimination against blacks, preference in hiring and promotion should be given to blacks. Others say preferential hiring of blacks is wrong *because it gives blacks advantages they haven't earned.* What about your opinion . . . ?

AFFIRMATIVE ACTION – REVERSE DISCRIMINATION FRAME

Some people say that because of past discrimination against blacks, preference in hiring and promotion should be given to blacks. Others say preferential hiring of blacks is wrong *because it discriminates against whites.* What about your opinion . . . ? (Emphasis added.)

When, in the first case, the item refers to unfair advantages to blacks, whites' feelings of "symbolic racism" are engaged as correlates of opposition to affirmative action, but when, in the second case, the question refers to discrimination against whites, whites' attitudes concerning group competition between blacks and whites become engaged. Although overall levels of white opposition to affirmative action are unaffected by choice of question frames, the particular whites who opposed this policy – "symbolic racists" in the first frame, whites who feel in competition with blacks for jobs in the second – varied as a function of question frame.

A question-wording experiment from the 1989 NES pilot provides another example of this phenomenon. Respondents were randomly selected to respond to one of three questions about oil drilling in Alaska. The questions were

OIL DRILLING – BARE BONES

Do you favor or oppose drilling new oil fields on federal lands in Alaska?

OIL DRILLING – FOREIGN DEPENDENCY FRAME

There is a lot of talk these days about a plan to allow more drilling for oil on federal lands in Alaska. Some people are opposed to this drilling. They say the Alaskan wilderness should be preserved in its natural state for future generations. *Others say the drilling is necessary because the U.S. needs new energy sources to avoid becoming dependent on foreign oil.* What is your opinion? Do you favor or oppose drilling new oil fields on federal lands in Alaska?

OIL DRILLING – ECONOMIC COSTS FRAME

There is a lot of talk these days about a plan to allow more drilling for oil on federal lands in Alaska. Some people are opposed to this drilling. They say there would be no need for this oil if we made better use of our existing energy resources. Others support the drilling. *They say that without new sources of oil, working people will be hurt by higher gasoline prices and there will be further layoffs in American factories.* What is your opinion? Do you favor or oppose drilling new oil fields on federal lands in Alaska? (emphasis added)

In responding to the first and second form of the question, respondents showed no concern about a possible link between oil drilling in Alaska and the cost of conservation to the economy. In particular, there was no correlation between social class – a common indicator of sensitivity to economic costs – and attitudes toward drilling. However, in the third form of the question, which explicitly raises potential economic costs, people's identification as working class or middle class becomes a strong correlate of attitudes toward oil drilling.[2] The overall level of support for oil drilling also rises, mainly among members of the working class, when the third form of the question is used. Thus, it is not true, as one might suppose from responses to the first two questions, that Americans are entirely unconcerned about the possible economic costs of conservation; it is

2 In addition, respondents' attitudes toward environmentalism were more strongly engaged in the second and third frames than in the first.

just that few people happened to think of them – until prodded to do so by the question frame. (Technical details for this experimental finding are available upon request.)

The reason that priming occurs in these examples is that different question frames raise the salience of different ideas, thereby engaging different "gatekeeper" attitudes as the correlates of people's attitude reports. Question frames can produce priming effects in one other way: by providing background information that makes the question more intelligible, especially to the unaware, who are most likely to lack it.

A pair of questions concerning U.S. spending on the Contra guerrillas in Nicaragua demonstrate this effect. The questions, each asked of a random subsample of respondents to the 1989 NES pilot survey, were as follows:

CONTRA AID – BARE BONES

Would you like to see aid to the Contras in Nicaragua increased, decreased, or kept about the same?

CONTRA AID – FRAMED

Here is another question about foreign policy. As you know, the U.S. has been giving aid to the Contras, a guerilla group that wants to overthrow the Communist government of Nicaragua. Some people say we should stop aid to the Contras because the U.S. has no business in the internal affairs of Nicaragua. Others think the U.S. should continue the aid because the Contras are freedom fighters trying to stop the spread of Communism in Central America. Would you like to see aid to the Contras in Nicaragua increased, decreased, or kept about the same?

As we saw in Chapter 2, few of the politically unaware knew who the Contras were or what they stood for. Hence, when unaware persons answered the bare bones version of the Contra question, they tended to see it as a question about government spending: Poorly informed people who favored most domestic spending programs were also more positive on aid to the Contras, while people who opposed domestic spending also opposed spending on the Contras. Further, attitudes toward Contra spending were completely uncorrelated with attitudes toward anticommunism, as measured elsewhere in the survey.

When responding to the framed question, however, poorly informed persons were able to recognize the Contra issue as involving anticommunism. Hence their attitudes toward domestic spending now had no effect on their attitude reports, while their general feelings on anticommunism were strongly engaged as a determinant of attitudes toward Contra spending. Meanwhile, question form had no impact on politically aware persons, who knew what the Contras stood for whether the question carried this information or not. Technical details of these tests are given in Table 5.1.

To summarize: The key point here is that which considerations are brought to bear in answering survey questions may depend on which have been recently primed, or made accessible to the respondent. Priming may be accomplished by (1) elite discourse over a period of months (as in the example of Iran–Contra's effect on the correlates of evaluations of Reagan), (2) a particular news story one

Table 5.1. *Effect of question form on support for Contra aid*

	Level of political awareness		
	Low	Middle	High
Intercept	0.93	0.93	0.04
Anticommunism attitudes	0.03 (0.34)	0.36 (3.70)	0.51 (5.24)
Domestic spending attitudes	−0.37 (2.01)	−0.50 (2.32)	0.54 (3.16)
Form (1 = communism frame, else 0)	−0.51 (2.25)	−0.29 (1.34)	0.26 (1.46)
Form x anticommunism attitudes	0.34 (1.91)	0.01 (0.04)	−0.10 (0.69)
Form x domestic spending attitudes	0.50 (1.63)	0.31 (0.98)	−0.10 (1.01)
Adjusted r^2	0.07	0.15	0.38
N	97	114	119

Note: T-ratios are in parentheses. Variables, all scored in the liberal direction, are described in Measures Appendix.
Source: 1989 NES pilot survey.

has recently seen or read (as in the experiments by Iyengar, Kinder, and others on how TV news changed the correlates of presidential evaluation), or (3) the way the question has been framed on the questionnaire, as we have just seen. In all of these cases, but especially the last,[3] priming effects may be explained by the assumption that individuals do not typically possess "just one attitude" toward issues, but several opinions (the Ambivalence Deduction), and that which of these potential opinions they report depends, here as elsewhere in this chapter, on the information that has been most recently made salient to them (*D19*).

Milburn (1987) has documented yet another way in which priming effects can be induced: by the order in which questions are presented. He found that asking respondents, "Tell me everything that comes to mind when you think of a Liberal (Conservative)" caused subsequent attitude reports to be more ideologically consistent with one another than were the attitude reports of a control group. Milburn obtained this effect, however, only for persons who had either liberal or conservative leanings to begin with. Price (1991) has recently replicated these findings in an experiment conducted on college students and in nonexperimental data from national samples. In both cases, Price finds that simply asking persons to place themselves on a liberal–conservative rating scale increased the ideological consistency of responses to subsequent policy items – but, again,

---

3 The first two effects may also involve the formation of some new considerations, which takes us into the domain of attitude change, which is treated in later chapters.

only for those who possessed a clear ideological leaning (that is, who were not centrists or unable to place themselves on the self-rating scale).

This type of priming or question-order effect is also explainable from the RAS model. Having had their ideological orientations made salient to them just prior to answering policy items, those respondents who have such an orientation are more likely to rely on it as a consideration in formulating responses to subsequent policy questions, thereby making those responses more strongly correlated with their ideological positions and hence also more ideologically consistent with one another (*D20*).

EFFECTS OF THOUGHT ON THE RELIABILITY OF ATTITUDE REPORTS

Within the framework of the RAS model, the effect of political awareness or intellectual engagement with politics is to enhance the quality of attitude reports. They lead to greater stability in one's attitude reports and to attitude reports that more reliably reflect underlying predispositions (Chapter 6). But these awareness effects involve habitual or long-term political awareness. We shall see in this section that certain kinds of artificially induced increases in intellectual engagement can produce quite opposite effects.

If someone were completely uncritical in response to the flow of political communications, he would fill his head with a mixture of whatever conflicting considerations were carried in the mass media. These considerations would tend to be mutually canceling much of the time, so that attitude reports based on them would tend to be centrist. This type of situation should occur most often for less aware persons, who tend to lack the cueing messages and contextual information necessary for a critical response to political communications. Thus, we should expect them to be relatively centrist in their attitude reports.

With increases in political awareness, however, come increases in critical capacity and hence in the internal consistency of the considerations one forms. We should therefore expect more politically aware persons to be more noncentrist – or extreme – in their attitude reports (*D21*). This basic expectation has been strongly confirmed (Sidanius, 1988; Lusk and Judd, 1988).

This so-called extremity effect of awareness might be more appropriately conceptualized as a reliability effect. For there is no reason to believe that less politically aware persons are, on average, more or less extreme than highly aware persons in terms of underlying predispositions. The difference simply is that, owing to lessened critical capacity, less aware persons are less able to reliably convert their predispositions into noncentrist attitude reports.

This deduction leads directly to another. If political awareness is a cause of extreme attitude reports, we ought to find that individuals can report extreme attitudes more quickly – that is, with less hesitation before answering – than less extreme ones. The reasoning for this deduction is as follows: A3, the Accessibility Axiom, contends that considerations that have been more recently activated take less time to locate and call to the top of the head for use. Political awareness, from its definition as intellectual engagement with politics, ought to be associated with more recent activation of one's political thoughts and hence with quicker reporting of one's attitudes. Since these attitudes are, as we just saw, likely to be more extreme, extreme attitudes ought to be more quickly reported (*D22*).

Psychologists, who can measure response times in fractions of seconds, have confirmed that more extreme attitudes are indeed reported more quickly (Judd et al., 1991).[4]

Let us now move from habitual, long-term political engagement with politics to short-term engagement. Suppose that survey respondents could be induced temporarily to increase their normal level of engagement with an issue just at the moment of responding to a question about it. What would be the effect of such heightened engagement or "extra thought"?

More thought at the moment of answering a question could not affect the mix of considerations in a person's head, since considerations are, according to the model, formed from the internalization of arguments from the mass media and elite discourse. Short-term increases in engagement could, however, increase the amount of time one devotes to searching one's memory and thereby raise the number of considerations used in formulating one's attitude report.

One intent in designing the stop-and-think probes in the 1987 NES pilot was to create exactly this sort of temporary increase in engagement with issues. By requiring individuals to discuss what a question means to them before answering it, the questionnaire would encourage them to call to mind and take account of a wider range of ideas than they normally would. One would expect that responses formed by averaging over a larger number of considerations would be better indicators of the population of underlying considerations than responses based on just one or two considerations, and hence more reliable.

There are two standard indicators of response reliability: stability of response over time, and strength of correlation between the response and related attitudes, which may be called predictive reliability. Both would be expected to be higher among respondents engaging in the stop-and-think procedure than among those answering questions in the normal fashion (*D23, D24*). Let me deal first with predictive reliability.

To test the expectation of greater reliability, a series of social welfare items was used to build a general measure of left–right tendency. This scale was expected to be more strongly related to the target items (jobs, government services, and aid to blacks) in the stop-and-think condition than in the retrospective

4 The Judd et al. article is only incidentally concerned with extremity and response time. One of its two important findings is that when people respond to questions about two related issues (for example women's rights and abortion), their responses to the second question will be quicker for whichever question is answered second. This is also explainable from the RAS model: The first question raises considerations that are, having just been used, extremely accessible as considerations for use in answering the second question, thereby enabling faster response to it.

Table 5.2. *The effect of stop-and-think on ideological consistency*

	Low awareness	High awareness
Intercept	0.01	-.20
Ideology measure	0.89	0.62
	(4.23)	(4.43)
Form	-0.36	0.00
	(1.71)	(0.0)
Ideology x Form	-0.24	0.62
	(0.89)	(2.38)
N	434	437

Note: *T*-ratios are in parentheses. Data are from Wave 1, except when don't know was given in that wave. Measures are described in Appendix.
Source: 1989 NES pilot survey.

condition. This relationship was tested by means of the following interactive logit model, where Form refers to question form:

$$\text{Response} = b_0 + b_1 \text{Form} + b_2 \text{Ideology} + b_3 \text{Form} \times \text{Ideology}$$

When this model was estimated for respondents scoring in the upper 40 percent of the measure of political awareness, it was found that the critical coefficient, b_3, ran in the expected direction for all three items but achieved statistical significance in only one case. To increase the statistical power of the interaction test in the small sample, the model was reestimated under the constraint that all coefficients be equal across the three items. The results of this test, shown in the right-hand column of Table 5.2, confirmed expectations: The effect of ideology is twice as large in the stop-and-think condition, a difference that achieves statistical significance.

The interaction model was estimated under the same constraints for respondents scoring in the bottom 40 percent of the awareness measure. Here the stop-and-think exercise not only failed to produce an increase in reliability but may have reduced it slightly.

The results for low-awareness respondents thus appear to contradict expectations, but unfortunately the apparent contradiction is confounded with a methodological artifact. Owing to the use of an explicit ''no interest'' option in the retrospective condition but not in the stop-and-think condition, respondents in the retrospective condition gave many more no-opinion responses, and low-awareness persons were most affected by this question difference. Their no-opinion rate averaged 38 percent in the retrospective condition and only 4

Table 5.3. *The effect of stop-and-think on test–retest correlations*

	Level of political awareness					
	Low		Middle		High	
	Retro-spective	Stop and think	Retro-spective	Stop and think	Retro-spective	Stop and think
Job guarantees	.68	.45	.64	.41	.70	.55
N	(40)	(62)	(29)	(60)	(39)	(51)
Government services	.56	.43	.48	.38	.61	.58
	(41)	(58)	(31)	(51)	(37)	(48)
Aid to blacks	.79	.53	.81	.51	.70	.86
	(53)	(57)	(33)	(58)	(32)	(45)

Note: Cell entries are test–retest correlations.
Source: 1989 NES pilot survey.

percent in the stop-and-think condition.[5] This means that stop-and-think respondents, especially less aware ones, are a less selected group and would, for this reason, be expected to be less ideologically reliable than their retrospective counterparts. Hence, the apparent decrease in predictive reliability among low-awareness persons in the stop-and-think condition cannot be taken as definitive.

Note, however, that the artifactual problem does not undermine the first part of the test: The *increase* in reliability among politically aware persons runs against the grain of the artifact, and so is likely to be real.

The second test of the stop-and-think treatment involves the stability of attitude reports over time. Here the expectation is that the stop-and-think treatment will cause attitudes to become more stable, simply because sampling more considerations should make the sample average more reliably representative of the underlying population of considerations.

The stop-and-think treatment failed to produce this expected result. It left attitude stability among highly aware persons unchanged, while greatly *reducing* attitude stability among people with middle and low levels of awareness. The results are shown in Table 5.3 in the form of test–retest correlations.

D24 thus appears to be disconfirmed. As before, however, the disconfirmation is tainted by selection bias. That is, the less selected respondents in the stop-and-think condition might have been less stable precisely because they were less selected.[6]

I propose, nonetheless, to accept the disconfirmation of D24 and the partial disconfirmation of D23 as probably real. Part of the reason is the magnitude of the apparent disconfirmation in Table 5.3; but more important, this pattern of

5 By contrast, the difference in no-opinion rates across forms averaged 13 percent (16% vs. 3%) in the highest information quintile.
6 Note that the difference in no-opinion rates across the two forms, as described previously, is compounded by the fact that respondents must twice answer the policy questions in order to test the stability of their opinions over time.

results is not only intelligible in light of recent psychological research, but could have been predicted from it. To see how, it is necessary to review this research in detail.

In a compelling series of experiments, Timothy Wilson and colleagues have shown that asking people to "analyze the reasons" for their feelings often has a *disruptive* effect on the predictive reliability of attitude reports.[7] A typical Wilson experiment is the following: College students were given a choice of several free posters of the type that are commonly hung in dorm rooms and student apartments. A random half was asked to analyze the reasons for their likes and dislikes before making a choice of which poster to take home; the other half was not required to do this. Follow-up interviews several weeks later found that the students who analyzed their feelings before making choices were *less* likely to report satisfaction with their posters than were people who simply took the poster they liked (see Wilson, Dunn, Kraft, and Lisle, 1989).

Similar evidence of the disruptive effects of thought have been obtained in attitude reports concerning presidential candidates, strawberry jam, and even dating partners. In explaining these results, Wilson, Dunn, Kraft, and Lisle (1989) argue that

when people attempt to explain an attitude, they do not always know exactly why they feel the way they do. Therefore, the reasons they come up with sound plausible, but might not correctly explain their feelings. . . . Unaware that their reasons are incomplete or incorrect, people view them as representative of their feelings and adopt the attitude they imply (pp. 296–7).

In the case of the posters, for example, students faced a choice between prints of Impressionist paintings and humor posters (such as a cat on a tightrope with the caption, "Gimme a break"). Students found it easy to articulate things they disliked about the Impressionist paintings ("fuzzy images") and easy to think up things they liked about the humor posters ("it's funny"). So, following the logic of their own reasons, they often chose (and subsequently grew tired of) a humor poster. Meanwhile, students in the control condition, arriving at evaluations by whatever means they normally do, overwhelmingly chose and were subsequently more satisfied with a print of an Impressionist painting.

It is important to notice that these results tend, in a fairly direct way, to confirm the central assertion of the RAS model, which is that people's attitude reports (and even behaviors) reflect the ideas that are at the top of the head at the moment of decision rather than any deeper type of "true attitude." In fact, it is precisely because attitude reports do depend on immediately salient ideas that

7 Wilson et al. have also found that asking people to analyze the reasons for their attitude reports lowers the stability over time of reported attitudes (see Wilson, Dunn, Kraft, and Lisle, 1989, for a summary of findings). However, this finding is not comparable to those presented here, since the Wilson et al. stability tests usually involve asking people to analyze reasons at their T2 but not at their initial T1 attitude measurements. What Wilson's studies of attitude stability examine is really the comparative equivalence, across treatment groups, of two somewhat different methods of measurement. Much more significant, to my mind, are Wilson's results on predictive reliability, as reviewed in the text.

extra thought, in bringing new and possibly unrepresentative ideas to the top of the head, often proves disruptive.

Yet, the findings on the disruptive effects of thought also present a problem, for nothing in the RAS model can explain why inducing people to utilize a larger base of considerations should *undermine* reliability. Indeed, the expected finding is the reverse, as I have indicated.

The crux of the problem, according to Wilson's argument, is that people bring somewhat different considerations to mind when asked to give the reasons for their attitudes than they do otherwise. As a result, attitude reports made after a "reasons analysis" may fail to predict the attitudes and behaviors that are based on a normal memory search. The problem, thus, is not with the extra thought per se, but with extra thought that fails to mimic the normal process by which people search their memories for relevant considerations.

For further evidence on this point, consider the following study by Millar and Tesser (1986). They observe that people may undertake actions either for the pleasure they afford (consummatory behavior) or for their practical benefits (instrumental behavior). Decisions concerning the former are likely to be based on feelings about the attitude object, while decisions about the latter are likely to be more cognitively driven.

Given this, and still assuming that people base attitude reports on whatever ideas are immediately salient in their minds, one would expect that inducing people to think about the *reasons* for their attitudes prior to making an attitude response should lead to a report that correlates well with instrumental behavior toward a given object but poorly with consummatory behavior. Similarly, inducing people to think about their *feelings* prior to making an attitude report should lead to a report that correlates well with consummatory behavior but poorly with instrumental behavior. In a cleverly designed experiment, this is exactly what Millar and Tesser found.[8]

---

8 Subjects were given five types of puzzles to work with (e.g., try to find the next letter in a sequence). Half were told to "analyze WHY you feel the way you do about each type of puzzle," and half were told to "analyze HOW you feel." Also, half were told that they would take a test of "analytic ability" after playing with the puzzles, and that the puzzles would be good practice for it; the other half was not led to believe the puzzles would be useful for anything. After practicing with the puzzles, all subjects gave a rating to each puzzle and were then given a period of free time in which to play with whichever puzzles they wished. The amount of time spent playing with each puzzle in free time was the dependent variable in the analysis. Subjects who were told to analyze the reasons for their feelings, and who believed they were about to take a test of analytic ability, had ratings of the puzzles that correlated well with the amount of time spent playing with them. Thus in this condition, an attitude report that followed a "reasons analysis" correlated with an instrumental behavior. Similarly, for students who analyzed how they felt about puzzles and who did not think they would be completing a test of analytic ability, there was also a strong correlation between rating and behavior. Here, an attitude report that followed a "feelings analysis" correlated with consummatory behavior. But in the other two conditions – reasons analysis and consummatory behavior, and feeling analysis and instrumental behavior – correlations between rating and behavior were low. Thus, the effect of thought depends on the degree of match or mismatch between the kind of thought undertaken and the kind of behavior one is attempting to predict.

Let us now turn to the 1987 pilot study, which asked half of the respondents "What kinds of things come to mind when you think about [a given issue]?" Such a probe appears more likely to induce an analysis of reasons than an analysis of feelings. Thus, the treatment should enhance reliability of attitude reports if people base their attitude reports on reasons, and lower it if they base them on feelings.

There is, as it happens, evidence from Sniderman, Brody, and Tetlock (1991) that less aware persons place heavier weights on feelings in their attitude reports, whereas more aware persons tend instead to stress ideological principle. From this it follows that the particular inducement to greater thought used in the 1987 pilot, with its emphasis on reasons rather than feelings, should prove disruptive to the attitude reports of the less aware and helpful (or at least nonharmful) to the attitude reports of the more aware, which is the pattern that has been obtained in Tables 5.2 and 5.3.[9]

What this line of argument suggests is the need for a method to induce extra thought that mimics rather than cross cuts people's normal ways of thinking about issues. In the meantime, it seems to me, D23 and D24 cannot be said to have been adequately tested, and hence have been neither confirmed nor disconfirmed.

But however this may be, the psychological studies we have been examining have been extremely useful. They show, at least as clearly as any of the survey-based evidence, that closed-ended attitude reports depend to a surprising degree on ideas at the top of the head at the moment of response – and that this remains true even when the procedures used to bring the ideas to the top of the head are rather artificial, and even when the attitude reports involve something as personally important as one's dating partner or lover (see Seligman, Fazio, and Zanna, 1980). This evidence adds up to support for the central claim of the RAS model if not for every implication of this claim.

CONCLUSIONS

Nature of public opinion

This chapter and the last have covered a great deal of ground, but nearly all of the theoretical work has been done by two ideas: the Ambivalence Deduction,

---

9 More aware persons are, as we have seen, more consistent in the considerations they form than are less aware ones. If, as this suggests, their reasons and feelings are more consistent than those of less aware persons, this would be another reason why a reasons analysis would not prove disruptive to the attitude reports of more aware persons.

Wilson, Kraft, and Dunn (1989) have shown that a "reasons analysis" disrupts the attitude reports of less politically aware persons, as found here, but does not increase the reliability of attitude reports of more aware persons, as expected by my line of argument. However, their more aware respondents are persons scoring in the top half of a measure of political awareness; the beneficial results found in Table 5.2 involve persons scoring in the top 40 percent of an awareness scale. It would be useful to replicate both their results and mine on a sample of persons more uniformly high on political awareness.

which asserts that individuals feel differently toward different aspects of most issues; and the Response Axiom, which asserts that individuals base their survey responses on the considerations that are, for any reason, most immediately salient to them.

These two ideas were initially put to use explaining response instability. The argument was that if people don't normally have any fixed attitude on most issues but instead answer questions on the basis of the particular considerations most immediately salient to them, a certain amount of response instability over time is bound to occur. Several implications of this general argument were developed and tested, including, most importantly, the expectation that those who were most consistent in their considerations with respect to an issue (as measured by open-ended discussions of it) would be most stable in their responses to closed-ended questions about it.

It was further argued that, given a situation in which people are both internally conflicted and answering questions off the top of their heads, any factor that systematically affects the salience of ideas in people's minds should also affect their survey responses. Among the seemingly irrelevant features of the interview situation that have this effect are question order, race of interviewer, the invocation of a relevant reference group, recent viewing of a relevant news story, and question framing.

The argument concludes with close examinations of priming effects and the effects of extra thought on response reliability. The former occur because any of several factors – elite discourse, recent news stories, or question frames – can change the types of considerations that people use in responding to an issue, thereby also changing the predispositional correlates of responses. The latter were expected to occur because responses based on an average of multiple considerations should be a more reliable indicator of the population of underlying considerations.

Of the two ideas that have done the work of these chapters, the Ambivalence Deduction – including its corollary, that individuals don't normally have a single, fixed attitude on issues – is probably the more unfamiliar and hence potentially controversial. It both contradicts the dominant theories of mass political attitudes, those of Converse and Achen, and violates commonsense notions of public opinion, which implicitly assume that members of the public have real attitudes on most issues. I therefore close this chapter with an argument that may, in light of the empirical evidence just presented, help to make this idea seem less surprising and more intuitively plausible.

Both in survey questions about issues and in elite debate of these issues, policy questions tend to be framed in terms of *summary judgments* – whether abortion should be permitted or not, whether schoolchildren should be bused to promote racial integration or not – so that the making of these judgments requires an aggregation of one's feelings across frequently diverse concerns. There is absolutely no reason to suppose that a person must feel consistently about each of the elements that he aggregates across when making summary judgments.

Someone who supports a woman's right to control her reproductive schedule need not also feel comfortable with killing fetuses; a person who desires racial integration need not also believe that busing children between communities is an attractive means to achieve it. A person may react angrily to a news report of welfare fraud and then, a few weeks later, become equally distressed over other news reports of impoverished children and homeless families.

Thus, people may have one reaction to an issue that would cause them to favor it and another that would cause them to oppose it, but – and here is the heart of the argument – for most people, most of the time, there is no need to reconcile or even to recognize their contradictory reactions to events and issues. Each can represent a genuine feeling, capable of coexisting with opposing feelings and, depending on momentary salience in the person's mind, controlling responses to survey questions.

Analysts of public opinion have long been aware that few citizens are "ideologically consistent" in their responses to different issues (Converse, 1964). The argument here is that many citizens are, in effect, equally inconsistent in their reactions to different aspects of the same issue.

Although all this may seem innocuous enough, its implications are not. The most important is, as I have stressed, that individuals do not typically possess "true attitudes" on issues, as conventional theorizing assumes, but a series of partially independent and often inconsistent ones. Which of a person's attitudes is expressed at different times depends on which has been made most immediately salient by chance and the details of questionnaire construction, especially the order and framing of questions.

The notion that citizens have "just one" attitude on typical issues is made to look foolish every time multiple polling agencies become involved in trying to measure opinion on some issue. What they find is not evidence of the public's "true attitude," but of its many different attitudes. In the buildup to the Persian Gulf War, for example, support for a war against Iraq fluctuated greatly – not over time, but across the different questions used by different polling organizations trying to measure the same attitude. Thus, two journalists, attempting to characterize mass opinion three weeks before the fighting began, observed that "[d]epending on how questions are framed, support for a hard line can be depressed to the 40 percent to 50 percent range or increased to 70 percent to 80 percent" (*Washington Post*, December 23, 1990, p. C1).

To take a person's response to any one question as evidence of a theoretical true attitude seems a grievous simplification. What is needed is conceptual machinery to enable the analyst to recognize the diversity of feelings that people frequently harbor, and the limited information that can be revealed by responses to any one formulation of an issue at one point in time. Such machinery is what the RAS model attempts to supply.

I should repeat here a point made earlier but that might by now have been forgotten: Nothing in my argument suggests that every member of the public is ambivalent on every issue, or that everyone is ambivalent to the same degree.

On the contrary, some people feel no ambivalence at all on some issues, so that, for them, every consideration that comes to mind impels them in the same direction. Such unusual nonambivalence can be readily explained by the model provided that, as will often be the case, it is accompanied by high levels of attention to the issue.

Public opinion and democracy

When the University of Michigan's 1956–58–60 NES Panel Study turned up huge amounts of response instability in political attitudes, Converse explained it with his famous "nonattitudes" thesis: Large segments of the electorate, he said, often simply had no attitudes to report.

The implications of this argument are rather bleak. If Converse's nonattitudes thesis is correct, Achen wrote, "Democratic theory loses its starting point" (1975: p. 1227). In contrast, the implication of Achen's empirical investigation was more optimistic: Most members of the public have "true attitudes" that are almost perfectly stable. The disturbingly high levels of response change noted by Converse are due only to the vague questions of survey researchers rather than the vague minds of citizen respondents.

My position falls somewhere between the Converse and Achen positions. It agrees with Converse that there is a great deal of uncertainty, tentativeness, and incomprehension in the typical mass survey response. The problem, it further contends, is much deeper than vague questions. And yet, with Achen, it rejects the premise of Converse's black-and-white nonattitudes model, which is that most response fluctuation is due to essentially random guessing by people who have no meaningful opinions.

My claim is that even when people are temporally unstable, expressing completely opposing positions at different times, they may still, like the vacillating teacher profiled in Chapter 4, be expressing real feelings, in the sense that they are responding to the issue as they see it at the moment of response. Although perceptions of the issue may change over time, the responses they generate are not, for that reason, lacking in authenticity.

Purely random guessing, on the basis of no feelings about the issue whatsoever, would vitiate the political significance of the responses given, in the sense that it would relieve political leaders of any reason to pay attention to them. But purely random fluctuation between opposing positions, each of which is sincerely held, would have significance, in that it would accurately indicate the balance of the person's true feelings – and, when aggregated in a large national survey, the balance of the public's true feelings.

Yet, given the logic of my argument, I must take care not to carry any argument about true feelings too far. The thrust of my argument has been to deny the existence of any such true position, either at the level of individuals or at the level of the public as a whole.

The reason for the denial should by now be clear: What gets measured as public opinion is always and unavoidably dependent on the way questions have been framed and ordered. If different frames or different question orders produce different results, it is not because one or the other has distorted the public's true feelings; it is, rather, because the public, having no fixed true opinion, implicitly relies on the particular question it has been asked to determine what exactly the issue is and what considerations are relevant to settling it.

None of this is to deny that the public has hopes, fears, values, and concerns that are, to a large extent, independent of elite discourse (though see Chapters 6–10). The claim, rather, is that the public's feelings are, in their unobserved state, unfocused and frequently contradictory. Which of these feelings becomes activated for expression as public opinion depends on a complex process in which pollsters, among others, are key players.

If accepted, this view of the nature of political attitude statements makes the measurement of public opinion in a poll (or any other way) difficult to defend as a completely neutral act. Also, if there was ever any doubt, it renders pollsters a part of the political elite. Thus, as Kinder and Sanders (1990) note in discussing the effects of different ways of framing the issue of affirmative action, "those of us who design surveys find ourselves in roughly the same position as do those who hold and wield real power: public officials, editors and journalists, newsmakers of all sorts. Both choose how public issues are to be framed, and in both instances, the choices seem to be consequential" (p. 99).

In my experience, most pollsters, at least academic ones, do not relish being in the political spotlight in this way. Like Walter Cronkite, who used to conclude his newscasts with the solemn assurance "That's the way it is," pollsters like to think of themselves as unobtrusively measuring "what the public really believes." What this ideal comes down to in practice is asking the public to choose between the major opposing positions in the ongoing elite debate on an issue.

The effect of pollsters' desire to be unobtrusive, then, is to pass the buck for framing the expression of public opinion back to the larger political community – to the politicians, issue activists, interest group leaders, journalists, and media consultants, many of whom clearly do relish the opportunity to actively shape the expression of public opinion. It is their public discourse, always conducted with one ear cocked to hear how the public is responding, that creates the specific "issues" on which "public opinion" is then collected and published.

I am obviously not the first to observe that elites regularly attempt to frame issues in a manner helpful to their causes (see Edelman, 1964; Bennett, 1980; Gamson and Modigliani, 1987). But I have provided a novel microexplanation for why framing and other manipulations of symbols often make the difference that they often do.

Framing and symbol manipulation by elites are sometimes discussed in conspiratorial tones, as if, in a healthy democratic polity, they would not occur. But from my perspective they are, whether healthy or not, unavoidable. For, given a public that has no fixed attitude toward what it wants done, but simply a range of only partially consistent considerations, someone has got to play the role of crystallizing issues in a way that can lead to action.

Consider, in this connection, Douglas Arnold's recent book, *The Logic of Congressional Action* (1990). Arnold shows that Congress often takes blatantly contradictory actions. It favors a balanced budget when this is the issue, and favors increased spending when asked to vote on particular spending provisions. Likewise, it favors "tax incentives" when asked to vote on them one item at a time, and also tax simplification when asked to vote on tax reform. The key to these and numerous other inconsistencies in Congress's record, according to Arnold, is how issue entrepreneurs frame the given issue, thereby linking it to one rather than another potential distribution of public opinion. Success in congressional politics turns on the ability to get one's colleagues and other elites, especially in the press, to think about one's issue in a way that will produce majority support for it rather than, as might be the case under a different issue frame, majority opposition.

A similar argument might be made for leadership in general. Political leaders are seldom the passive instruments of majority opinion. Nor, as it seems to me, do they often attempt openly to challenge public opinion. But they do regularly attempt to play on the contradictory ideas that are always present in people's minds, elevating the salience of some and harnessing them to new initiatives while downplaying or ignoring other ideas – all of which is just another way of talking about issue framing.

I suggest, then, that my account of an ambivalent public is not only more faithful to the wealth of microevidence examined earlier in this chapter, but also more faithful to the complex role of public opinion in democratic politics.

All of the analysis in this and the last chapter involves the form and nature of attitudes rather than the content of people's opinion statements and the process by which they are formed. The next five chapters are concerned with drawing out the implications of the model in these latter areas.

6

The mainstream and polarization effects

With the national inflation rate approaching the then-startling level of 7 percent, President Nixon went on television in late summer 1971 to announce a surprise decision to impose wage and price controls on the economy. Although such controls were a major departure from administration policy, the decision was immediately hailed by commentators across the political spectrum as a necessary step in the battle against inflation.

By good luck, there exist excellent data on the effect of Nixon's speech on public attitudes. A Columbia University survey of political activists happened to be in the field at the time of Nixon's announcement, and Gallup surveys on price controls bracketed the speech. The Columbia study found, first of all, that the speech had little effect on Democratic activists, who tended to favor wage and price controls even before Nixon spoke. But the effect of the speech on Republican activists was dramatic. Virtually overnight, support for controls among Republican activists shot up from 37 percent to 82 percent, a rise of some 45 percentage points (Barton, 1974–5). The Gallup surveys, meanwhile, showed that the public as a whole became about 10 percentage points more favorable toward price controls in the weeks following the Nixon speech.

This case suggests that a popular president backed by a unified Washington community can have a powerful effect on public opinion, especially that part of the public that is most attentive to politics.

This is the first of a series of chapters that aims at accounting for the effects of such elite communications on mass attitudes. In this chapter we examine two simple ideal typical situations, one type in which elites achieve a consensus or near consensus on a value or policy, so that virtually all communications take the same side of the given issue, and another type in which elites disagree along partisan or ideological lines, so that there is a roughly even flow of communications on both sides of the issue. The case of wage and price controls is an example of the first type of situation, and the nearly unified support of American elites for the war in Vietnam in 1964 is another. The sharply ideological division of elites over Vietnam in the late 1960s is an example of the second. The RAS model, as we shall see, leads us to expect that these two types of situations will have regular and predictable effects on public attitudes.

Later chapters will examine more complicated cases, ones in which the pattern of elite messages switches from mainly consensual to mainly conflictual, and others in which elites are divided, but in which the relative intensity of communications changes over time. Such changes in the flow of elite communications produce quite interesting and nonintuitive patterns of change in mass attitude reports, as will become apparent.

MAINSTREAM EFFECT

What, we may now ask, would be the theoretically expected effect on public opinion if elites across the political spectrum were to achieve a consensus in support of a particular "mainstream" policy? Or, to ask the same question in the language of the model: What would be the expected effect on public opinion if virtually all the persuasive messages carried in political media on a particular policy were favorable to that policy, and if there were no cueing messages to alert people that the policy was inconsistent with their values?

Axiom A1 suggests, first of all, that the greater a citizen's level of political awareness, the greater the likelihood of reception of persuasive messages on this hypothetical mainstream issue. If all of the cueing messages on this policy were favorable, no one would have any basis via A2 for resisting it. From this we can deduce that the greater a person's level of political awareness, the greater the number of mainstream messages the person would internalize in the form of considerations and hence, all else equal, the greater the person's level of expressed support for the mainstream policy (*D25*).

Researchers working on a variety of substantive problems have reported support for this implication of the model. In fact, though using different vocabularies, several have made roughly the same argument as here. For example, in *Public Opinion and American Democracy* (1961), V. O. Key, Jr., wrote that a person's level of formal education may be an indicator of the extent to which the person has been influenced by society's traditional or "official" values. Key wrote:

Probably a major consequence of education for opinion consists in the bearing of education on the kinds of influences to which a person is subjected throughout his life. The more extended the educational experience, the more probable it is that a person will be exposed to the discussions of issues as they arise. When, as so often occurs, the current discussion is heavily loaded on one side, it might be expected that this educationally conditioned exposure would have some bearing on the direction of opinion. (1961: p. 341)

Noting that education was associated with greater support for racial equality, private health insurance, and tolerance of nonconformists, Key explained that "formal education may serve to indoctrinate people into the more-or-less official political values of the culture" (p. 340).

Writing a few years later, Gamson and Modigliani (1966) noted a substantial correlation between political information and support for the government's foreign policies (see also Sigelman and Conover, 1981). Their explanation for this paralleled Key's argument. Information measured "one's attachment to the mainstream and the resultant exposure to influences such as the mass media" (1966: p. 189). McClosky and Brill's (1983) argument that education promotes the "social learning" of libertarian ideals, and Mueller's (1973) claim that better educated persons were more likely to support the Vietnam War because they were better "followers" of official policy likewise appeal to the notion that exposure to "mainstream" values tends to enhance support for them. More recently, the tendency of better educated persons to be more opposed to the quarantining of AIDS victims (Sniderman et al., 1991) appears to reflect the internalization of a medical consensus that such action is unnecessary to prevent the spread of the disease (Colby and Cook, 1991).[1]

In a comparative study of the United States and Britain, Cain, Ferejohn, and Fiorina (1987) turned up a finding that nicely illustrates the "indoctrinating effect" that exposure to a particular elite culture often produces. Citizens in both countries were asked whether elected representatives should "support the position their parties take when something comes up for a vote, or should they make up their own minds regardless of how their parties want them to vote." In Britain, where Parliament depends on a high degree of party discipline, college-educated persons were more likely than those with only high school education to say that representatives should hew the party line. But in the United States, with its antiparty and individualist political tradition, college-educated persons were more likely to say that representatives should vote their own opinions. Thus, the better educated in each country are the more faithful adherents of their country's respective national traditions.

If the mainstream argument is correct, correlations between awareness and support for a policy should be strongest when elite consensus is strongest and less strong when elite consensus is less strong or nonexistent (*D25*). Much published evidence (to be supplemented later in this chapter) supports this expectation. For example, Mueller notes that the correlation between education and support for the Vietnam War was strong early in the war, when most elites supported it, and weak in the late phases of the war, when party and ideological elites became deeply divided. In a systematic test of this hypothesis in the domain of civil liberties, McClosky and Brill (1983: p. 421) classified more than 100 civil liberties items according to the degree of support for the libertarian option in relevant Supreme Court decisions and in the attitudes of some 2,000 elites they had surveyed. They found that for items on which the Court and other elites had strongly endorsed the civil liberties position, members of the general public who had attended college were, on average, 24 percentage points more libertarian than were those with less than a high school education. Yet education had a progressively weaker effect in inducing support for libertarian policies as elite support for them declined, until finally, education had a slightly negative

---

1 This is my interpretation of the education effect reported by Sniderman, Brody, and Tetlock (1991, chap. 4). For a further discussion of this point, see Chapter 12.

association with support for civil liberties on those (few) items on which the pre-Rehnquist Court and most elites took an antilibertarian position (for example, civil disobedience).[2]

It is widely supposed that political awareness – whether measured by knowledge, participation, or education – engenders resistance to elite influence rather than, as assumed in the mainstream model, susceptibility to it. As will become clear in Chapters 7–11, this supposition has some validity. Political awareness does appear to engender resistance to the political communications of governing authorities. But awareness does so less by engendering resistance per se than by increasing the person's sensitivity to the communications of countervailing elites, especially the ideological opponents of the regime. Thus, for example, it will turn out in Chapter 9 that a major source of opposition to the Vietnam War was the exposure of politically aware citizens to antiwar communications that were too faint to be picked up by the less aware. The notion that politically aware persons resist all forms of political persuasion is highly dubious.

One other comment. There are in every society ideas on which virtually everyone agrees. In such cases, the idea is unlikely to become the object of studies of public opinion, except perhaps in studies of culture. Such "motherhood issues" in the United States might include maintenance of free elections, tax-supported public schools, and state-organized attempts to repulse an invading enemy. The mainstream model is less useful for policies of this type than for policies on which there is popular reluctance to go along with an elite consensus, such as tolerance of disliked groups, or support for war when the nation is not immediately threatened.

THE POLARIZATION EFFECT

There are, of course, many cases in which political elites heatedly disagree, so that no "mainstream" exists. In cases of this type, the RAS model leads us to expect quite different patterns of mass attitudes.

To see why, let us assume a situation in which elites are roughly evenly divided on a partisan issue, with one partisan camp sponsoring persuasive messages favoring the liberal position and the other sponsoring messages in support of the conservative position. We further assume that each camp sponsors cueing messages indicating why the given policy is or is not consistent with liberal (or conservative) values. Finally, let us assume that all of these messages are equally intense in that a person at a given level of political awareness would be equally likely to encounter and take in any one of them.

Within the general public, increases in awareness will lead to increased reception of persuasive messages favoring both the liberal position and the conservative position (from A1) and also increased reception of cueing messages concerning the issue. Let us focus first on how this affects liberals. Since politically aware liberals will be likely to possess cueing messages that enable them

2 See also Chong, McClosky, and Zaller, 1984.

to see the ideological implications of the messages they receive, they will be likely to reject conservative arguments on this issue; these cueing messages will not, however, impede their internalization of liberal messages. Less politically aware liberals, by contrast, will be exposed to few persuasive messages, and, owing to their low reception of cueing messages and the lower accessibility of these cues in memory, will be less selective about the persuasive messages they internalize.

In consequence of this dynamic, the most aware liberals will fill their heads, so to speak, with a large number of considerations that are, on balance, favorable to the liberal side of the issue. Less aware liberals, for their part, will fill their heads with a smaller number of considerations, and these considerations will not consistently favor the liberal side of the issue.

The same argument, *mutatis mutandis,* applies to conservatives. Highly aware conservatives should fill their heads with mostly conservative considerations, while less aware conservatives should fill their heads with a smaller number of considerations that are less consistently conservative.

Our expectation, then, is that for cases in which there is a roughly even flow of opposing partisan messages, the ratio of ideologically consistent considerations to ideologically inconsistent ones should increase as political awareness increases.

Figure 4.1 has already confirmed this expectation. As shown there, the ratio of consistent considerations to total considerations increases from about .5 among the least informed persons to about .80 among the most informed. Two of the slopes in Figure 4.1 are statistically significant at the .01 level and the third is significant at the .10 level.[3]

One may expect that an increasing ratio of ideologically consistent to inconsistent considerations should translate into differences in people's attitude statements: More aware liberals will be more likely to call to mind considerations favorable to the liberal position and hence will be more likely to support it. Less aware liberals will be less likely to be able to recall considerations of any kind, which will lead to higher no-opinion rates, and less likely to endorse the liberal position when they do offer an opinion.[4]

The logic of this argument again applies equally to conservatives. That is, increases in awareness make mass conservatives increasingly likely to make conservative attitude statements when asked about the issue.

Thus, in the case of an evenly divided partisan elite and a balanced flow of partisan communications, the effect of political awareness is to promote the

3 The relationships depicted in Figure 4.1, however, apply to the sample as a whole; closer inspection of the data reveals that the expected relationships hold only for liberals, where they hold very strongly. For conservatives, there appears to be little change in the ratio of consistent-to-inconsistent considerations as awareness increases. The reason for this complication appears to be that the assumed conditions for the test have not been met, namely, a roughly even division of elite support for the opposing policy alternatives. For none of the three options is the division of mass opinion close to 50–50, as it ought to be in the case of an equal elite division. See Chapter 8 for further tests of the effect of awareness and ideology on the internalization of considerations.
4 See Krosnick and Milburn, 1990, for a review of the evidence on the effects of political awareness on no-opinion rates.

polarization of attitude reports as more aware liberals gravitate more reliably to the liberal position and more aware conservatives gravitate more reliably to the conservative position (*D26*).

Empirical support for the polarization effect

Much empirical evidence supports the expectation of an awareness-induced polarization of liberals and conservatives on partisan issues. The polarizing effect of political awareness on partisan (as against mainstream) issues was first noted by George Belknap and Angus Campbell (1951–2) and was incorporated into the Michigan school's classic, *The American Voter* (Campbell et al., 1960: pp. 186, 207). Using different theoretical vocabularies, Gamson and Modigliani (1966) and Chong, McClosky, and Zaller (1984) have noted the same effect. They examine public attitudes toward numerous issues on which elites disagree, issues ranging from foreign policy to civil liberties to welfare to race to economic policy. In each case, increases in political awareness were associated with a sharper polarization of attitudes between liberals (or Democrats), on one side, and conservatives (or Republicans), on the other.[5]

The data in Figure 6.1 illustrate both the mainstream and polarization effects of political awareness. When, in 1964, American elites nearly all supported the Vietnam War, increases in awareness led nonelite liberals and conservatives to become more supportive of the "mainstream" war policy. Yet when, in 1970, American elites had become deeply divided about the war, increases in awareness are associated with greater polarization of the attitudes of mass liberals and conservatives.[6]

The Persian Gulf War affords another opportunity to observe both the mainstream and the polarization effect. From the Iraqi invasion of Kuwait in August 1990 through the fall 1990 congressional election, there was only light criticism of President Bush's handling of the crisis and, in particular, virtually no articulate opposition to the policy of sending U.S. forces to the region. Thus, as J. W. Apple wrote on the eve of the election,

[A] midterm election campaign has taken place with war threatening in the Persian Gulf, and . . . the major foreign policy issue confronting the nation has generated almost no debate among the candidates about what the U.S. should do.
    Instead, President Bush has traded insults with Saddam Hussein of Iraq, and the Democrats have barely mentioned the subject. (*New York Times,* 6 November 1991, p. A1)

5 In Gamson and Modigliani, these findings are the basis for a "cognitive consistency" model of opinion formation; in McClosky et al., they are the basis for a "contested norms" model of opinionation. Yet in both cases, the empirical regularity being explained, as well as the operational constructs in the models, are the same as in the Belknap and Campbell polarization model.

6 To validate these claims concerning elite consensus and division, I asked a research assistant to classify cover stories on Vietnam in *Newsweek* and *Time*. In 1964 prowar cover stories outnumbered antiwar ones by a margin of approximately 3 to 1; in 1970, the ratio was close 1 to 1. (See also Hallin, 1986.)

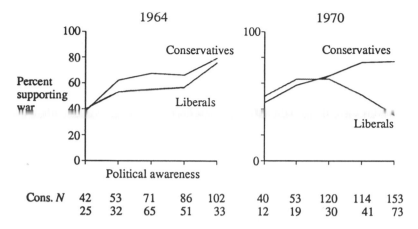

Cons. N   42   53   71   86 102   40   53 120 114 153
          25   32   65   51   33   12   19   30   41   73

Figure 6.1. An illustration of the mainstream and polarization models. Liberals are defined as persons who rated liberals fifteen or more points higher than conservatives on separate 100-point feeling thermometers; conservatives are persons who exhibited the reverse pattern. Persons supporting the war are those who said either that the United States should "keep troops in Vietnam but try to end the fighting," which was the position of both the Johnson and Nixon administrations, or that the U.S. should take a stronger stand on the war. The awareness measure is described in the Measures Appendix. *Source:* 1964 and 1970 CPS surveys.

Two days after the election, however, Bush announced a decision to send several hundred thousand additional troops to the gulf. This decision sparked strong congressional criticism, leading to congressional hearings in which administration policy was harshly criticized and later to a congressional vote on a war policy resolution. As in the Vietnam case, Democrats were the most salient critics of the administration's hawkish policies and Republicans were the most salient defenders.

In view of this, we should expect, in the period before Congress reacted critically to Bush's troop announcement, to find evidence of the mainstream effect; after criticism began, we should expect to observe the polarization pattern.

By good luck, the 1990 National Election Study went into the field on the day after the election and was able to complete more than 250 interviews before congressional criticism of Bush's military buildup began. It also carried a question asking whether "we did the right thing in sending U.S. military forces to the Persian Gulf, or should we have stayed out?"

Results, which are derived from a maximum likelihood logistic regression that controls for political awareness, party attachment, gender, race, and Jewish ethnicity are shown in Figure 6.2.[7] (The coefficients on which the figure is based are in Table 6.3 of the appendix to this chapter.) As expected, the data

7 Democrats and Republicans in the figure are constructed as persons with a score of ±1.3 on the party variable, where party ranges from −2 (strong Republican) to +2 (strong Democrat). Awareness scores in the figure run from −1.8 SD to +2.57 SD.

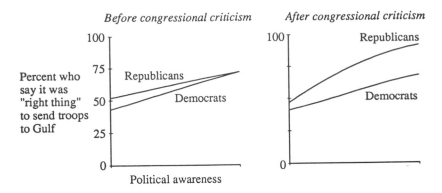

Figure 6.2. Partisans become more polarized over time on "right to send troops." Estimates are derived from coefficients in Table 6.3. *Source:* 1990 NES survey.

betray little evidence of partisan polarization in the period prior to the congressional criticism of Bush's policies, but clear polarization afterward. Public division does not appear to be as sharp as in the Vietnam case, but this is probably because elite polarization on Persian Gulf policy did not approach that of the Vietnam period in terms of either duration or intensity.

Before continuing the analysis of opinion on Persian Gulf policy, I must discuss a methodological issue. In creating Figure 6.2 from the coefficients in a logistic regression model, I had to make certain coding decisions. For example, to show the effects of political awareness, I manipulated scores from roughly the 1st percentile on political awareness to the 98th percentile. Since I need to make many similar decisions about how to create graphs from coefficients in the next several chapters, I want to standardize my procedures in an intelligible set of conventions. A summary of these conventions, which will be used for the rest of the book, is given in the accompanying box.

The 1990 NES survey carried one other question which is useful for gauging public opinion on the gulf crisis. It reads:

Which of the following do you think we should do now in the Persian Gulf:

Pull out U.S. forces entirely.

Try harder to find a diplomatic solution.

Tighten the economic embargo.

Take tougher military action.

All but the first of these options imply support for the basic United States policy of military involvement in the Persian Gulf. Since, with the possible exception of the congressional Black Caucus, virtually all of Bush's elite critics accepted this policy, we should expect to find that, among the public, political

Conventions of graphical analysis

For graphs showing the relationship between political awareness, political pre-dispositions, and a political attitude or attitude change, the following conventions will apply in the remainder of the book:

Basic design. In all cases, political awareness will be treated as the principal independent variable and plotted against the x axis. The dependent variable, usually the probability of a political attitude or attitude change, the will be plotted against the y-axis, as in Figure 6.2. The effect of differences in political dispositions (such as, being a Democrat rather than a Republican) will be shown by separate lines within the graphs, as in Figure 6.2.

Range of political awareness. Except as noted, graphs depict the simulated effect of moving from about the 1st percentile to about the 98th percentile on political awareness. This range leaves about 1 percent of the cases outside each endpoint, though, of course, lumpiness in the data makes it impossible to achieve this range in every case. Because different awareness scales have different skews, the range of political awareness scores will not always correspond to a particular z-score range, such as ±2 SD. The particular z-score ranges used in the simulations will be provided in footnotes.

Range of simulated attitude scores. With one clearly noted exception, graphs showing probabilities or proportions will use a scale of 0 to 1.0. When means are used, graphs will reflect the range of mean values in the data. Thus, in the case of means, the ranges can vary from figure to figure. However, unless explicitly noted, identical scales will be used in figures that are being compared to one another.

Range of predispositional variables. Throughout the analysis, party attachment is coded from −2 (strong Republican) to −1 (weak or independent Republican) to +1 (weak or independent Democrat) to +2 strong Democrat, with all others assigned to the score of zero. In graphs that depict the effect of being a Republican or Democrat, partisans are simulated by scores of either −1.3 or +1.3, as appropriate. The effects of other predispositional measures (such as equalitarianism, hawkishness) are simulated differently in different cases, depending on how many measures are available for use in a given model. For example, if only one measure is used in a model, the range may be ±2 SD for that variable; if three measures are used, their joint effect – that is, the effect of identical movements on all three variables – will be depicted over a smaller range. The exact values are provided in each case. The aim will be to approximate the raw data, insofar as the raw data can be directly observed.

awareness is associated with greater support for keeping U.S. forces in the Gulf – which is to say, greater levels of rejection of the "pullout" option in favor of one of the other three response alternatives. This expectation is confirmed in Figure 6.3 (see Table 6.3, the chapter appendix, for coefficients). Even within the group most resistant to using military action against Iraq – black Democratic women – rejection of the pullout option rises from about 54 percent in the lowest awareness category to about 92 percent in the highest

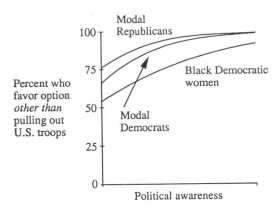

Figure 6.3. Support for keeping U.S. troops in the Persian Gulf. Estimates are derived from coefficients in Table 6.3. *Source:* 1990 NES survey.

category.[8] The trends in Figure 6.3 were about the same throughout the period of the survey.[9]

It is difficult to be certain what to expect from the three response options – more diplomacy, a tighter embargo, and tougher military action – that I have counted as implying support for military involvement in the Gulf. Certainly, Democrats en masse would be expected to reject the choice of "tougher military action," since the Democratic party in Congress was clearly identified with opposition to this idea. The problem is that it is not clear that Republicans should be expected to embrace it. For Bush's public position, especially in the early months of the crisis, was that an embargo, in combination with skilled diplomacy, would make it possible to avoid the use of force. In mid-December, however, the Bush administration rejected a proposed January 12th meeting in Baghdad on the grounds that it was too near the United Nations deadline for Iraqi withdrawal from Kuwait to be useful for averting military action. By that point, therefore, it was clear at least that *willingness* to use force was a key feature of Bush policy. One might therefore expect that at about that time opposing partisan groups in the public became increasingly polarized over the question of military force.

Figure 6.4 appears to support this expectation. Highly aware Democrats and Republicans were apparently more polarized over the use of force after December 15 than they had been before. Despite this, however, the increase in po-

8 In separate regressions for blacks and whites, political awareness is associated with rejection of the pull-out option at least as strongly among blacks as among whites. (In a simple linear regression of this question [scored 0–1] on political awareness, the intercept and slope for blacks are .55 and .047, respectively; for whites, the intercept and slope are .78 and .022, with all terms highly statistically significant; the range of political awareness is 0 through 13.) See Chapter 9 for additional discussion of the effects of elite opinion leadership on Afro-Americans.
9 Insofar as there was a time trend, it was toward less party polarization, but the trend did not approach either statistical or substantive significance.

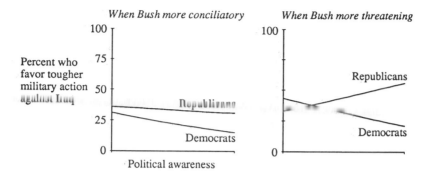

Figure 6.4. Partisans become more polarized over time on use of military force. Estimates are derived from coefficients in Table 6.3. *Source:* 1990 NES survey.

larization does not achieve statistical significance and must therefore be taken as equivocal support for my expectation (coefficients shown in Table 6.3).

The key point here is that exposure to public affairs, as measured by tests of political awareness, has important effects on mass attitudes, but that these effects differ across policies and across time, depending on the positions taken by political elites and reflected in the mass media. Awareness is associated with support for those aspects of government policy that have the consensual support of political and media elites, but is associated with higher levels of polarization over policies on which elites are divided.[10]

To demonstrate this point more rigorously, I selected items from the 1972–74–76 NES survey that seemed on their face to exemplify mainstream policies and partisan policies of the early 1970s.[11] Table 6.1 contains a list of these items. Selection of the items was based on my judgment of the positions of liberal and conservative elites, political party elites, and the mass media at the time of the NES study. To confirm these judgments, I asked a research assistant to read the platforms of the Democratic and Republican parties in 1972, and to rate each party on each issue. The research assistant was unaware of my expectations and did the ratings on the basis of instructions that were conveyed in writing.[12] I expected that both parties would explicitly endorse the policies I had identified as mainstream policies, and would take sharply opposing positions on policies I had identified as partisan policies. These expectations were largely

10 In showing that the public became more polarized in its attitudes toward Vietnam and Persian Gulf policy, I have been, in effect, examining mass opinion change. The actual patterns of change occurring in these cases are, however, considerably more complicated than I have been able to demonstrate in this initial treatment. For further examination of opinion change on Vietnam, see Chapter 9; for a treatment of opinion change on Gulf war policy along the lines sketched in Chapter 7, see Zaller (1992).

11 I used the panel data because this test was part of a study to test the comparative ability of political knowledge, education, political interest, media exposure, and political participation to specify relationships that a good measure of political awareness should specify. It turned out that political knowledge outperformed all of the alternative measures (see Zaller, 1990).

12 The written instructions are available from the author upon request.

Table 6.1. *Question stems for opinions on mainstream and partisan issues*

Mainstream issues

This country would be better off if we just stayed home and did not concern ourselves with problems in other parts of the world.

Do you think that mainland China should be a member of the United Nations, or do you think it should not?

Should farmers and businessmen be allowed to do business with Communist countries or should they be forbidden to do business with Communist countries?

Should the government support the right of black people to go to any hotel or restaurant they can afford, or should it stay out of this matter?

Recently there has been a lot of talk about women's rights. Some people feel that women should have an equal role with men in running business, industry, and government. Others feel that women's place is in the home.

Partisan issues

There is much discussion of the best way to deal with racial problems. Some people think achieving racial integration of schools is so important that it justifies busing children to schools out of their neighborhoods. Others think letting children go to their neighborhood schools is so important that they oppose busing.

Some people feel the government in Washington should see to it that every person has a job and a good standard of living. Others think the government should just let each person get ahead on their own.

Do you think we did the right thing in getting into the fighting in Vietnam or should we have stayed out?

Source: 1972 NES survey.

confirmed. The one exception involved an item about whether the federal government should guarantee blacks the right to equal treatment in hotels and restaurants. A provision on equal accommodations was a key part of 1964 Civil Rights Act, which, Senator Barry Goldwater notwithstanding, passed the Congress with majority support from both the Democratic and Republican parties. The Democratic platform, as I had expected, explicitly endorsed this policy, but the Republican Party, although professing general support for equal rights, made no direct reference to it. I continue, in light of the bipartisan history of the Civil Rights Act and the fact that even Southern opposition to it had collapsed by 1972, to consider equal accommodations in hotels and restaurants a mainstream government policy.[13]

13 In addition to the items in Table 6.1, I asked my research assistant to rate an item on whether the government should act against inflation. There was strong endorsement of this principle by both parties, but a ceiling effect on mass support for the policy prevented a test on the effect of political awareness on support for this idea.

The model used to estimate the effect of awareness on each of these policy items was as follows:

Prob(Lib. Response) = Prob(Opinionation) × Prob(Lib. | Opinionation)

That is, the probability of a liberal response is the probability of offering any opinion at all, times the probability of making a liberal response, given that an opinion has been offered. The two parts of the model have been estimated separately.

The probability of a liberal opinion, given that an opinion statement has been made, has been modeled as a logit function of awareness, ideological self-designation,[14] party identification, and standard demographic variables (race, age, income, and residence in a Southern state). In addition to these variables, the initial specification of each equation contained an interaction term for Awareness × Ideology and Awareness × Party. This equation was estimated separately for each of the five mainstream and three partisan issues. To maximize comparability of results across different item formats, each item was coded to a three-point scale running from 0 to 0.5 to 1.0.[15]

The expectation from the model is that for partisan policies, the two Awareness × Values interaction terms will be strong, but that for mainstream policies these interactions will be anemic. The second expectation is that awareness will have an important positive impact on support for mainstream policies.

The first of these expectations is largely confirmed. The Ideology × Awareness term gets coefficients that are large for the three partisan issues and trivial for the five mainstream issues, exactly as expected. The Party × Awareness term behaves erratically, but its coefficients are either statistically insignificant or too small to have much impact, thus leaving the ideology interaction term to dominate the results. Let us look first at results for the three partisan issues.

The coefficients for the three partisan issues are shown in the left-hand side of Table 6.2, and a graphical analysis of these coefficients is shown in the top half

14 The question asked respondents to place themselves on a seven-point scale that ran from "extremely liberal" to "liberal" to "slightly liberal" to "moderate, middle of the road" to "extremely conservative." The question was asked in all three waves of the survey, and in the test reported below, responses over all three waves were averaged. People who gave no opinion in one year were assigned their average for the other two years; people who gave a response in only one year were assigned their response from that year. People who gave a no-opinion response all three times were assigned to the sample average. This way of including respondents with missing data would be expected to produce differences in item reliabilities across different respondents, but since this difference is constant across all dependent variables, and since the key hypothesis involves differences in the effect of ideology across different items, it would not be expected to produce biased results. Omitting respondents with any missing data would, on the other hand, undermine ability to detect the effect of awareness on support for mainstream policies, since the people omitted would be mainly less-informed persons.
15 When the original item was an agree/disagree item, "in between" responses were coded to .5 and other responses were coded zero or one. The jobs and women's rights items were originally seven-point scales; 4 was coded to .5 and the other points were coded to zero or one. Busing was also originally a seven-point scale, but it was so skewed in the antibusing direction that it was necessary to transform it; the far conservative position, which contained 68 percent of all respondents, was coded to zero, the next most conservative position was coded to .5, and the remaining five scale points were coded to one.

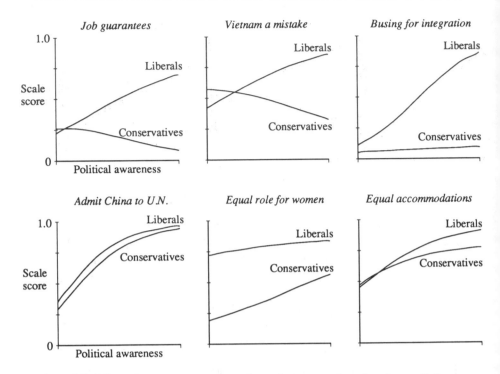

Figure 6.5. Effect of awareness on support for mainstream and partisan issues. Estimates are derived from coefficients in Table 6.2. "Liberals" in this figure have been constructed as persons who score +6 on a seven-point ideology variable and +1.3 on the party attachment scale; "conservatives" have been constructed from scores of +2 and −1.3 on these variables. Political awareness in this figure runs ±2 SD. See footnote 14 for additional information. Adapted from figure 2 of Zaller (1990). Original variables have been recoded to have roughly equal variance on a 0−.5−1 scale, with the liberal or mainstream pole coded high. See footnote 15 for additional information. *Source:* 1972 wave of NES panel survey.

of Figure 6.5. The results in the top half of Figure 6.5 are consistent with expectations: Increases in political awareness are associated with more polarized scale scores (see note 15) on all three issues.

The second expectation, concerning the effect of awareness on support for mainstream policies, was difficult to confirm because of the presence of severe multicollinearity. For all five of the mainstream policies – equal accommodations, women's equality, trade with communist nations, admission of China to the U.N., and antiisolationism – the estimated coefficient for awareness was correlated with the coefficient for Awareness × Ideology at the level of .96 or higher. Because of this, neither awareness, ideology, nor their interaction achieved statistical significance in some of the equations.

Table 6.2. Coefficient estimates for partisan and mainstream issues

	Partisan issues			Mainstream issues				
	Job guarantee	Vietnam war	School busing	Equal accom.	Women's rights	China in UN	Comm. trade	Anti-isolation
Direction of response function[a]								
Intercept	-1.99	-0.57	-3.52	0.62	-0.74	1.33	0.40	2.28
Awareness (standardized)	-0.84*	-0.71*	-0.71*	0.26*	0.50*	0.65*	0.73*	1.12*
Ideology (7-point scale)	0.37*	0.27*	0.60*	0.18*	0.33*	0.13	0.14	-0.11
Awareness × ideology	0.18*	0.19*	0.30*	b	-.07**	b	b	-0.07
Party (range +2 to -2))	0.01	-.07	0.07	-0.09**	0.31*	0.01	0.01	0.01
Awareness × party	0.06	0.01	-0.13**	0.13*	0.02	b	b	-0.06
Opinionation function								
Intercept	1.98	2.70	2.48	2.64	2.83	2.68	1.35	5.01
Awareness	0.89*	0.62*	0.80*	0.99*	0.51*	1.32*	0.73*	1.58*

[a] Coefficients are from logistic equation described in text. Estimation was by nonlinear least squares. Equations also included controls for race, age, South, and income; these coefficients are the same as those used, but not reported for reasons of space, in Zaller (1990).
b Term omitted after F-test showed that coefficient had no statistical effect on equation; nonsignificant terms were omitted only when they caused severe multicollinearity; see text for further discussion.
* Significant at .01 level.   ** Significant at .05 level.

Source: 1972–74–76 NES panel survey.

However, multicollinearity can greatly reduce the precision of estimates even when the true effect of one of the collinear variables is zero.[16] To test whether the Awareness × Value interaction terms had any real effect on the mainstream policies, I reestimated each equation without the interaction terms and did an F-test to see if the omissions had a significant effect on the residual sum of squares. For antiisolationism, women's rights, trade with communist nations, and admission of China to the United Nations, the F-test indicated that the interaction terms did not contribute significantly to the fit of the model. Moreover, with the interactions omitted, awareness took on a statistically significant positive coefficient in all four cases, as expected. In the fifth case, equal accommodations, the Party × Awareness coefficient remained significant, but with the nonsignificant Ideology × Awareness term omitted, awareness had the expected positive effect on support for this mainstream race policy.[17]

The right-hand side of Table 6.2 and the bottom half of Figure 6.5 present the results for the mainstream issues. Two mainstream issues – antiisolationism and trade with communist nations – are not shown in Figure 6.5 but closely resemble the pattern for the item on admission of China to the United Nations, which is shown in the figure.

Of the five mainstream issues, only the women's role item raises any doubts about the performance of the model. Though awareness does, as expected, have a positive effect on support for gender equality, the effect on liberals in this interactive model is modest. Moreover, the effect of ideology is quite large, especially if, as I maintain, elite messages consensually favored an equal role for women.

One explanation for these results is that, despite the endorsement of the two parties in 1972, women's rights was not really a mainstream issue at that time; if so, it is no problem for the model, which takes elite consensus as an initial condition. Other explanations, however, appear more plausible. The modest slope for liberals, first of all, is the result of a ceiling effect among liberals. It would be hard to get very much positive slope in view of the fact that support among low-awareness liberals starts out at 71 percent. With respect to the large effect of ideology, recall that 1972 was near the highwater mark for radical feminism, a viewpoint that had little mass support and may have had deleterious spillover effects on support for equal rights for women (Mansbridge, 1986). Recall also that the Republican Party, although endorsing equal rights for women in 1972, was shortly to withdraw its support for the Equal Rights Ammendment. All this makes the women's role issue a particularly tough test of the mainstream hypothesis. And yet the hypothesis is, in the end, upheld in the sense that there is an important positive effect for awareness.

Altogether, then, the mainstream results, along with those for the three partisan issues, support the two basic deductions of the model: In cases of elite

16 See Hanushek and Jackson, 1977: pp. 231–3; Rao and Miller, 1971: ch. 3.
17 It is not permissible to do a parallel test omitting the direct awareness term, since awareness must be in the equation if awareness × ideology is included.

consensus, political awareness leads to increased support for the mainstream policy, and in cases of elite division, political awareness leads to increased polarization among groups having opposed value orientations.[18]

ATTITUDE CONSTRAINT AND MASS BELIEF SYSTEMS

An extensive research literature has documented that people who are liberal (or conservative) on one issue tend to be relatively liberal (or conservative) on a range of other issues. This tendency is most commonly explained by means of the concept of "attitude constraint," which implies that one sort of attitude (ideological orientation) constrains other attitudes (policy preferences), thereby linking a range of attitudes into a cohesive "belief system." The classic statement of this argument is Philip Converse's famous paper, "The nature of belief systems in mass publics" (1964).[19]

As it happens, the logic of the polarization argument is isomorphic with the logic of Converse's account of attitude constraint in his 1964 paper. Thus in explaining mass attitude polarization on partisan issues, the RAS model has also explained attitude constraint.

This point is easily demonstrated. According to Converse, ideologies originate among a "minuscule" number of "creative elites" and subsequently diffuse through the public. Elites, thus, are the source of mass ideologies. Converse argues, however, that the diffusion of elite-created belief systems is highly imperfect. Only the politically aware pay enough attention to elite discourse to find out the ideological implications of different policies – in Converse's terms, to learn "what goes with what." As a result, attitude constraint of the conventional liberal–conservative type develops mainly among the more politically aware strata.

Compare this argument to the representation of the polarization model in the upper half of Figure 6.5: Highly aware liberals and conservatives (or Democrats and Republicans) look to appropriate partisan elites to find out "what goes with what." Having acquired this information, they are able to become consistently liberal or consistently conservative across a range of issues. The less aware, as shown in Figure 6.5, are less likely to acquire the attitude that is conventionally appropriate to their partisan orientation, and hence less likely to develop "attitude constraint" across issues. The well-established finding of belief systems studies – that average interitem correlations among issues are higher

---

18 Mainstream norms are determined not by what all elites actually believe, but by what the elites who have regular access to the public say in their public utterances. If, for example, there were many Southern elected officials who continued to oppose equal accommodations for blacks in 1972 but who had no access to the media to express this view, and if, on the other hand, supporters of equal accommodations had good access to the mass media to publicize their side of the issue, then equal accommodations would be classified as a mainstream norm. The elites who count as shapers of public opinion in this model are those who have or control access to the mass media.

19 For the most recent work and bibliographies of the vast literature in this area, see Wyckoff (1987) and Jacoby (1991).

among more aware citizens – is just a generalization of this pattern to a cluster of ideologically charged issues (see, for example, Stimson, 1975; Jacoby, 1991).[20] Thus the existence of attitude consistency across issues, and the well-documented tendency for consistency to become stronger with increases in awareness, can both be explained by the RAS model (*D27, D28*).[21]

This account of attitude consistency does not, so far as I can tell, differ in any important way from Converse's. It is simply a somewhat more fully specified statement of his general argument.

I shall have more to say about attitude constraint in Chapter 9, where I show how it develops and changes in situations in which the flow of communications is not, as I have assumed it to be in this chapter, either stable over time or evenly balanced between liberal and conservative messages.

ALTERNATIVE EXPLANATIONS

There are alternative explanations for the empirical regularities noted in this chapter, and it is instructive to review them, for they illustrate the fragmented state of the public opinion field of which I complained in the opening chapter. For example, Cantril (1944) found that persons scoring high on a measure of political knowledge were more likely to support American involvement in World War II, including numerous particular policies of the Roosevelt administration, such as the foundation of a United Nations organization upon the defeat of the Axis powers. Cantril's explanation for this pattern is that better informed Americans are likely to have a correct understanding of their true interests. Stouffer (1954) argues that better educated persons are more supportive of civil liberties because they are more likely to give a "sober second thought" to freedom issues; Allport (1954: p. 405) cites the greater personal security of better educated persons as a possible explanation for their greater racial liberalism; Bobo and Licari (1989) contend that education promotes political tolerance because it is associated with "more sophisticated modes of reasoning"[22]; and

20 Lane (1973) and Marcus, Tabb, and Sullivan (1974), among many others, criticize Converse's belief-systems argument on the grounds that it overlooks idiosyncratic ways in which individuals may structure their attitudes, and that it arbitrarily equates ideological consistency with sophistication. My account accepts the first point, claiming, in effect, that political awareness drives a socialization process that overrides idiosyncratic attitude structures. My account does not, however, equate consistency with sophistication except in the possibly perverse sense that an ideologically "consistent" individual has managed to absorb a particular set of conventions.

21 Even critics of Converse's position find evidence that constraint varies by political awareness (see Wyckoff, 1987). Wyckoff concludes with an excellent analysis of the conditions under which attitude constraint is most likely to appear.

22 In their study of *Political Tolerance and American Democracy*, Sullivan, Pierson, and Marcus (1981) maintain that better educated persons are *not* more tolerant, once dislike for the target group is controlled for. Two comments are in order here. The first is that the mainstream model would expect better educated people to be more tolerant only when a traditionally protected civil liberty is at stake – as in the case of freedom of political speech, which has been well protected by the Supreme Court in recent years. But the mainstream model would not predict education to be associated with support for civil liberties that have not achieved mainstream status, such as the right of members of a self-proclaimed terrorist group, like the Symbionese Liberation

Hamilton(1968) and Hahn (1970) suggest that higher levels of support for the Vietnam War among educated persons may be due, as Hamilton puts it, to "upper-middle class authoritarianism" (p. 446). Each of these arguments is perhaps plausible on its face, but none generalizes easily to other issues. The more parsimonious explanation of the RAS model would be that better educated and otherwise more politically aware persons have been in each case more heavily exposed to mainstream elite values. (Although the work necessary to establish the existence of mainstream norms in some of these cases has not been done, I believe it could be.)

In a careful piece of work, Jackman (1978) notes that education is associated with liberalism on some race items (such as "strict segregation" of the races) but not on others (such as busing). She concludes from this that, contrary to much past research, education promotes only "superficial" learning of democratic values rather than genuine commitment to them. The alternative argument of the RAS model, of course, would be that the first type of item taps a mainstream policy and the second a partisan policy.[23]

The explanation of the RAS model, which follows from Key's observation on the "indoctrinating effect" of exposure to elite discourse, is preferable in each of these cases because it is embedded in a theory having a wider range of applications. In particular, it can explain why awareness has a polarizing effect in some cases and a mainstream effect in others, even when the substantive issue domain is the same.[24]

There also exist alternative explanations for attitude constraint. Most stress the internal sources of constraint – that is, schematic associations that develop within the mind as a result of thought about the particular issues. These explanations also stress that more politically aware persons (often described as political "experts") are more ideologically consistent than are less aware persons

Army, to teach in the public schools. In looking for a global effect of education, Sullivan et al. fail to distinguish between cases in which the mainstream model would expect to find educationally induced tolerance and cases in which it would not. (From table 5.2 of Sullivan et al., it appears that the effect of education on tolerance is large in the case of free speech for one's most disliked group, but that the effect of education is nonexistent when it comes to being "pleased" at having one's child date a member of one's least liked group; it may be that citizens in a democracy ought, in some sense, to be tolerant of having their children date members of their least liked political group, but nothing in the mainstream model would predict that better educated people would be more likely to be so pleased than less well-educated ones.) Second, even if the better educated people are more tolerant in part because they are less frightened of certain groups, which appears to be the case, the support they give to mainstream civil liberties remains politically significant. It is, moreover, quite possible that learning to discount one's fears of radical groups is simply another element of mainstream civil liberties norms that is better learned by better educated persons. For example, learning to discount one's irrational fears of domestic communism seems to have been a principal "mainstream" lesson of the so-called McCarthyism period.

23 For a critique of Jackman that uses different conceptual machinery to reach essentially the same conclusion, see chapter 4 of Sniderman, Brody, and Tetlock, 1991.

24 The fact that, as Duch and Gibson (n.d.) point out, the effect of education on tolerance varies substantially from one nation to another is further reason to believe that it measures differences in socialization rather than differences in cognitive capacity or psychological adjustment.

(novices) because they think more about politics (Fiske and Kinder, 1981; Judd and Krosnick, 1989). Though approaching the problem quite differently, Luskin's (1987) treatment of the relationship between attitude constraint and political sophistication likewise stresses connections between idea-elements within a person's mind.

Though not denying the importance of intrapsychic connections and the individual's own thought in developing them, the RAS model manages to explain attitude consistency without referring to such mental organization. It instead stresses the extrapsychic or external sources of constraint, namely the pattern of elite division or nondivision on the given issue. In maintaining this external focus, the RAS model is able to explain the quite different effects that awareness has in different contexts, as in Figures 6.1 and 6.5. Also, the RAS model can better explain phenomena, including random response variation and response effects, that affect novices and experts alike. Finally, the present model, as shown in the next four chapters, adds a dynamic element to our understanding of how awareness (or expertise) affects attitude statements, namely an account of attitude change.

APPENDIX

Table 6.3. *Coefficients for Gulf War opinion*

	Right to send troops	Reject pullout of troops	Tougher military action
Intercept	−0.02	−2.19	1.33
Awareness (standardized)	−0.24 (.17)	−0.73 (.09)	0.13 (.07)
Party (range −2 to +2)	0.09 (.14)	0.28 (.07)	0.19 (.06)
Party x awareness	−0.03 (.14)	0.12 (.07)	0.06 (.06)
Time[a]	−0.18 (.19)	−	−0.42 (.19)
Gender (female = 1, else 0)	−.60 (.13)	−0.35 (.16)	−0.81 (.14)
Race (black = 1, else 0)	1.04 (.20)	0.69 (.17)	0.84 (.25)
Ethnicity (Jewish = 1, else 0)	0.19 (49)	−0.15 (.63)	−0.27 (.49)
Time x party x awareness	0.15[b] (.15)	−	−0.12 (.17)
Time x party	0.23[b] (.15)	−	−0.05 (.15)
Time x awareness	−0.18[b] (.19)	−	−0.12 (.21)
N	1976	1987	1987

Notes to Table 6.3

Note: Cell entries are coefficients from ML estimation of logistic regression model, with standard errors shown in parentheses. First dependent variable is whether the U.S. did the right thing in sending troops to the Persian Gulf (0–1); the second is whether U.S. should pursue some policy *other than* a pullout of troops from the gulf region; the third is whether the United States should take tougher military action against Iraq.

[a] For the "right thing" question, time is coded 0 in the period through November 9, when congressional criticism of American involvement began, and 1 afterward. For the "tougher military action" question, time is coded 0 in the period through December 15, at which time President Bush rejected an Iraqi meeting proposal, thereby signaling clear intent to enforce a January 15 pullout deadline, and 1 afterward.

[b] Block of three coefficients is statistically significant on F-test at $p < .01$.

Source: 1990 NES survey.

7

Basic processes of "attitude change"

Within the RAS model, "attitudes, " in the conventional sense of the term, do not exist. Rather, people make "attitude reports" or "survey responses" on the basis of momentarily salient considerations. Attitude change, then, cannot be understood within the RAS model as a conversion experience, the replacement of one crystallized opinion structure by another. It must instead be understood as a change in the balance of positive and negative considerations relating to a given issue. To model it, one must represent the process by which new considerations are added to the pool of existing considerations in the person's mind, thereby permanently altering long-term response probabilities on the issue. *Permanent alterations in long-term response probabilities* are the RAS model's equivalent of attitude change. Since this phrase is a cumbersome one, my discussion of the phenomenon will retain the more standard locution, attitude change. However, the reader should keep in mind that I am using it as a phrase of convenience, and am actually referring to an alteration in long-term response probabilities that has been brought about by the acquisition of new considerations.

Attitude change, understood in this way, makes an enormously more interesting subject of study than cross-sectional opinion. When adequate opinion data are available, as they are in a handful of cases, the analyst is no longer forced to infer a dynamic process from a static distribution of opinion, as was done in Chapter 6, but can directly observe the processes that are shaping opinion. This permits a more challenging and stimulating test of the RAS model than has been possible so far. It will, in particular, enable us to see in detail whether the effects of exposure to streams of opposing information flows, are, as claimed, major forces in shaping mass attitudes.

This chapter deals with the basics of attitude change, including some initial tests of the argument. More demanding and revealing tests of the model appear in later chapters. Although I will continue to use the RAS model in this chapter to deduce expected patterns in the data, the deductions will be fewer and easier to keep track of. Hence, I will cease numbering them as in earlier chapters.

MODELING ATTITUDE CHANGE

The defining axioms of the RAS model have strong implications for how attitude change, as just defined, may be expected to occur. To develop these implications, we return to the fundamentals of the model.

Suppose that, after some interval of time, public opinion on a certain issue has changed. From the perspective of the RAS model, such change can only have occurred because the relative salience of liberal and conservative considerations in people's minds is different from what it was previously; this, in turn, may have come about by one of only two routes.

The first is that recent events or information may have increased the salience of preexisting liberal or conservative considerations, thereby bringing about changes in people's attitude reports, as discussed under the rubric of salience effects in Chapter 5. Although salience effects may persist for any period of time, depending on how long the events or information causing them remain current, they involve no changes in people's feelings toward the issue itself and hence do not fit the definition of attitude change. Salience effects that persist may be more appropriately described as "mood changes."

Mood changes may be difficult to distinguish empirically from attitude change, except in a laboratory experiment that alters a person's general state of mind without exposing her to any new ideas. Nonetheless, I conjecture that the well-known presidential "rally-round-the-flag effects," whereby the job performance ratings of U.S. presidents shoot up in times of international crisis (Mueller, 1973; Brody, 1991), may be partially due to mood shifts in the public. That is, the public may lay greater stress on the president's leadership function in times of threat, and evaluate him differently even though the considerations underlying the evaluations are unchanged. However, I stress that shifts in the national mood can be, at most, only a partial explanation for rally effects, since, as Brody (1991) has shown, the timing and magnitude of rallies is dependent on the extent to which other political elites support the president in time of crisis. Owing to the lack of data, I shall have nothing further to say about mood effects in this study.

The other way in which the RAS model allows changes in the public's response to an issue is as follows: Some members of the public have been exposed to persuasive communications and accepted them as considerations, thereby altering the balance of liberal and conservative considerations in their minds and hence their long-term response probabilities. This type of change fits the definition of attitude change, as given a moment ago. Attitude change, thus, depends on a two-step process involving *reception* of new ideas and *acceptance* of some as new considerations, thereby altering the balance of considerations in people's minds.

Note that people may form *both* new liberal and new conservative considerations during a period of attitude change. All that is logically required for attitude change to occur is that, if overall opinion has moved, say, in a conservative direction, the relative prevalence of conservative considerations in people's minds has increased. If, as ought normally to be the case, the initially existing balance of considerations reflects the balance of competing conservative and liberal messages in the preceding period, the relative prevalence of conservative considerations will increase if the *relative intensity* of the conservative message has increased.

To take an example: Suppose that, every week, the news media broadcast nine liberal stories on a given issue and one conservative story, each having equal prominence and credibility. Then suppose the media begin broadcasting eight liberal and two conservative messages every week. This would count as a gain in the relative intensity of the conservative message and would create a movement of opinion in the conservative direction.

It is helpful at this point to drop references to liberal and conservative messages and to recast the argument in terms of dominant and countervailing messages. Thus, the message that is more intense during the period of attitude change is defined as the *dominant* message, and the less intense message is the *countervailing* message. Opinion change may sometimes occur in the direction of the countervailing, or less intense, message if the less intense message, though remaining less intense, has nonetheless gained in relative intensity (as in the example in the preceding paragraph). Most often, however, opinion change probably runs in the direction of the more intense or dominant message.

Let us say that the probability a given individual will express support for the dominant position at time 1 is[1]

$$\frac{D_1}{C_1 + D_1}$$

where C_1 and D_1 are the number of considerations in the person's mind initially favoring the countervailing and dominant positions, respectively. So if some individual has three dominant and two countervalent considerations, and if she responds to survey questions on the basis of the first consideration that comes to mind, the probability of stating a dominant opinion is $3 / (3 + 2) = .6$.

Over the next time period, persons may, in response to the political communications they encounter, form new considerations. New considerations favoring the dominant message will be designated D_2, and new considerations favoring the countervailing position will be C_2. Given this, change in long-term response probability – that is, "attitude change" – can be specified as the difference between the proportion of considerations favoring the dominant position at time 2, and the proportion favoring this position at time 1, as follows:

$$\text{Change in response probability} = \frac{(D_1 + D_2)}{(C_1 + C_2) + (D_1 + D_2)}$$
$$- \frac{D_1}{C_1 + D_1} \qquad (7.1)$$

This equation, which simply claims that changes in long-term response probabilities depend on changes in the mix of considerations relating to an issue, is the foundation for all of this study's subsequent investigation of attitude change.

---

1 Again, I assume that individuals respond on the basis of the first consideration that comes to mind, and also that some consideration always comes to mind – that is, people do not respond "no opinion."

From Equation 7.1, we can see that the incidence of attitude change in response to dominant and countervailing messages depends on four quantities: C_1, D_1, C_2, and D_2.

In beginning to think about the incidence of attitude change, it is useful to focus on *resistance* to change in the direction of a dominant message, given exposure to dominant and countervalent messages. Such resistance can take three forms, which I will describe as partisan resistance, inertial resistance, and countervalent resistance. Each depends on one or more of the terms in Equation 7.1, as follows:

Partisan resistance. Individuals may refuse to internalize new dominant messages that they recognize as inconsistent with their underlying predispositions, where such recognition depends (via axioms A1–A3) on the possession and accessibility of contextual information from a relevant cueing message. By rejecting dominant messages, persons ensure that D_2 is a small number or perhaps zero, which reduces change in the direction of the dominant message. Because such outright rejection of the dominant message is rooted in a person's predispositions, I refer to it as predispositional or partisan resistance.

Inertial resistance. Individuals, especially well-informed ones, may possess large stores of preexisting considerations, C_1 and D_1, so that even if some new considerations, D_2, are internalized, their effects will be swamped by the effects of previously formed considerations. Because this form of resistance depends on the inertial mass of preexisting considerations, I refer to it as inertial resistance to persuasion.

Countervalent resistance. Individuals may internalize countervalent considerations, C_2, during the period of attitude change. The effect of these considerations in counteracting newly formed dominant considerations is what I call countervalent resistance.

It follows from the logic of the RAS model that the incidence of *each type of resistance* is likely to increase with increasing levels of political awareness. To see why this is so, we can consider the example of how liberals would be affected by a dominant conservative message and a countervailing liberal message.

Obviously, liberals will be more likely than conservatives to reject the dominant conservative message – if they possess the contextual information that enables them to recognize it as inconsistent with their predispositions. Because more aware liberals will, by the Reception Axiom, be more likely to possess the contextual information necessary to achieve such recognition, they will be more likely to reject the dominant messages which they receive, thereby exhibiting greater *partisan resistance* than less aware liberals.

The most politically aware liberals will also tend to have the largest stores of existing liberal considerations, thereby making them most likely to exhibit *inertial resistance.* The reason is that, as highly aware persons, they will have been more heavily exposed to liberal messages previously, and, as liberals, they will likely have internalized many of them as considerations.

Finally, highly aware liberals will be most heavily exposed to the countervailing liberal message during the period of attitude change and, as liberals, they will be likely to accept it. Hence they will be most likely to internalize new liberal considerations, thereby exhibiting *countervalent resistance* to change.

Note that, in this example and throughout my discussion of attitude change, resistance to change means resistance to change in long-term response probabilities. Thus, the highly aware may internalize some conservative messages but yet, because they also form some new countervalent considerations or exhibit inertial resistance, remain unchanged in their long-term probability of giving a conservative response.

More generally, resistance to a dominant communication flow can take quite different forms. People may resist either by *rejecting* uncongenial messages at the point of encountering them, or, if some are accepted, by *counteracting the effects* of the dominant messages by means of countervalent and inertial considerations.

Since each of the three forms of resistance to persuasion produces distinctive effects, it will be possible to demonstrate that each makes an independent contribution to resistance to attitude change. Chapters 8 through 10 develop the evidence of these independent resistance effects.

This chapter, however, takes a different tack. It will develop a model of attitude change that makes no direct reference to any of the three resistance mechanisms, and no direct reference to countervalent communications. It will be, therefore, a "one-message" model of attitude change, where the one message is the one that is gaining in relative intensity and thereby bringing about attitude change. The one-message model will serve to introduce the reader to the complex patterns of attitude change that can be expected within the RAS model; it will also be capable of functioning as a sort of "reduced form" model of attitude change in the majority of situations in which the data necessary to observe the independent effects of inertial, countervalent, and partisan resistance are unavailable.

A RECEPTION-ACCEPTANCE MODEL OF ATTITUDE CHANGE

From the preceding discussion, attitude change requires, at a minimum, reception and acceptance of one or more new considerations. Accordingly, I will represent attitude change as the outcome of the following probabilistic reception-acceptance process:

$$\text{Prob(Change)} = \text{Prob(Reception)} \times \text{Prob(Acceptance | Reception)} \quad (7.2)$$

where

Prob(Change) = probability of change in long-term response probability

Prob(Reception) = probability of reception of a change-inducing message; by reception is meant that the person has been exposed to and comprehended the message

Prob(Acceptance | Reception) = probability of accepting (or internalizing) the message, given reception

Thus if, for example, an individual has a .5 probability of receiving a message and a .5 probability of accepting it (having received it), his probability of attitude change, according to this model, is simply the product of these reception and acceptance probabilities, that is, .5 × .5 = .25.

As is obvious, this formulation of the attitude change process omits any reference to "considerations," which cannot be easily measured in most attitude change situations, and refers instead to the probability of change in a person's summary attitude report. It also omits any reference to countervalent messages, even though they will often be present in attitude change situations. These are significant simplifications. Yet, Equation 7.2 does depict a reception-acceptance process, as required by the RAS model, and the equation can, as we shall see, be filled out in a way that implicitly accommodates the *effects* of both considerations and countervalent messages on the incidence of attitude change.

Let us begin filling out Equation 7.2 by more fully specifying the reception and acceptance functions that jointly constitute it. From previous chapters, we know that the probability of reception of change-inducing messages is positively associated with a person's level of general political awareness. Thus we can stipulate that Prob (Reception) in Equation 7.2 is an increasing (positive) function of political awareness.

With respect to the acceptance function in Equation 7.2, we know from the previous section that – owing to their greater attention to cueing messages, their larger stores of considerations and their greater exposure to countervalent messages – more aware persons are relatively more resistant to the effects of dominant messages that are inconsistent with their predispositions. We can therefore use awareness, a measured variable, to capture the effects of these three difficult-to-observe resistance mechanisms. More specifically, we can specify an acceptance function for Equation 7.2 in which acceptance rates decline as awareness and ideological distance from the message jointly increase.

Before completing specification of the reception and acceptance functions, it will be useful to provide illustrations of the ideas developed so far and to sketch their principal implications. Consider the following hypothetical data, which give probabilities of reception, acceptance, and attitude change for persons having different levels of political awareness:

Attitude change in response to a hypothetical message

	Level of awareness		
	Low	Middle	High
Prob(Reception)	.10	.50	.90
Prob(Accept | Reception)	.90	.50	.10
Change (Reception × Acceptance)	.09	.25	.09

In the first row, reception probabilities increase from .10 to .50 to .90 as political awareness increases from low to middle to high. These numbers capture the notion, central to the RAS model, that reception increases with awareness. In the second row, acceptance probabilities decrease from .90 to .10 as awareness increases from low to high. These hypothetical numbers capture the notion, developed in the preceding section, that acceptance levels tend to decline with increases in awareness. The resulting change probabilities, which are formed by multiplying reception rates by acceptance rates within each column, are shown in the third row. As can be seen, persons in the middle levels of awareness are most likely to experience attitude change in this hypothetical case.

Thus, the model implies that the relationship between awareness and attitude change may be nonmonotonic, that is, that persons at middle levels of awareness may be most likely to change. As was indicated in the brief discussion of congressional elections in Chapter 2, and as much more evidence will attest, nonmonotonic patterns of attitude change turn up with considerable regularity in opinion data. Hence, Equation 7.2, with further elaboration of the reception and acceptance functions, will be central to the explanation of attitude change over the next four chapters.

It must immediately be added, however, that attitude change does not always conform to a nonmonotonic pattern. Markedly different patterns of change are expected, depending on how various message-level and individual-level factors interact. Thus, a *nonmonotonic pattern of attitude change is simply one special case among many possibilities.* These different possibilities do not occur at random but adhere to a definite theoretical model. This point is best made by reviewing the work of William McGuire (1968, 1969), the social psychologist who first proposed a reception-acceptance model of attitude change having the form of Equation 7.2.

PATTERNS OF ATTITUDE CHANGE

McGuire began with a problem that had long vexed social psychologists, namely the relation between personality and persuasibility. McGuire noted that several personality traits – self-esteem, intelligence, and freedom from anxiety – had been shown to be associated with nonmonotonic patterns of attitude change in experimental studies of persuasion in laboratory settings. To explain this occurrence, he suggested that these personality traits might be positively associated with reception of persuasive communications but negatively associated with disposition toward acceptance, given reception.[2] In the case of the expected positive relationship between self-esteem and reception, for example, one might argue that high self-esteem is associated with low need for ego defense, greater capacity for focusing one's attention, and lower levels of anxiety – all of which conduce toward a higher probability of reception of persuasive communication.[3] As regards the expected negative relationship between self-esteem and accep-

---

2 McGuire's term for what I am calling acceptance was yielding.
3 For evidence that self-esteem is associated with exposure to political values in a nonlaboratory setting, see Sniderman, 1975.

tance of the communications which one has received, one could argue that people possessing little self-esteem tend to yield uncritically to whatever communications they happen to encounter.

Having thus posited that self-esteem has a positive relationship with reception and a negative relationship with acceptance, McGuire proposed the logic of the reception-acceptance process, as embodied in Equation 7.2 and illustrated in the hypothetical data just examined, to explain why the expected relation between self-esteem and attitude change is, under certain conditions, nonmonotonic.

McGuire goes on, however, to show that Equation 7.2 can account for a variety of other patterns of opinion change. In fact, the great value of the reception-acceptance model proposed by McGuire is that it enables the analyst to explain results that seem at first to be contradictory. Consider a typical "hard learning" situation, which is defined as a situation in which the persuasive message is, for some reason, difficult to receive. The factors making for difficulty of reception might include background noise, the presence of distractions, or the inherent difficulty of the message. A prototypical hard learning situation is a college lecture in physics. All physics students may be presumed to have a high disposition toward acceptance of the contents of the lecture, but only the most intelligent may be able to understand it.

One can capture this situation by saying that everyone has a 1.0 probability of accepting the contents of the physics lecture, given reception of it. But effective reception of the physics lecture will be positively correlated with intelligence. When we represent these ideas in a reception-acceptance table, like the one following, we find (in the bottom row of the table) that the most intelligent students are most likely to undergo "attitude change" in response to the instructor's "persuasive argument."

Attitude change in a "hard learning" situation

	Levels of intelligence		
	Low	Middle	High
Prob(Reception)	.10	.20	.30
Prob(Accept I Reception)	1.0	1.0	1.0
Change (Reception × Acceptance)	.10	.20	.30

As will be seen below, there are also political situations in which messages have so little intensity, or are so difficult to comprehend, that, like some physics lectures, they reach only the most aware persons. In such cases, which might also be called "hard learning" situations, the most aware persons are most likely to change. Although generally resistant to persuasion, they are the only people who will have been effectively exposed to any new information.

Now consider an entirely different kind of persuasion situation, an "easy learning" situation in which someone stands in front of a large audience and repeats suggestively, "Your head is moving back and forth, back and forth." What makes this an easy learning situation is that the persuasive message is so extremely simple and clear that we may assume that essentially everyone, except perhaps the hard of hearing, receives it. To capture the dynamics of such an easy learning situation, we set everyone's reception probability to 1.0. If, as shown below, we assume that acceptance probabilities in this situation would be negatively correlated with intelligence, and then carry out the multiplication of rows in accord with the model, we find that people with the least intelligence should be most likely to begin swaying their heads back and forth.

Attitude change in an "easy learning" situation

	Levels of intelligence		
	Low	Middle	High
Prob(Reception)	1.0	1.0	1.0
Prob(Accept | Reception)	.90	.50	.10
Change (Reception × Acceptance)	.90	.50	.10

McGuire cites numerous studies whose results, though once apparently contradictory, make sense when interpreted in light of this model. For any individual trait variable that is positively correlated with reception of persuasive communications and negatively correlated with likelihood of uncritically accepting them, the relation between the trait and attitude change can be positive, negative, or nonmonotonic, depending on whether the persuasion situation stresses the capacity of subjects to receive the message (as in the educational or "hard learning" situations), their willingness to accept the message (as in the case of the easy but repetitive message), or both (which may sometimes produce a nonmonotonic pattern of change).

Political awareness, like the personality traits that McGuire examined, would be expected to be positively correlated with reception of persuasive communications and negatively correlated with likelihood of uncritical acceptance. Hence, the relation between awareness and attitude change may be positive, negative, or nonmonotonic. In fact, whole families of curves can be generated in theory and matched to actual data, depending on how an individual's predispositions and awareness interact with particular messages.

What gives rise to *families* of curves, rather than a single curve pattern, is that persuasive communications vary continuously from very hard (or "low intensity") to very easy ("high intensity"), and as message intensity changes, the shapes of the attitude change curves generated by the messages change incrementally. Similarly, resistance to a message may differ incrementally in different groups, depending on the fit between their partisanship and the partisan coloration of the message source. This was a type of factor that McGuire did not consider, but it can greatly affect the shape of the attitude change curves that one observes. Let me offer some illustrations.

The following set of tables illustrates how patterns of reception and acceptance of a *liberal message* among three ideological groups – liberals, centrists, and conservatives – might come together to form a family of attitude change curves:

Attitude change in response to a liberal message within three ideological groups

	Among liberals			Among centrists			Among conservs.		
	Low	Middle	High	Low	Middle	High	Low	Middle	High
Prob(Reception)	.10	.50	.90	.10	.50	.90	.10	.50	.90
Prob(Accept | Reception)	.90	.85	.80	.90	.55	.20	.90	.46	.02
Change(Reception × Acceptance)	.09	.425	.72	.09	.275	.18	.09	.23	.018

Level of awareness

Within all three groups, reception of the liberal message increases from .10 to .50 to .90 as political awareness increases; this is shown in the top row of each part of the table and indicates that the intensity of the persuasive message is the same for all three groups. Also within all groups, acceptance rates decline with awareness. Yet the decline in acceptance rates is much steeper for conservatives (where it falls from .90 to .02) than among liberals (where it declines only from .90 to .80), with centrists falling in between. The result is that attitude change is expected to follow different patterns in the two groups: Change rises with awareness among liberals (from .09 to .425 to .72) but is nonmonotonic with respect to awareness among centrists and conservatives.

Because these patterns reappear in various guises throughout the rest of the book, generally resembling actual estimates of reception and acceptance rates, as shown in Figures 7.4 and 10.1, it is essential for the reader to be entirely clear about how the nonmonotonicity comes about: Conservatives and centrists having low levels of awareness do not change much because only 10 percent of them are ever exposed to any change-inducing messages. Highly aware conservatives and centrists are very likely to be exposed to the liberal message (their reception rate is 90 percent), but their acceptance rates are so low (2 and 20 percent, respectively) that few end up changing their attitudes. This leaves moderately aware conservatives and centrists most susceptible to change: They pay enough attention to be likely to receive the liberal message but are not sufficiently aware to be able to reject it as inconsistent with their values. The shapes of the nonmonotonic change curves among conservatives are, as can be seen, somewhat different than among centrists, because the negative effect of awareness on acceptance is stronger in the former case than in the latter.

A question that arises in this example is why, among liberals, there is *any* tendency for awareness to create resistance to persuasion by a liberal message. Indeed, might not acceptance rates *rise* with political awareness when the message is a congenial one?

My answer to this question is empirical: When a model is designed to allow for this sort of interaction, there turns out always to be a negative relation between awareness and probability of acceptance, even when the message is ideologically congenial. The effect of awareness on acceptance may be slight, as in this example of liberals responding to a liberal message, but it seems always to be negative.[4] What this indicates is that, perhaps for reasons of inertial resistance, more aware persons are always somewhat more resistant to change, given reception of a change-inducing message, than are less aware persons.

INITIAL TESTS OF THE MODEL

Even though development of the abbreviated reception-acceptance model is not yet complete, it is useful to demonstrate that the simulations just outlined resemble cases of attitude change that actually occur in the political world. I will take two such cases, one involving opinion change in a liberal direction and the other change in a conservative direction.

The first case involves public attitudes toward defense spending. In the 1980 and 1982 election studies, the NES asked the following question:

Some people believe we should spend much less money for defense. Others feel that defense spending should be greatly increased. Where do you stand on this issue, or haven't you thought much about it?

Respondents were then asked to place themselves on a seven-point scale, from greatly reduced spending at point 1 to greatly increased spending at point 7.

During the two-year interval between surveys, coverage of the defense issue in the press was heavily unfavorable toward defense spending. As discussed in Chapter 2, a content analysis of stories in *Newsweek* found that stories favoring cuts in spending outnumbered pro-spending stories by a ratio of about 2 to 1. Thus, although countervalent communications were present, there was a dominant, anti–defense-spending message in this period. Presumably as a result of this dominant message, the percentage of persons favoring cuts in defense (persons who took point 1, 2, or 3 on the defense scale) in the two NES surveys rose from 10 percent to 28 percent.[5]

The second example involves U.S. policy in Central America. The question, which was asked in the fall of 1986 and again to a subsample of the same respondents in June 1987, was as follows:

Some people feel that the United States should become much more involved in the internal affairs of Central America. Others feel we should become much less involved. Where do you stand on this issue, or haven't you thought much about it?

The Iran–Contra controversy emerged in November, as the National Election Study went into the field, and hit full stride over the next few months. At the heart of the controversy were allegations that the Reagan administration had illegally used funds from the sale of weapons to Iran to support the Contra guerrillas,

4 In particular, there is no tendency for awareness to interact with ideology in the acceptance process so as to produce a positive awareness slope for one ideological group and a negative one for the other. Except in Tables 7.3 and 9.1, I have not reported the results of such tests, because I have regarded them as exploratory.
5 In the period from 1978 to 1980, coverage of the defense issue in the same magazine favored *increases* in defense spending by about the same ratio it favored *decreases* in spending over the period 1980 to 1982. However, the NES surveys did not begin to carry parallel measures of attitudes toward defense spending until the 1980–2 period.

who were fighting to overthrow the communist government of Nicaragua. The Senate's Iran–Contra hearings were under way at the time of the reinterview in June. As we will see in the next chapter, this controversy brought a steep decline in President Reagan's popularity. But it also brought increased publicity to the President's Central America policy, as exemplified in the defiant testimony of Lieutenant Colonel Oliver North at the Senate Contra hearings. The result was increased public support for American involvement in Central America. In the 1986–7 NES surveys, the increase was from 28 percent support to 38 percent support.[6]

Given that mass attitude change has occurred, the reception-acceptance model gives us definite expectations concerning the patterns of the change. When opinion changes in response to a predominantly *liberal* message, as in the case of defense spending, we expect that, for liberals, there will be a positive relation between political awareness and likelihood of change, as in the preceding example. For conservatives responding to a liberal message, we expect a nonmonotonic pattern in which moderately aware conservatives are most likely to change, as also indicated in the preceding. But when, as in the Central America issue, mass attitude change occurs in response to a *conservative* message, our expectations for liberals and conservatives reverse: We anticipate a positive relation between awareness and change among conservatives, and a nonmonotonic relation with awareness among liberals.

To test these expectations, we need, for each survey, a measure of political awareness and a measure of individuals' values or partisanship. Awareness can be readily measured in both surveys with tests of neutral political knowledge. For the surveys capturing attitude change on Central America, an excellent measure of political values is available, namely, the Hurwitz–Peffley items on anticommunism and military vigilance (Hurwitz and Peffley, 1988).[7] For the 1980–2 surveys, the most appropriate measure of values carried on both surveys is the traditional measure of party attachment. Since differences between Democrats and Republicans on defense spending were one of the major elements of interparty conflict in the early 1980s, party attachment is a reasonable measure of individual predispositions on this issue.

The results of the tests are shown in Tables 7.1. and 7.2.[8] Let us look first at Table 7.1, which deals with the defense spending issue. The table shows rates of

6 See Sobel (1989) and Bowen (1989) for evidence on commercial polls of similar increases in support for U.S. involvement in Central America.
7 The 1986 NES postelection study carried a question on U.S. involvement in Central America. This question was repeated in the June wave of the 1987 NES pilot study, which reinterviewed 457 people from the fall survey. Hurwitz–Peffley (1988) militarism items were carried in the second wave of the pilot survey, which began in August and was able to reinterview only 360 of the original 457 pilot respondents. Since the militarism scale is necessary to the analysis, the analysis will be based on the fall 1986 and June 1987 interviews of respondents who agreed to be interviewed in the second wave of the pilot study in August.
8 Both the defense spending and Central America items were originally asked in the form of seven-point scales. For purposes of this analysis, positions 1, 2, and 3 on the defense scale have been collapsed into support for greater cuts; positions 5, 6, and 7 on the Central America scale have been collapsed into support for greater U.S. involvement.

Table 7.1. *Support for cuts in defense spending, 1980 and 1982*

| | Level of political awareness | | | |
	Low			High
Democrats				
1980	12[a]	11	12	20
N	(318)	(131)	(129)	(123)
1982	16	36	41	57
	(304)	(185)	(128)	(153)
Change rate 1980 to 1982[b]	4%	28	33	46
Republicans				
1980	8[a]	12	3	4
	(134)	(78)	(125)	(161)
1982	10	23	29	14
	(113)	(103)	(100)	(128)
Change rate 1980 to 1982[b]	2%	13	27	10

[a] Cell entries give percent who favor defense cuts.

[b] Change rate is calculated as $(\text{Opinion}_{82} - \text{Opinion}_{80})/(100 - \text{Opinion}_{80})$.

Source: 1980 and 1982 NES surveys.

support for cuts in defense spending, separately in 1980 and 1982, for Democrats and Republicans by level of political awareness. Thus, it can be seen that in 1980, 12 percent of Democrats in the lowest awareness category favored cuts in defense spending; but in 1982, 16 percent of Democrats in the low-awareness category favored such cuts. This amounts to a difference of 4 percentage points. Meanwhile, the most highly aware Democrats went from 20 percent in favor of defense cuts to 57 percent in favor, a difference of 37 percentage points.

Our interest here is in the probabilities of attitude change, that is, the probability that a person not already committed to cuts in defense spending would switch to favor such cuts in the second survey. Thus if 20 percent of highly aware Democrats favored cuts in 1980 and 57 percent did so in 1982, then the percentage of persons not initially favoring cuts who switched was

$$\text{Percent change} = \frac{[\text{Time}_2 - \text{Time}_1]}{[100\% - \text{Time}_1]} = \frac{[57\% - 20\%]}{[100\% - 20\%]} = 46\%$$

Change rates, calculated in this way for Democrats at each level of awareness, are displayed in the third row of Table 7.1. As can be seen, they generally fit

Table 7.2. *Support for greater U.S. involvement in Central America, 1986 and 1987*

	Level of political awareness			
	Low			High
Hawks				
1986	22[a]	30	43	60
1987	33	48	50	80
Change rate 1986 to 1987	14%	26	12	50
N	(18)	(40)	(44)	(15)
Centrists				
1986	17[a]	08	18	21
1987	23	30	38	21
Change rate 1986 to 1987	7%	24	24	00
	(30)	(37)	(40)	(14)
Doves				
1986	20[a]	10	08	08
1987	20	10	18	19
Change rate 1986 to 1987	0%	0	11	12
	(15)	(31)	(50)	(26)

[a] Cell entries give percent who favor greater U. S. involvement in Central America.

Source: 1986 NES survey and 1987 NES pilot survey.

expectations: More aware Democrats are more likely to have switched to a position of favoring defense cuts.

The lower panel of the table provides parallel data for Republicans. Note the change figures for Republicans in the bottom row of the table; as can be seen, change levels run from 2 percent in the lowest awareness category to 13 percent in the next category to 27 percent in the third category and then down to 10 percent in the highest category, a relationship that is, as expected, nonmonotonic. Altogether, then, the results from the defense spending issue conform well to theory.

Table 7.2 presents comparable data for the Central American issue. The fit to expectations here is fairly good but, at least at first glance, not perfect. Among "hawks" there is a positive relationship between political awareness and change in the direction of greater support for American involvement in Central America. Among "centrists" this relationship is sharply nonmonotonic, a result that is quite in the spirit of the model.

There is, however, a problem with the "doves." As would be expected, doves were much less responsive to the pro-Contra message than were either hawks or centrists. But contrary to expectation, the tiny handful of doves who did move in a conservative direction were not moderately aware doves, but very highly aware doves.

This departure from expectation is more apparent than real. For one thing, the number of cases in the critical cells is such that small departures from expectations should not be taken too seriously.[9] (Different responses by just two individuals in the cell for highly aware doves would have brought the change rate in this group down to .04.) Table 7.2 also shows the effect of only one predispositional variable; there may be other predispositions that need to be controlled before we can get a clear picture of how attitudes were changing.

The need for controls and statistical tests highlights the limitations of tabular analysis for testing the RAS model. To address these needs, it is necessary to develop a statistical model of the attitude change process. Since variants of this model will be at the center of my analysis in the remainder of the book, I will fully describe each step of the model development. This will involve detail that statistically accomplished readers may find tedious, but that others will, I hope, find useful.

A STATISTICAL MODEL OF ATTITUDE CHANGE

The basis of the statistical model will be Equation 7.2, repeated below:

$$\text{Prob(Change)} = \text{Prob(Reception)} \times \text{Prob(Acceptance} \mid \text{Reception)}$$

Attitude change, thus, is a multiplicative function of separate reception and acceptance functions. To make this equation a statistical model of attitude change, we need to specify the nature of these reception and acceptance functions.

From earlier discussions, we have a fair amount of information about what these specifications must be. We know, first of all, that political awareness is positively associated with reception of persuasive communications, and we know that awareness and political values (and perhaps other variables) are negatively associated with the likelihood of uncritical acceptance. But to make full use of this information, we must know the *functional form* of the relationships between these independent variables, on one side, and the dependent variables, reception and acceptance, on the other. We need to know, in other words, whether the form of these relationships is strictly linear, exponential, or something else.

If this seems an arcane issue, consider the following problem. Suppose that we have tested several million schoolchildren from kindergarten through grade twelve on the question, "What is the square root of 4?" And suppose that we now want to model the relationship between years of schooling and the proba-

9 In evaluating this table, it is useful to keep in mind that, for a difference of means test with $p = .20$ and $n = 25$, the standard error of the mean difference is 0.11.

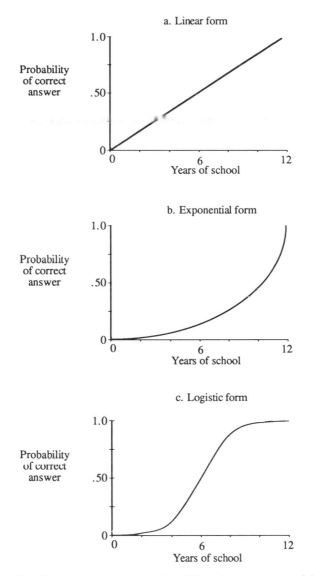

Figure 7.1. Three functional forms for relations between two variables.

bility of getting the correct answer to this question. Obviously, we would expect to find a positive relationship. That is, more years of schooling would be associated with a higher chance of getting the answer right. But as Figure 7.1 shows, there are several forms this relationship could take. The top panel depicts a strictly linear relationship: Each additional year of school increases the probability of a correct response by a constant amount. The middle panel depicts an exponential relationship: Schooling affects knowledge of square roots slowly at first, but has an increasingly powerful effect as one goes further in school. Thus going from the first to the second grade has scarcely any effect, but going from eleventh to twelfth grade has a very large effect. The bottom panel of Figure 7.1 claims that the relationship between schooling and math knowledge follows the form of a logistic function: The earliest and latest years of school have little effect, but the middle years of school have a substantial effect.

The point here is that in order to model the relationship between two variables, one must know more than just the fact that they are positively correlated. One must know – or at least be able to make a plausible guess about – the *form* of their relationship. To resolve this problem in the present example, we would use our background knowledge of how education is organized in the United States. Knowing, that is, that square roots are normally taught between the third and eighth grades, we would assume that little learning about square roots occurs in the very early or very late years of school, and hence that the logistic functional form best describes the relationship between years of school and correct answers on this particular test question.

The choice of functional form in the case of awareness and reception is also fairly clear. Since we are dealing with *probabilities* of reception, we would like to have a function that varies naturally between 0 and 1. The logistic form meets that requirement. The lowest value it can take is 0 and the largest value is 1. Empirical studies of the diffusion of ideas also often find that logistic functions (or close equivalents) provide a good fit to the actual data (Price, 1961; Neuman, 1990).[10]

For all these reasons, I will assume that the relationship between awareness and reception can be represented by the following logistic function:

$$\text{Prob(Reception)}_i = 1 - \left[\frac{1}{1 + f + e^{(a_0 + a_1 \text{ Awareness}_i)}} \right] \qquad (7.3)$$

where

Prob(Reception)_i = the probability that individual (i) will receive a persuasive message

a_0 = coefficient designating the intensity of message

a_1 = coefficient designating strength of relationship between awareness and reception

f = floor parameter

e = the natural logarithmetic base, 2.7214

10 In tests of individual differences in ability, such as IQ tests, researchers regard each question as a "test" that some people will "pass" and others will "fail," depending on their general levels of ability. They next argue, from elementary statistical considerations, that the relationship between any particular test item and a general measure of ability should be described by the normal ogive function, which is a close approximation of the logistic function (Torgerson, 1958; Lord and Novick, 1968). In a similar fashion, one can regard reception of a particular persuasive message as a "test" that some will pass and others will fail, depending on their general levels of political awareness. By analogy to test theory, it would then follow that the relationship between reception of a particular persuasive message and general levels of political awareness should be described by a logistic function.

Equation 7.3 can be equivalently written as

$$\text{Prob(Reception)}_i = 1 - [1 + f + \text{Exp}(a_0 + a_1\text{Awareness}_i)]^{-1} \quad (7.3')$$

Since many readers will not be greatly familiar with this type of logistic function, and since it will be heavily and somewhat unconventionally used in my examination of attitude change, it is worth digressing to gain some familiarity with the function and its associated parameters.

The "a_1" parameter is, first of all, a measure of the strength of the relationship between political awareness and reception of a particular message. Thus, it is the analogue of the slope in a standard linear regression. The top panel of Figure 7.2 shows how the relationship between awareness and reception varies for a typical range of values of a_1: ($a_1 = .5$, $a_1 = 1.0$, $a_1 = 2.0$).[11] The higher the value of a_1, the stronger the relationship between awareness and reception. For the case in which $a_1 = 2.0$, reception levels are near zero at low awareness, begin a sharp rise at about -2, and approach a ceiling of 100 percent by the time awareness reaches a level of $+2$ units.

Political awareness in Figure 7.2 has been scored in standard units. The measures of political awareness that I will use in modeling attitude change have also been expressed in standard units. Since the awareness measures usually have a roughly normal distribution, this means about 96 percent of individuals will usually have awareness scores that fall within an interval of ± 2 units on Figure 7.2. Knowing this, the reader can interpret the magnitude of the coefficients reported in later sections of this book by referring back to Figure 7.2. For example, for a case in which the awareness coefficient is 1.0 and a_0 is near zero, Figure 7.2 implies that reception levels rise from about 10 percent at low levels of awareness to 90 percent at high levels of awareness. Relationships of this strength or greater will be common in the empirical analyses reported below.

The a_0 parameter captures the difficulty or the "loudness" of the particular message, and is the analogue of the intercept in standard regression. The middle section of Figure 7.2 shows how reception varies with information at three different values of a_0 (and a fixed value of $a_1 = 2.0$). High values of a_0 indicate high levels of reception at given levels of awareness, which in turn indicate "high-intensity" messages. If appropriate care is taken in the construction of variables, the a_0 coefficients can be compared across models to see which involve the most intense message.

This brings us to the f parameter. All of the projections in the top and middle panels of Figure 7.2 set the floor parameter, f, to zero. When f takes on positive values, it sets minimum or "floor" levels of reception, regardless of an individual's level of awareness. The bottom panel of Figure 7.2 shows three reception curves that are identical to those in the middle panel, except that the floor parameter is set to .30. Thus, instead of rising from a floor of zero, reception rises from a floor determined by f.[12]

11 These examples assume that Political Awareness runs from -3 to $+3$.
12 On the use of floor parameters in such situations, see Lord and Novick (1968: ch. 17).

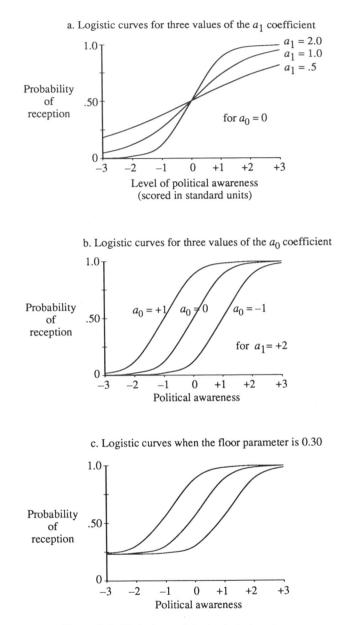

a. Logistic curves for three values of the a_1 coefficient

Figure 7.2. Variations of the logistic function.

Floor parameters are necessary in situations in which people may respond to survey questions without having received any information about the question – which, in many cases, probably means guessing. Without a floor parameter to assign "reception" scores to guessers, the model I am developing would have no way of accommodating the fact that such persons give answers to survey questions. The f parameter, thus, is a nuisance term that improves the fit of the model to the data without conveying substantive significance. As Figure 7.2 shows, it has an effect only at lower levels of awareness, where guessing is likely to be most common.[13]

The probability that an individual will accept a persuasive message (having received it) decreases with awareness and ideological distance from the message. Again assuming that the logistic function describes the form of this relationship, we may write

$$\text{Prob(Accept} \mid \text{Reception)}_i = [1 + \text{Exp}(-b_0 - b_1\text{Awareness}_i$$
$$- b_2\text{Predispositions}_i \ldots)]^{-1} \qquad (7.4)$$

where

$\text{Prob(Acceptance}\mid\text{Reception)}_i =$ the probability that individual (i) will accept the persuasive message, having received it

$b_0 =$ coefficient designating the difficulty or credibility of message

$b_1 =$ coefficient designating the effect of awareness on resistance to persuasion

$b_2 =$ coefficient designating the effect of predispositions on resistance to persuasion

Equation 7.4 differs from Equation 7.3 in two important ways. First, its form has been altered so as to make its coefficients more intelligible. In particular, Equation 7.4 has been set up so that if, as expected, higher levels of awareness are associated with lower acceptance rates, the coefficient on awareness will take a negative sign.[14] The second difference is that the acceptance function contains a term for differences in political predispositions, that is, ideology, party, religiosity, or whatever.

An important feature of logistic functions is that whenever two or more variables are used, the variables *automatically interact with one another* – which is to say, the effect of one variable depends on the values taken by the others. Thus, in Equation 7.4, the effect of awareness will always depend on the effect of the predispositions variable(s). It is necessary to allow for such Awareness × Predispositions interactions because the RAS model holds that predispositions have no effect unless the individual is sufficiently politically aware to possess the contextual information that enables resistance to uncongenial messages. Thus,

13 The f parameter may also be thought of as creating a more flexible, three-parameter reception function. Or again, it might be thought of as specifying floor levels of reception that are independent of political awareness.

14 In earlier work with this model (Zaller, 1989, 1991; Geddes and Zaller, 1989), the acceptance function was specified in such a way that obtaining a *positive* coefficient on awareness in this function indicated a *negative* relationship between awareness and probability of acceptance. In this book, I have changed the specification of the acceptance function to avoid this possibly confusing outcome.

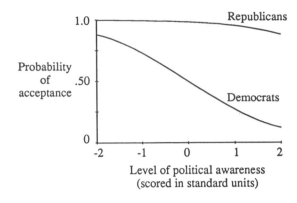

Figure 7.3. The automatically interactive nature of the logistic function. Values of the logistic function are $b_0 = 2$, $b_1 = -1$, $b_2 = -1$, with scores of -2 and $+2$ on the predispositions variable for Republicans and Democrats, respectively. The model is Equation 7.4.

as we saw in Table 7.1, unaware Democrats and Republicans did not differ much in their resistance to anti–defense-spending communications: The former became 4 percent less favorable toward defense spending, while the latter became 2 percent less favorable. Yet party attachment had a large impact on resistance to antidefense messages among highly aware partisans: Democrats became 46 percent less favorable and Republicans 10 percent less favorable. The same sort of Predisposition × Awareness interaction arose, *mutatis mutandis,* for hawks and doves in response to a conservative message, as shown in Table 7.2.

Figure 7.3 shows how Equation 7.4 handles Awareness × Predisposition interactions. In this figure, b_0 is set to -2, b_1 is set to -1, and b_2 is set to -1; party is scored -2 for Republicans and $+2$ for Democrats. These values, as will be seen below, fall within the range of the values obtained empirically from the application of Equation 7.4 to actual data. The figure shows that increases in awareness lead to lower acceptance rates among both Democrats and Republicans, but to a much steeper decline among Democrats. Thus, the effect of awareness on acceptance depends on whether the person is a Democrat or Republican. (This interaction would occur only when the change-inducing message was a conservative message; for a liberal message, the sign on b_2 would reverse, thereby causing awareness to have a greater effect on the acceptance rates of Republicans.)

The reader may wonder why, since the RAS model expects this type of interaction, I do not simply include a specific term for Awareness × Predispositions in Equation 7.4. The reason is practical: Most of the time such interaction terms contribute little or nothing to the fit of the model but nonetheless introduce large amounts of troublesome multicollinearity. Or, to put it differently, Equation 7.4 normally picks up interaction effects without the need for specific interaction terms (see Table 7.3). However, in one case, reported in Chapter 9, I found interaction terms helpful and so did include them in an acceptance function.

I would, incidentally, encourage readers who have access to a spreadsheet program to replicate the results in Figures 7.2 and 7.3, to experiment with other parameter values, and to plot the results of the more complex functions I shall report here. Doing this will greatly enhance understanding of the claims I make on behalf of the RAS model.

We are now ready to bring the reception and acceptance functions together. Substituting Equations 7.3 and 7.4 into Equation 7.2, we get

$$\text{Prob(Change)} = (1 - (1 + f + \text{Exp}[+a_0 + a_1\text{Awareness}])^{-1}) \times (1 +$$
$$\text{Exp}[-b_0 - b_1\text{Awareness} - b_2\text{Predispositions} \dots])^{-1} \quad (7.5)$$

The first term in Equation 7.5 is a monotonically increasing function of awareness, while the second is a similarly decreasing function of awareness and value distance from the message.

There is an important and nonobvious feature of this formulation of the reception-acceptance model. It is the implicit assumption that a person's predispositions, although affecting acceptance of persuasive messages, do not affect reception. This assumption is signaled by the fact that predispositional variables are included only in the acceptance function. This specification of the model would be inappropriate if, as early opinion research indicated, individuals engaged in "selective reception" of political information – if, that is, they exposed themselves mainly to ideas they thought they were likely to find acceptable and avoided exposure to uncongenial ideas. However, more recent research has been unkind to the notion of selective reception (Sears and Freedman, 1967; McGuire, 1969; Wicklund and Brehm, 1976; Cotton, 1985; Patterson and McClure, 1974; Patterson 1980). Most people, this research maintains, are simply not so rigid in their information-seeking behavior that they will expose themselves only to ideas that they find congenial. To the extent selective exposure occurs at all, it appears to do so under special conditions that do not typically arise in situations of mass persuasion.[15]

The likely reasons for the relative unimportance of selective reception are several. First, most people inform themselves by means of exposure to a fairly wide variety of outlets, most of which are "common carriers" of a national communications flow (Key, 1961). Second, selective reception requires a level of concerned vigilance much greater than most citizens, who are relatively apathetic about politics, are likely to make (Graber, 1984: p. 128). And third, most news events important enough to engage the attention of survey researchers

15 For example, the one case in which, according to Cotton (1985), selective exposure has been rigorously documented in a nonlaboratory setting involved new car purchasers. The new car purchasers were more likely than ones who had bought their cars a year earlier to look at advertisements for the car they had just purchased than ads for a car they had examined but decided not to buy.

   Recently, Price and Zaller (1990) have turned up some evidence of selective exposure effects in reception of new stories. The effects were typically small to nonexistent, but were large in two cases, both involving minor news stories. (For laboratory evidence of selective exposure, see Markus and Zajonc, 1985.)

are major, continuing stories such as the Vietnam War or the Iran–Contra scandal, so that people who pay any significant degree of attention to politics are unlikely to remain unaware of them even if they are not avidly interested in each new detail.

The selective reception hypothesis cannot be entirely false. After all, it would be extremely surprising if, say, liberal ideologues were as likely to subscribe to *National Review* as to *Nation*. But, by the available evidence, selective reception apparently does not occur on a sufficiently broad scale to affect the diffusion of major political ideas, and hence poses little danger to my formulation of the reception-acceptance model.[16]

Although Equation 7.5 is a model of attitude change, it requires adaptation before it can be applied to the two cases under examination here. There are three reasons for this. The first is that, in the defense spending case, we have no individual-level data on attitude change; rather, we have separate cross-section surveys in which *similar* individuals, rather than the *same* individuals, are compared across time. (Thus, for example, the low-awareness Democrats in the 1980 survey in Table 7.1 were not reinterviewed in 1982 to find out whether their attitudes had changed; rather, a separate sample was drawn in 1982 to measure the attitudes of low-awareness Democrats.) From this sort of data one can calculate aggregate-level change rates across different types of persons, as in Table 7.1, but not individual-level change rates of the type required by Equation 7.5.

The second limitation of equation 7.5 is that it accommodates change in one direction only – the direction of the dominant message. This creates a problem even when individual-level change data are available, as it is in the Central America case. If, as here, support for a hawkish policy rises from 28 percent to 38 percent, Equation 7.5 implicitly assumes that 10 percent of the sample has changed its attitude in the direction of the dominant message and the other 90 percent has remained stable. Owing, however, to random response variability (see Table 2.1), the actual pattern of change is more complicated. Thus, in the Central America case, 22 percent changed in the direction of the dominant hawkish message while 12 percent changed in a dovish direction, for a net change of 10 percent. Equation 7.5 cannot accommodate such two-way patterns of change.

A final difficulty is that if, as in Equation 7.5, one models only individual-level change rates, one is inefficiently discarding information about the baseline and final distributions of opinion. This information is often essential for gaining leverage on the overall reception-acceptance process.

16 The reader may wonder why I do not subject these arguments about selective reception to an empirical test by entering measures of political predispositions in the reception function. If they attract significant coefficients, it would indicate that selective reception occurs; if not, it would show that there is no problem. The reason is that Equation 7.5 would not be identified if all predispositions variables were entered in both the reception and acceptance functions. There would then be complete collinearity between the two functions, and hence no ability for the model to distinguish the separate effects of variables on the reception and acceptance steps.

For these reasons, then, we need a model of the attitude change process that is capable of capturing change between a baseline distribution of opinion and a subsequent opinion distribution, and that does so without implicitly assuming that all individual-level change runs in the direction of the dominant persuasive message.

One can develop such a model by making separate estimates of baseline attitudes at time$_1$ and the probability of attitude change, so that time$_2$ attitudes are a function of baseline attitudes and change probabilities, as follows:

$$\text{Prob(Opinion}_2) = \text{Prob(Baseline Opinion)} + \text{Prob(Change)}$$
$$* (1 - \text{Baseline Opinion}) \qquad (7.6)$$

That is, the probability of holding a particular opinion at time$_2$ is the probability of holding it at the baseline period, plus the probability of converting to the opinion if not already holding it at time$_1$.

The baseline and change functions can be specified straightforwardly as separate reception-acceptance models, each having the form of Equation 7.5. That is, baseline opinion is the outcome of a reception-acceptance process that is captured by Equation 7.5, and attitude change is also the outcome of a reception-acceptance process that is captured by Equation 7.5.

This model must be estimated simultaneously on data from both the time$_1$ and time$_2$ periods, as follows:

$$\text{Prob(Opinion)}_t = \text{Prob(Baseline)} + \text{Dum}_t * \text{Prob(Change)}$$
$$* (1 - \text{Baseline}) \qquad (7.7)$$

where Dum$_t$ takes the value of 0 at time$_1$ and the value of 1 at time$_2$. Thus, opinion at time$_1$ depends on the baseline reception-acceptance process only, while opinion at time$_2$ depends on both the baseline and the change models. Since the f parameter in the reception function is intended to pick up the effects of guessing, and since these effects are absorbed in the baseline model, it is unnecessary to include an f parameter in the reception function of the change model.

Coefficients from the application of Equation 7.7 to the data on defense spending are shown in the left column of Table 7.3. The dependent variable is a 0–1 variable that distinguishes those who support cuts in defense spending from all others, including those who make no-opinion responses.[17] To facilitate

17 This scoring of the dependent variable has advantages and disadvantages. The obvious disadvantage is that it throws away information from the original seven-point scales by making everyone either a zero or a one. This poses an efficiency problem. But on the other hand, to keep information from the seven-point scale, I would have to discard no-opinion respondents as missing data. No-opinion respondents, whose typically low political awareness scores indicate they have failed to receive any information that would enable them to have an opinion, help to define the effect of awareness on reception. Hence to discard them would introduce bias. A second advantage of 0–1 scoring is that it enables me to retain the natural metric of "percent supporting" a given position, which adds to the intelligibility of the results (note the relationship of Figure 7.4 to Figure 8.2). I return to this issue in Chapter 11.

Table 7.3. *Coefficients for opinion change on defense spending*

	No constraints	One constraint	With interaction
Baseline reception function			
Intercept (a_0)	–4.18	–3.51	–4.29
Awareness (a_1)	1.24	0.96	1.35
(standardized)	(.82)	(.66)	(.85)
Floor parameter (f)	0.10	0.10	0.10
	(.03)	(.03)	(.02)
Baseline acceptance function			
Intercept (b_0)	6.56	1.96	6.25
Awareness (b_1)	–0.59	–0.41	–2.31
	(0.49)	(.40)	(2.63)
Party attachment (b_2)	6.12	2.03[a]	5.81
	(6.96)	(.46)	(5.06)
Party x Awareness	–	–	–1.65
			(2.52)
Change reception function			
Intercept (a_0)	–1.07	–1.16	–1.13
Awareness (a_1)	1.03	0.91	0.97
	(.19)	(.14)	(.16)
Change acceptance function			
Intercept (b_0)	2.37	3.70	3.80
Awareness (b_1)	–1.39	–1.65	–2.08
	(0.53)	(.64)	(1.02)
Party attachment (b_2)	1.23	2.03[a]	2.26
	(.37)	(.46)	(1.07)
Party × Awareness	–	–	–0.52
			(0.57)
Residual sum of squares	538.23	538.97	537.94

Note: Model is Equation 7.7, estimated by maximum likelihood. The dependent variable is a 0–1 variable distinguishing support for defense cuts from all other responses, including no opinion. Party is scored in Democratic direction. See chapter appendix for details of estimation. Standard errors are in parentheses. The Time$_1$ N is 1602; Time$_2$ N is 1402.
[a] Coefficients constrained to be equal.
Source: 1980 and 1982 NES surveys.

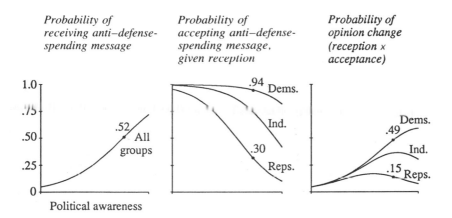

Figure 7.4. Estimated effects of reception and acceptance on changing support for defense spending. Estimates are derived from the change function in Equation 7.7 and the coefficients for the unconstrained model in Table 7.3. *Source:* 1980 and 1982 NES surveys.

replication of these results, I include in the appendix to this chapter the SAS program code used to produce them.

The coefficients in Table 7.3 all have good magnitudes, as can be seen by comparing them to the coefficients used to produce Figure 7.2, and signs that run in the theoretically expected directions. However, there is a great deal of statistical imprecision in the coefficients in the acceptance function of the baseline model. The reason for the imprecision in this subfunction appears to be that there is little variance in support for cuts in defense spending in 1980, as can be seen in Table 7.1. To reduce this imprecision, I constrained the value of the most unstable coefficient, that of party, to be equal in both the baseline and change models. This resulted in a more stable set of estimates, as shown in the center column of Table 7.3. The constraint did bring about a statistically significant reduction in the statistical fit of the model to the data (F (1, 2,993), 4.12, $p < .05$), but did not affect the visual or qualitative fit of the model to the raw data, as shown earlier in Table 7.1.

The right-hand column of Table 7.3 shows the coefficients that are obtained when Awareness × Party terms are put into the model. The inclusion of these terms did not significantly improve the statistical fit of the model, and I present them only to satisfy the interest of readers who might wonder about the effect of interaction terms on the performance of the model.

There is little more to be learned about the dynamics of attitude change from simple visual inspection of the coefficients from the model. I have, therefore, used the coefficients, in conjunction with Equation 7.7, to construct graphical representations of the implied effects of these coefficients. These graphs, based on coefficients from the unconstrained model and using the graphing conventions set forth in Chapter 6, are shown in Figure 7.4.

Figure 7.4 decomposes the attitude change process into its components: reception, acceptance, and attitude change. In the left-hand panel, the figure shows estimated rates of reception of anti–defense-spending messages between 1980 and 1982. These estimates have been obtained by plugging the reception coefficients from the change model in Table 7.3 into the reception function, Equation 7.3, and calculating reception rates at different levels of political awareness. As expected, reception of anti–defense-spending information increases as political awareness increases.[18]

Acceptance rates, given reception, are shown in the center panels of the figure. They have been obtained by plugging the acceptance coefficients from Table 7.3 into the acceptance function, as given in Equation 7.4. As can be seen, these rates differ markedly for Republicans and Democrats. Among Republicans, political awareness generates much lower rates of acceptance of antidefense information – or alternatively, much higher levels of resistance; among Democrats, awareness also produces higher resistance rates, but only barely so. Thus, as expected, awareness interacts with political predispositions to generate selective resistance to persuasion.

Multiplication of the reception rates on the left of Figure 7.4 by the acceptance rates in the center yields estimated rates of attitude change on cuts in defense spending, which are shown on the right. To illustrate how this works, the figure focuses on a hypothetical Republican and Democrat who are somewhat above the median level of political awareness. Each has a 52 percent chance of exposure to antidefense information, but their acceptance rates are quite different: 30 percent for the Republican and 94 percent for the Democrat. Multiplication of these reception and acceptance rates yields attitude change rates, as shown on the right. For the Republican, the change rate is $.52 \times .30 = .15$. These estimated rates of attitude change agree well with the raw data on attitude change, as shown in Table 7.1.

Let us turn now to the issue of U.S. involvement in Central America. Coefficient estimates for the application of Equation 7.7 to the data from this issue are shown in Table 7.4. Owing to the much smaller sample involved, these estimates are even less precise than those for the defense spending issue, and here the instability extends to both the baseline and change models. Of the six substantive coefficients, only two reach statistical significance. In order to improve the statistical precision of the fit, I constrained the coefficients on political awareness to be the same in both the baseline and change models. That is, awareness was constrained to have the same effect on reception in both periods and the same effect on acceptance in both periods. These constraints brought the theoretically important coefficients of awareness to statistical significance at the .05 level, as can be seen in Table 7.4, and did so without producing a significant reduction in the fit of the model to the data (F [2, 707], .43, n.s.). Also, the qualitative fit of the constrained model to the data is as good as the fit of the unconstrained model.

18 The z-scores on the awareness variable in this graph run from -1.86 to $+1.96$; these scores correspond to about the 1st and 98th percentiles on political awareness.

Table 7.4. *Coefficients for opinion change on U.S. involvement in Central America*

	No constraints	Two constraints
Baseline reception function		
Intercept	-1.15	-1.77
Awareness	2.52	2.13[a]
(standardized)	(1.69)	(1.20)
Floor parameter	0.37	0.35
	(.17)	(.16)
Baseline acceptance function		
Intercept	-0.33	-0.19
Awareness	-0.76	-0.80[a]
	(.42)	(.37)
Hawk–dove	-1.38	-1.42
(standardized)	(.43)	(.46)
Reagan fall disapproval	-0.30	-0.33
(range -2 to +2)	(.19)	(.20)
Change reception function		
Intercept	-1.40	-0.60
Awareness	1.17	2.13[a]
	(1.16)	(1.20)
Change acceptance function		
Intercept	1.50	-0.10
Awareness	-1.39	-0.80[a]
	(1.56)	(.37)
Hawk–dove	-0.66	-0.52
	(.93)	(.47)
Reagan disapproval	-0.29	-0.14
	(.47)	(.28)
Residual sum of squares	155.99	156.18

Note: Model is Equation 7.7, estimated by maximum likelihood. The dependent variable is a 0–1 variable indicating support for greater involvement in Central America. Other political variables are scored in liberal direction. Standard errors are in parentheses. The $\text{Time}_1 N$ and $\text{Time}_2 N$ are 360.

[a] Coefficient constrained to equal another coefficient.

Source: 1986 and 1987 NES surveys.

It is interesting that hawk–dove attitudes appear about four times more important as a determinant of Central America attitudes than approval of presidential job performance.[19] (Since the hawk–dove scale has been standardized and the approval measure runs from -2 to $+2$, the two variables have approximately the

19 Hawk–dove attitudes remain dominant if party attachment is substituted for Reagan approval.

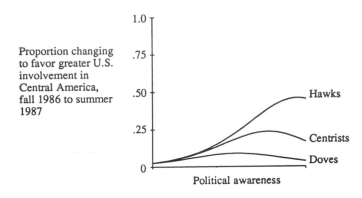

Figure 7.5. Attitude change on U.S. involvement in Central America. Estimates are derived from the change function in Equation 7.7 and the coefficients for unconstrained model in Table 7.4. *Source:* 1986 and 1987 NES surveys.

same range.) Thus, it was not Reagan supporters per se who mainly rallied behind U.S. involvement in Central America during the Iran–Contra controversy; it was people having hawkish values. (For additional discussion of this issue, see the appendix to Chapter 8.)

The estimated patterns of attitude change in the Central America case are shown in Figure 7.5.[20] These patterns, which are derived from the change model in Table 7.4, are highly similar to those for the defense-spending issue. The only important difference is that, for the Central America issue, it is the left-wing group that is resistant to change, whereas in the defense case, the right-wing group is more resistant. Thus, together, the defense and Central America cases show that the model works as well when opinion swings to the right as when it swings to the left.

In order to be certain the reader understands what is and is not being shown in Figure 7.5, I present Figure 7.6, which displays the Central America data from a different viewpoint. Rather than show *rates of change* between two points in time, as in Figure 7.5, it shows absolute *levels of support* in each period. Thus, 79 percent of the most aware hawks supported greater U.S. involvement in the fall, while 89 percent did so in the summer. This absolute difference of 10 points ($89 - 79 = 10$) amounts to a conversion rate of about 50 percent for highly aware hawks not already supporting greater U.S. involvement in the fall ($10/[100 - 79] = 10/21 = 48$ percent). Meanwhile, there is an 11-point shift among hawks scoring just below the median on political awareness ($46 - 35 = 11$). This 11-point shift represents the conversion of only 17 percent

20 The z-score values for awareness in this graph are -1.87 and $+1.92$ SD. The higher awareness score leaves about 2 percent of cases, rather than the usual 1 percent, in the upper tail; this cutoff has been used because it more accurately represents the actual data. Hawks and doves are defined as scores of ± 2 on the hawk–dove scale and ± 1.5 on Reagan disapproval, which has been scored from -2 to $+2$.

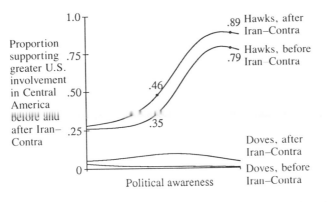

Figure 7.6. Estimated support for greater U.S. involvement in Central America before and after Iran–Contra. Estimates are derived from Equation 7.7 and the coefficients for unconstrained model in Table 7.4. *Source:* 1986 and 1987 NES surveys.

(11/[100 − 35] = 17 percent) of hawks at this level of political awareness. These conversion rates are what I have plotted in Figure 7.5. The reception-acceptance model, thus, does not deal in the *absolute magnitudes* of opinion change within subgroups; it deals in conversion *rates* among the unconverted members of particular groups. The difference is great.

Figure 7.6 makes another important point. It might seem odd that the Iran–Contra controversy produced attitude change in a proinvolvement direction. Yet if it were instead asserted that Iran–Contra further polarized public attitudes about U.S. involvement in Central America, the assertion would not seem odd at all. What Figure 7.6 also shows is that a critical effect of the controversy was, in fact, to further polarize hawks and doves. If polarization produced greater overall support for the proinvolvement position, it was because the public was, at the beginning of the Iran–Contra affair, so one-sidedly opposed to U.S. involvement in Central America that polarization entailed gains in support for the pro-involvement position.

Before closing the chapter, I should note that the wide confidence intervals for coefficients of the unconstrained model are worrisome, and that I discuss this problem in my concluding evaluation of the model in Chapter 11. In the meantime, let me say briefly that there appear to be two reasons for the problem. They are multicollinearity arising from the fact that awareness must be entered in the model four times (in the reception and acceptance subfunctions of both the baseline and change models), and the dependence of some coefficients on a small subgroup of respondents, namely people who both rank high on political awareness and appear predisposed to resist a given message. Although neither of these problems is a problem with the model itself, they make testing the model difficult. Some steps to maximize the efficiency of future tests are also discussed in Chapter 11.

CONCLUDING REMARKS

This chapter has developed some basic principles of attitude change, proposed a simplified model that is broadly consistent with these principles, and undertaken simple tests of the models. The most important of the points made in this chapter is that attitude change may be understood as a two-step process involving, first, reception of persuasive communications and, second, acceptance or nonacceptance of their contents.

The reception step in this process depends on the individual's level of political awareness: The greater the person's awareness, the greater his or her chances of receiving – that is, being exposed to and comprehending – a given change-inducing message.

The acceptance step is more complicated, but the central idea is that politically aware persons are better able to resist persuasive communications that are inconsistent with their basic values than are less aware persons. The magnitude of the awareness-induced resistance effect depends on the value distance of the individual from the persuasive communication. When the distance is minimal, awareness may have little or no effect in inducing resistance to change, as in the case of Democrats responding to the anti–defense spending message in Figure 7.4. But when the distance is great, awareness is strongly associated with resistance to change, as in the case of Republicans responding to the same liberal message in Figure 7.4.

Later chapters will fill out this argument in several ways. One important step that remains to be taken is an examination of the effects of messages of different intensities. As McGuire's analysis of easy-learning and hard-learning situations indicates, the expected pattern of mass attitude change is markedly different when the persuasive message saturates, or nearly saturates, a population, than when the message has so little intensity that it can reach only the most politically aware members of the group.

Another complexity concerns the novelty or freshness of the issue that the persuasive message addresses. If the issue is an extremely familiar one, most citizens will have relatively large stores of existing considerations, and this will produce high overall levels of inertial resistance to the message. Such resistance will not only lessen the aggregate *amount* of attitude change that occurs in response to a message of given intensity, but also alter the *pattern* of change.

Yet another task that remains is to develop evidence that the dynamics of the attitude change model hold at the level of the most basic element of the RAS model, the formation of considerations in response to persuasive communications. I have made specific claims concerning the role of considerations in the change process but have yet to produce direct evidence that the claims are valid.

Finally, the model proposed in this chapter assumes that attitude change results from the exposure of the public to a single, dominant flow of communications. This, as I have made clear, is a major simplification. Indeed, in the case of U.S. involvement in Central America, where proinvolvement change took place amid the Iran–Contra scandal, the simplification is so extreme as to be entirely implausible. The assumption of a one-sided information flow is less extreme in the case of defense spending, where, as I was able to report, the flow of information in the media predominantly favored cuts in defense spending. But even here, the public was exposed to some countervalent information from the Reagan administration, which sought to justify its policy of increased spending. Taking full account of the existence of such two-sided information flows is perhaps the most interesting complication to be added to this intitial discussion of attitude change.

APPENDIX

This appendix explains how to obtain maximum likelihood (M L) estimates of Equation 7.7.

Equation 7.7 takes the general form

$$\text{Prob}(y = 1) = f(X, \beta).$$

where y is a 0–1 dependent variable, X is a vector of independent variables, and β is a coefficient vector. The first step is to write out the likelihood function, as follows:

$$L = \Pi\, D1 * f(X, \beta) \times \Pi\, D2 * (1 - f(X, \beta))$$

where $D1$ takes the value of 1 if $y = 1$ and zero otherwise, and $D2$ takes the value of 1 when $y = 0$ and 0 otherwise. The log of the likelihood function is then

$$\text{Log}(L) = \sum D1 * \log[f(X, \beta)] + \sum D2 * \log[1 - f(X, \beta)]$$

The aim is to maximize the value of $\text{Log}(L)$. Because the log of a number between 0 and 1 is negative, and because $0 < f(X, \beta) < 1$ since it gives probabilities, this expression can be rewritten as

$$-\text{Log}(L) = \left(\sqrt{-\sum D1 * \log[f(X, \beta)] - \sum D2 * \log[1 - f(X, \beta)]}\,\right)^2$$

Because nonlinear regression will find the coefficient values of a right-hand expression that minimize the sum of *squared* residuals from a left-hand variable, one can find the values of B that minimize the *nonsquared* value of $-\text{Log}(L)$ – which is the same as maximizing the nonsquared value of $\text{Log}(L)$ – if one uses nonlinear regression to estimate

$$0 = \sqrt{-D1 * \log[f(X, \beta)] - D2 * \log[1 - f(X, \beta)]} \qquad (7.8)$$

This algorithm for producing maximum likelihood estimates, which has wide utility but has not been previously published, was suggested by Doug Rivers of Stanford University.

In order to apply Equation 7.8 to data on attitude change between two time periods for a case in which $f(X, \beta)$ equals Equation 7.7, it is necessary to combine the data from the two periods into a single stacked data file, with a 0–1 dummy variable to indicate which data are from time$_1$ and which are from time$_2$. The following SAS program language can then be used to produce ML estimates from such a data file. This example involves the case of changes in attitudes toward defense spending between 1980 and 1982, where the value of 1 on DEFSPN indicates support for cuts in spending, and the value of 1 on YEAR indicates attitudes in 1982:

```
DATA;
INFILE MYDATA;
INPUT   AWARE 1-11   DEFSPN 12-19   PID 20-27   YEAR 28-35;
IF DEFSPN EQ 1 THEN D1=1;
IF DEFSPN EQ 0 THEN D1=0;
IF DEFSPN EQ 0 THEN D2=1;
IF DEFSPN EQ 1 THEN D2=0;
VAR1=0;
PROC NLIN METHOD=DUD;
PARMS   B99=.10   B0=-3.9   B1=1.2   B2=4   B3=-.6   B4=4
B10=-1.1   B11=1   B21=2.4   B31=-1.4   B44=1.2;
T1   =   (1-(1/(1+B99+EXP(B0+B1*AWARE))))*
(1/(1+EXP(-B2-B3*AWARE-B4*PID)));
T2   =   (1-(1/(1+EXP(B10+B11*AWARE))))*
(1/(1+EXP(-B21-B31*AWARE-B44*PID)))*
P1   =   T1+YEAR*T2*(1-T1);
MODEL VAR1   =   (-D1*LOG10(P1) -D2*LOG10(1-P1))**.5;
```

It is also possible to use nonlinear regression to estimate the simpler expression: MODEL DEFSPN = P1

This will give estimates that are unbiased and consistent but inefficient; also, the standard errors will be incorrect, owing to heteroskedasticity arising from a 0–1 dependent variable.[21]

21 The only difficulty in implementing this estimation technique is the selection of good starting values for parameters in the model. In small datasets, this can be a serious problem, since nonsensical estimates will be generated unless the starting values for most parameters are reasonably close to actual values. My approach to finding starting values is as follows: First, confirm by visual inspection of the raw data, as organized in the manner of Table 7.1, that there is reason to believe that the reception–acceptance model will apply. That is, confirm the existence of clear nonmonotonicities in the data; if the appropriate patterns are not apparent, further modeling is unlikely to be helpful. Second, eliminate all but the essential variables from the model; in most cases, this will mean using only awareness in the reception function, and only awareness and one predispositions variable in the acceptance function. Third, fix the parameter values for these three variables to plausible values; if all three have been standardized and if the predispositions variable has been scored so that high values indicate resistance to change, plausible values are +1, −1, and −.4, respectively. Then, using starting values of 0 for the intercepts in the reception and acceptance functions, estimate the baseline function for data from the initial time period alone. Once intercept estimates for the baseline model have been obtained, they can be used as starting values. As constraints are serially loosened, remaining pieces of the model are put back and additional variables are added.
     An alternative approach is to use a spreadsheet to manually fit the model to the data by choosing appropriate parameter values, where the data have been organized in the form of Table 7.1. I suspect that many researchers wanting to use the reception–acceptance model will need to learn to manipulate it on a spreadsheet before they are able to use a statistics package to fit it to data.

8

Tests of the one-message model

The purpose of Chapter 7 was to familiarize the reader with the basic logic of the reception-acceptance process and to develop a model capable of capturing the essentials of the process as it manifests itself in the limited attitude change data that are available in typical surveys. The present chapter develops and tests the model's deductive implications, including some nonintuitive ones. The aim is to convince the reader that the success of the model in its initial tests was not merely fortuitous but arises from a significant congruence between its structure and the actual dynamics of mass opinion.

The chapter has three parts. The first analyzes two message-level determinants of attitude change: the intensity of the change-inducing messages, and whether the messages deal with a familiar or unfamiliar issue. These factors create predictably different patterns of opinion change. The second part examines the dynamics of resistance to persuasion at the level of the RAS model's primitive term, considerations. Finally, the chapter uses the model to shed light on a classic problem of opinion research, generational differences in receptivity to new ideas.

I should warn that, in the course of developing these diverse tests of the reception-acceptance model, the chapter skips from one empirical example to another – from public support for foreign wars to presidential approval ratings to racial attitudes – without developing a comprehensive picture of opinion in any single domain. This makes the chapter a bit of a hodgepodge to read, but I see no alternative if I am to exploit fully the limited data that are available to test the model.

CHARACTERISTIC PATTERNS OF ATTITUDE CHANGE

The analysis of attitude change has so far concentrated on how two types of *individual-level* factors, differences in habitual political awareness and in political predispositions, interactively affect attitude change. This section will bring into play two *message-level* factors that also systematically affect patterns of attitude change.

The first of the message-level differences is the penetrating power or *intensity* of change-inducing messages. The idea here is that some messages have greater capacity than others to transfuse a public that is differentially attentive to politics. A few messages have such great penetrating power that they reach virtually everyone, regardless of their level of attention to politics. Communications concerning the U.S. policy of opposing Germany and Japan in World War II are an example of such very high-intensity messages (Cantril, 1944). But many messages reach only persons who are relatively attentive to politics. Most congressional actions, Supreme Court decisions, and presidential directives, even those that make the front pages of newspapers and arouse some controversy, fall into this category, as we shall see.

One might suspect that the capacity of a message to penetrate the consciousness of members of the public, which is what I mean by intensity, is wholly a function of the amount of broadcast time or front-page space that the news media devote to it. There is, however, a factor that is at least as important: how much people already know and care about the issue that the message addresses. The greater their concern and initial knowledge, the more likely they are to notice and comprehend additional information that comes their way.

This can be seen from the 1989 NES pilot study, which measured the diffusion of particular news stories through the public. The following three news stories broke just before or during the pilot survey:

> Lieutenant Colonel Oliver North was given a suspended sentence, a fine, and 1,200 hours of community service for his conviction of crimes in connection with the Iran–Contra controversy. North's sentencing was a highly discrete event that was the lead story on the national television news and in most newspapers for one day.

> Speaker Jim Wright resigned his speakership and left the House of Representatives amid allegations of scandal. Wright's resignation was the final act in a long drawn-out political controversy that was at or near the top of the news for several months.

> The U.S. Supreme Court ruled that juveniles and mentally retarded persons could be executed for the crime of murder. Like North's sentencing, this was a discrete event that was at the top of the national news for a short time and then disappeared from view.

In the survey, respondents were questioned to find out what, if anything, they had learned about these news messages. For example, on the Wright story, people were asked:

Have you heard or read any stories on the resignation of Congressman Jim Wright from the House of Representatives?

(IF YES) Do you happen to recall why he resigned?

Persons who could give a minimally correct answer to the follow-up question – for example, any mention, however vague, of scandal or accusations of wrongdoing – were counted as having "received" the story of the Wright resignation. From such data, it can be estimated that approximately 75 percent of the public learned of North's sentence, about 45 percent became aware of the Wright affair, and 25 percent heard of the Supreme Court's death penalty decision (Price and Zaller, 1990).

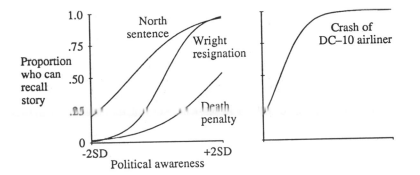

Figure 8.1. Diffusion of political news. Estimates are derived from Equation 7.3 and the coefficients in Table 8.6. *Source:* 1989 NES pilot survey.

The only way to explain these data is to assume that the penetrating power of a message may be as much a property of the audience that does or does not find it interesting as it is of the amount of media coverage devoted to it. Thus, the story of Oliver North's sentencing achieved wider recognition in one day than the Wright scandal achieved in several months. Similarly, when former President Ronald Reagan fell off his horse while vacationing in Mexico, more people learned about it than learned the reason for the Wright resignation, even though the horse incident occurred on a Saturday and received minimal coverage in lightly watched weekend news shows.[1] Thus, when I refer to the intensity of a message, the reader should keep in mind that I am making a statement about both the message itself and the audience that does or does not become interested in it.[2]

The diffusion patterns of these differently intense news stories are worth examining more carefully because, unlike the cases of attitude change we have examined, they enable us to measure reception of particular messages independently of whether the messages brought about attitude change. Thus, we can see very clearly just how different pieces of information diffuse through the public.

Data on the diffusion of the North, Wright, and death penalty stories are shown in Figure 8.1. There is, as expected, a strong relationship between people's habitual levels of political awareness and their reception of particular news stories. Some members of the public (those who score high on habitual political awareness) learn about virtually all important political news, while others learn about almost none of it.[3] (The curves in Figure 8.1 are derived from logistic

1 More complex stories may also have less penetrating power than simple stories. However, it seems to me that the stories mentioned here are all fairly simple, and that differences in people's interest in them are therefore the key to the observed differences in penetrating power.
2 In principle, one could obtain separate measures of intensity of coverage of an issue and the public's familiarity with it, but such data are not available for the present study.
3 Compare these results with those of Tichenor, Donohue, and Olien (1970).

regressions of the form of Equation 7.3; the associated coefficient estimates are shown in Table 8.6 in the appendix to this chapter.)

The righthand panel of Figure 8.1 contains comparison data on the diffusion of a nonpolitical story, the crash of a DC-10 airliner while trying to make an emergency landing. The disaster, which killed more than 100 persons, was captured on videotape and shown repeatedly on television for several days. It was prominently featured in all the nation's political media – local and national TV news, the newsweeklies, radio, and press. In view of the amount of this coverage, the intrinsic interest of the story, the vividness of the accompanying television and still pictures, and the simplicity of the plotline, it is striking that a large number of people nonetheless remained unaware of its existence. These must be persons either who were entirely cut off from the news media or who manage to remember almost nothing of what they encounter in the media.

The diffusion patterns for the four differently intense news stories in Figure 8.1 have the utmost importance for the study of attitude change. The attitude change curves we saw in the last chapter take markedly different shapes, depending on whether they involve a story that has the penetrating power of the DC-10 crash, the North sentencing, or the Supreme Court's death penalty decision.

If messages can vary in their intensity, they can also vary in the extent to which they address issues on which the public has a large store of existing considerations. This is the second message-level variable that systematically affects patterns of attitude change. According to our earlier discussion of inertial resistance, large stores of preexisting considerations act to dilute the effects of any new message. For this reason, messages addressing issues that are, in this particular sense, familiar to the public are likely to produce less attitude change, all else equal, than messages that address novel or unfamiliar topics.[4] They also affect the expected patterns of change, as depicted in attitude change curves of the type examined in Chapter 7.

The attitude change model embodied in Equation 7.5, repeated below, has been designed to capture these two message-level variables:

$$\text{Prob(Change)} = (1 - (1 + f + \text{Exp}[+a_0 + a_1\text{Awareness}])^{-1})$$
$$\times (1 + \text{Exp}[-b_0 - b_1\text{Awareness}$$
$$- b_2\text{Predispositions}])^{-1} \qquad (7.5)$$

Differences in message intensity are captured by the a_0 parameter in the reception function; higher values of a_0 indicate that people at the same level of political awareness will have higher levels of reception of the given message, all else equal. (Compare the middle panel of Figure 7.2 with Figure 8.1.) Differences in message familiarity, which affect acceptance rates, are captured by the b_0 coefficient in the acceptance function; lower levels of b_0 indicate lower levels of acceptance, at given levels of reception of persuasive messages.

4 Note that message intensity, as discussed here, and message familiarity are not entirely independent, since both depend on the public's prior level of information about the topic of the message.

Because the reception-acceptance model is highly interactive – because, that is, the effect of one variable depends on the values of all other variables – the effects of shifts in a_0 and b_0 ramify throughout the model. In order to illustrate their effects, I have constructed a typology, shown as Figure 8.2, to illustrate characteristic patterns of attitude change. The typology has been constructed from Equation 7.5 by using typical values for the parameters on individual-level variables (awareness and predispositions) while varying the message level parameters, a_0 and b_0, to capture typical differences in intensity and familiarity.[5] To facilitate exposition of the typology, I assume the diffusion of a liberal message through subpopulations that are liberal, centrist, and conservative in their predispositions, but other metrics of distance between message sources and message receivers, such as those associated with religion or ethnicity, would produce the same theoretically expected patterns.

Look first at the top panel of Figure 8.2. It shows expected patterns of attitude change on "less familiar" topics for messages of low, medium, and high intensity, where levels of message intensity roughly correspond to the intensity of stories on the Supreme Court's death penalty decision, the Wright resignation, and the DC-10 crash, as depicted in Figure 8.1.

When the change-inducing message has low intensity, as in panel A, attitude change is concentrated among the most highly aware persons. This is because highly aware persons are the only ones who meet the first requirement for attitude change: reception of a relevant message. But as the change-inducing message becomes more intense, as in panel B and especially C, attitude change becomes common among moderately aware and finally modestly aware persons. One can see from these graphs that, in general, *the lower the intensity of the message, the smaller the proportion of attitude change that occurs among less-aware persons.* Conversely, the higher the intensity of the message, the higher the proportion of attitude change that occurs among less-aware persons.

Note that the patterns of attitude change on the issue of U.S. involvement in Central America, as depicted in Figure 7.5 of the last chapter, roughly correspond to the pattern in panel B of this figure. This correspondence will be a critical element in tests of the validity of the typology later in this section.

The lower panel of Figure 8.2 uses the same parameter values as in the top panel, except that the b_0 coefficient has been set higher to indicate attitude change on a "more familiar" topic. The increase in issue familiarity has two effects on attitude change. The first is that, as would be expected, messages on more familiar subjects produce less overall attitude change. Second and more subtly, *a higher proportion of the attitude change on more familiar issues (compared to less familiar issues) is concentrated among less-aware persons.* This

5 The values used in constructing the typology are $a_1 = 1.25$ and $b_1 = -1.25$; a_0 for low-, middle-, and high-intensity messages are -2.5, 0, 2.5, respectively; b_0 for low-familiarity and high-familiarity messages are $+3$ and 0, respectively; liberal, centrist, and conservative persons had additional resistance effects of $+1.5$, 0, and -1.5, respectively. The f parameter is 0. In constructing the simulated change scores, awareness runs from -2 to $+2$. These values, when substituted into Equation 7.5, will precisely reproduce the curves shown in Figure 8.2.

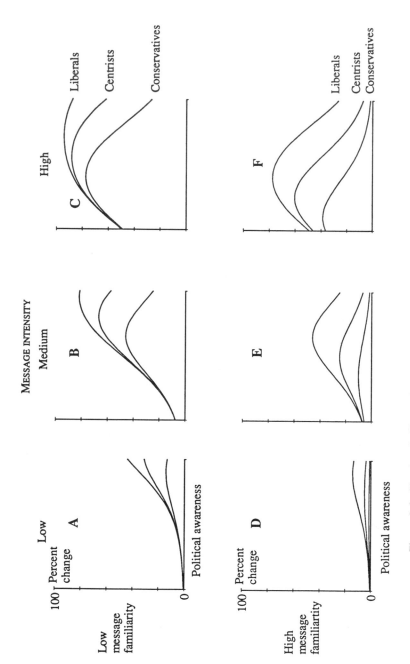

Figure 8.2. Simulated effects of message intensity and familiarity on opinion change.

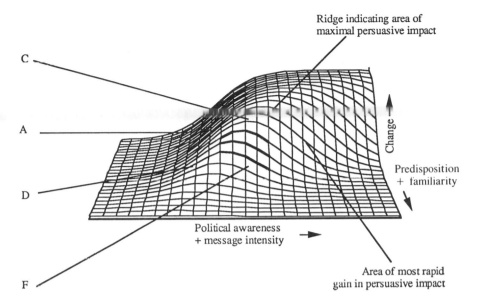

Figure 8.3. Simulated effects of message intensity and familiarity on opinion change (three dimensional).

can be seen by noting the peak level of change on each curve and comparing it with its vertical counterpart; the peaks are more toward the low-awareness end of the spectrum in the bottom panels.[6]

Obviously, the curves depicted in Figure 8.2 do not exhaust the patterns of attitude change that might be generated by Equation 7.5 and observed in actual data. In particular, one might encounter messages that are even more intense than those depicted here, in which case the change rates among the least aware persons in panels C and F of Figure 8.2 would be even higher. Alternatively, one might encounter issues that are even less familiar than those examined in the figure, in which case there would be even larger amounts of attitude change, especially among highly aware persons. The important point about Figure 8.2, then, is not that it tells us exactly what to expect in every possible situation, but that it gives us a basis for projecting how, in a general way, changes in message intensity and issue familiarity interact with each other and with individual-level factors in the attitude-change process.

Since, as this discussion indicates, the particular attitude-change curves derived from the model depend on the particular parameter values used to construct them, I wanted to make sure that the typology is not overly dependent on the particular parameter values I chose. Accordingly, I constructed Figure 8.3, which generalizes Figure 8.2 to three dimensions and, in the process of doing so, shows the joint effects of message intensity and issue familiarity across a much

6 Given that awareness has both reception and acceptance effects.

wider range of parameter values. (As a visual aid to interpretation, the regions of Figure 8.3 that correspond to the different cells of Figure 8.2 are labeled accordingly.) I found that three-dimensional representations of the model, of the type shown in Figure 8.3, retain the same general shape over all plausible values of a_0 and b_0,[7] provided that awareness remains positively associated with reception of change-inducing messages and negatively associated with acceptance to roughly the same degree. Figure 8.3, thus, depicts the general patterns of attitude change that can be expected if Equation 7.5 has accurately captured the dynamics of the attitude-change process.

The typologies of expected patterns of attitude change in Figures 8.2 and 8.3 create the potential for tests of the reception-acceptance model that are, by the standards of social science, rather demanding, as the next section will show.

The case of presidential popularity

Confirmation of the empirical value of the typology in Figure 8.2 requires independent measurement of the two message-level variables, intensity and familiarity. This is no easy task. With respect to intensity, the problem is that, as indicated, intensity involves more than the amount of media attention to an issue, which could by itself be fairly easily measured. Intensity, as used here, also involves the degree to which the public finds the subject an inherently interesting and engaging one. Although one might be able to capture this less tangible factor by measuring how much the public knows or cares about different issues, the data necessary for making such comparative measurements are currently unavailable.

With respect to issue familiarity, the measurement problem is essentially the same. It would be fairly easy to use surveys to gather data on what the public knows about different issues, and to use this as a measure of aggregate levels of issue familiarity. But, at the moment, such data are unavailable. Comparative rates of no opinion, as utilized in Bartels's 1988 analysis of voter knowledge of different candidates, might be a plausible indicator of aggregate levels of issue familiarity, except that different question formats raise different hurdles to the expression of no opinion on different issues.

Although rigorous measurements of intensity and familiarity are, for these reasons, impossible in the present study, informal but plausible comparative measurements can be made for at least some issues. My method will be to take the issue of U.S. involvement in Central America as a baseline case, and to judge other cases in relation to it. So let us begin with a close examination of this case.

U.S. involvement in the guerrilla wars of Central America was frequently enough in the news through 1986 and 1987 to indicate serious media attention. For example, both *Time* and *Newsweek* devoted cover stories to it during these

---

7 That is, a_0 and b_0 values between ± 10.

two years. Yet it is implausible to claim that this was an issue that really gripped the public mind. One indication of this is that the public's level of factual information on this issue, as gauged by direct tests of information, was notoriously low. For example, only 38 percent of Americans knew in 1986 that the United States was supporting the Contra guerillas and not the Nicaraguan government (Shipler, 1986).

As we saw earlier, attitude change on the Central America issue conformed to the pattern indicating a message of middle intensity and a lower level of issue familiarity (Figure 8.2b). Let us therefore stipulate the Central America case to have defined the standard for middle-intensity persuasive messages and low issue familiarity. To the extent that other cases differ from these standards, they will be classified as having more or less intensity, and more or less average familiarity within the public.

The first case to be examined in light of these standards is the decline in President Reagan's job performance rating over the course of the Iran–Contra controversy. In the period between late November 1986 and June 1987, Reagan's disapproval rating rose from 32 percent to 48 percent in response to charges that the president had known about the illegal diversion of government funds to the Contra guerrillas in Nicaragua. What can be said about message intensity and issue familiarity in this case?

In comparison to the intensity of messages concerning the Central America issue, messages on Reagan's job performance must be classified as more intense. First, with respect to the sheer amount of media attention, the Iran–Contra scandal was the major continuing news story in the United States for several months, which is a status that the Central America issue, by itself, never achieved. Second, with respect to public interest, President Reagan was in this period the country's leading political figure and the focal point of a large fraction of the news broadcast in the United States on a day-to-day basis (Grossman and Kumar, 1981; Iyengar and Kinder, 1987). It is therefore likely that his conduct of the presidency was a more interesting issue than a guerrilla war whose principal adversaries were not even widely known.

Americans would also be expected to have larger amounts of stored information about Reagan, who was then in his sixth year as president, than about affairs in Central America. If so, the issue of Reagan's job performance would have been a more familiar issue.

Given that the case of Reagan's job performance involved messages of higher intensity and higher familiarity, in the particular senses indicated, than messages on Central America, it follows that the pattern of attitude change on Reagan's job evaluation should differ from the Central America pattern in roughly the way that Figure 8.2b differs from Figure 8.2f.

The attitude change data necessary to evaluate this expectation are presented in Figure 8.4. These data show the probability of a change toward disapproval of President Reagan's job performance between November 1986 and June 1987, as captured in the regular NES postelection survey and the 1987 NES pilot study.

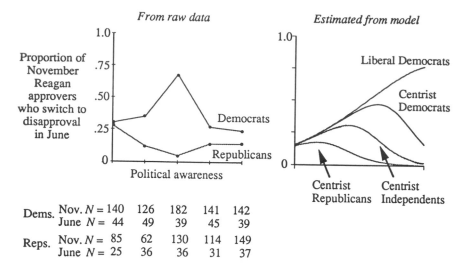

Figure 8.4. Opinion change on Reagan approval following Iran–Contra controversy. Estimated change rates are derived from Equation 7.7 and the coefficients in Table 8.5. *Source:* 1986 and 1987 NES surveys.

The change curves on the left have been calculated from raw data in the manner of Tables 7.1 and 7.2. As can be seen, the match between Figure 8.2f and the raw data is reasonable.

The change curves on the right have been estimated from the reception-acceptance model, as expressed in Equation 7.7. The model controls for party identification, egalitarianism, and attitudes toward U.S. involvement in Central America, as measured in the baseline survey. (The coefficients from which Figure 8.4 is derived, along with a discussion of their estimation, are contained in the appendix to this chapter.) When the effects of the two value measures are controlled – as in the three curves in Figure 8.4 for centrist Republicans, centrist Independents, and centrist Democrats – the patterns of attitude change closely resemble both the raw data and the theoretically derived patterns in cell F of the typology. (Centrist Democrats are defined as persons who have a mean party identification of 1.3 and who score at the population mean on egalitarianism and the hawk–dove scale.)

Yet when we examine the fourth curve in Figure 8.4, that of liberal Democrats,[8] the typology appears to fail. For in this case there is no evidence of nonmonotonicity. Moreover, there appears to be a conflict with the raw data on the left-hand side of Figure 8.4, which shows a strongly nonmonotonic pattern among Democrats. What is going on?

8 Liberal Democrats are defined as persons having a mean party identification of 1.3 and who score 1 SD above average on egalitarianism and dovishness. Political awareness in Figure 8.4 ranges from −1.87 SD to +2 SD.

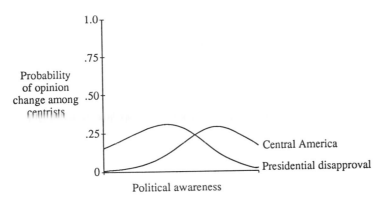

Figure 8.5. Patterns of opinion change among centrists on two issues. Estimates are transposed from Figures 7.5 and 8.4.

With respect to the apparent conflict with the raw data, there is a compositional problem. The raw data show patterns of attitude change *among Democrats who were capable of exhibiting attitude change in an anti-Reagan direction,* that is, among Democrats who did not already disapprove of Reagan's job performance in fall 1986. This group did not contain many liberal Democrats, since most liberal Democrats, especially those high on political awareness, already disapproved of Reagan's performance at that time. Thus, the simulated attitude change curve for liberal Democrats does not attempt to explain what was going on among the majority of Democrats in the fall who were available for conversion to an anti-Reagan position. The one for centrist Democrats does, and this curve generally agrees with the raw data.

But if the patterns of attitude change that occur at any point depend on the ideological composition of the group available for attitude change, can we still make a fair test of the typology?

Yes, provided we control for partisan composition. Figure 8.5 imposes such a control by comparing the attitude-change curves of centrists on the issues of presidential popularity and of Central America involvement, the defining instance of a medium-intensity and low-familiarity issue. With partisan composition controlled, we can see that – even though the total amount of attitude change is about the same on both issues – the anti-Reagan message was louder, since it was more successful in penetrating the lower awareness strata. We can also see that the anti-Reagan message was more familiar, since it encountered greater resistance among highly aware persons, as is expected for more familiar issues.

It is striking that, among the most politically aware centrists, the Iran–Contra controversy had virtually no effect on Reagan's approval rating. It is tempting to attribute this stouthearted resistance to the effects of ideology, but since we are dealing with centrists, this is hard to do. An alternative explanation is that we are seeing the effects of the inertial resistance that develops on familiar issues.

Six years into the Reagan presidency, these politically attentive centrists had already acquired so much information that the revelations of the Iran–Contra hearings made little additional impact. Rather, the scandal had its greatest impact on those whose initial information about Reagan, as judged by their overall levels of political awareness, was relatively modest.

Opinion formation on new issues

This section applies the reception-acceptance model to three additional cases; the formation of attitudes toward federal involvement in school desegregation in the mid–1950s, the formation of popular judgments on the performance of the national economy at the time the country appeared to be coming out of the recession of 1981–2, and the formation of attitudes toward a proposed freeze on nuclear weapon production in the early 1980s. Each of these cases has considerable intrinsic interest, but the main purpose in examining them is to provide further tests of the typology of characteristic patterns of attitude change as depicted in Figure 8.2.

Note, however, that the previous paragraph refers to cases of attitude *formation* rather than, as earlier, to attitude *change*. The reason is that here I am dealing with attitudes that were formed and measured early in the life of the given issue, at the point when the issue was just emerging on the national agenda and beginning to attract the attention of pollsters. In such situations, attitude change cannot be measured against a baseline of prior opinion because, at least in these cases, the issues were so new that there were no prior measurements and quite possibly no prior opinions. I will therefore assume that most of the opinion in favor of the new issue has been formed in response to recent communications, and, more importantly, that opinion has formed in accordance with the usual reception-acceptance process. I will assume, in other words, that *attitude formation* is a type of attitude change that depends on a two-step process in which political awareness is positively associated with reception of messages on the new issue, and in which acceptance of these messages depends on awareness and on political values.

Consider school desegregation in the 1950s. Until the Supreme Court's ruling on *Brown v. Board of Education* in 1954, the idea that the federal government should take the leading role in desegregating the public schools of the South was simply not a subject of salient public controversy. Neither of the two major parties had advocated it in its platforms, no major legislation on the subject had come close to passage in Congress, and no major politician was identified with it. School desegregation was still largely a "nonissue," in the sense of Bachrach and Baratz (1962). Hence, no polling agency attempted to measure public attitudes on the issue until the Supreme Court suddenly thrust school desegregation onto the national agenda.[9]

9 Page and Shapiro, in press: ch. 3.

In 1956 the Center for Political Studies at the University of Michigan posed the following agree–disagree question in a national survey:

The government in Washington should stay out of the question of whether white and colored children go to the same schools.

Given the novelty of this issue, one may reasonably conclude that most of the persons (except for blacks) who favored federally mandated school desegregation in this poll were fairly new adherents to this view.[10]

A parallel argument can be made for the other two issues to be examined here:

Nuclear freeze. The notion of a freeze on the production of nuclear weapons enjoyed a brief but intense vogue in the early 1980s. Television talk shows debated it, a spate of new books was devoted to it, and both houses of Congress passed resolutions favoring it. Although no national polling organization carried a question on this issue until its emergence as an issue in 1981, popular support for it was strong in all of the early polls on the subject. In the fall of 1982, the NES asked the following question:

Do you think the United States should freeze the production of nuclear weapons on its own, do so only if the Soviet Union agrees to a freeze as well, or do you think that the United States should not freeze production of nuclear weapons at all?

Support for a nuclear freeze, as captured by the first two options, could only have been new support, since the idea for a "freeze" on nuclear weapons production had been self-consciously invented by antiwar activists only a few months before the issue emerged in the national limelight (Pringle, 1982).

The economy. Through the first six months of 1982, the country was mired in the deepest recession since the Great Depression of the 1930s. By the fall, however, there began to be reports in the mass media that the economy was turning around and heading toward a period of expansion. These mainly took the form of news reports about various economic indicators and of prognostications by economic forecasters. In November and December of that year, the NES asked the following question:

Over the past year, has the economy gotten worse, stayed about the same, or improved?

Given the bleakness of the economy in the earlier months of 1982, such support as existed for the proposition that the economy was improving at the time of the fall survey may be considered new support for this view.

10 It is true, as Page and Shapiro (in press) point out, that American public opinion had been moving steadily leftward on race since at least the mid–1940s, presumably at least partly in response to other Supreme Court decisions on race, President Truman's efforts to achieve fair employment for blacks, and agitation by Hubert Humphrey and others within the Democratic Party. One might therefore take the sum of media reports of these activities as "the message" which, filtering through the reception-acceptance process, produced the degree of support for school desegregation that existed in 1956.

In order to test patterns of attitude formation on these topics against the typology in Figure 8.2, it is necessary to make rough judgments about the intensity and issue familiarity of each of these three issues.

To begin with issue intensity: The segregation and freeze issues seem, from my casual examination of the periodical literature of the 1950s and 1980s, to be typical instances of controversial issues. That is, they received significant press coverage, sometimes as the lead story of the day, but did not dominate the Washington community and political news for months at a time. They seemed, thus, to involve political communications of roughly middle intensity, much as in the case of U.S. policy in Central America. The news on the economy seems, by comparison, significantly less intense than coverage of the Central America issue. Most of it was carried as second-level news, worthy of a 30-second spot well back in the national evening news or a headline in the business pages, but never of major story status.

With respect to general familiarity, I would judge race to be, by far, the most familiar. This issue is, as many observers have noted (for example, Converse, 1964; Carmines and Stimson, 1982, 1989), one of the few political subjects on which Americans are likely to have well-crystallized opinions. The nuclear freeze issue, however, seems at the other pole of issue familiarity, a completely novel twist on a subject that is, however important, still a foreign policy issue that is relatively remote from most people's lives.

The familiarity of news on the economy is, by my lights, the most difficult to evaluate. On the one hand, the performance of the economy is something that touches everyone's lives and is, in this sense, highly familiar; but on the other hand, few people keep close tabs on technical indicators of economic performance, which means that any new information of this type would not encounter a large store of preexisting considerations.[11] In view of the difficulty of classifying economic news on issue familiarity, I will leave this classification open.

From the foregoing, we expect patterns of attitude formation on the freeze to resemble cell B of the typology (middle intensity and low familiarity) and the segregation issue to resemble cell E (middle intensity and high familiarity). Patterns of economic judgment should resemble one of the low-message-intensity cells (a or d).

The attitude curves necessary for evaluating these expectations are reported in Figure 8.6. These curves have been derived from a straightforward application of Equation 7.5 to data on each of the three issues (coefficients for these applications may be found in Table 8.7 in the appendix to this chapter). As can be seen, the fit with theoretical expectations is reasonable.[12]

Note that for the two liberal issues, the freeze and school desegregation, there is, as we would expect, a positive relationship between awareness and support

11 For example, only about 15 percent of respondents to the 1985 NES pilot study were able to identify Paul Volker as chairman of the Federal Reserve.
12 Awareness runs from -2.54 to $+1.35$ for the school issue and -1.86 to $+1.96$ for the other two. To achieve equivalence across cases, scores on the two scales in the school case have been set at $-.85$ and $+.85$; for the other two issues, scores on the solo scales range ± 1.5. Ranges for the party and approval variables are ± 1.3. Age is set at 45.

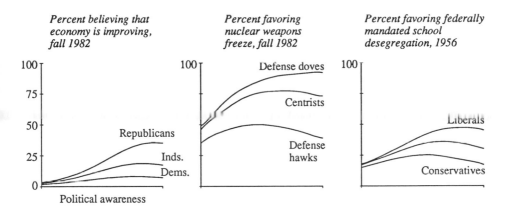

Figure 8.6. Estimated patterns of opinion change on three new issues. Estimates are derived from Equation 7.5 and coefficients in Table 8.7. *Source:* 1982 NES survey and 1956–58–60 CPS survey.

for the new idea among liberals, and that this same relationship is nonmonotonic among conservatives. With respect to the economy, where the news of the improving economy had a conservative valence (''Reaganomics is working''), these patterns reverse: There is a positive awareness relationship for conservatives and a nonmonotonic one for liberals.

Evaluating the attitude-change typology

Along with the results of the previous chapter, these data lend significant support to the reception-acceptance model and to expectations of characteristic patterns of attitude change derived from it. In particular, they lend support to these deductions from the model:

> The diffusion of a liberal message through a very liberal group, or a conservative message through a very conservative group, will produce a monotonic pattern of attitude change in which the most aware persons are most likely to change, at least in cases in which the issue is a relatively unfamiliar one.

> The diffusion of a moderately intense liberal message through a conservative group, or a moderately intense conservative message through a liberal group, will produce a nonmonotonic pattern of attitude change in which moderately aware persons are most likely to change.

> Low-intensity messages, as compared to high-intensity ones, will produce a higher proportion of change among highly aware persons, as in Figure 8.2.

> Attitude change on less familiar issues, as compared to more familiar issues, will more often occur among highly aware persons, as in Figure 8.2.

The evidence in support of the first two of these deductions seems quite strong, and more supporting evidence will be reported below. That is, there is presently a significant number of cases in which there exist monotonicities and nonmonotonicities in the expected places, and it seems likely that more such cases will accumulate in the future.

The complex series of deductions embodied in the typology of attitude change is less strongly supported, for two reasons: weak measurement of the key independent variables, intensity and familiarity; and a scarcity of cases that can, even by the weak measurement used here, be plausibly assigned to particular cells. Still, the available evidence is supportive: As expected, a low-intensity message (on the economy) produced a higher proportion of its change among highly aware persons than the more intense message (on Central America).[13] Also as expected, a larger proportion of change on the two more familiar issues (segregation and Reagan approval) occurred among moderately aware persons than occurred among these persons on less familiar issues. But confident confirmation that the typology holds, especially in connection with the putative effects of message familiarity, awaits stronger evidence.

Before leaving this topic, it is necessary to repeat an important caveat: Throughout this and the last chapter, I have sought to model the diffusion of a single message, that is, a message in which all communication favors one side of the issue. When, as often occurs, mass opinion changes in response to information flows that carry opposing messages – and especially when the opposing messages differ in intensity from each other and across time – the expected patterns of attitude change can be quite different.

As in the previous chapter, none of the cases examined meets the requirement of a strictly one-sided information flow. Satisfactory resolution of this problem awaits development of a "two-message model" of attitude change to replace the simple "one-message" model that I have been using so far. That will come in Chapter 9. In the meantime, it is apparent that the one-message model is robust to fairly substantial departures from its assumption of a strictly one-sided information flow, which means that it can be a useful theoretical tool in cases in which the data necessary for testing a more elaborate two-message model are unavailable.

MICROFOUNDATIONS OF RESISTANCE TO PERSUASION

A central feature of the reception-acceptance model is that greater political awareness is associated with greater resistance to ideas that are inconsistent with one's political values, and that the amount of added resistance due to awareness increases as value distance from the message increases. Although there can be little doubt, in light of the evidence already presented, that awareness has such resistance effects under at least some circumstances, the reasons for the resistance are yet to be made clear. Early in Chapter 7, three explanatory mechanisms were proposed:

---

13 The middle-intensity message on race also produced a higher proportion of its change among highly aware persons than the more intense message on presidential performance. However, a confounding factor here is that race is probably a more familiar issue than presidential performance; the effect of this difference is to reinforce rather than cross cut the effect of the intensity difference, which makes it difficult to be certain whether the apparent difference is due to intensity or familiarity or both.

More aware persons are more likely to possess and have available in memory the cueing messages that enable them to recognize messages that are inconsistent with their values.

More aware persons are likely to have larger stores of preexisting considerations on most issues. This "informational ballast" counteracts the effects of any new messages that might be accepted.

More aware persons are more likely to be exposed to relatively esoteric communications which run counter to the dominant message in the political environment. The acceptance of such countervalent communications counteracts the effects of any dominant messages that might also be internalized.

These three forms of resistance, each rooted in the RAS model, were described as partisan resistance, inertial resistance, and countervalent resistance, respectively. The aim of this section is to search for evidence of the empirical validity of the first two types of resistance. I will continue this effort in Chapters 9 and 10, where I will also provide evidence of countervalent resistance.

Preexisting considerations and inertial resistance

It would obviously be highly valuable to make direct observations of the stored considerations which, as the RAS model claims, are the basis of inertial resistance to persuasion. There is only one case of attitude change for which such observations are available: the decline in President Reagan's approval ratings over the course of the Iran–Contra controversy of 1986–7. As we saw earlier, Reagan suffered his greatest losses among persons of moderate political awareness. Highly aware persons, though more heavily exposed to the damaging news of Iran–Contra, were relatively resistant to change. So the question to be asked is: Is there evidence that the inertial effects of previously formed considerations contributed to the resistance of highly aware persons?

A measure of considerations affecting Reagan's job evaluations can be found in the June wave of the 1987 NES pilot study. Respondents were asked to rate Reagan's performance and then immediately afterward were asked the following open-ended question:[14]

Still thinking about the question you just answered, I'd like you to tell me what ideas came to mind as you were answering that question. Exactly what things went through your mind? (Up to three follow-up probes of "Any others?")

14 The Reagan approval item used here was included near the end of the survey as part of a priming experiment. That is, several items ahead of the approval item were a series of questions that made salient either favorable or unfavorable aspects of Reagan's job performance. The open-ended probes were included in order to directly assess the effects of the primes

The priming experiment failed in the sense that it failed to produce a shift in marginal approval rates for Reagan. However, half of the sample was primed with information concerning the Iran–Contra controversy, and these persons were slightly more likely to mention Iran–Contra in their open-ended remarks. Hence all persons from this half-sample have been eliminated from the analysis that follows.

Note that the approval item used to measure attitude change on presidential approval is a separate item that was carried early in the survey and hence was unaffected by the failed priming experiment.

The majority of remarks elicited by these probes could be comfortably accommodated within the standard NES candidate master codes (these are the codes used for classifying responses to questions asking for the respondents' likes and dislikes about the candidates in the regular NES surveys). However, some remarks concerning Reagan's job performance had never come up in connection with other candidates and hence required new codes. Three of these new codes seem to involve direct or indirect reference to the Iran–Contra scandal:

Uninformed; doesn't (seem to) know anything about the issues/what is going on in the country/government.

Doesn't work (hard) at job; not involved (enough) in the work of his office; delegates too much authority to others; has chosen poor/incompetent aides; his aides have not performed well.

(Involvement in) *Diversion of money* to the Contras (in violation of the law).[15]

Remarks falling into any of these new categories, plus direct references to attempts to free hostages (which were accommodated within an existing code), have been combined into a simple index that may be considered a rough indicator of the considerations relating to Iran–Contra that entered into people's calculations of Reagan's approval rating.

This index, it must be emphasized, is a very rough indicator. First, there are many things that people might have said about Reagan that were inspired by Iran–Contra (such as "He is dishonest") but that would not have been captured by these special codes. Second, some people, notably highly aware Democrats, may have had so many more important (to them) reasons for disapproving of Reagan that they failed to mention Iran–Contra even though it weighed in their minds as a negative consideration. Third, it is possible that people are unable to recall on a moment's notice all of the ideas that have influenced their evaluations, as maintained by Lodge, McGraw, and Stroh (1989). For these reasons, the index almost certainly understates the influence of the scandal on Reagan's ratings.

Nonetheless, these data do enable us to test notions about how information about Iran–Contra interacted with other information about Reagan's job performance to affect his overall job rating. What exactly, then, do we want to test?

If stored information engenders resistance to persuasion among highly aware persons, we should find, first, that highly aware persons have large stores of non-Contra considerations, and second, that these non-Contra considerations serve to offset the impact of scandal-related considerations. As can be seen in Table 8.1, the first expectation is strongly supported. The more attention people paid to politics, the better able they were to recall non-Contra considerations on which to judge Reagan. The second expectation is also supported; as can be seen in the bottom row of Table 8.1, the ratio of Contra to non-Contra considerations

15 By inadvertence, codes for the open-ended Reagan remarks were not included in the codebook for the 1987 pilot. However, the new codes have been permanently incorporated into the existing NES master codes, and so can be found in the party/candidate master codes in the early-release codebook for the 1988 election study. They are distinguished from preexisting codes by an asterisk.

Table 8.1. *Relationship between political awareness and remarks on Reagan job performance*

	Level of political awareness				
	Low		Middle		High
Mean number of remarks *not* related to Iran–Contra affair	0.68[a]	1.21	1.30	1.55	1.63
Mean number of remarks related to Iran–Contra affair	0.09[a]	0.23	0.41	0.42	0.28
Ratio of Contra remarks to all remarks	0.08[b]	0.15	0.23	0.21	0.13
N	44	52	54	38	46

[a] Cell entries in this row represent mean number of remarks of type indicated. Cells include all respondents, including those who had no opinion on Reagan job approval.

[b] Cell entry in this row is the average of an individual-level measure.

Source: 1987 NES pilot survey.

is highest among persons in the middling levels of political awareness. This non-monotonicity, which easily achieves statistical significance,[16] has come about in part because the large number of non-Contra considerations in the minds of highly aware persons has been able to dilute the effects of Contra-related ones. Thus, Table 8.1 is consistent with the notion that stored information concerning Reagan's overall performance as president helped to offset the effects of negative news concerning Iran–Contra.

There are two additional points to notice in Table 8.1. One is the very low level of spontaneous mention of the controversy in the least aware strata of the public; even allowing for some undermeasurement, 9 percent is a low level of penetration for a controversy of the magnitude of Iran–Contra. This, presumably, is why there was relatively little change in popularity ratings among the least aware, as shown earlier. The other point to notice is the pattern of non-monotonicity in spontaneous references to the scandal. This nonmonotonicity contributed to the nonmonotonic ratio in the bottom row of Table 8.1; its explanation is considered in the next section.

Partisan resistance at the level of considerations

Inertial resistance is, as we have seen, a mechanism for diluting the effects of newly acquired considerations. A more efficient form of resistance to persuasion, however, is outright rejection of new considerations at the point of first encountering them, if they are inconsistent with one's predispositions.

16 This can be confirmed by regression analysis. If ratio is the dependent variable, and information and information-squared are the independent variables, the coefficients on both independent variables are significant at the .05 level, one-tailed.

Within the RAS model, people can reject ideas only when they possess cueing information to let them know that a particular idea is inconsistent with their values, and they are more likely to possess this information and have it available for use if they are politically aware (see Table 4.4). Hence we should expect greater partisan resistance to uncongenial communications among well-informed persons.

From this reasoning, we should find that, for typical partisan issues, the incidence of inconsistent considerations – considerations that are inconsistent with the person's ideology – tends to be nonmonotonic with respect to political awareness. The reason stems from now familiar logic: Highly aware persons will, in the normal course of events, be heavily exposed to inconsistent messages but, being highly aware, they will possess the contextual information necessary to recognize and reject these messages. Very unaware persons will be exposed to few messages of any kind and hence also form few inconsistent considerations. This would leave moderately aware persons as most likely to form inconsistent considerations: They pay enough attention to politics to be fairly heavily exposed to inconsistent messages, but often lack the message cues necessary to recognize inconsistency.

In addition, we would expect a positive relationship between awareness and acquisition of consistent considerations – that is, considerations consistent with a person's ideology. The reason is that there is, as always, a strong exposure effect from awareness and, in this case, no awareness-induced resistance effect.

Thus we have a dual expectation: All else equal, political awareness should have a positive relationship with the acquisition of consistent considerations and a nonmonotonic association with inconsistent considerations. Or, more generally, the typology in Figure 8.2 should apply to the formation of new considerations as well as to attitude change.

To test the expectation, I return to data from the 1987 Pilot study. This survey, it will be recalled, contains measures of considerations for three issues: job guarantees, government services, and aid to blacks. Each consideration has been classified as either consistent or inconsistent with the person's liberal-conservative orientation (see Measures Appendix for description of measure); thus, for a liberal person, any consideration that might induce the person to give a liberal response has been classified as a consistent consideration and any that would tend to induce a conservative response has been classified as an inconsistent consideration. Separate indices have been created to tally the number of consistent and inconsistent considerations each person mentioned. To maximize chances that these indices would capture the full range of considerations in people's heads, they were built to include all relevant remarks over both waves of the study. The data are from the stop-and-think probes since, as will be recalled, these probes were intended, *inter alia,* to elicit as many as possible of the considerations present in people's minds.

The data on consistent and inconsistent considerations are arrayed in Figure 8.7. To compensate for the small number of cases and the high level of error in

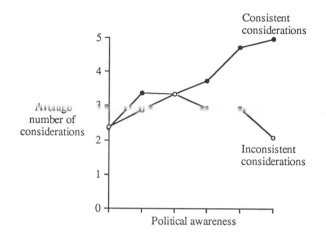

Figure 8.7. Effect of political awareness on formation of consistent and inconsistent considerations. See Table 8.2 for data on which figure is based. *Source:* 1987 NES pilot survey.

these data (see discussion in Chapter 4), this figure presents results that have been aggregated over all three items. As can be seen, these data are consistent with expectations. When the same data are examined at the level of individual items, as shown in Table 8.2, the results are rather ragged but still essentially consistent with expectations.[17]

The nonmonotonic pattern of references to the Iran–Contra controversy in Table 8.1 also suggests the existence of partisan resistance. The most informed persons were obviously heavily exposed to news of Iran–Contra, but they were apparently less likely to internalize it than were moderately aware persons.

We should expect, however, that highly aware Republicans would be much more resistant to Iran–Contra news than highly aware Democrats. Thus if we look separately at Republicans and Democrats, we should find a nonmonotonic relationship between awareness and Iran–Contra mentions among Republicans, and a positive relationship among Democrats. As can be seen in Table 8.3, this expectation is supported by the data.

Altogether, then, the expected patterns of monotonicity and nonmonotonicity have been obtained separately for a group of three social welfare items and for presidential popularity ratings, and were especially clear in the latter case. This pattern of results could have been obtained by chance alone only about six times

17 Table 8.2 has folded the ideology scale at the midpoint, so that considerations for liberals and conservatives can be examined at the same time, thereby boosting the number of cases for analysis. The expected relationships, however, are much stronger for liberals alone than they are for liberals and conservatives together, as in Table 8.2. My attempts at simulation suggest that something like this pattern could be produced if the conservative messages on these social welfare issues were more intense (reflecting the nation's tradition of economic individualism) and more credible (i.e., lower values on the b_0 coefficient in the acceptance function) than the liberal messages. (For an argument that this is so, see Feldman and Zaller, 1992.)

Table 8.2. *Ideology, awareness, and consistency of considerations*

	Low		Middle			High
			Level of political awareness			
Job guarantees						
Consistent considerations	1.50	2.82	3.14	3.68	3.37	4.23
Inconsistent considerations	2.08	2.94	2.79	2.54	2.57	1.31
N	(12)	(17)	(34)	(37)	(30)	(13)
Government services						
Consistent considerations	2.62	3.57	2.95	3.25	4.73	5.29
Inconsistent considerations	1.46	1.95	3.16	2.64	3.03	1.86
N	(13)	(21)	(37)	(36)	(30)	(14)
Aid to blacks						
Consistent considerations	2.92	3.70	4.26	5.42	6.06	5.36
Inconsistent considerations	3.58	3.70	4.09	3.58	3.23	3.07
N	(12)	(20)	(34)	(38)	(31)	(14)
Unweighted mean						
Consistent considerations	2.34	3.36	3.33	3.74	4.72	4.96
Inconsistent considerations	2.37	2.86	3.35	2.92	2.94	2.08

Note: Cell entries are mean number of remarks of the type indicated.
Source: 1987 NES pilot survey.

in a hundred.[18] Thus the results presented in this section offer helpful but not clinching evidence for partisan resistance at the level of considerations as a type of resistance mechanism. Further evidence on this point will be developed in Chapter 10.

AGE AND RESISTANCE TO CHANGE

My analysis so far has examined the effects on attitude change of several kinds of political predispositions: party attachment, dovishness, egalitarianism, and so forth. However, the predispositions that regulate attitude change need not be manifestly political.

One important but not manifestly political predisposition is chronological age. Research has produced abundant evidence of generational differences in susceptibility to new ideas (Abramson, 1983; Glenn, 1977).

---

18 Taking the summary data from Table 8.2 and the results from Table 8.3, there are four opportunities to observe the expected patterns of monotonicity and nonmonotonicity, and expectations are upheld in all four cases. The probability of observing this outcome by chance alone is $.5^4 \sim .06$. Note that the numbers of cases on which the individual tests are based are quite small.

Table 8.3. *Relationship among party, awareness, and remarks on Iran–Contra*

	Level of political awareness			
	Low	Middle		High
Republicans	0.25	0.33	0.30	0.23
N	(30)	(18)	(30)	(26)
Democrats	0.07	0.28	0.41	0.46
N	(27)	(32)	(32)	(26)

Note: Cell entries are mean number of negative references to Iran–Contra affair.
Source: 1987 NES pilot survey.

If the RAS model is a truly general model of attitude formation and change, it ought to specify the effects of generational differences in susceptibility to persuasion as well as it specifies the effects of other predispositional factors. We ought, then, to be able to observe the same kinds of interactions between political awareness and age that we found between awareness and other predispositional variables.

It is, however, by no means obvious than this will be the case. Consider the issue of racial equality. There are well-established generational differences in support for racial equality, with younger cohorts exhibiting greater racial liberalism. Insofar as chronological age represents the distillation of a person's life experience with an issue – in this case, the fact that most older Americans grew up in a period in which both political norms and everyday practice permitted or even required racial discrimination – age might retard a trend toward racial liberalism, regardless of political awareness or any other factor in the RAS model.

But suppose, as I suggested in Chapter 2, that racial equality is not some sort of amorphous trend, but a new norm created by various elites and transmitted to the public via the political media. If so, the more politically aware members of each cohort should be more heavily exposed to the new idea, thereby creating at least the potential for greater attitude change among the most aware.

Suppose also that the ability to defend one's predispositions against novel influences depends on the possession of relevant contextual information. If so, older highly aware persons who were exposed to pro-equality communications might be better able to reject them than their less aware counterparts. If this reasoning is correct, age ought to interact with political awareness in the RAS model to explain susceptibility to new ideas about race.

Let me, then, examine the effect of age in conditioning responses to three historic changes in American public opinion: the conversion of the public from the isolationist attitudes that predominated prior to World War II to "liberal internationalism" in the late 1940s and 1950s, the retreat of much of the public during the Vietnam War from the original doctrines of liberal internationalism, and the acceptance by much of the public of the new norm of racial equality in the 1950s. In each case, I will pay particular attention to why political awareness might interact with age to enhance resistance to persuasion.

Resistance to liberal internationalism

Throughout the 1930s and early 1940s, the Democratic Party, especially its liberal wing, was the party of "internationalism." It favored an activist foreign policy in which U.S. military power was seen as necessary to defend American interests and to keep the country's enemies in check. Foremost among these enemies, of course, were Nazi Germany and Stalinist Russia. Meanwhile, the Republican Party, especially its conservative wing, was the party of isolationism. The United States had no need for an internationalist foreign policy, it claimed; we could remain peacefully secure behind our ocean buffers, leaving other nations to look after their own interests.

During and after World War II, the Republican Party largely abandoned its isolationist posture. Wartime experience had, as it seemed to the leaders of the war effort, proven that America could no longer remain aloof from world affairs without suffering disastrous consequences. So, under the leadership of Senator Arthur Vandenberg, the Republican Party supported Democratic President Truman's initiatives on the economic rebuilding of Europe, a system of military alliances in which the United States was always the key member, American membership in the United Nations, and, finally, American intervention in the Korean War.

With the Republican Party largely in a supporting role, liberal internationalism was by the 1950s a "mainstream" policy norm in the United States. In the terminology of the RAS model, there was a steady stream of messages favoring this policy and few cueing messages indicating inconsistency between internationalism and conservatism.[19] Within most segments of the population, then, we expect the standard mainstream pattern, namely, a strong positive association between political awareness and support for the mainstream norm.

But what of highly aware older Republicans? Might not they have resisted the mainstream tide? Throughout the 1920s and 1930s and even part of the 1940s, they had been exposed to a steady stream of party communications opposing liberal internationalism in the most strenuous terms. Presumably they had internalized many of these arguments in the form of considerations, and presumably some of these considerations were still alive in their minds in the early 1950s, thereby providing the basis for resistance to the new policy of mainstream internationalism.

If so, our expectations concerning patterns of support for internationalism among Republicans circa 1950 should be as follows. Among younger Republi-

19 It is true that some Republicans, led by Senator Bricker, continued to oppose liberal internationalism. Cohen (1963), however, maintains that most of the press in this period regarded isolationism as a "provincial" view and hence tended to ignore it.

cans, who had little direct familiarity with Republican isolationism in its heyday in the 1930s, there should be a positive relationship between awareness and support for mainstream internationalism. Among older Republicans, however, we may expect a nonmonotonic relationship with awareness: The least aware pay too little attention to be exposed to messages favoring the new mainstream norm and hence mainly fail to support it. The most aware also resist, not because they don't know about it, but because they possess (from the 1930s) the contextual information necessary to reject the new idea, and perhaps also because they possess larger inertial stores of isolationist considerations from previous decades. Support for internationalism, then, should be greatest among moderately aware older Republicans: They pay enough attention to receive messages favoring the mainstream norm but do not possess sufficient contextual information and informational ballast to enable them to resist.

A 1951 survey by the Center for Political Studies at the University of Michigan permits a test of these expectations. A rarity among surveys of this period, it contained a measure of political information, as well as several items on American foreign policy. The toughest test of liberal internationalism in this period was Truman's Korean War policy, which required major American "sacrifices" in the interest of what was, from the isolationist perspective, unimportant Asian real estate.

Since the 1951 survey was a one-shot survey, we do not have data on attitude change over time. But since any support for American involvement in Korea must have been relatively new support, expectations derived from the reception-acceptance model ought to apply.

The measure of support for Truman's war policy was disagreement with the assertion that the United States "should get out of Korea now and stay out." The model used to estimate support for the Truman policy is a straightforward application of Equation 7.5, except that an age variable has been added.

The results, although based on a small number of cases in the critical cells, sustain expectations (see Figure 8.8). Among all Democrats (data not shown) and among younger Republicans, there is a strong positive relation between awareness and support for American intervention in Korea. Among older Republicans, but no other segment of the population, this relationship is strongly nonmonotonic, the result presumably of resistance to a new policy on the part of highly aware Republicans who had not yet forgotten their party's old isolationist line. Although some coefficients in the model do not achieve conventional levels of statistical significance, the critical coefficient on the age variable is significant at the .07 level (see Table 8.7 in the appendix to this chapter for coefficient estimates).

Resistance to the liberal anti–Vietnam War movement

The Vietnam War provides a parallel case for further tests of the effects of age. The only important difference is that in Vietnam the shoe is on the other foot: It

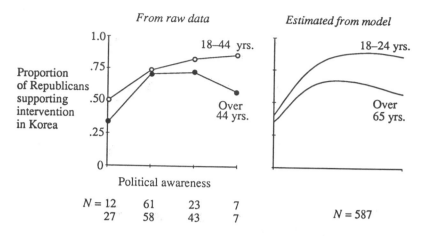

Figure 8.8. Cohort differences among Republicans in support for Korean War. Estimates are derived from Equation 7.5 and coefficients in Table 8.7. *Source:* 1951 CPS survey.

is highly aware older *liberals* who were forced to accommodate themselves to a shift in partisan norms.

The basic outline of the change in liberal ideology during the Vietnam War is well known. For at least a generation prior to the war, liberal ideology was, as just indicated, closely identified with an activist foreign policy. Thus, older liberals would have experienced the "lessons of Munich," the most important of which was that "appeasement" of aggressor nations only encourages further aggression; they would have witnessed the communist "takeovers" of eastern Europe and China in the period before the resolve of the United States stiffened; and they would have "seen" in Korea, Greece, Turkey, and West Berlin that a display of strength can deter aggression. If these older liberals (and, increasingly, older conservatives too) were following partisan interpretations of these events, they would therefore have encountered numerous arguments on the need to "stand up to communism" in places like Vietnam. Younger, politically aware liberals might also have encountered some of these "lessons," but would have had fewer opportunities to learn them than older liberals.

Over the course of the Vietnam War, liberal support for internationalism at first weakened and then reversed. Liberalism came to be associated with the view that American intervention in Vietnam was a tragic and unwarranted intrusion into the internal affairs of a sovereign nation.

So here we expect the dynamics of generational difference to be played out within the liberal camp.[20] That is, we expect that among younger liberals, there will be a positive relation between political awareness and attitude change in the direction of the new liberal norm. Among older liberals, we instead expect a nonmonotonic relation in which highly aware liberals exhibit inertial resistance

20 I refer to changes in "liberalism" rather than changes in the Democratic Party because liberal ideology appeared to shift more rapidly than did the Democratic Party, which included a large conservative wing.

to the new policy, thus leaving moderately aware older liberals most susceptible to change.

The data for testing this expectation are much stronger than in the Korean case in that they enable us to examine patterns of actual change over time (rather than, as earlier, support for a new partisan policy in a single cross-sectional survey). In each of its four election surveys between 1964 and 1970, the Center for Political Studies asked its respondents a question on support for the Vietnam War, thereby permitting the direct assessment of attitude change. The question was

Which of the following do you think we should do now in Vietnam?

Pull out of Vietnam entirely.

Keep our soldiers in Vietnam but try to end the fighting.

Take a stronger stand even if it means invading North Vietnam.

The second option, because it represents the official policy of both the Johnson and Nixon administrations (Gelb with Betts, 1979), will be counted as "war support" in the analysis that follows, as will the third response option. The "pull out" option will be counted as opposition to the war.

The data on changing support for the war between 1966 (which was high tide for support of the war) and 1970 among three cohorts of liberals are shown in Table 8.4. Through the noise created by small cells,[21] the table clearly supports the expectation of inertial resistance among highly aware older liberals. Among younger liberals, there is a positive relationship between political awareness and reduced support for the war, but among middle-aged and especially older liberals, this relationship is nonmonotonic. (The measure of ideology used in this table is discussed in detail in Chapter 9 in connection with a more extended examination of attitudes on the Vietnam War.)

The reader should note that there is a significant anomaly in these data, namely the −6 percent change in support for the war among the least aware older liberals. This number indicates that unaware older liberals actually became more supportive of the war between 1966 and 1970. In the next chapter we shall see evidence that this contrarian change – that is, change that runs contrary to the direction of change in most of the rest of society – is probably quite real. To explain it, a more complicated model is needed than has been developed so far. In the meantime, however, the data in Table 8.4, in conjunction with the Korean data just examined, indicate that the RAS model helps to specify the effect of age on susceptibility to attitude change.

Generation and race

I have already developed the rationale for expecting age to interact with political awareness in determining resistance to the new norm of racial equality. Because, as we have seen, ideology is also an important resistance factor with respect to

---

21 For a difference of means test between two cells which have $N = 25$ and a true mean of .40, the standard error is .14; and 95 percent confidence interval is then ±.28.

Table 8.4. *Generational differences in support
for Vietnam War among liberals, 1966 to 1970*

	Level of political awareness			
	Low			High
Youngest cohort				
War support in 1966	60%	89	86	92
N	(30)	(47)	(22)	(50)
War support in 1970	50	67	54	43
	(38)	(33)	(35)	(49)
Change rate 1966 to 1970	17	25	37	53
Middle cohort				
War support in 1966	44	71	92	83
	(59)	(52)	(36)	(59)
War support in 1970	43	61	54	57
	(51)	(38)	(41)	(51)
Change rate 1966 to 1970	2	14	41	31
Oldest cohort				
War support in 1966	32	75	73	79
	(54)	(36)	(15)	(24)
War support in 1970	34	56	21	67
	(47)	(39)	(19)	(21)
Change rate 1966 to 1970	−6	25	71	15

Note: Youngest cohort is age 21 to 35 in 1966; middle
cohort is age 36 to 55; oldest cohort is age 56 and above.
Liberals are persons who score in upper 40 percent of
dove measure described in Chapter 9. Change rate is
calculated as 100 x (Support$_{66}$ −Support$_{70}$)/Support$_{66}$.
Source: 1966 and 1970 CPS surveys.

racial equality, we should expect a triple interaction, as follows: Among people
who are both liberal and young, there should be little or no resistance to racial
equality; hence within this group − and only within this group − there should be
a positive linear relationship between awareness and racial liberalism. As age
and conservativism increase, the relationship between awareness and support for
racial equality should become increasingly nonmonotonic. Figure 8.9 tests this
expectation by showing levels of support for school desegregation by age cohort, ideology, and political awareness.[22] The estimates are derived from the

22 The 1956–58–60 NES panel carried a question on desegregation in all three waves, and some
pro-integration change occurred between 1956 and 1958, perhaps in response to President Eisenhower's use of federal troops to enforce a desegregation order in Little Rock. There was, however, too little change to show a distinct pattern.

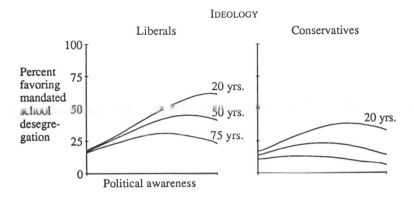

Figure 8.9. Cohort differences in support for school desegregation in 1956. Estimates are derived from Equation 7.5 and coefficients in Table 8.7. *Source:* 1956–58–60 CPS survey.

same model reported in Figure 8.6, except that here age differences are shown rather than suppressed. As can be seen, the data conform to expectation.

But what exactly, one may still wonder, would make highly aware older liberals relatively resistant to court-mandated school desegregation in the South? Why would not their prior experience as liberal ideologues rather than as older citizens have predisposed them to be especially supportive of federal involvement in this issue?

The answer to these questions, though perhaps obscure to persons living in the late twentieth century, would, I believe, have been quite obvious to midcentury liberals. From the late nineteenth century until Franklin Roosevelt's attack on the Supreme Court in the late 1930s, judicial activism in the United States almost invariably served conservative interests; in these same years, the principles of states' rights and judicial self-restraint most often served to protect liberal policies from federal judicial interference. This was because liberal-minded state legislatures in the Northeast and Midwest were passing economic regulations that the Supreme Court, acting in the name of constitutional principle, regularly invalidated. Upset by this, liberals stressed the "democratic" principle that the judiciary should defer to the popular branches of government – especially state and local governments. Thus, just as highly aware older liberals in the 1960s had learned the "lessons of Munich" too well to oppose the Vietnam War, so highly aware older liberals in the 1950s had learned the "dangers of judicial activism" too well to be entirely comfortable with *Brown v. Board of Education.*[23] (There may be a parallel to this phenomenon in the attitudes of some

---

23 See White, 1976, for an account of the discomfit that race and civil liberties issues in the 1950s caused one older liberal, Felix Frankfurter. As a Supreme Court justice, Frankfurter appears to have been torn between his attachment to the doctrine of judicial self-restraint, formed in his young adulthood, and his equally strong commitment to racial and civil liberty.

contemporary liberals who personally fought to end racial discrimination but now oppose affirmative action on the grounds that racial selectivity is never justifiable.)

General effects of age

I have examined these three cases in some detail in order to show why exactly the effects of age on susceptibility to new ideas can be specified by the RAS model. However, if, as I have suggested, age is a predispositional factor like any other, no special case-by-case justification is necessary. If older people are more or less predisposed toward some idea – whether for reason of past learning, physiological condition, self-interest, life circumstances, general conservativism, or anything else – the logic of the RAS model should apply. That is, more aware older persons should be more heavily exposed to change-inducing political communications, and they should also be better able to resist ideas that are contrary to their predispositions.

There is, I should add, no reason to believe that age will be generally associated with greater resistance to change. If a proposal to increase Medicare benefits became a highly salient political issue, the elderly would not be expected to be unusually prone to resist. Support for the idea among the elderly might increase with levels of political awareness without any sign of resistance among the most aware. Resistance, if there were any, would be expected among the politically aware young.

My argument in this section, then, is not that age is associated with resistance to new ideas; it is that the predispositional effects of age, whatever their direction, can be specified by the RAS model.

SUMMARY

This chapter has shown that the one-message model of attitude change, although a significant simplification of what must occur in reality, has sufficient internal complexity to generate interestingly different expectations in different circumstances, and sufficient validity that these expectations can remain plausible even after empirical testing. More specifically, the chapter has shown that different patterns of attitude change arise for different types of issues and communications, that the formation of the considerations that underlie people's closed-ended survey responses also appear to follow the logic of the one-message model, and that the one-message model specifies the effect of one important type of nonpolitical predisposition, namely, age.

A variety of different kinds of evidence, no one piece of which is conclusive, is accumulating in support of the RAS model. The next two chapters add to this cumulation in the context of chapter length examinations of two substantive problems, attitudes toward the war in Vietnam and evaluations of candidates in partisan elections.

APPENDIX: ESTIMATING THE PRESIDENTIAL
POPULARITY MODEL

Although Reagan's approval ratings fell sharply in early November in response
to revelations concerning the Iran-Contra matter (Brody, 1991), they remained
steady through most of November in the sample of the NES postelection survey,
which began on November 6 and continued through January. There appears to
have been a sharp break in the data series on November 28, which is the day
after Thanksgiving and three days after Attorney General Edwin Meese announced that the administration was beginning a self-investigation of Iran–
Contra allegations. Prior to November 28, Reagan's disapproval rating stood at
32 percent in the NES sample, with no indication of a time trend; from November 28 until the end of the NES interviewing period, disapproval averaged 39
percent, a change that is highly statistically significant. In the 1987 pilot survey,
which reinterviewed 457 of the fall NES respondents, Reagan's disapproval rating was 48 percent. In light of these data, I used the pre–November 28 period as
my baseline period and the June 1987 as my postchange period.[24]

The estimation of Equation 7.7 on these data is shown in the left column of
Table 8.5. As can be seen, all theoretically important coefficients have good
magnitudes, but their standard errors are large, as in earlier applications of the
model. Hence I added two constraints to the basic model. First, I removed the
floor parameter, which clearly was going beyond its intended effect of picking
up the effects of guessing and which had a huge standard error. I also constrained awareness to have the same effect on reception in both the baseline and
change subfunctions. These two constraints did not significantly diminish the
overall fit of the model to the data (F, [2, 1905], 1.6, n.s.) and also did not no-
ticeably affect the qualitative fit of the model, as analyzed graphically. The constraints did, however, bring stability to the results; in particular, they brought
coefficient estimates for the two most theoretically important coefficients –
those depicting the effect of awareness on reception and acceptance in the
change model – into the range of conventional statistical significance.

An interesting feature of these results is that the effects of the predispositions
variables – party, egalitarianism, and attitudes toward U.S. involvement in Central America – on Reagan's evaluations appear to have increased over the period. Of these apparent increases, only that associated with Central America
attitudes survives an F-test of statistical significance. This case is an important
one, however, because it confirms the analysis of Krosnick and Kinder (1990),

24 I also examined attitude change within the 457-person NES pilot sample, using the sample's
own fall interviews as the baseline. Using the small pilot sample, it was impossible to discard
that portion of the panel that had been interviewed after November 27. Thus, this dataset was not
only smaller than the one just described; it also contained less real attitude change. Despite this,
the patterns of change in the raw pilot data were essentially similar to those found in the larger
comparison. However, I was unable to get the model to reliably fit the smaller dataset, and chose
instead to use as my baseline the pre–November 27 portion of the whole NES postelection study,
as described.

Table 8.5. *Coefficients for model of change in presidential job approval*

	No constraints	Two constraints
Baseline reception function		
Intercept	0.62	2.12
Awareness (standardized)	3.35 (4.39)	0.79[a] (.43)
Floor parameter	2.84 (4.18)	–
Baseline acceptance function		
Intercept	–0.88	–0.92
Awareness	0.03 (.14)	0.07 (.15)
Party attachment (range –2 to +2)	0.94 (.11)	0.91 (.10)
Equalitarianism (standardized)	0.35 (.09)	0.36 (.08)
Central America attitudes[b] (standardized)	0.28 (.09)	0.23 (.09)
Change reception function		
Intercept	–0.25	–0.22
Awareness	0.68 (.39)	0.79[a] (.43)
Change acceptance function		
Intercept	1.24	0.68
Awareness	–2.68 (2.16)	–2.17 (1.22)
Party attachment	2.02 (1.59)	1.76 (.94)
Equalitarianism	1.81 (1.71)	1.64 (1.14)
Central America attitudes	3.67 (3.00)	3.10 (1.74)
Residual sum of squares	421.21	421.91

Note: Model is Equation 7.7, estimated by maximum likelihood. Dependent variable is disapproval of job performance (0–1). The Time$_1$ N is 1463; Time$_2$ N is 457. Standard errors are in parentheses.

[a] Coefficients constrained to be equal.

[b] The items were Contra spending and United States involvement in Central America, as measured in 1986.

Source: 1986 and 1987 NES surveys.

who found that the Iran–Contra controversy had "primed" people's attitudes on Central American policy, thereby leading these attitudes to become more strongly engaged as determinants of presidential approval ratings.

Tables 8.6 and 8.7 contain the coefficients for the remaining figures in the chapter.

Table 8.6. *Coefficients for diffusion of news*

	North sentence	Wright resign	Death penalty	DC–10 crash
Intercept (a_0)	0.88 (.11)	−0.42 (.10)	−1.96 (.17)	3.48 (.65)
Awareness (a_1)	1.12 (.12)	1.92 (.18)	1.03 (.15)	2.43 (.51)

Note: Model is equation 7.3, estimated by nonlinear least squares. Standard errors are shown in parentheses.
Source: 1989 NES pilot survey.

Table 8.7. *Coefficients for opinion formation on school desegregation, economic news, nuclear freeze, and Korea*

	School desegregation	Nuclear freeze	Economic news	Korean War
Reception function				
Intercept	0.35	2.14	−1.02	1.52
Awareness	0.72	1.15	1.21	1.58
	(.32)	(.31)	(.28)	(.41)
Acceptance function				
Intercept	2.17	2.05	1.35	3.59
Awareness	−.71	−0.33	−0.61	−0.35
	(.40)	(.22)	(.34)	(.46)
Age[a]	−0.038	−0.008	−.033	−1.60
	(.017)	(.008)	(.01)	(1.09)
Domestic policy attiudes (standardized)	0.55 (.23)	–	–	–
Foreign policy attitudes (standardized)	0.38 (.22)	0.91 (.20)	–	–
Reagan job approval (range −2 to +2)	–	0.08 (.08)	–	–
Party attachment (range −2 to +2)	–	–	−0.66 (.16)	–
Economic attitudes (standardized)	–	–	−0.13 (.13)	–
Vote in 1948[b] (1 = Dewey, 0 = Truman)	–	–	–	−0.77 (.60)
N	848	1400	1413	596

Note: Model for all issues is Equation 7.5, estimated by maximum likelihood. Dependent variables are 0–1, as follows: disagreement that the federal government should stay out of school desegregation (V74); support for joint or unilateral freeze (V305); statement that economy has improved in last year (V327); disagreement that the United States "should get out of Korea now and stay out." Other political variables are coded in liberal direction, except vote for Dewey; see Measures Appendix for additional information. Standard errors are shown in parentheses.

[a] Age was entered in years, except for Korea, where a five-point cohort variable on 0–1 range was used because age in years was unavailable.
[b] Nonvoters from 1948 are excluded from the analysis because their political predispositions are unknown.

Sources: For school desegregation, 1956–58–60 CPS study; for freeze and economic news, 1982 NES survey; for Korean War, 1951 CPS survey.

9

Two-sided information flows

Until this chapter, I have modeled attitude change as a response to a one-sided stream of communications – for example, the negative effects of Iran–Contra on presidential popularity, or the argument for liberal internationalism in the post–World War II era. Much has been learned about the dynamics of attitude change from this approach because, in many cases, the flow of political communications really is, at least for a time, heavily one-sided. Yet it is rarely *completely* one-sided over any appreciable length of time. Even amid the Iran–Contra scandal, for example, some Republican senators defended the president, and their remarks may have had some effect in preventing even greater damage to President Reagan's approval ratings.

The burden of this chapter is to develop a model that is capable of capturing the effects of two-sided information flows which change public opinion – that is, information flows that consist of both a dominant message pushing much of public opinion in one direction, and a less intense, countervalent message that partly counteracts the effects of the dominant message. Such a model is possible because, as will be shown, dominant and countervalent messages can have different effects in different segments of the population, depending on citizens' political awareness and ideological orientations and on the relative intensities of the two messages.

But the larger purpose of this chapter is to integrate the work of earlier chapters into a general statement of the effect on mass opinion of two-sided information flows. We saw in Chapter 6 that when elite discourse one-sidedly favors a given policy, it produces a "mainstream pattern" in which the most aware members of the public subscribe to the elite consensus most strongly, and further, that when elite discourse divides along partisan lines, the effect is to generate a "polarization" of mass opinion. The present chapter extends this analysis by showing how the mainstream and polarization patterns form and change over time in response to changes in the intensities of competing messages in a two-sided information flow. The chapter further shows how changes in the relative intensities of opposing messages can produce not only the patterns of attitude change observed in Chapters 7 and 8, but more complicated ones as well.

More generally, then, this chapter seeks to show that public opinion can be understood as a response to the relative intensity and stability of opposing flows of liberal and conservative communications. (Again, I stress that use of these ideological labels is meant to convey only the directional thrust of the message.) Whether public opinion is momentarily stable in the mainstream or polarization pattern, or undergoing attitude change, depends on whether the opposing communication flows are one-sided or evenly balanced, and whether they are stable or changing over time.

Unfortunately, there are few issues for which the relative intensity of opposing messages changes clearly and crisply over a short period of time, and only one case of which I am aware in which the resulting changes in mass attitudes have been adequately captured by a series of high-quality surveys. This case, however, is an important and intrinsically interesting one: popular support for and opposition to American involvement in the Vietnam War. This case will provide most of the illustrative material for the argument of this chapter.

To accomplish the goals of this chapter, it will be necessary to engage in some statistical modeling and a fairly extensive discussion of the data employed. To make it easier to see where the technical work is going, I have included a simple illustration of the effects of two-sided information flows at the beginning of the chapter. Then, in the middle section of the chapter, I develop a statistical model that is capable of capturing attitude change in response to changes in a two-sided information flow. The final section describes the measures used in testing the model and the results of the modeling effort.

EBB AND FLOW OF SUPPORT FOR THE VIETNAM WAR

The case of the Vietnam War presents an unusually fertile opportunity for examining the dynamics of public opinion. Among its attractive features are the following:

> Rapid change in elite positions on the issue. Liberal opinion leaders overwhelmingly supported the war in 1964, but mainly opposed it in 1970. Conservative elites, by contrast, continued to support the war throughout the period of American involvement.

> Changes in the intensity of the dominant message. President Johnson made far more strenuous efforts to promote public support for the war after the increased commitment of U.S. ground troops in 1965 than he had a year earlier, when he was in the midst of an election campaign.

> Changes in the intensity of the countervalent message. The antiwar message was virtually nonexistent in 1964 and was still hardly more than a whisper in 1966. By 1970, however, it was probably as intense, and perhaps more intense, than the prowar message.

> Transformation of Vietnam from a mainstream issue in 1964 to a polarization issue in 1970.

The election studies conducted by the Center for Political Studies (CPS) at the University of Michigan during the Vietnam War provide excellent data on the public's response to this issue. An almost identical question, quoted in Chapter 8, was asked in four different surveys, and each of these surveys carried

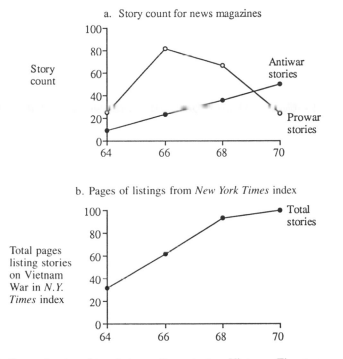

a. Story count for news magazines

Story count

Antiwar stories

Prowar stories

b. Pages of listings from *New York Times* index

Total stories

Total pages listing stories on Vietnam War in *N.Y. Times* index

Figure 9.1. Two estimates of trends in media content on Vietnam. The story count measure gives the count of pro- and antiwar stories associated with cover stories on the Vietnam War in the period 1963 to 1970 in *Life, Time,* and *Newsweek* magazines.

a good selection of explanatory variables, especially political awareness and political values.

Before turning to the opinion data, however, it is useful to examine the sources of mass opinion on the war, namely the flow of political communications on Vietnam. I have developed several indicators of these communications. First and most important, I asked a research assistant to undertake a content analysis of war reporting in *Time, Newsweek,* and *Life* magazines for the period 1963 to 1970. The research assistant was unaware of my expectations as to what the analysis might reveal. Following instructions, he identified all magazine issues in which the Vietnam War or related events (such as antiwar protests) were featured on the cover and read all stories in these magazines relating to the war. The stories selected in this way may be considered a reasonable sample of the war reportage that was most salient to the public. The research assistant rated each as predominantly prowar in its slant, predominantly antiwar, or fairly evenly balanced. The resulting estimate of trends in war coverage are depicted in Figure 9.1a.

By these data, the prowar message was only moderately prominent in 1963–4, averaging about four stories per year per magazine in association with a cover on Vietnam. (There were, of course, many non–cover-related stories on Vietnam.)

But the prowar story was nonetheless far more intense than was the antiwar story, which averaged about 1.5 cover-related items per magazine per year. A close examination of these early antiwar stories shows, in addition, that they did not portray partisan opposition to the war, as did much of the later coverage; rather, they reported difficulties in the conduct of the war that might have been interpreted as reasons for strengthening the U.S. commitment.

As can also be seen in Figure 9.1a, the prowar message gained considerably in intensity between 1964 and 1966, maintaining this higher level of intensity through about 1968. After 1968 the prowar message declined rapidly, falling almost to 1964 levels of intensity. Meanwhile, the antiwar message gained in intensity each year and appears to have caught and even overtaken the prowar message in intensity by 1970.

A peculiarity of these data is the overall fall-off in news coverage of the war in 1970. Did the volume of war coverage really decline in 1970, even though levels of U.S. troop commitment remained near peak levels, or did war news simply cease to be featured in periodical publications?[1]

To check the latter possibility, I did a simple count of pages in the *New York Times Index* devoted to stories about Vietnam. The results, displayed in Figure 9.1b, suggest that the total volume of war coverage remained high in the later years of the war. What seems to have happened, thus, is that war coverage lost its novelty in later years of the conflict, and so tended to drop out of the trendier periodical literature. In another medium, however, the overall volume of coverage remained high.

As a further check on information flow during the war, I examined Hallin's (1984) published analysis of prowar and antiwar statements in the television news. A central finding of his study was that "spokesmen for administration policy were heavily predominant during the early period [prior to spring, 1968], while after Tet there was relative parity between the administration and its critics" (1984: 9). Hallin also reports (personal communication) that the overall volume of war coverage on television increased through about 1966 and remained roughly steady until after 1970.

One can also take the actions of leading political figures as an indicator of trends in political communications on the war. For example, when in 1964 President Johnson sought congressional authorization for his Vietnam policy in the Gulf of Tonkin resolution, it passed 414 to 0 in the House of Representatives and by a margin of 88 to 2 in the Senate. These congressional actions suggest, as did the media analysis for this period, that political communications in the early phase of the Vietnam War predominantly favored American involvement.

As U.S. involvement in the war increased in 1965 and 1966, President Johnson devoted more of his public utterances to promoting his war policy. However, real congressional debate over the Vietnam War, including the first hints of opposition to it, also emerged in this period, most prominently in hear-

---

1 A separate count of Vietnam articles in the *Readers Guide to Periodical Literature* shows a similar decline across a wider range of media outlets.

ings conducted by Senator William Fulbright in 1966. Beginning in 1967, there were also some attempts in Congress to cut off funding for the war. Yet these initial efforts were soundly defeated, indicating continued strong support for the war by congressional elites.[2] So again, the actions of leading political figures are broadly consistent with the trends in media coverage, as depicted in Figure 9.1a.

The years 1969 and 1970 marked the height of heavily covered antiwar protests, but they were also a time in which the Nixon administration sought by its well-publicized "Vietnamization' program to show that U.S. policy was succeeding, and a time in which attempts in Congress to cut off war funding continued to be defeated, though by closer margins than previously.[3] Here, then, we find a discrepancy between the two indicators of communications flow. Although the news magazine data suggest that the flow of communications favored the antiwar position by 1970, the actions of political officeholders show that there remained a stream of communications that was, on balance, supportive of American involvement.

Taking all of these indicators together, it appears that both the prowar and the antiwar messages became more intense between 1964 and 1966, with the prowar message initially far more intense but losing this advantage by 1970. The flow of pro- and antiwar communications may have been roughly even by 1970, and probably still quite high in overall volume.

This is a more complicated pattern of change in the flow of political communications than has been examined so far, and one which cannot be fully accommodated in the simple model developed in Chapter 7. To capture its effects, a "two-message model" of opinion change is necessary.

The central idea in a two-message model is that citizens are exposed to two communication flows, one on each side of the issue. These opposing communications may have different effects in different segments of the population, depending on the relative intensity of the messages. For example, in the period between 1964 and 1966, one might expect the antiwar message, which was still very low in intensity even in 1966, to have had its greatest impact on the most politically aware liberals: Their high levels of awareness would ensure reception of the message, and their liberalism would make them sympathetic to it. By contrast, the increase in the prowar message from 1964 to 1966 might be expected to have a relatively larger impact on persons of moderate or low political awareness: The prowar message was, as just shown, already fairly intense in 1964, and so would probably have reached most highly aware persons at that time. Hence the increase in its intensity would mainly affect persons who had not yet gotten the message in 1964, that is, moderately aware or less-aware persons.

2 A 1966 proposal to repeal the Gulf of Tonkin resolution was defeated in a Senate vote by a margin of 92 to 5; a 1967 House amendment barring funds for military operations over North Vietnam was defeated 372 to 18. See Jack McWethy, *The Power of the Pentagon* (1972: p. 112).

3 In 1970 the Cooper–Church amendment, barring funds for U.S. military operations in Cambodia, passed the Senate 58 to 37, but was defeated in the House 237 to 153. Later in 1970 the McGovern–Hatfield amendment, setting a deadline for U.S. withdrawal from Vietnam, was defeated in the Senate by a vote of 55 to 39; the measure did not come to a vote in the House (ibid.).

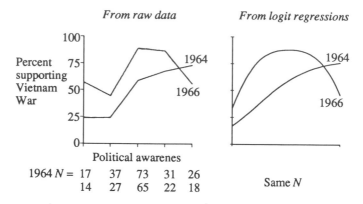

Figure 9.2. Patterns of support for the Vietnam War among liberals in 1964 and 1966. Logit estimates for the figure on right are constructed from a model in which awareness and awareness squared were the only independent variables. The awareness scores used in constructing this figure are given in footnote 15. The measure of support for the war is described in Chapter 8. For reasons discussed in connection with Figure 9.6, this analysis is limited to whites. *Source:* 1964 and 1966 CPS surveys.

These suppositions, as can be seen in Figure 9.2, nicely fit the changing patterns of support for the Vietnam War among liberals between 1964 and 1966. (The measure of liberal or dovish values used in this figure will be described later in the chapter.) Support for the war among less aware doves rose between 1964 and 1966, presumably because they had finally begun to be heavily exposed to prowar arguments; notwithstanding this, the most aware doves began to turn against the war between 1964 and 1966, presumably because they encountered and accepted an antiwar message that was still inaudible to less attentive doves.

This account of attitude change between 1964 and 1966, though rough and informal, is the clearest illustration I have for the main point of this chapter: Public attitudes on major issues change in response to changes in the relative intensities of competing streams of political communications, as filtered through the reception-acceptance process. As I have indicated, however, this account is preliminary. To make it fully credible, it will be necessary to explain not only attitude change among doves between 1964 and 1966, but attitude change in the whole population between 1964 and 1970. (The CPS item on Vietnam was changed after 1970, which is why my analysis ends at that point.)

A TWO-MESSAGE MODEL OF ATTITUDE CHANGE

The basic claim of the RAS model is that people respond to survey questions on the basis of whatever considerations are present in their minds and immediately accessible in memory. The formation of considerations, for its part, depends on the flow of communications in the political environment. Hence, changes in the relative intensities of the opposing messages determine people's relative propensities to form liberal and conservative considerations, which in turn determine their survey responses.

In order to test this basic claim, it is necessary to introduce some simplifying assumptions in the RAS model. First, it is not possible to measure reception and acceptance of each of the discrete communications – official speeches, press releases, news stories, and so on – that constituted the real-world prowar and antiwar messages of the Vietnam era. Hence, I will assume that, within each two-year period, all communications concerning the war fell into a fixed but reasonably small number of categories, which I will take to be "messages." I further assume that all of the messages of a given direction and time interval are equally intense. Thus, within each two-year time period, there will be N prowar messages of uniform intensity, and N antiwar messages of different but uniform intensity. Since real-world communications are too numerous and varied to be actually measurable or, if organized into a manageable number of topics, merely abstract entities anyway, nothing of importance seems lost by this simplification.

The second simplifying assumption is that no consideration remains active in a person's mind for more than two years unless it is reinforced by reception and acceptance of an identical argument, in which case it is the same as a new consideration. The value of this assumption is that, once it has been made, public opinion in each of the four Vietnam surveys can be modeled as a response to communications in the preceding two years, which eliminates the need to take account of the lagged effects of communication from earlier time periods.[4] Although there is no doubt that communications have effects that can last longer than two years, the four surveys of the Vietnam dataset do not provide sufficient leverage to determine what the lagged effects are. Hence, again, it does not seem that anything has been lost by the simplifying assumption.

The final simplifying assumption is that individuals respond to survey questions on the basis of the first consideration that comes to mind rather than on the basis of whatever considerations are accessible, as allowed in axiom A4. This assumption greatly simplifies the formal structure of the model without, again, giving up anything about which we have information in the present data.

We can now begin development of a model for the diffusion of competing liberal and conservative messages about the Vietnam War. The model is based on a two-step process in which individuals are exposed to political communications that, if received and accepted, become considerations for them. I begin with a model of the reception process, as follows:

$$\text{Prob(Reception)}_{ikt} = 1 - [1 + f + \text{Exp}(a_{0kt} + a_1 * \text{Awareness}_i)]^{-1}$$
$$= RE_{ikt} \qquad (9.1a)$$

Equation 9.1a is a standard logistic function, that is, one that varies between a floor of zero and a ceiling of 1.0. The subscript i indicates individual-level differences. The subscript k refers to the ideological coloration of the message

4 See Appendix B to Chapter 10 for a model that permits lagged effects of previous communications.

(prowar and antiwar) while the t subscript refers to the time of the survey (64, 66, 68, 70). Since the a_0 parameter carries these kt subscripts, shifts in the intercept of the logistic function vary by message and by time, thereby allowing shifts in the intensity of each message across time. If the reader reviews my discussion of the basic reception function in Chapter 7, this will be seen as an appropriate way of specifying shifts in message intensity.[5]

Since there are four time periods and two messages, these kt subscripts indicate that we will be estimating eight different a_0 parameters, one for the intensity of the pro- and antiwar messages in each time period. Thus I have, in effect, made the intercept of the logistic function into a variable for capturing time-related differences in message intensity.

I turn now to a model of the acceptance process. The Resistance Axiom holds that people reject political messages that are inconsistent with their predispositions, but only if they possess contextual information concerning the relationship between their predispositions and the message. From axioms A1 and A3, respectively, both the reception and the accessibility of cueing information (given reception of it) will be associated with higher levels of habitual political awareness. Hence, rates of acceptance of incoming messages, given reception of them, ought to decline as a joint function of political awareness and ideological distance (a phrase I will use instead of "predispositional distance") from the message. The following logistic function meets these requirements:

$$\text{Prob(Accept | Recept)}_{ikt} = [1 + \text{Exp}(-b_{0k} - b_{1t}*\text{Awareness}_i$$
$$- b_{2t}*\text{Distance}_i]^{-1}$$
$$= \text{Accept}_{ikt} \qquad (9.2)$$

As in Equation 9.1a, the subscripts in this equation embody definite claims about the opinion formation process. First, the k subscript on the intercept parameter b_0 indicates that some messages may encounter more resistance than others. For example, one might suspect that the liberal antiwar message would encounter more resistance, at given levels of awareness and ideological distance, than would the conservative prowar message, because it runs contrary to an established policy. Or, the liberal message might be, for reasons of patriotism or rhetoric or political association, an inherently less attractive or persuasive message. The subscript k enables the model to capture such message-level variation in overall acceptance notes.

Second, there are t subscripts for time on the coefficients for awareness and ideological distance from the message. Since, as I have argued, the effects of these variables depend on cueing messages from elites, and since these cues

5 An argument might be made that the a_1 coefficient, which captures the strength of relationship between reception and awareness independently of message intensity, should also be subscripted by time or by message. If, for example, a message was carried exclusively through political media in its early phases, but was carried through entertainment and political media in a later phase, it would be appropriate to allow for a stronger relationship between exposure and awareness in the earlier period. Since, however, the Vietnam data are not strong enough to make credible tests of the null hypothesis, I have specified a time-invariant a_1 parameter.

changed as liberal elites began to oppose the war starting in about 1966, this specification will enable us to test whether ideological distance and awareness became, as expected, more strongly associated with resistance to persuasion after that time.

With the reception function in Equation 9.1a and the acceptance function in Equation 9.2, we have precise statements about how individuals respond to the political communications they encounter, selectively internalizing some of these communications as new considerations. What remains is to state how they transform considerations into survey responses.

The RAS model, as indicated, assumes that individuals sample whatever consideration is "at the top of the head" at the moment of response. Let R_i be defined as a function giving the likelihood that a typical consideration, having been formed, will be accessible for answering survey questions, and let it be assumed that R_i varies directly with political awareness and nothing else, as follows[6]:

$$\text{Prob(Recall)}_i = 1 - [1 + \text{Exp}(c_0 + c_1 * \text{Awareness}_i)]^{-1}$$
$$= R_i \qquad (9.3)$$

Note that because this function carries no kt subscripts, it applies to each consideration in a person's mind, so that regardless of when a consideration has been formed or which side of the issue it favors, it is equally likely to be sampled. One can readily imagine more complicated or ideologically biased sampling functions, but the available data provide neither means for testing more complicated formulations nor reason to try them, since the present specification turns out to work quite well.

With the new R_i term, we can write an expression for the probability that a message to which an individual has been exposed will be immediately accessible in memory as a consideration. This is simply the probability that an individual has received the message, times the probability that he has accepted it, times the probability that he has it accessible in memory at the moment of responding to an attitude question, as follows:

$$\text{Prob(Accessible)}_{ikt} = RE_{ikt}(\text{Accept}_{ikt})R_i$$
$$= AC_{ikt} \qquad (9.4)$$

Since we have already assumed that there are N prowar arguments ($k=P$) and N antiwar arguments ($k=A$), the relative accessibility of prowar considerations is equal to

$$\frac{\sum^N RE_{iPt}(\text{Accept}_{iPt})R_i}{\sum^N RE_{iPt}(\text{Accept}_{iPt})R_i + \sum^N RE_{iAt}(\text{Accept}_{iAt})R_i} \qquad (9.5)$$

6 In principle, of course, any variable that affects attention to an issue would also affect recall ability; however, nothing of value except general awareness is available in the Vietnam data series.

Also, it would follow from axiom A3 that recall ability varies inversely with the time since a consideration has been formed. However, I omit this idea from Equation 9.3 because it has no observable implications in the context of the present problem.

This expression can be simplified in two ways. First, the R_i terms appear in both the numerator and denominator, so they cancel and can be omitted. Second, because there are, by assumption, equal numbers of prowar and antiwar messages, and because all messages of each type are assumed to be equally intense, the summation signs also become superfluous. This leaves

$$\frac{RE_{iPt}(\text{Accept}_{iPt})}{RE_{iPt}(\text{Accept}_{iPt}) + RE_{iAt}(\text{Accept}_{iAt})} \tag{9.6}$$

as our measure of the relative accessibility of prowar considerations P over antiwar considerations A in the mind of individual i at time t, where the reception and acceptance functions are given by Equations 9.1a and 9.2. Equation 9.6 is intuitively quite simple: Relative accessibilities depend on the reception-acceptance ratios of the two messages, where these ratios vary by time and by differences among individuals in awareness and ideological distance.

One problem remains: namely, what to do about "No opinion" responses. In the Vietnam case as in others, large numbers of the public reported that they had no opinion. Presumably, people make such responses when they are unable to call to mind any consideration that would give them a reason for supporting one rather than the other side of the issue. If the chance that any particular consideration is accessible in the memory of the ith individual is AC_{ikt_N} (from Equation 9.4), then the chance that someone would have none of the $2N$ possible considerations readily accessible in memory is

$$\text{Prob(No opinion)}_{it} = (1 - AC_{ikt_1})(1 - AC_{ikt_2})(1 - AC_{ikt_3}) \ldots (1 - AC_{ikt_{2N}})$$

Assuming, as I have, an equal number of liberal and conservative messages, this becomes

$$\text{Prob(No opinion)}_{it} = \Pi^N(1 - AC_{iPt}) \, \Pi^N(1 - AC_{iAt})$$
$$= \Pi^N(1 - RE_{iPt}\text{Accept}_{iPt} \, R_i) \, \Pi^N(1 - RE_{iAt}\text{Accept}_{iAt} \, R_i)$$

The probability of having some opinion, then, is

$$\text{Prob(Opinion)}_{it} = 1 - \Pi^N(1 - AC_{iPt})\Pi^N(1 - AC_{iAt}) \tag{9.7}$$

Putting this expression for opinionation together with the expression for the relative accessibility of prowar arguments, we obtain the basic statistical model for estimating support for the Vietnam War:

Probability
of prowar
response$_{iPt}$ = (Probability of recalling any consideration at all) $\times$

$$\left(\frac{\text{Accessibility of prowar considerations}}{\text{Accessibility of prowar considerations} + \text{Accessibility of antiwar considerations}} \right)$$

$$= (1 - \Pi^N(1 - AC_{iPt})\Pi^N(1 - AC_{iAt}))$$

$$* \frac{RE_{iPt}\text{Accept}_{iPt}}{RE_{iPt}\text{Accept}_{iPt} + RE_{iAt}\text{Accept}_{iAt}} \tag{9.8}$$

This equation, in conjunction with appropriately modified expressions for anti-war and "No opinion" responses, is my model for fitting the opinion data on Vietnam.

This two-message model is obviously quite different in form from the one-message model developed in Chapter 7, which was intended as a simplification of the basic attitude-change process. However, both models are capable of capturing, in essentially similar fashion, many types of attitude change, as will be shown below. The two-message model is, however, by far the more versatile and powerful, as will also be apparent.

The model developed in this section is not, I might add, the only form that a two-message model could take. In Appendix A to this chapter, I derive an alternative form which, because it omits any reference to considerations, is mathematically simpler.

Before estimating the two-message model on the CPS data series on the Vietnam War, I must describe certain features of the data. Despite their generally high quality, there are some problems in adapting them for use by the two-message model.

DATA AND RESULTS

None of the major CPS surveys conducted from 1964 to 1970 were reinterviews with the same respondents. The analysis of mass attitudes across time therefore requires comparisons of particular types of persons across time – comparison, for example, of war support among "highly informed doves" in 1964 with war support among "highly informed doves" in 1966, 1968, and 1970. This, in turn, requires the construction of highly similar measures of awareness and values in all four surveys, so that similar subgroups of people can be located in each survey.

With respect to awareness, this is easy to do. As discussed in the Measures Appendix, each survey contains a set of information items sufficient to build an awareness scale with an alpha reliability of .80 or better. Although most of the information items vary from year to year, there is no reason to believe that they vary in consequential ways. Just as one could rank order individuals in terms of spelling ability with one randomly selected set of twenty words about as well as with another randomly selected set of twenty words, so the different information tests used in the different CPS surveys should all serve roughly equally well.

Building comparable measures of political values is more difficult. One possible measure of values is a person's "ideological" position on the left–right continuum, which can be measured in the CPS surveys as the difference in "feeling thermometer" scores for liberals and conservatives. This measure, however, has a major difficulty. Although ideology must function as an exogenous cause of opinion toward the war in Vietnam, it is possible that influence runs partly in the other direction. It is possible, that is, that people form evaluations of liberals and conservatives partly on the basis of their opinion on the Vietnam issue rather than vice versa.[7]

Another possibility is to use people's general feelings of hawkishness or dovishness as the measure of predispositions to support or oppose the war. The advantage of hawk–dove opinion is that it is the dimension of left–right orientation most likely to affect opinions toward the Vietnam War. The problem is that the 1964–70 CPS surveys contain no direct measure of it.

The problem is not, however, as intractable as it might seem. One can use Franklin's (1989) two-sample instrumental variables technique to construct a proxy measure of hawk–dove attitudes. This technique, which uses information from one dataset to build an instrumental variable in another dataset, produces measures that are asymptotically unbiased and efficient.

The technique works as follows. First, we locate a dataset that has a good measure of hawk–dove values. The one I use here is the 1988 National Election Study, which asked several questions of the following type:

Which do you think is the better way for us to keep the peace – by having a very strong military so that other countries won't attack us, or by working out our disagreements at the bargaining table?[8]

A battery of these items can be used to predict a person's general predisposition to support foreign wars. The next step is to locate a set of "auxiliary" demographic and issue variables – gender, religion, racial attitudes – which are related to the measure of hawk–dove values in the 1988 dataset and which are carried in identical form in the Vietnam datasets. Having done this, one does a regression in the 1988 dataset to determine the relationship between hawk–dove values, on one side, and the auxiliary variables, on the other. The assumption behind the regression is that the coefficients it generates, even though based on 1988 data, capture a *time-invariant* relationship between hawk–dove values and the auxiliary variables.

We then go back to the Vietnam datasets, where we use the auxiliary variables (the same ones that were carried in the 1988 dataset) to make predictions about which people were likely to be hawks and doves in the 1960s. Thus, if women, Quakers, and racial liberals were doves in 1988, we will predict that women, Quakers, and racial liberals were likely to have been doves in the 1960s as well.

But how do we combine scores on numerous auxiliary variables to predict a person's overall likelihood of having been a hawk or dove in the 1960s? This is where the coefficients from the 1988 regression come in. If the coefficients

7 Party attachment could substitute for ideology; however, party is a weaker predictor of war attitudes, while suffering the same endogeneity problem.
8 A series of hawk–dove items of this type were developed and validated by Hurwitz and Peffley (1988).

have, as assumed, captured a time-invariant relationship between the auxiliary variables and hawk–dove values, they should predict how exactly the auxiliary variables were related to hawk–dove values in the Vietnam era. So we use these coefficients as weights on the auxiliary variables to combine them into a new "instrumental variable." The new variable, a weighted combination of the information on numerous auxiliary variables, should predict who was likely to have been a hawk or a dove in the 1960s.

A limitation of this approach, as with any use of instrumental variables, is that the instrument is only as good as the auxiliary variables that have been used to construct it, which, in the present case, is not very good, since the *r*-square on the first stage regression is only 0.14. Despite this, the measure turns out to perform extremely well, as will be shown below. (See Appendix B of this chapter for further details and discussion of the measure; see also footnote 14.)

One final measurement issue needs to be addressed. Although, as I indicated, the Michigan surveys asked essentially the same Vietnam question over four surveys, there is one noteworthy discontinuity. In 1964 and 1966 all respondents were asked whether they had been "paying attention to what is going on in Vietnam," and only those who responded affirmatively were subsequently asked whether they supported or opposed American involvement. In 1964 some 20 percent of the respondents failed this minimal test of interest and were not asked whether they supported or opposed the war; in 1966 persons failing to pass the initial interest screen fell to 7 percent. Then, in 1968 and 1970, the interest screen was dropped, so that only those volunteering a "No opinion" response are counted in that category.

This discontinuity makes it difficult to offer confident estimates of the changes in "No-opinion" rates between 1966 and 1968. Yet the trajectory of decline from 1964 to 1966 in no-attention responses (from 20 percent to 7 percent) suggests that the number of such respondents still having no interest in 1968 was probably small. And, of course, respondents could still volunteer a "No-opinion" response to the Vietnam item itself. Some 7 percent did in 1968, which was down from 9 percent in 1966 and 13 percent in 1964. The fact that volunteered rates of "No opinion" continued to fall from 1966 to 1968 despite removal of the interest filter, as well as other published data (Pierce, Beatty, and Hagner, 1982: p. 142), make it clear that "No opinion" rates did actually continue to decline between 1966 and 1968. But the CPS data probably overestimate the amount by which they did so.

This problem can be accommodated by adding a time subscript to the "floor parameter" in the reception function, as follows:

$$\text{Prob}(RE)_{ikt} = 1 - [1 + f_t + \text{Exp}(a_{0kt} + a_1 * \text{Awareness}_i)]^{-1}$$
$$= RE_{ikt} \tag{9.1b}$$

where f_t can take different values in 1964–6 and 1968–70. The subscripted f-parameter permits different floor levels of opinionation, depending on the presence or absence of a "No-opinion" filter.

Estimation of the model

The model makes multinomial estimates of response probabilities for three categories: support for the war, opposition to it, and no opinion.[9] These estimates are made across four datasets having 5,002 respondents. Initial estimation of the model indicated that patterns of opinion change were different among Anglo whites than other groups. A separate analysis was therefore undertaken for blacks and is reported below; however, Hispanic and Asian-American respondents have been omitted because there are too few cases for separate analysis.

My first estimates of the model produced plausible values for all coefficients, but a graphical analysis showed that the estimated coefficients "underfit" the raw data, in the sense that trends which were clearly apparent in the raw data, as in Figure 9.2, were not adequately represented. The underfitting was not dramatic, but it was quite noticeable. To remedy the problem, I added a term for awareness times values in the acceptance function, and this enabled the model to do a better job of fitting the raw data, though underfitting remains a problem.[10]

Maximum likelihood coefficient estimates of Equation 9.8 for whites are shown in the first column of Table 9.1. The coefficients in the table are described both in terms of the substantive variable to which they refer and the subfunction in which they occur. The standard errors for all coefficients, which are also shown, should be regarded as approximate.

The most notable aspect of these coefficient estimates is their lack of statistical precision, which is to say, the very high standard errors that are associated with them. There are two fairly obvious reasons for this problem. The first is that the data have given the model no indication of the actual intensities of the communication flows that are supposedly shaping opinion – except that they differ by year and by message – or the number of discrete messages citizens were exposed to. This creates severe multicollinearity: There might have been few messages of high intensity, or many messages of low intensity, and the model has no way of telling. Second, political awareness has three separate roles to play – namely, mediating memory search, reception, and resistance. On top of this, awareness appears in several interaction terms in the acceptance function. The effect, once again, is severe multicollinearity.

In an effort to reduce the multicollinearity, I introduced some plausible constraints in the model. Before presenting results from the constrained model, however, it is instructive to examine the unconstrained coefficients.

---

9 As explained in the last chapter, the war support option combines two separate response options – keeping U.S. troops in Vietnam while trying to end the fighting, and taking a stronger stand even if it means invading North Vietnam. The first represents the consistent position of the Kennedy, Johnson, and Nixon administrations; the latter was the preferred strategy of some right-wing critics of the administration. Hawks and doves differed in expected ways in their choices between the two prowar options, and it would be desirable to build a "three-message model" capable of capturing this variation.

10 I should add that none of the substantive conclusions of this chapter would have to be changed if the Awareness × Values terms were omitted; their inclusion serves only to enhance the visual clarity of the simulations, as in Figure 9.4.

Table 9.1. *Coefficients for diffusion of prowar and antiwar messages on Vietnam War*

	Unconstrained model	Constrained model
Reception function (Equation 9.1b)		
Right dummy intercepts (a_{0kt})	See Figure 9.3	
Message intercept[a]	–	−5.68
		(1.29)
Message slope	–	1.71
		(0.64)
Awareness	0.51	0.50
(standardized)	(0.32)	(0.17)
Floor 64–66 (f_t)	0.008	0.01
	(0.11)	(0.02)
Floor 68–70 (f_t)	0.04	0.06
	(0.53)	(0.03)
Acceptance function (Equation 9.2)		
Conservative message intercept (b_{0k})	1.43	2.31
	(2.36)	(1.48)
Liberal message intercept	−1.06	−1.23
	(3.83)	(0.43)
Awareness	−0.08	0.06
	(1.09)	(0.50)
Awareness x time	−0.27	−0.43
(Time = 0 in 1964, 1 afterward)	(0.78)	(0.51)
Hawk–dove[b]	0.11	0.19
(standardized)	(0.26)	(0.30)
Hawk–dove x awareness[b]	0.01	−0.07
	(0.27)	(0.32)
Time	0.29	0.47
	(2.55)	(0.41)
Hawk–dove x time[b]	0.19	0.14
	(.33)	(0.30)
Hawk–dove x awareness x time[b]	0.09	0.22
	(0.27)	(0.35)
Male	−0.18	−0.05
(1 = male)[b]	(0.21)	(0.16)
Recall function (Equation 9.3)		
Intercept (c_0)	3.19	3.47
	(2.48)	(2.36)
Awareness (c_1)	1.66	1.75
	(.94)	(.94)

Number of messages　(N)	35.2	24
	(560)	(fixed)
Degrees of freedom	9980	9987
Residual sum of squares	1643.67	1650.77

Note: Dependent variable is a multinomial item on Vietnam policy: support for the war, opposition to it, and no opinion. The model is Equation 9.8, with subfunctions specified by Equations 9.1b, 9.2, and 9.3. Estimation is by maximum likelihood. N of cases is 5002.
a In the unconstrained model, changes in message intensity over time are captured by eight dummy intercepts in the reception function, one for the liberal and conservative message in each of the four years, as plotted in Figure 9.3. In the constrained model, the message intercept and slope operate on the eight logged story counts shown in Figure 9.1 to produce eight estimates of message intensity.
b Coefficient is negative in acceptance function for conservative message (indicating lower acceptance among liberals) and positive in acceptance function for liberal message.
Sources: 1964, 1966, 1978, and 1970 CPS surveys.

Note first that, in the acceptance function, the effects of both ideology and awareness appear to increase markedly from the period in which there was a mainstream elite consensus (1964) to the period in which the war provoked elite disagreement (1966 through 1970). The direct effect of values increased by a factor of 1.7, the direct effect of awareness increased by a factor of 3.4, and the awareness × values interaction increased by a factor of 9.[11]

These results support a key point in my argument, namely that the effects of values and awareness on political attitudes are not automatic but depend on elite cues for activation.

As explained in the previous section, the model uses changes in the intercept of the reception function, in the form of the a_{0kt} coefficients, to estimate the intensities of pro- and antiwar communications that would have been necessary to produce the observed patterns of opinion on the war. The values of these coefficients are shown in Figure 9.3 (rather than in Table 9.1). Their absolute values have little meaning, but changes over time indicate changes in the relative intensities of the two messages and therefore do have meaning. Thus, the model estimates that the prowar message increased in intensity from 1964 to 1966, fell back moderately in 1968, and declined once again in 1970. Meanwhile, the model estimates that the antiwar message, though initially very weak, steadily gained in intensity until 1970, when it finally became more intense than the prowar message.

11 In my earlier analysis of opinion on the Vietnam War (Zaller, 1991), awareness had positively signed effects in the acceptance function. This difference is due to a change in the form of the acceptance function, as explained in footnote 14 of Chapter 7.

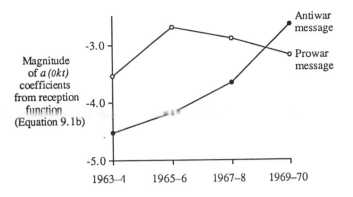

Figure 9.3. Estimated intensities of prowar and antiwar messages, 1963–1970.

The correspondence between these estimated message intensities – which, I stress, have been inferred by the model from trends in opinion data alone – with the actual count of pro- and antiwar stories in national newsmagazines in Figure 9.1a is remarkably good. Indeed, it may be a little too good. As discussed earlier, different indicators of media coverage yield somewhat different results than those shown in Figure 9.1a, and a different version of the two-message model, as described in Appendix A to this chapter and applied to the Vietnam data (Zaller, 1991), produced somewhat different estimates of the pro- and antiwar information flows.[12] Even so, the basic result, very high agreement between two completely different types of estimates of communication flow, amounts to an important achievement for the two-message model.

In reestimating the model, I imposed two constraints. The first is that I required the a_{0kt} coefficients to be a linear function of the logged story counts shown in Figure 9.1a. Thus, the intensities of the pro- and antiwar messages are no longer completely free to take any value in a given year, but are constrained to reflect an actual count of pro- and antiwar stories appearing in the media. Second, because the number of messages in a two-year period is a purely theoretical entity, I arbitrarily constrained it to the number of months between surveys, 24. This constraint increased the residual variance in the model (but only slightly, since any number of messages between about eight and sixty seems to produce an almost equally good fit) while greatly decreasing estimates of standard errors.[13]

12 The correlation between the eight a_{0kt} coefficients reported in Zaller (1991) and the log of the story counts in Figure 9.1 is 0.79; for the version of the two-message model used in this book, the correlation is 0.89.

13 Another advantage of the constrained model is that it converges much more quickly to final parameter estimates. The unconstrained model took several hundred (expensive!) iterations to converge on what seemed to me like firm estimates, even though the initial starting values were fairly good. The greater computational efficiency of the constrained model makes it feasible to do F-tests on particular coefficients, which must still be done in some cases.

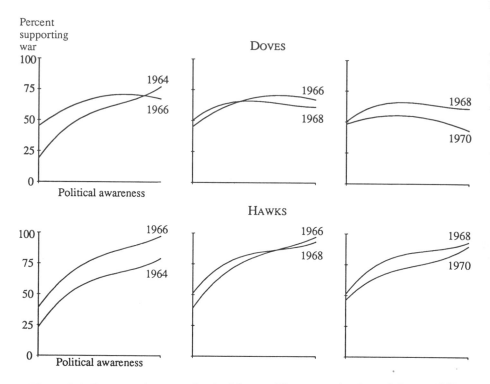

Figure 9.4. Patterns of support for the Vietnam War among hawks and doves, 1964–1970. Estimates are derived from media-constrained coefficient estimates in Table 9.1. See footnote 15 for additional information on the coding of variables in this figure. *Source:* 1964, 1966, 1968, and 1970 CPS surveys.

Estimates from the constrained model are shown in the right-hand column of Table 9.1 As can be seen, the precision of the coefficient estimates is greatly improved. All but one of the coefficients in the reception and recall functions is now statistically significant, and the exception, the floor parameter f in 1964–6, was not expected to diverge from zero.

The coefficients in the acceptance function, however, remain quite imprecise. Yet on a series of F-tests, the important coefficients all emerged as statistically significant. Thus, awareness, values, and Awareness × Values had no overall effect (these apply only to 1964), but the block of coefficients capturing the increased effect of these variables in the period 1966 through 1970 – Awareness × Time, Values × Time, Awareness × Values × Time, and Time – were all statistically significant ($F[4, 9987]$, 2.39 $p < .05$). The interaction terms for awareness and values – Awareness × Values and Awareness × Values × Time – were also statistically significant on an F-test.

What all this means in plain English is that awareness and values had significant effects on resistance to pro- and antiwar communications, but only after elite divisions over the war activated the public's predispositions toward support or opposition.

Of the substantively interesting variables, only male gender is insignificant in the constrained model. This is surprising, since a gender effect is visibly present in the raw data (see Zaller, 1991). I guessed that the problem might be that gender is an important contributor to the hawk–dove instrument and so is, in a sense, being entered into the acceptance function twice. I therefore substituted a more direct measure of ideology – the difference in each respondent's ratings of liberals and conservatives on 100-point feeling thermometers, as described above – into the acceptance function and reestimated the model. In this model, gender was statistically significant on an individual coefficient F-test $(F,[2,9987], 13.68, p < .01)$.[14]

Patterns of support for and opposition to the war

More important than the fit of the model to the data is the substantive story implied by the data and the model. The story emerges readily from a graphical analysis, as shown in Figure 9.4.[15] (This and subsequent figures are based on results from the constrained model.)

Let us examine first the attitudes of doves. Figure 9.4 shows that in 1964 political awareness had a roughly linear relation with support for the war. This result exemplifies the mainstream or "follower" model of opinion formation, as discussed in Chapter 6.

By 1966, however, the Johnson administration was attempting to counter an incipient antiwar movement through "peace offensives," condemnations of "communist aggression," and other publicity ploys. The effects of the louder

14 Multicollinearity among the other variables in the acceptance function affected the precision of the intercept, which in turn affected the precision of the gender coefficient.

    Interestingly, the decrease in residual variance from using the feeling thermometers, despite the problem of endogeneity, as the measure of values over using the hawk–dove instrument is modest. This indicates both a slight level of endogeneity in the feeling thermometers and an impressively good performance by the hawk–dove instrument.

15 Hawks and doves are persons having a score of ±1.85 on the hawk–dove variable; for comparison, the mean score of the doves depicted in Figure 9.2 was just over +2. The following table gives the z-score ranges for the awareness scores that were used in constructing Figure 9.4. Also included are the extreme values of each awareness measure in each year.

z-score values of awareness scales

	1964	1966	1968	1970
Minimum value	−2.51	−1.57	−2.58	−2.14
5th percentile	−2.03	−1.57	−2.00	−1.70
98th percentile	1.61	2.24	1.61	2.13
Maximum value	1.84	2.66	1.96	2.57

Note that the lower range awareness scores represent the 5th percentile in this figure rather than the 1st as in most other figures. The reason is that the lowest z-score on the 1966 awareness scale is −1.57, a score attained by 7.7 percent of the sample. To maintain rough comparability between this lower end value and those of other years, I used a 5th percentile cutoff in the other years.

prowar message register mainly among respondents in the middle to lower ranges of the information spectrum; these are people who previously had been only lightly exposed to the prowar message and were now readily converted to supporting it. Meanwhile, the antiwar message, though barely audible to most of the public, had begun to reach and convert the most politically informed doves, who were the one segment of the public to become less supportive of the war between 1964 and 1966.

The top middle panel of Figure 9.4 shows that, as late as 1968, a small prowar trend is still evident among the least informed doves (though this effect is statistically uncertain) who were still just getting the prowar message, but that the small prowar trend at the low end of the awareness scale is offset by a much larger antiwar movement in the middle and upper ranges of the awareness scale. Thus the balance of pro- and antiwar messages that had mainly favored the war in 1966 was working against it in 1968. Finally, as the top right panel of Figure 9.4 shows, all segments of the dove subgroup were turning against the war by 1970.

Note that the biggest antiwar shift in liberal opinion occurred after Richard Nixon took over the presidency in 1969. With the war effort being led by a Republican rather than a Democrat, many doves found it easier to oppose the war, an observation first made in Mueller's (1973) account of changing patterns of support for the war. Yet it is also notable that the two-message model quite nicely picks up the acceleration in liberal antiwar opinion after 1969 without including a special term for change in presidential leadership; the only source of opinion change on Vietnam in this period is change in the pattern of pro- and antiwar information in the media, as shown in Figure 9.1a.

Changing patterns of war support among hawks generally parallel those among doves, with the conspicuous exception that war support among the most aware hawks never really declines. Between 1964 and 1966, support for the war grows in all awareness groups, including those scoring at the very top of the awareness scale. In 1968 gains in support for the war among the less informed roughly balance small losses among the most informed. And in 1970, despite the growing intensity of the antiwar message, support for the war among hawks declines only slightly – mainly among moderately aware hawks. Thus, throughout the war, political awareness remains positively associated with what is, among hawks, a strong partisan norm.

It is interesting to compare the effects of political awareness on hawks and doves. First of all, the least informed within each camp behave similarly. Owing to their habitual inattentiveness to politics, they are late to support the war and also late to respond to antiwar information. Moderately aware hawks and doves also behave fairly similarly: They fail to support the war in its initial stage because they have not been sufficiently propagandized; as the prowar message heats up, they become more supportive of the war, but then just as quickly begin to abandon the war when the antiwar message becomes loud

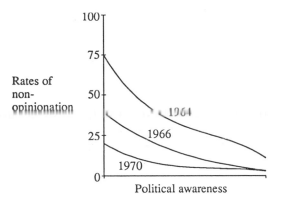

Figure 9.5. Estimated "No-opinion" rates among doves, 1964–1970. Estimates are derived from media-constrained coefficient estimates in Table 9.1. *Source:* 1964, 1966, 1968, and 1970 CPS surveys.

enough to reach them. The most politically aware ideologues, meanwhile, behave very differently. Highly aware doves begin turning against the war as early as 1966; highly aware hawks, by contrast, largely hold their ground, so that they are almost as likely to support the war in 1970 as they were at the start of the conflict. The explanation, of course, is that hawks were sustained by a steady flow of ideologically congenial prowar messages and were, at the same time, highly resistant to the ideologically inconsistent antiwar message.

Although my analysis has focused on differing rates of support for the Vietnam War, the model also accounts for trends in opposition to the war and in "No opinion" rates. The latter are rather interesting, as depicted in Figure 9.5. There is, as would be expected, a strong relationship between "No opinion" rates and political awareness. But the relationship is much steeper early in the war, when most politically unaware persons had no opinion on the war, than it was in later years, when most citizens had opinions. The model is able to accommodate these changing "No opinion" rates because the opinionation function carries information (via Equation 9.4) about the intensity of communications on the war,[16] and more intense messages are, of course, associated with lower rates of the "No opinion" response.

Although it is not shown in Figure 9.5, the model predicts an increase in "No opinion" rates between 1968 and 1970. This projected increase is small, about 2 percentage points in the lowest awareness group and even smaller in other groups, and so does not show up in the raw data. However, Pierce, Beatty, and Hagner (1982: p. 142) report that, across several surveys, "No opinion" rates did begin to creep upward in 1971, a reflection perhaps of a decline in the intensity of communications on the war.

16 More specifically, the RE_{ikt} terms in Equation (9.4) carry the a_{okt} coefficients.

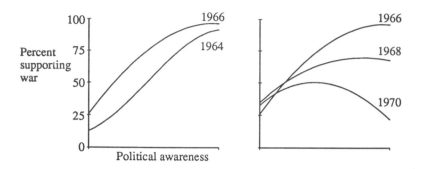

Figure 9.6. Trends in black support for the Vietnam War, 1964–1970. Trend lines have been derived from logistic regressions. The awareness measure in the figure runs ± 1.75 SD. *Source:* 1964, 1966, 1968, and 1970 CPS surveys.

AFRO-AMERICANS' SUPPORT FOR THE WAR

The small number of Afro-Americans available for analysis in the CPS datasets (despite black oversamples in some years) makes it difficult to make a confident assessment of black trends in support for the war. Nonetheless, the available data reveal some highly suggestive patterns, as shown in Figure 9.6. (The data in this figure have been constructed from simple polynomial regression in order to smooth out lumpiness arising from sampling error.)

The data in the left panel of Figure 9.6 show patterns of war support among blacks in 1964 and 1966. These patterns generally resemble those of white conservatives, rather than white liberals, in Figure 9.4; there is, in other words, a generally positive relationship between awareness and support for the war, with an increase in support between 1964 and 1966 that registers mainly among less-aware and moderately aware persons. The jump in war support presumably reflects the increase in the intensity of prowar communications. Contrary to some analyses, these data offer no indication that blacks were initially reluctant to support the Vietnam War.[17]

After 1966, however, black attitudes toward the war begin to resemble those of white liberals, as can be seen from a comparison of the right-hand side of Figure 9.6 with trends among liberals in Figure 9.4. That is, support for the war declined significantly, especially among highly and moderately informed blacks, as a result of the gradual diffusion of the antiwar message.

Nothing in these opinion data can, by itself, explain why black attitudes toward the war should resemble those of white conservatives until 1966 and those

17 There is a significant tendency for blacks to be less supportive of the war in both years, but it disappears once a control for political awareness has been imposed. A close inspection of the data further suggests that highly aware blacks were more supportive of the war than highly aware white conservatives (or any other group) in both 1964 and 1966; at the same time, however, less informed blacks were less supportive of the war than less informed white conservatives (or any other group) in each year. These apparent racial differences, however, are unreliable because of very small numbers of cases at the extremes of high and low information.

of white liberals after that time. There seems, nonetheless, to be an obvious explanation: The Vietnam War was led by President Lyndon Johnson, who in 1964 and 1965 won congressional approval for two historic civil rights bills and who launched the ambitious War on Poverty program. In light of this, members of the black public were likely to attach greater credibility to Johnson's statements on the war than were other types of persons. By 1968, however, Johnson's civil rights achievements were well behind him and many members of the black civil rights leadership group, including the recently assassinated Martin Luther King, Jr., had come out against the war.[18] In this situation, blacks became more susceptible to the increasingly intense antiwar message.

Thus, blacks appear to have been as responsive as whites to the flow of pro- and antiwar information on Vietnam, but blacks evaluated this information in light of somewhat different leadership cues.

IMPLICATIONS

The results of this chapter have advanced our understanding of the dynamics of opinion change in several respects. First, they provide the first clear evidence of countervalent resistance, most strikingly in the period 1964 to 1966. They show, that is, that highly aware doves were able to resist the dominant prowar message of this period in part because they were exposed to the countervalent antiwar message. This message, though less intense than the prowar message in the early stage of the war, not only neutralized the prowar message, but actually induced some of the most aware doves to buck the national trend by becoming less supportive of the war.

The reason that the effects of countervalent communications are so clear in the case of Vietnam is that the countervalent message was becoming more intense at a time when the dominant message was also becoming more intense, so that each message could produce converts in a different part of the public. This pattern of information flows is probably unusual (though see Figure 10.5). But it is likely that there are many other cases in which countervalent communications, though not quite strong enough to produce movements against a predominant national trend, are nonetheless important in inducing resistance to such a trend. We shall see further clear evidence of the effects of countervalent communications in the next chapter.

Second, these results enable us to see that attitude change in response to a two-sided message can take different forms at different points in time, depending on the relative intensities of the opposing messages and the prior distribution of opinion. We see also that some of these patterns do not match those developed in the typology proposed in Chapter 8, a typology that was constructed

---

18 Johnson's approval ratings fell more rapidly among blacks than among whites in the period from 1966 to mid-1968, but then rebounded at the time of the election. (See Dawson, Brown, and Cohen, n.d.)

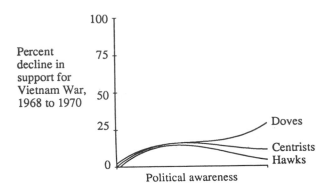

Figure 9.7. Changes in support for the Vietnam War, 1968–1970. Figure shows percentage of persons supporting the war in 1968 who no longer supported it in 1970. These estimates are derived from the support scores shown in Figure 9.4. *Source:* 1968 and 1970 CPS surveys.

under the assumption that opinion change is a response to a one-sided information flow.

What, then, do we make of the typology in Chapter 8? Although I cannot say precisely, my simulations of attitude change with Equation 9.8, along with the empirical results reported in Chapter 8, suggest that the typology is, despite its focus on one-sided information flows, a good approximation to a wider variety of cases. The typology appears to be an especially good approximation to the patterns of change that may be expected when one of the opposing messages remains equally intense or loses intensity over time, while the other message gains in intensity. This pattern of changes in a two-sided information flow is perhaps the most common form of stimulus to mass attitude change; in fact, all cases of mass attitude change of which I am aware, except the 1964 to 1966 period of the Vietnam War, appear to have been produced by this type of stimulus. For example, late in the Vietnam War, when the prowar message was roughly stable or losing intensity and the antiwar message was gaining in intensity (see Figure 9.3), the typology provides an approximation of the patterns of attitude change that actually occurred, as can be seen in Figure 9.7.

Nonetheless, it remains the case that the patterns depicted in the typology in Chapter 8 strictly hold only under conditions of a one-sided communication flow. These conditions would seem most likely to hold when the period between attitude measurements is short, and when the gain in the relative intensity of one of the messages is large.

Third, the results presented in this chapter, along with the discussion of age effects on the Vietnam issue, constitute an unusually detailed account of how mass belief systems form and change over time in response to a complex stimulus.[19] The leading theoretical account of this general phenomenon has long been Converse's "The nature of belief systems in mass publics" (1964). His argument, it will be recalled, was that certain "creative elites" manufacture wide-ranging belief systems – which is to say, clusters of attitudes that are widely perceived as "going together." These belief systems then diffuse imperfectly through the public, such that only the most aware members of the public manage to fully absorb them.

The argument of this chapter has filled in important details of this general argument and, in so doing, has somewhat altered it. It has documented, first of all, how a new element – an antiwar posture on Vietnam – became gradually incorporated into the liberal belief package, where liberalism itself is operationally measured as general tendencies toward hawkishness or dovishness. (The same patterns of attitude change arise more sharply if a direct measure of ideology – scores for liberals and conservatives on 100-point feeling thermometers – are substituted for the hawk–dove instrument that I used.) The story of this incorporation is largely in the spirit of Converse's analysis: The most politically attuned liberals were the first to adopt the new belief element, while highly aware conservatives tended, in general, to resist it.

There are, however, some unexpected turns. In Converse's theory, ideology operates as a "constraint" on the organization of one's attitudes. Thus, if one is a liberal, one is expected to embrace all of the elements of the liberal belief package. That argument does not, however, readily apply to the highly aware, older liberals who continued to resist the antiwar element of the liberal belief package as late as 1970. As they presumably saw it, the constraints of liberal ideology cut the other way – toward *support* of the Vietnam War as another case of post–World War II liberal internationalism. Such lags in adopting policies to which individuals are presumably predisposed by their general philosophy represent an interesting and heretofore unglimpsed aspect of the notion of ideological constraint in a dynamic setting.

Another unexpected turn is the back-and-forth movement of moderately aware and less aware liberals. The liberals who moved in a prowar direction between 1964 and 1966 may have thought, if they stopped to reflect on it, that they were moving in a *liberal* direction. After all, internationalism had been a core element of the liberal belief package for some thirty years, and the principal advocate of the prowar policy was the liberal Democratic president, Lyndon Johnson. Yet, if, as seems most reasonable, ideology is defined by the preferences of its avant garde elites, this is another case in which persons were "constrained" by what they took to be liberalism to adopt a policy attitude that was, for its time, rapidly becoming a litmus test of conservative values.

The analysis of changing attitudes on the Vietnam War thus affords a rare opportunity – rare because the direction of elite cues on most issues is stable from year to year – to observe the evolution of mass ideologies. Although this

19 For other treatments of the evolution of mass belief systems, see Miller and Levitan, 1976; Carmines and Stimson, 1989; and Hurwitz and Peffley, in press.

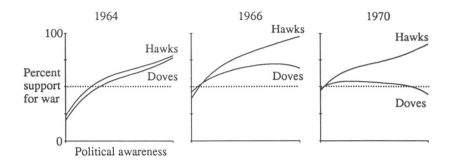

Figure 9.8. Partisan polarization on the Vietnam War. Estimates are a rearrangement of the data appearing in Figure 9.4. *Source:* 1964, 1966, 1968, and 1970 CPS surveys.

case has involved foreign policy attitudes, it is likely that ideological cues on other issues sometimes undergo similar changes in "what goes with what," and that when they do, they produce similar changes in the pattern of mass attitudes.

There are, it should be added, no contradictions between my analysis of the Vietnam case and the general theory outlined by Converse. Vietnam has simply provided examples of how, in a dynamic situation, various types of lags may lead to unexpected forms of ideological constraint.

Finally, and most importantly, the results of this chapter provide credible evidence for a very strong claim: that public attitudes toward major issues are a response to the relative intensity of competing political communications on those issues. When elites unite on a mainstream issue, the public's response is relatively nonideological, with the most aware members of the public reflecting the elite consensus most strongly. When elites come to disagree along partisan or ideological lines, the public's response will become ideological as well, with the most politically aware members of the public responding most ideologically. The degree of mass ideological polarization on an issue reflects the relative intensity of the opposing information flows. Thus, when, in the case of the Vietnam War in 1966, the conservative message was much more intense than the liberal, the degree of polarization was both modest and skewed in the direction of the conservative position; as the opposing information flows became more nearly balanced, overall support for the conservative position fell and ideological polarization became more intense. These points are highlighted in Figure 9.8, which is a reorganization of data presented earlier in Figure 9.4.[20] (Polarization is sharper if the ideology thermometers rather than an instrument are used to measure predispositions; see Zaller, 1991, figure 8.

20 It is interesting that even though the model estimates the antiwar message to have been more intense than the prowar message in 1970, it also indicates that public support for the war was greater in that year than opposition. This is possible because the model also maintains that there was more resistance to the antiwar message, at comparable levels of reception, than to the prowar message; this difference is captured in the intercept difference in the acceptance functions of the two messages, as shown in Table 9.1.

Although the two-message model used in this chapter has made "considerations," defined as discrete reasons for favoring or opposing an idea, its primitive unit of analysis, no measurements of public opinion on Vietnam were made at the level of considerations. As a result, I have been unable to provide direct evidence that the dynamics of the model hold at the intrapsychic level at which people either internalize or fail to internalize particular messages they encounter. The next chapter fills out this part of the argument by showing how the relative intensity of opposing communication flows determines the formation of new considerations, which in turn determines the summary preference statements people make.

APPENDIX A: AN ALTERNATIVE FORM OF TWO-MESSAGE MODEL

In this appendix, I derive an alternative form of two-message model. The alternative omits any reference to considerations, but is otherwise similar to the model developed in the text.

Let us assume a political world in which, within every time period t and with respect to every political issue, citizens are presented with two information flows, or "messages," one tending to push mass opinion in a liberal direction and the other in a conservative direction. The two messages represent the sum of all directionally valenced communications relating to a given issue in the period.

The following three-axiom model shows how, in such a world, temporal variations in the intensities of the liberal and conservative messages can explain both the cross-sectional distribution of mass opinion at any one time and changes in opinion over time.

1. *RECEPTION AXIOM. An individual's probabilities of receiving the liberal and conservative messages within any given time period t are independent, increasing functions of general level of political awareness.*

The mathematical form of this axiom is Equation 9.1*b*.

2. *ACCEPTANCE AXIOM. The probability that an individual will resist – that is, refuse to accept – a message, given reception of it, increases with (1) distance between the values of the individual and the value coloration of the message, and (2) the likelihood that individuals will be aware of the elite-supplied "contextual information" that gives messages their colorations.*

The form of this axiom is given by Equation 9.2.

Before stating the third axiom, I define "supporting messages" as those consistent with an existing opinion and "opposing messages" as those that are inconsistent. The final axiom can now be stated:

3. *CHANGE AXIOM. Two types of opinion change, conversion and decay, may occur:*
   A. When a person accepts an opposing message (having received it) and does not accept a supporting message (whether receiving it or not), the person converts to the opposing view.

B. If a person accepts no messages in a given period, or accepts both a supporting message and an opposing one, the person's initial opinion decays toward "no opinion" with a fixed probability of d.

We can use these axioms to write an expression for the probability that, following some time period, an individual who initially holds a liberal opinion or no opinion will change to a conservative opinion. From axioms 1 through 3A, that probability must be

$$
\begin{aligned}
P_{i \to C_{t+1}} = \ & \text{Probability that an individual will switch} \\
& \text{to a conservative opinion following time period } t \\
= \ & [RE_{iC_t}(1 - RE_{iL_t})]\text{Accept}_{iC_t} + RE_{iC_t}RE_{iL_t} \\
& [\text{Accept}_{iC_t}(1 - \text{Accept}_{iL_t})] \hspace{2cm} (9.9)
\end{aligned}
$$

The first term on the right-hand side is the probability that the individual will receive only a conservative message – $RE_{iC_t}(1 - RE_{iL_t})$ – times the probability that the person will accept it, having been exposed, Accept_{iC_t}. The second term is the probability that the individual will receive both messages – $RE_{iC_t} RE_{iL_t}$ – but accept only the conservative one – $\text{Accept}_{iC_t}(1\text{-Accept}_{iL_t})$. The term $P_{i \to L_{t+1}}$ can be similarly defined.

One can also write out the probability that the response of an individual initially holding an opinion will decay to no opinion. That probability is d times the probability of either accepting no messages or accepting both a supporting and opposing message, as follows:

$$
\begin{aligned}
P_{i \to \text{Non}_{t+1}} = \ & d[(1 - RE_{iC_t})(1 - RE_{iL_t}) + RE_{iC_t}(1 - RE_{iL_t}) \\
& (1 - \text{Accept}_{iC_t}) + RE_{iL_t}(1 - RE_{iC_t})(1 - \text{Accept}_{iL_t}) \\
& + RE_{iC_t}RE_{iL_t}\text{Accept}_{iC_t}\text{Accept}_{iL_t}] \\
= \ & d(1 - P_{i \to C_{t+1}} - P_{i \to L_{t+1}}) \hspace{2cm} (9.10)
\end{aligned}
$$

At some initial moment, everyone has a fixed probability of holding a liberal or conservative opinion or no opinion. Let us call these probabilities $\text{Lib}_{(t)}$, $\text{Con}_{(t)}$ and $\text{Non}_{(t)}$. The probability that someone initially holding a liberal opinion will still hold a liberal opinion at time $t + 1$ is then

$$
\begin{aligned}
\text{Lib}_{(t+1)} = \ & \text{Lib}_{(t)} - [P_{\to C}\text{Lib}_{(t)}] - [P_{\to \text{Non}}\text{Lib}_{(t)}] \\
& + [P_{\to L}(\text{Con}_{(t)} + \text{Non}_{(t)})] \hspace{2cm} (9.11)
\end{aligned}
$$

A parallel expression can, of course, be written for conservative opinion at $t+1$.

With some algebraic manipulation, Equation 9.11 can be rewritten as a difference equation that gives the probability of a liberal opinion after N time periods, as follows:

$$
\text{Lib}_{(t+N)} = \text{Lib}_{(t)}X^N + P_{\to L}\frac{1 - X^N}{1 - X} \hspace{2cm} (9.12)
$$

where $X = 1 - P_{\to C} - P_{\to L} - d + d(P_{\to C} + P_{\to L})$

One may conceptualize time as consisting of an infinitude of arbitrarily tiny time units. If so, N is infinity, in which case the term X^N in Equation 9.12, which is a proportion raised to an infinite power, goes to zero. This leaves

$$
\text{Lib}_{(t+N)} = P_{\to L}\frac{1 - X^N}{1 - X}
$$

$$
= \frac{P_{\to L}}{P_{\to C} + P_{\to L} + d - d(P_{\to C} + P_{\to L})} \tag{9.13}
$$

Thus, opinion at any point in time represents an equilibrium outcome that is independent of starting values. This equilibrium depends, at the aggregate level, on the intensities of the competing information flows, and, at the individual level, on people's attention to politics and their values. Opinion change in response to persuasive information, a central topic of my analysis, can be captured as a difference over time between equilibrium points, where changing equilibria depend on change in the competing information flows.

This model has been used (Zaller, 1991) to estimate the effect of ideology and awareness on support for the Vietnam War, producing results that are highly similar to those reported in this chapter. The main difference is that this model does less well in estimating the intensities of the antiwar and prowar messages to which the public was exposed, in the sense that its estimates correspond less well with the story counts shown in Figure 9.1. See footnote 12.

APPENDIX B: MEASUREMENT OF HAWK–DOVE ATTITUDES

Franklin's instrumental variables technique provides "a method of estimating relationships between variables not measured in the same dataset" (1989: p. 23). The method is as follows: One has a measure of variable X in dataset A but not dataset B; however the dependent variable of interest, variable Y, is in dataset B. One then locates a set of auxiliary variables carried in both datasets. The X variable is regressed on these auxiliary variables in dataset A, an instrument for X is built from the resulting coefficient estimates, and this instrument is used in dataset B as an independent predictor of variable Y. In the present case, the X variable is a measure of hawk–dove attitudes, as measured in the 1988 National Election Study; the Y variable is opinion toward the Vietnam War, as measured in the CPS surveys of 1964 to 1970. Provided appropriate assumptions are met, Franklin's technique makes it possible to build an instrumental measure of hawk–dove attitudes in the CPS datasets from information contained in the 1988 NES.

The most important of these assumptions are that both datasets be samples of the same population, and that relationships between the auxiliary variables and the X variable be the same in both datasets. The latter assumption is obviously the more worrisome, since the datasets were created eighteen to twenty-four years apart. Nonetheless, it is not implausible to believe that the types of persons most likely to be doves in 1988, such as females, atheists, and civil rights liberals, were likely to be doves in the 1960s as well, provided they were given appropriate leadership cues. And, in fact, all of these variables are correlated

Table 9.2. *First stage regression estimates for hawk–dove instrument*

	Coefficient	T-ratio
Agnostic or atheist	0.40	4.04
Catholic	0.15	2.51
Fundamentalist[a]	−0.18	2.54
Jehovah's Witness	0.98	1.05
Jew	0.55	2.99
Pacifistic religion[b]	0.43	1.53
Church attendance[c]	0.08	3.57
Too slow on civil rights (V845)[d]	0.50	6.01
Too fast on civil rights	−0.38	6.75
Border state	−0.01	.16
Southern state	−0.13	1.91
Union member	−0.11	1.68
N	1441	
Adjusted r^2	.14	

Note: Dependent variable consists of five items, combined by principal components analysis into a scale: Strong military or bargain for peace (V966); importance of strong military (V967); United States stay most powerful (V972); Communist takeovers always threat (V973); United States must stop communism (V974). High scores indicate dovish responses.
[a]Codes 130 to 149, and 152 on V527.
[b]Codes 153, 155, and 156 on V527.
[c]V530, range 1–4.
d It was necessary to subsitute Aid to Minorities, appropriately recoded, in construction of the Form II instrument of the 1970 CPS study.
Source: 1988 NES survey.

with opinions toward the Vietnam War in the expected directions. Hence, despite some concern, it is reasonable to assume that the conditions necessary to apply the Franklin technique have been met.

Two variables require comment, however. First, age is associated with greater hawkishness in 1988, as measured by general hawk–dove items of the type shown in the text, but less support for the Vietnam War in the 1960s. This does not, however, appear to represent change over time, since older persons, though presumably still tending to be hawkish in 1991, were also less likely to support U.S. military involvement in the Persian Gulf crisis.[21] Second, education is as-

21 *New York Times,* December 14, 1990, p. A8.

sociated with less hawkishness in 1988 but greater support for the Vietnam War, especially in the early phase of the war. This reversal is best explained by Mueller's (1973) observation that better educated persons, though not dispositionally hawkish, are more susceptible to elite opinion leadership, since they are more heavily exposed to what elites are saying. And again, this does not seem to represent a change in the last twenty years, since education was positively associated with support for mainstream policy in the nation's most recent war even though it was negatively associated with hawkishness, as measured by the NES in 1988.[22] But even though no sign changes appear to have occurred over time, the "wrong-way" correlations of age and education with hawkishness indicate that they should not be used in building an instrumental measure that is intended to measure predispositions to support the Vietnam War.

The OLS coefficients used in building the hawk–dove instrument, along with information concerning the auxiliary variables, are shown in Table 9.2.

22 Ibid.

10

Information flow and electoral choice

Election campaigns are attempts by competing partisan elites to reach citizens with political communications and persuade them to a point of view. In this essential respect, election campaigns resemble the ongoing campaigns to shape public opinion that we have examined in previous chapters. One may therefore suspect that the dynamics of contested elections are much like those we have already seen. One may suspect, that is, that citizens vary in their susceptibility to influence according to their general levels of political awareness and their predispositions to accept the campaign messages they receive.

The aim of this chapter is to test this suspicion. I will examine four types of contested elections: elections for the House of Representatives and U.S. Senate, general presidential elections, and presidential primary elections. In so doing, I will try to shed light afresh on the question of how citizens choose their elected representatives. No attempt will be made, however, to develop a comprehensive account of electoral behavior in these four types of elections. Rather, my primary effort will be to use systematic differences that exist among them to increase understanding of how, in general, mass attitudes form and change in response to competing flows of political information. Capitalizing on the fact that most congressional campaigns are dominated by incumbent officeholders, I shall be especially interested in the process by which citizens resist dominant campaign messages.

The great advantage of electoral attitudes, for the purposes of this book, is that more resources have been devoted to studying them than to any other kind of political attitude. In consequence, there exist datasets with strong measures of all of the key variables in the RAS model – including, most importantly, the "considerations" that underlie people's opinion statements, which in this case are reports of vote decisions. There is also wide and readily measurable variability in the relative intensity of the competing messages (the political campaigns) to which people are exposed.

One of the richest of the election datasets, from the perspective of data needs of the RAS model, is the 1978 NES congressional election study. The study carries identical individual-level measures of awareness, ideology, and attitudes toward candidates across seventy-seven widely different contested elections. Thus, whereas in the case of attitudes toward the Vietnam War we had just four surveys in which to observe the effects of competing messages of differing intensity, here we have, in effect, seventy-seven.[1]

The availability of such strong data will enable us to undertake a relatively full examination of how the basic resistance mechanisms of the RAS model, especially inertial and countervalent resistance, operate in a dynamic setting. In addition, we will encounter further instances of differential information flow, that is, cases in which competing messages generate cross-cutting opinion formation in different segments of the public, depending on levels of attentiveness and the relative intensities of the two messages. The outcome of these analyses will be a much clearer picture of how complex information flows affect the formation of citizen preferences.

Because the largest single part of this chapter is devoted to exploiting the House election data, I begin with a brief review of current research on House elections.

INERTIAL RESISTANCE TO INCUMBENT-DOMINATED HOUSE CAMPAIGNS

A central research problem in congressional elections in recent years has been the dynamics of incumbent advantage. Since David Mayhew raised the puzzle of the "vanishing marginals" in a famous 1974 paper, scholars have turned out a torrent of papers attempting to explain why politically marginal districts – that is, districts carried by the winning party by a margin of five points or less – have tended to disappear over the past two decades. Much of this research has focused on the incumbent's skill in constituency service and image building, by which the member creates a "personal vote" that is significantly independent of normal party attachments in the district (Erikson, 1971; Fenno, 1978; Fiorina, 1977; Mann, 1978; Cain, Ferejohn, and Fiorina, 1987).

Inasmuch as House members must reach and persuade members of an electorate that vary in both attention to politics and partisan predispositions, the reception-acceptance model would seem ideally suited to studying the process by which incumbents develop their mass followings.

Let us begin with the reception of proincumbent information. Some of the self-promotional efforts of House members take the form of case work (for example, chasing after lost social security checks) that will come to the attention of voters independently of their general political awareness. But most of what House members do to publicize themselves is likely to reach mainly people who are chronically attentive to politics. This includes sending out newsletters (which are more likely to be read by the politically aware), efforts to bring particularistic benefits to the district (which depend on newspapers and civic groups to get the word out), collecting political endorsements, and giving speeches and attending rallies. When, on the other hand, politically apathetic persons happen to

---

1 The NES study covered 108 districts, but my analysis focuses on the 77 in which an incumbent House member sought reelection against an opponent from the other party.

encounter information about their House member, they may forget, ignore, or otherwise fail to react to what they see; this, after all, is what it means to be politically apathetic.

So, meaningful exposure to the activities of House members is likely to be positively associated with habitual political awareness. And given that most House elections are low-key contests in which only the incumbent manages to mount a serious campaign, most of what politically aware people encounter during and between campaigns will have a strong proincumbent bias (Jacobson, 1991).

But this is only half the story. People who are politically aware may also be better able to resist the appeals of a dominant campaign message, if they are predisposed by party or ideology to do so. This is because, as we have seen, such persons are likely to possess prior information that acts to dilute the effects of new ideas. They are more likely to receive countervalent messages (in this case, the campaign information of the congressional challenger) and more likely to possess the contextual information necessary to recognize and reject outright communications that are inconsistent with their predispositions. In other words, more aware persons are more likely to exhibit inertial, countervalent, and partisan resistance to the blandishments of the incumbent House member.

If more aware persons are more heavily exposed to the dominant campaign of the incumbent, and also more capable of resisting its messages (given reception), we might expect from the logic of the reception-acceptance process to find a nonmonotonic relationship between awareness and vote defection, such that persons who are *moderately* politically aware will be most likely to defect to the incumbent, thereby creating a "personal vote" for him or her.

As many readers will recall, Philip Converse found evidence of such nonmonotonicity in his classic study of the 1952 presidential election, "Information flow and the stability of partisan attitudes" (1962). He explained it in these now-familiar terms: Highly aware persons are heavily exposed to the persuasive appeals of the campaign, but, owing to the strength of their preexisting attitudes, they are difficult to influence. At the same time, persons who pay little attention to politics are also relatively stable – not because they have strong partisan commitments, but because they pay so little attention to politics that they rarely encounter communications that can change their preferences. Finally, moderately aware people pay enough attention to politics to be exposed to partisan communications but are not sufficiently committed to their initial preferences to be immune to conversion. Hence this group tends to be the most volatile of the three.

Converse's explanation for why politically aware persons might be more difficult to persuade, despite their high levels of exposure to the campaign, is also familiar:

the highly informed voter operates with a large storage of political lore, and the uninformed voter is characterized by poor retention of past political information. Our repeated observations of the staggering differences in information level in the electorate, then, are observations of the great differences in this "mass" from voter to voter. And *the probability that any given voter will be sufficiently deflected in his partisan momentum to cross party lines in a specified election . . . varies inversely as a function of the mass of stored information about politics.* (pp. 140–1, emphasis in the original)

If, as seems reasonable, one substitutes the phrase "preexisting considerations" for "mass of stored information," Converse's explanation for awareness-induced resistance to persuasion corresponds almost exactly to my notion of inertial resistance. Converse makes no reference, however, to concepts resembling my notions of countervalent or partisan resistance.

In his "Information flow" article, Converse looked briefly at data from the 1958 House elections, but he turned up no evidence of a nonmonotonic pattern of partisan instability. Converse's quite plausible explanation was that news about congressional elections was so "extremely weak" that it went "unheeded by all but the most avid readers of political news" (p. 143). Hence defection rates in House elections were very low, and such defection as did occur was concentrated among the more politically aware voters.

But Converse's analysis was based on congressional elections as they existed three decades ago. House campaigns have gained intensity in recent decades, enough intensity perhaps that they now reach voters who are only moderately attentive to politics. Certainly the recent explosion of television advertising and the appearance of the new nonstop reelection campaigns would justify the assumption that House campaigns now reach a larger fraction of the electorate than they did in the 1950s.[2] And if this is true, it might turn out that people of moderate political awareness are now more susceptible to the appeals of congressional campaigns than are the most attentive voters.

A look back to Chapter 8 will reveal that the difference between Converse's account of the 1958 House elections and my expectations for the 1978 elections is perfectly captured by the difference between cell A and cell B in the typology of attitude change in Figure 8.2; cell A refers to the effects of low-intensity messages, whereas cell B refers to medium-intensity messages.

Let us turn, then, to the data to see whether the basic reception-acceptance dynamic holds in House elections as in other political contexts, and, if so, whether, as Converse thought, "stored information about politics" plays a critical role in the generation of resistance to persuasion.

Defection patterns in House elections

In House elections in which an incumbent seeks reelection, the incumbent normally dominates the flow of political communications, with the result that almost all defections are defections to the party of the incumbent (Abramowitz,

2 Despite this, the ability of constituents to freely recall the name of their congressional representative has not changed since the 1950s (Nelson, 1978–9). Evidence of more intense campaign activity is nonetheless abundant (Fiorina, 1977; Mann, 1978). It is possible, as Mann and Wolfinger (1980) suggest, that name recognition has increased even though recall has not.

1980; Jacobson, 1991; especially at p. 115). The present analysis, then, will limit itself to defections to the incumbent from members of the opposing party.

These defecting "outpartisans" hold considerable political interest: They are precisely the voters who, by abandoning their normal party in order to support the incumbent, are most responsible for the "vanishing marginals" and the rise of the "personal vote." The defectors also hold theoretical interest: They have succumbed to the message of a dominant campaign despite its inconsistency with their political predispositions. Our task is to find out why exactly they have done so.

My approach will be to model defection as the outcome of a standard reception-acceptance process, where the source of persuasive communication is the dominant campaign of the incumbent. The model, thus, will take the following form:

$$\text{Prob(Defection)} = 1 - (1 + \text{Exp}[a_0 + a_1\text{Awareness} + \ldots \text{others}])^{-1}$$
$$\times (1 + \text{Exp}[-b_0 - b_1\text{Awareness} \ldots \text{others}])^{-1} \quad (10.1)$$
[adapted from Equation (7.5)]

An attractive feature of House elections, from the point of view of exercising the reception-acceptance model, is that the intensity of the dominant incumbent campaign varies markedly from one district to another, and does so in ways that are readily measured by such variables as campaign spending. The intensity of the challenger's campaign – which is to say, the intensity of the countervalent information flow – also varies in readily measurable ways.

To capture the effects of this variation in information flow, I have included the following variables in the two subfunctions of the model:

Reception function	*Acceptance function*
Political awareness	Political awareness
Intensity of media coverage	Strength of party attachment
Incumbent's spending	Inertia (preexisting considerations)
Challenger's spending	Challenger's spending
Years in office (seniority)	
Seniority × Challenger's spending	

Each set of variables requires comment, beginning with the reception variables. Note, first of all, that there is only one individual-level reception variable, political awareness. The rest – media coverage, incumbent's spending, challenger's spending, and seniority – are aggregate-level variables intended to capture the flow of communications in the political environment. Use of a logistic function to model the reception process means that the aggregate variables will interact with individual differences in political awareness to determine how much information different people receive.

To measure the general intensity of media coverage of a given race, I begin with responses to the following question:

How many newspaper articles did you read about the campaign for the U.S. House of Representatives in your district – would you say you read a good many, several or just one or two?

The mean of responses to this question has been calculated for respondents in each congressional district and purged of the effects of district-level variation in political awareness.[3] These purged means, which ranged from a low of 0.6 to a high of 1.9, can be used as an aggregate-level measure of the intensity of media coverage.

Years in office has been included among the reception variables on the theory that more senior incumbents have had more time to get their message out to the public via newsletters, appearances, case work, and news events, and hence will be more effective in attracting defectors from the opposition party. Seniority, thus, is intended as a proxy for the interelection communications by which incumbents gradually build a personal following in their districts.

Seniority, it will turn out, has the effect expected, but only in lightly contested races. In the most heavily contested races, long service in office seems to hurt rather than help the incumbent. I sought to capture this cross-cutting effect by including a term for seniority times challenger's spending.[4]

I turn now to the acceptance function. The most interesting variable here is inertia, by which I mean the mass of considerations that cause voters to lean toward their chosen party, and that the incumbent campaign must overcome if it is to win the votes of partisans of the opposing party.

Throughout my discussion of the one-message model, I have maintained that political awareness is associated with resistance to persuasion in part because it is a proxy for inertial resistance. In adding the inertia variable to the acceptance function, I am able, for the first time, to make a direct test for inertial resistance.

To measure inertia, I use the standard NES "likes/dislikes" questions about the political parties. These are open-ended probes in which voters are asked what they like and dislike about each party, as follows:

I'd like to ask you what you think are the good and bad points about the two national parties. Is there anything in particular that you like about the Democratic [Republican] party? What is that? Anything else? [Up to five responses were coded.]

Is there anything in particular that you don't like about the Democratic [Republican] party? What is that? Anything else? [Up to five responses were coded.]

Inertia can then be measured as follows:

$$
\text{Inertia} = +\sum(\text{Outparty likes}) + \sum(\text{Incumbent party dislikes})
$$
$$
- \sum(\text{Outparty dislikes}) - \sum(\text{Incumbent party likes})
$$

---

3 If individuals in one district are, say, very well educated, the mean number of articles about the House race that are reported for that district may be high even if there was only a light campaign. These are the sorts of individual-level effects I have purged from the district-level means.

4 This term represents an ad hoc adaptation to the presence of a substantial antiincumbent information flow in high-intensity races. Such adaptations are needed because Equation 10.1 is essentially a one-message model. As the challenger campaign becomes more intense, Equation 10.1 becomes less capable of capturing what is going on in a theoretically coherent way. A two-message model, along the lines of that proposed in Chapter 9, is needed here.

Table 10.1. *Coefficients predicting vote for House incumbent among outpartisans*

Reception function		Acceptance function	
Intercept	−1.71	Intercept	3.39
Awareness	2.24	Awareness	−1.01
(standardized)	(1.20)		(.41)
Incumbent spending	−0.11	Party strength	−1.32
(in $10 thousands)	(.09)		(.48)
Challenger spending	0.28	Partisan inertia[a]	−0.22
(in $10 thousands)	(.18)		(.12)
Media coverage	3.51	Challenger spending	−0.05
(range .59 – 1.9)	(2.72)		(.02)
Seniority	2.84		
(logged)	(2.13)		
Seniority x challenger	−0.41	N	277
spending	(.26)		

Note: Model is Equation 10.1, estimated by maximum likelihood. Standard errors are in parentheses. Dependent variable is vote for incumbent among outpartisans.

[a] High scores run in direction of challenger party.

Source: 1978 NES survey.

The higher an outpartisan's score on the inertia variable, the more difficult it should be, at a given level of exposure to an incumbent dominated campaign, to deflect her or his vote to the party of the House incumbent.

The final variable in the acceptance function that requires comment is challenger's spending. The idea here is that outpartisans will be less likely to accept the incumbent's message if they are being concurrently exposed to a strong campaign by a challenger. Thus, the challenger's spending variable in the acceptance function is an attempt to capture the effects of countervalent information.

Altogether, then, Equation 10.1 specifies a complex interaction between individual-level differences in propensities for reception and acceptance of communication, and aggregate-level differences in the intensities of a dominant and countervalent communication flow. As should be apparent, however, Equation 10.1 is not fully a two-message model – it does not contain separate reception and acceptance functions for each message, as did the model used for estimating Vietnam attitudes in Chapter 9. But, like the one-message model proposed in Chapters 7 and 8, it does attempt, in the ways I have indicated, to capture the effects of a two-sided information flow (see footnote 4).

The coefficients obtained from estimating the model are shown in Table 10.1. Although the interpretation of these coefficients requires, as usual, a graphical analysis, some information can be gleaned from visual inspection.

Because there are only 277 cases available for analysis, namely the outpartisans who voted in a race in which an incumbent was opposed for reelection, many of the coefficients in Table 10.1 lack statistical precision. Nonetheless, all of the individual-level variables achieve statistically significant coefficients, thereby confirming the basic applicability of the RAS model to this case.

The significant negative coefficient on awareness in the acceptance function is especially noteworthy.[5] In the RAS model and especially in Converse's "Information flow" model, political awareness is important as a resistance factor in part because it is a proxy for the stored mass of precampaign considerations. With preexisting considerations controlled, as in Equation 10.1, one might therefore have expected awareness to have little or no direct effect on resistance. The fact that awareness continues to do so indicates that there is something about awareness, beyond its effect as a proxy for preexisting or inertial considerations, that engenders resistance to incumbent-dominated campaigns. The "something" will turn out, as my analysis unfolds, to be partisan resistance and especially countervalent resistance.

Meanwhile, the effect of inertia, although statistically significant, is only moderately large. This can be seen by comparing its effect to that of party. Given inertia's coefficient of $-.22$, it takes a net score of 6 on inertia, which is a very high score on this variable, to equal the effect of strength of party attachment, which has a range of one unit and is applied against a coefficient of -1.32. Omitting inertia from the model leads to a 2 percent increase in residual variation, but omitting strength of party attachment leads to a 4 percent increase.

It is notable that only one of the aggregate-level measures of campaign intensity achieves a statistically significant coefficient. However, a block F-test on all six of the aggregate measures indicates that their overall effect is statistically significant ($F[6,265]$, 2.62, $p < .05$).[6]

The most substantively interesting of the aggregate variables is seniority, which has a positive main effect but a negative interaction with challenger spending. This indicates, as suggested earlier, that seniority is helpful to incumbents in low-intensity races but tends to be harmful in high-intensity ones.

Because the apparently cross-cutting effects of seniority are both statistically marginal and not fully anticipated, the cautious reader may be inclined to discount them. However, an F-test on the two seniority terms indicates that their joint effect is close to statistical significance ($F[2, 265]$, 2.96, $P < .06$). There

5 In my earlier analysis of House elections (Zaller, 1989), awareness had a positive coefficient in the acceptance function. This difference is due to a change in the form of the acceptance function, as explained in footnote 14 of Chapter 7.

    In another matter, I have discovered a typographical error in the statement of the reception function in the earlier paper (Zaller, 1989); the A coefficients in Equations 2 and 4 should have negative signs.

6 Owing to the probable endogeneity bias of the spending variables, there is no point in trying to make a verbal interpretation of the individual coefficients. Rather, I will use graphical displays to depict their effects as part of a block of variables capturing overall campaign intensity.

is also corroborating evidence for both the direct and interactive effects of seniority, as will be reported. I propose, therefore, to accept the cross-cutting effects of seniority as probably real and to attempt over the course of the chapter to explain how they have come about.

I turn now to a graphical analysis of the implied effects of the coefficients in Table 10.1.[7] This analysis appears in Figure 10.1, which decomposes the process of electoral persuasion into its three component parts. That is, it shows estimated rates of reception of defection-inducing campaign messages (left panel), rates of acceptance of these messages among outpartisans (center panel), and defection rates to the incumbent among outpartisans (right panel). The figure shows these estimated rates for three types of "constructed outpartisans," defined as follows: A strong partisan identifies strongly with her party and has a score of +3 on the inertia variable; a disaffected partisan is a "not so strong" or independent-leaning party member and has a score of −3 on inertia (more dislikes of her party than likes); and finally, a modal outpartisan has a score of +0.7 on the inertia variable and a score of 1.30 on the party strength variable ("strong" partisans were scored as 2 and "weak" and "leaning" partisans as 1, so that 1.30 represents someone falling between these positions). The simulations in the top panel of Figure 10.1 involve a race in which the House incumbent has just two years of seniority; in the lower panel is a simulation for a race in which the incumbent has completed ten years in office. Both top and bottom panels involve a low-intensity race, namely, one in which the incumbent spends $25,000 (in 1978 dollars), the challenger makes no spending report, and media coverage is .75, which is near the bottom of its range. About 10 percent of all contested House elections involve campaigns of this type.

For the sake of illustration, let us focus on a "strong partisan" voter who scores at the 50th percentile of habitual awareness. The top panel of the figure shows that, for a race with a one-term incumbent, this type of voter has a 72 percent chance of reception of a defection-inducing message, a 56 percent chance of accepting it (given reception), and therefore a .72 × .56 = .40 chance of defecting to the incumbent House member. For a race with a five-term incumbent, the chance of reception of a defection-inducing message by the same type of voter rises to .97, which, all else equal, drives estimated defection rates up to 54 percent (.97 × .56 = .54).

With the organization of Figure 10.1 now clear, we can turn to substantive questions. Let us begin by looking more closely at how seniority affects defections to the incumbent. As noted earlier, House members conduct virtually non-stop campaigns for reelection. This enables them, over time, to reach even voters who are relatively inattentive to politics. Thus, as the two left-hand panels in Figure 10.1 show, low to moderately aware voters are much more likely to receive proincumbent messages when the incumbent has been in office five terms rather than one term. A typical voter of moderately low awareness has a

7 In Figures 10.1, 10.2, and 10.6, political awareness has been manipulated over the range from −1.88 to +1.8.

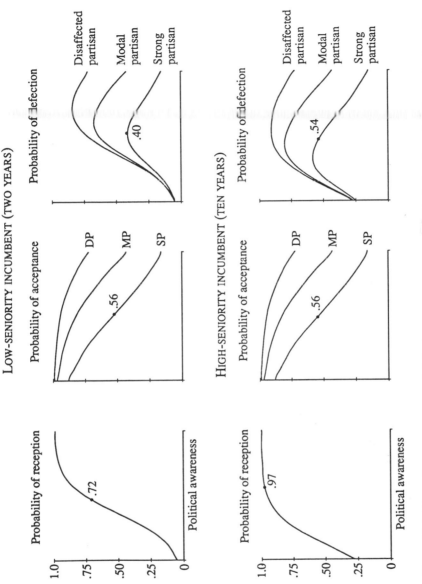

Figure 10.1. Reception, acceptance, and defection rates among outpartisans in low-intensity House elections. Estimates are derived from coefficients in Table 10.1. *Source:* 1978 NES survey.

roughly 25 percent chance of reception of a proincumbent message if he happens to reside in the district of a one-term House member; but this same voter, if residing in the district of a five-term incumbent, has a roughly 65 percent chance of receiving such a message.

These seniority-induced differences in reception of proincumbent communications lead to higher levels of defection by less aware voters to ten-year incumbents, as seen in the right-hand panels. Note, however, seniority produces no comparable increase in defection rates among the most aware voters, who, as the figure shows, reach a saturation point for effective exposure after the incumbent's first term.

In another vein, note that, in the center panels of Figure 10.1, estimated acceptance rates decline with *both* awareness and partisan orientation, which is here measured by both strength of party attachment and scores on the inertia variable. This is a visual restatement of the earlier point that habitual awareness contributes substantially to resistance even after controlling for partisan orientation. Without this independent acceptance effect of awareness, there would be no nonmonotonicity in the defection curves of the right-hand panels after controlling for partisanship and inertia.

One can also see from the center panels of Figure 10.1 that the effects of political awareness and partisanship are highly interactive. That is, the variables measuring partisanship have little effect on resistance, except at middle and high levels of political awareness, where the effect is large. This further underscores the importance of political awareness as a resistance factor.

Finally, note that the patterns of defection roughly correspond to the patterns of attitude change that would be expected in response to persuasive messages on an ''unfamiliar topic,'' as shown in the top half of Figure 8.2. The efforts of a two-year incumbent have the effect of a moderately intense message, as in cell B of the typology, while the efforts of a ten-year incumbent seem to constitute a high intensity message, as in cell C.

It is misleading, however, to suppose that many House elections constitute anything like a high-intensity message. Recall that Figure 10.1 depicts persuasion effects for persons who report having voted in a congressional election. If the whole population were included in the denominator from which defection rates were calculated, both the low-seniority and high-seniority cases would roughly resemble cell B of the typology. Thus, it is more reasonable to maintain that a typical incumbent-dominated campaign constitutes a ''moderately intense message on an unfamiliar topic.''

Before leaving the analysis of seniority effects in Figure 10.1, I emphasize that the analysis has involved only low-intensity races. Because of the interaction between seniority and campaign intensity, as shown in Table 10.1, the effect of seniority is quite different in high-intensity races. I have not presented a graphical analysis of this effect because there are too few races involving both high seniority and high campaign intensity to be confident what the visual pattern of the effect is. But although the visual form of the seniority effect in high-

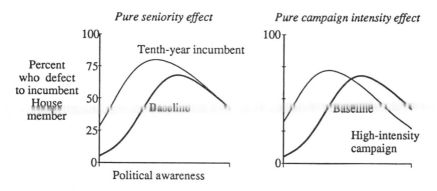

Figure 10.2. The effect of information flow on defections in 1978 House elections. Estimates are derived from coefficients in Table 10.1. Baseline is a race in which the incumbent has two years of seniority and is involved in a very low-intensity reelection campaign. Figures give estimates for modal outparty voters. *Source:* 1978 NES survey.

intensity races is uncertain, its direction is not: High seniority, in combination with high campaign intensity, reduces the number of defections that an incumbent can expect from members of the opposition party, as the Seniority × Challenger spending interaction coefficient in Table 10.1 indicates.

The basic point in Figure 10.1 was that seniority brings with it increased penetration of defection-inducing messages, thereby winning the incumbent greater support among voters who score moderate to low on political awareness. Seniority – or rather, the cumulated effects of cultivating a personal vote in one's district – is not, of course, the only source of defection-inducing messages. A high-intensity reelection campaign can accomplish roughly the same end, as shown in Figure 10.2. Let me explain how the figure works.

Baseline defection rates, shown in identical form in both the left and right panels of Figure 10.2, refer to defections by modal outpartisans to a two-year incumbent in a low-intensity campaign, as these terms were defined earlier. I refer to these as baseline rates because they are what occur when the flow of defection-inducing messages is at its minimum. (This minimal information flow is not, however, an especially low minimum, since first-term legislators work extraordinarily hard to build up a personal following among their constituents; Fenno, 1978; Hibbing, 1991.)

In the left-hand portion of Figure 10.2, we see, in relation to baseline rates, the effect of ten years of seniority on defection rates. If the data in this panel seem familiar, it is because they are a rearrangement of a portion of the data in Figure 10.1; I include them to facilitate certain comparisons, as will become apparent.

The new information in Figure 10.2 involves the effects of a high-intensity campaign, shown on the right. A high-intensity campaign is defined as one in which the incumbent spends $200,000, the challenger spends $150,000, and the media coverage variable is set to 1.25. These values constitute a race that falls at about the 90th percentile of overall campaign intensity.

Because my idealized high-intensity race involves an incumbent with exactly two years of seniority, differences in defection rates from baseline levels are purely the effects of the high-intensity campaign. As can be seen, the high-intensity campaign produces cross-cutting effects: higher-than-baseline levels of defection to the incumbent among less aware voters, and lower-than-baseline levels of defection among the most aware voters.

The existence of these cross-cutting effects defies the logic of a one-message model, which expects all change to run in the direction of the dominant message. What has produced the pattern of cross-cutting effects shown in Figure 10.2 is an interaction between a dominant incumbent campaign and a less intense, or countervailing, challenger campaign. That interaction, as later analysis will show, is as follows: The incumbent's high-intensity campaign manages to reach less aware voters, whereas the challenger's less intense campaign does not. Therefore the incumbent reaps big gains among the less aware – gains which, it appears, are roughly equivalent to those won from ten years of seniority, as shown on the left. But the challenger's campaign, although too weak to reach unaware outpartisans, can reach the politically attentive. Highly attentive outpartisans are, of course, also heavily exposed to the incumbent's campaign, but, as outpartisans, they are more likely to accept the challenger's message, thereby reducing their support for the incumbent to below baseline levels.

The difference between the left and right panels of Figure 10.2 is illuminating on this point. A high level of seniority generates no reduction in votes for the incumbent in any group because, in contrast to a high level of campaign intensity, it involves a mainly one-sided message, namely the incumbent's efforts to build up a personal vote. This type of message produces only one-directional change, at least in low-intensity campaigns. But a high-intensity campaign, because it carries two-sided messages, can produce cross-cutting patterns of change.

The cross-cutting effects of campaign intensity constitute another case of differential information flow. As in the early years of the Vietnam War, two messages produce different effects in different segments of the public, depending on an interaction between the relative intensities of the messages and people's levels of political awareness.

COUNTERVALENT AND PARTISAN RESISTANCE TO INCUMBENT-DOMINATED HOUSE CAMPAIGNS

The analysis so far has relied on a single blunt indicator of campaign influence: whether outpartisans voted for the party of the incumbent. The present section expands this analysis in two directions. First, it examines the effects of campaigns on people's evaluations of House candidates, both incumbent and challenger, and it does so at the level of positive and negative "considerations" formed with respect to each candidate. The greater information contained in such comparative candidate evaluations allows us to gain a much clearer idea of how campaign influence occurs. And second, because there is measurable variation in evaluations of the candidates among voters and nonvoters, and among inpartisans and outpartisans, the analysis in this section includes all respondents living in a given district. This greater inclusiveness greatly increases the number of cases available for study and hence the power of the tests that can be undertaken. This section, like the previous one, continues to examine only districts in which there was a dominant and countervalent campaign, that is, districts in which an incumbent sought reelection in a contested race.

The 1978 NES study contains excellent measures of citizens' evaluations of the House candidates. All respondents were asked, with respect to each candidate, the following open-ended likes/dislikes probes:

Next I would like to ask you some questions about the candidates who ran in this district for the U.S. House of Representatives. Was there anything in particular that you liked about [name of candidate], the Democratic/Republican candidate for the U.S. House of Representatives? What was that? Anything else? [Up to four responses were coded.]

Was there anything in particular that you didn't like about [. . .]. Anything else?

Responses to these questions may be taken as indicators of the positive and negative campaign messages that voters receive and accept as considerations. With respect to challengers, most of whom are neophytes, almost all of these messages will have reached voters during the House campaign itself. With respect to incumbents, some information will represent the effects of incumbents' interelection activities and some will represent campaign information. In both cases, however, differences between what voters know about candidates in very-low-intensity campaigns and what they know in higher-intensity campaigns can be taken as evidence of the effects of the campaigns.

There is, of course, some reason to be wary of using the likes/dislikes data as measures of the candidate information in people's heads. Obviously these data do not constitute a one-to-one and exhaustive mapping of every candidate-centered consideration in people's heads. Some individuals may, for example, fail to remember some pieces of candidate information that have importantly affected their votes (Lodge, McGraw, and Stroh, 1989); others may offer a large number of comments simply because they find it easy to talk about politics.

The limitations of the data should not be overdrawn, however. First, as will be shown, it is possible to control for individual differences in loquacity. More important, the volume of candidate remarks, as also demonstrated below, varies strongly across different campaign contexts, ranging from a simulated average of about 2.5 discrete remarks per respondent in heavily contested races to less than 0.5 remarks per respondent in low-intensity races. As long as one is willing to assume that this cross-district variation reflects more than individual-level differences in propensity to talk, as it obviously must, then it is possible to use the

Table 10.2. *Awareness and acquisition of electoral considerations*

	Low		Middle		High
Sum of all likes and dislikes	0.50	0.86	1.13	1.50	2.06
about two 1978 House candidates	(311)	(316)	(305)	(334)	(302)
Sum of all likes and dislikes	0.67	1.01	1.61	2.41	4.06
about two parties in 1978	(311)	(316)	(305)	(334)	(302)
Sum of all likes and dislikes	2.35	4.11	6.26	6.62	7.81
about 1984 presidential candidates	(518)	(466)	(398)	(426)	(434)

Note: Cell entries are mean number of summed likes and dislikes. Data from 1978 are derived from cases in which there was both an incumbent and a challenger. Number of cases is shown in parentheses.
Sources: 1978 and 1984 NES surveys.

likes/dislikes data to measure the diffusion of campaign information to different types of voters in different electoral contexts. Finally, the likes/dislikes data appear, on face inspection, to measure exactly what, according to the RAS model, we ought to be measuring, namely the discrete bits of positive and negative candidate considerations that have reached voters.

Despite some reason for concern, then, I regard these data as extremely well suited to the problem at hand; indeed, they constitute the best data of which I am aware for investigating the microfoundations of attitude formation and change in a dynamic political environment.

Table 10.2 gives us an initial look at these data. In the top panel is the sum of House candidate likes and dislikes, broken down by respondents' level of habitual political awareness. As would be expected, the people who are more politically aware are more likely to acquire information about particular House candidates. Politically aware people are also more likely to amass large stores of considerations about the two parties, as shown in the middle panel of the table. For purpose of comparison, Table 10.2 also contains data on the total number of likes and dislikes about the incumbent and challenger in the 1984 presidential election.

A salient feature of Table 10.2 is that voters have many more considerations about the two parties than about their two House candidates. An immediate question, therefore, is how much impact each type of consideration has on people's votes. If the impact of party considerations – the basis of the inertia variable examined in the previous section – is sufficiently great relative to that of candidate considerations, there might be no point in pursuing an investigation of the origins of candidate information.

The simplest way to address this problem is to perform a logistic regression analysis in which vote choice is the dependent variable and the two likes/dislikes

Table 10.3. *The effect of party and candiate information on vote for 1978 House incumbent among outpartisans*

Intercept	−.36
Net candidate likes and dislikes (candidate information)	−1.14
	(.19)
Net party likes and dislikes (party information)	−0.29
	(.11)
"Strongly" identified with party	1.11
(0–1)	(.41)
Political issues scale	0.06
(standardized)	(.06)
N	277

Note: Coefficients from maximum likelihood logistic regression in which incumbent vote among outpartisans in contested races was the dependent variable.
Source: 1978 NES survey.

measures, understood as indicators of party considerations and candidate considerations, are used as independent variables. Such an analysis is reported in Table 10.3. Since my focus is still on resistance to incumbent-dominated campaigns, the regression includes only partisans of the outparty. Party considerations are entered in the regression as the net of likes and dislikes, while candidate considerations are also entered as a net score, calculated as follows:

$$\text{Net candidate consideration} = +\sum(\text{Incumbent candidate likes})$$
$$+\sum(\text{Challenger dislikes})$$
$$-\sum(\text{Incumbent candidate dislikes})$$
$$-\sum(\text{Challenger likes}) \quad (10.2)$$

The regression in Table 10.3 controls for strength of party attachment ("strong" versus other) and position on a general measure of left–right issue orientation (with high scores indicating greater ideological distance from the incumbent, who is assumed to be liberal if a Democrat and conservative if a Republican; this measure is described more fully in the next section).

The logistic regression results indicate that candidate considerations are the most important single determinant of House voting. One additional like or dislike of one of the candidates has the same effect as identification as a strong member of the outparty, and about four times the effect of each party like or dislike. Ideological issue distance from the incumbent – though, as we shall see, indirectly important as a determinant of the acquisition of candidate considerations – seems to have virtually no direct effect on the vote.

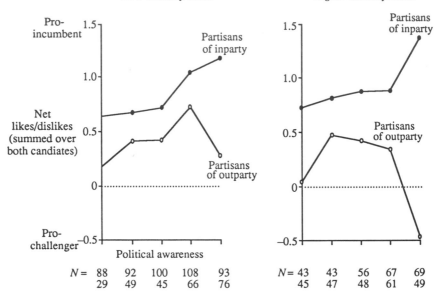

Figure 10.3. Formation of considerations in 1978 House elections. *Source:* 1978 NES survey.

These results provide further evidence that inertial considerations, which exist in voters' minds independently of any particular House campaign, play a role in preventing defections to incumbents, especially, as Figure 10.1 and Table 10.2 showed, among highly aware persons, who possess the largest stores of inertial considerations. But the results also show that the main action in House elections is in candidate considerations, which dominate the other measures.

Let us therefore proceed with our analysis of how voters acquire candidate considerations from political campaigns. We can learn a fair amount about how this occurs from simple graphical displays of the raw data, as shown in Figure 10.3. The figure presents separate summaries of net candidate considerations for lower-intensity and higher-intensity House races, with the cutpoint between the two set at $40,000. Focusing first on members of the incumbent's party, described in the figure as "partisans of inparty," we find, within both types of races, a strong positive relationship between political awareness and net considerations. Since the net considerations measure is scored in the direction of the incumbent, this indicates that, for inpartisans, greater exposure to the House campaign, as indexed by political awareness, is associated with steadily higher levels of proincumbent attitudes. Moreover, the positive trend lines contain no hint of the nonmonotonicity that arises from the resistance of the highly aware.

There is little surprise here. Highly aware inpartisans have no reason to resist the proincumbent communications to which they have been exposed in the campaign and, as is apparent, they do not.

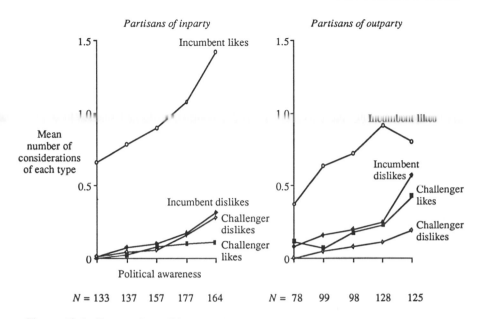

Figure 10.4. Types of candidate considerations formed in 1978 House campaigns. *Source:* 1978 NES survey.

For partisans who are not members of the incumbent's party, however, there exists a strong nonmonotonic relationship between political awareness and net candidate considerations. Note also that the curve for highly aware "outpartisans" is offset downward in higher-intensity races (on right), an occurrence which correctly indicates that their defections to the incumbent are lower in higher-intensity races. Clearly, highly aware outpartisans, though heavily exposed to the campaign, are more resistant to the predominantly proincumbent message than are moderately aware outpartisans, and they are especially resistant to the incumbent's efforts in higher-intensity races. Why is this?

To find out, let us disaggregate the net candidate consideration curves of outpartisans into their component parts, namely, the likes and dislikes of each candidate. When we do this, in Figure 10.4, we encounter a striking result: There is only slight evidence of the nonmonotonicity that arises from the heightened partisan resistance of the highly aware. One sees a hint of it in one of the curves (specifically, the incumbent likes curve of outpartisans), but the main message in Figure 10.4 is that the higher a person's level of political awareness, the more likely the person is to mention things she or he likes and dislikes about both candidates – *and to do so even when it goes against the partisan grain.*

This is a notable but also somewhat puzzling finding. If increases in political awareness are associated with increases in susceptibility to all types of influence, which is what Figure 10.4 seems to show, how does it occur that, as shown earlier, the relationship between awareness and vote defection is strongly nonmonotonic?

The answer is close at hand. The first point to notice in Figure 10.4 is the extent to which incumbent likes overwhelm all other types of considerations. Among the less aware members of the inparty, incumbent likes are almost the only type of response given. And even among outpartisans, reasons for liking the incumbent are four times as numerous as reasons for liking the challenger. Many House challengers, it appears, are all but invisible.

But challengers, though invisible to most, are visible to the highly aware. This, it turns out, is the key to explaining how highly aware outpartisans resist the dominant proincumbent message. Reception of countervailing considerations from the challenger's campaign, which only the most aware voters are able to achieve, gives highly aware outpartisans an informational basis for opposing the incumbent.

Highly aware outpartisans, it thus appears, do not simply resist the incumbent; they acquire countervailing information that enables them to positively support the challenger.

In the same vein, Figure 10.4 shows that the incidence of incumbent dislikes rises sharply with political awareness, especially among outpartisans. This gives highly aware outpartisans – but almost no one else – a further informational basis for opposing the incumbent.

Highly aware outpartisans, thus, are the only group in the electorate for whom proincumbent considerations do not overwhelm all others – the only group, that is, that pays enough attention to notice the relatively low-key campaigns of challengers and is also predisposed, on partisan grounds, to accept the information that challengers purvey. Thus, the capacity of highly aware outpartisans to resist the incumbent arises from their sensitivity to information flows that are too weak to reach the mass of less aware outpartisans.

All of this, of course, amounts to a clear and direct demonstration of countervalent resistance. It is the same mechanism that was invoked to explain the imperviousness of sophisticated liberals to the dominant prowar message of the early Vietnam War period; the only difference is that here, owing to the superior data available for House elections, we are able to observe directly the effects of the countervalent message at the level of considerations.

Focusing on partisan resistance

The analysis has so far focused on inertial and countervalent resistance to the dominant incumbent campaign, and has found evidence that both types of resistance are more common among those who are more politically aware.

But what about partisan resistance – that is, the tendency of people to refuse to accept considerations that are inconsistent with their political predispositions? Although I did not emphasize it, we have already encountered evidence of partisan resistance. It appeared most clearly in Figure 10.3, where we saw that partisans of the incumbent's party were far more likely than outpartisans to achieve proincumbent scores on the measure of net candidate considerations.

This occurred because partisans selectively accepted the congenial candidate information to which they were exposed while rejecting what was uncongenial.

What is not yet clear, however, is whether political awareness enhances partisan resistance. When we examined the relationship between awareness and candidate considerations in Figure 10.4, we found only slight visual evidence of the nonmonotonicity that arises from the greater partisan resistance of the more politically aware. This initial evidence needs to be more rigorously tested.

I propose to do this by making the likes and dislikes of each candidate the dependent variable of its own reception-acceptance model. That is, I will estimate four models having the general form of Equation 10.1, each specifying variations in one of the four candidate considerations measures as a function of individual- and aggregate-level influences. If the conclusions reached thus far are correct, we should find that aggregate variation in campaign intensity, along with individual-level differences in political attentiveness, have a major impact on the reception of candidate information, but that habitual awareness has little or no effect on acceptance rates. We should find, in other words, that awareness affects the formation of considerations mainly through its effect on the reception process, as suggested by Figure 10.4.

The model to be estimated is as follows:

$$\text{Net candidate considerations}_{ij} = \sum{}^4(\text{Like/Dislike})_n$$
$$= \sum{}^4 ((\text{Recept}_{ij})(\text{Accept}_{ij} \mid \text{Recept}_{ij}))_n \quad (10.3)$$

where the i subscript refers to individual-level differences, the j subscript refers to district-level variables, and n to the four summary measures of considerations. In estimating this model, I will assume that the reception and acceptance functions take the logistic form, as in Equation 10.1.

Measurement of the variables in this model is more complicated than usual and so requires some extra attention.

Measuring reception of campaign information. The *individual-level* variables affecting reception of campaign information in Equation 10.1 will be political awareness, measured in the usual way, plus expressed levels of interest in political campaigns and whether the person voted in the 1978 congressional election. The reason for adding the latter two measures is that the 1978 NES survey carried fewer and somewhat weaker political knowledge items than most NES surveys, which makes the use of supplements advisable.

The use of campaign interest and vote turnout as reception measures raises a subtle point. Throughout this book, I attempt to measure individuals' *habitual* levels of political awareness, by which I mean long-term awareness that is independent of the level of awareness of any particular campaign or issue. The reason for insisting on chronic, as against episodic, awareness is that a person stimulated to high levels of political attentiveness by a campaign may exhibit less partisan or inertial resistance to persuasion than someone who is habitually attentive to politics, even if both are paying equal amounts of attention to the campaign at a given moment.

This point is important because both expressed levels of political interest and vote turnout are slightly higher in districts in which an intense House race has occurred. This indicates that the campaign has stimulated people in these districts to score higher on these measures than they normally would. This difficulty, however, is easily remedied by purging both variables of their correlation with district-level measures of campaign intensity, as measured by media coverage. With this adjustment made, each can be taken as a measure of habitual awareness that is independent of any particular campaign.

The *district-level* variables affecting reception of campaign information are campaign spending by the incumbent and by the challenger, intensity of media coverage, and number of years the incumbent has served in the House. The spending variables require a brief comment.

As other research has shown, spending by the incumbent is determined, in part, by the level of the challenger's spending and by how well the incumbent did in his or her previous race. Spending by challengers, for its part, is determined in part by the quality of the challenger (as gauged by political skills or past experience, for example), in part by how well the incumbent did in the last race (weak incumbents tend to attract strong, heavy-spending challengers), and in part by the incumbent's record in office (Jacobson, 1980; Johannes and McAdams, 1987). Beyond this, newspaper coverage of congressional races varies as a function of the challenger's spending, incumbent's spending, and quality of the candidates (Westlye, 1991).

No one has yet been able to disentangle how exactly these several variables affect one another, and I cannot do so either. Hence in the analysis that follows, I will include all of the measures in the model in order to capture their reduced-form effects, but I will not attempt to draw conclusions from the relative magnitude of particular coefficients. Instead, I will use the entire set of coefficients to simulate the overall effects of certain types of races: higher-intensity races (high spending by both candidates, with heavy newspaper coverage), and lower-intensity races (moderate spending by the incumbent, low spending by the challenger, with light news coverage).

Measuring acceptance of campaign information. I will use four individual-level acceptance variables, each measuring a theoretically distinct concept. It is important to make clear exactly what these concepts are.

The first acceptance variable is *party identification,* as measured by the traditional party identification measure. A strong coefficient on this variable would indicate *a partisan bias in information processing* – that is, a tendency for partisans, all else equal, to accept favorable information about their party's candidate and to resist favorable information about the opposition's candidate. As usual, this variable has been coded to a five-point range, in which strong identifiers (±2) are distinguished from weak identifiers and independent leaners (±1) and pure independents (0). Scoring is in the direction of the challenger's party.

The second acceptance variable is *policy distance* from incumbent and challenger. The incumbent policy distance variable captures the left–right distance between the individual's policy preferences (as measured by NES issue questions) and the incumbent's voting record (as measured by the roll call ratings of Americans for Democratic Action and the American Conservative Union).[8] A large coefficient on this variable would constitute a further indication of partisan bias in the internalization of incoming messages.

Because data on the policy orientation of challengers are unavailable, I was unable to build as good a measure of policy distance from them. Since, however, Democratic politicians tend to be to the left of Republican politicians, liberal members of the public should tend to be closer to Democratic than Republican challengers, while mass conservatives should exhibit the opposite tendency. On this rationale, I use a measure of left–right issue orientation, scored to reflect whether the challenger is a Democrat or Republican, to capture policy distance from the challenger.

The third acceptance variable is *inertia*. This variable, the net of party likes and dislikes, measures an individual's mass of stored partisan considerations, as described earlier. A large coefficient on this variable would indicate that stored partisan information functions to fend off candidate information that is inconsistent with one's partisan orientation. Note that, within the RAS model framework, there is no expectation that preexisting considerations will affect acquisition of new considerations; they are supposed to create only inertial resistance, that is, to dilute the effects of new considerations.

The final acceptance variable is *political awareness*. In addition to being a proxy for stored considerations and reception of countervalent information, political awareness may enhance partisan resistance to dominant messages because it is associated with the possession of cueing messages that enable individuals to see the relationship between persuasive messages and their values. Because inertial considerations and reception of countervalent information are directly measured by other variables in the acceptance function, any remaining effect of political awareness can be attributed to its effect in enhancing partisan resistance.

There is one other issue to be discussed. It is, as earlier indicated, unrealistic to assume that an individual's volunteered likes and dislikes provide a complete report of the campaign messages he or she has internalized. One worrisome possibility is that, all else equal, some individuals are more talkative than others, perhaps because they are better able to search their memories for

---

8 This distance measure was created in the following steps: Build a measure of the left–right orientation of each survey respondent; average the ADA and ACA ratings of the incumbent over the previous two years; standardize both measures; subtract the two z-score scales; and take the absolute value of the difference. See the Measures Appendix for further information.

relevant information or perhaps because they are simply loquacious. To control for these individual differences, I took each person's total number of volunteered likes and dislikes (independent of directional thrust) about the political parties as a measure of memory and/or loquacity and used it as a nuisance variable in the acceptance function. People who have a great deal to say about the parties are expected, all else equal, to have more to say about the candidates. (Loquacity, as measured here, is confounded with an individual's level of political awareness, but since awareness is directly measured by other variables, this is not a problem.)

With these variables, we can model the diffusion of positive and negative considerations about each candidate as a function of several aggregate-level information flows – the challenger's campaign, the incumbent's campaign, media coverage, and the accumulated news of the incumbent's record in office (seniority). At the individual level, respondents may be more or less heavily exposed to these communication flows, depending on their levels of political attentiveness, and more or less resistant to the messages they receive, as determined by their party identification, policy orientation, preexisting considerations, and awareness.

The results of the estimation are shown in Table 10.4.[9] As with other models of the reception-acceptance process, a graphical analysis is necessary to convey the full significance of the coefficient estimates. Some information, however, can be gleaned from an examination of the raw coefficients, beginning with those from the reception function.[10]

---

9 The dependent variables of this analysis are the sum of all remarks of a given type, recoded to a 0–1 scale. On the theory that the intervals between a person's first, second, third, or fourth remarks might be unequal, I experimented with various transformations of the dependent variable, but this made no important difference in the results.

10 I would like to make a few comments on two variables from the reception function, incumbents' margin of victory in their last race and the number of days that elapsed between the election and the NES interview of a given respondent. Although tangential to the main analysis, both variables have intrinsic interest. Victory margin was included to pick up the reception effects of earlier, incumbent-dominated campaigns. The signs of this variable's coefficients indicate that it performed as expected: Incumbents who won their previous race by large margins are more often liked and less often disliked, all else equal, than incumbents who had a close race in their last outing. This effect, however, is statistically insignificant and substantively small. The implication of this essentially null result is that if a hard race in the previous election has any effect on the current election, it is because of its indirect effect on challenger quality and spending rather than because of a direct lingering effect on candidate evaluations. This conclusion is similar to the Jacobson and Kernell (1981) argument that the effect of the economy on congressional outcomes is largely mediated by its intervening effect on strategic politicians.

The other variable, days since election, was included to control for the possibility that the passing of time might lessen people's ability or motivation to explain what they liked and disliked about the candidates. The negative sign for this variable indicates that the variable performed as it would be expected to perform in three of the four cases; its effects, however, are neither large nor statistically significant.

I also note that loquacity – the count of party likes and dislikes – performs as expected: The more a person has to say about the two political parties, the more he or she is likely to say about the two House candidates. This effect is moderately large and statistically significant, but theoretically uninteresting. The ability to control for loquacity, however, improves the fit of the model and hence the ability to estimate other effects.

Table 10.4. *Coefficients for diffusion of likes and dislikes in contested 1978 House races*

	Incumbent likes	Incumbent dislikes	Challenger likes	Challenger dislikes
Reception function				
Intercept	−4.43	−8.92	−7.90	−8.21
Awareness (standardized)	0.58 (.08)	1.11 (.29)	0.71 (.18)	0.71 (.34)
General interest (range 1–3)	0.20 (.07)	0.06 (.15)	0.88 (.14)	0.43 (.14)
Voted in 1978 (range 0–1)	0.85 (.11)	0.74 (.24)	0.28 (.18)	1.05 (.24)
Incumbent spending (in logged $10,000s)	0.86 (.21)	2.36 (.58)	1.10 (.46)	1.54 (.45)
Challenger spending (in logged $10,000s)	−0.11 (.11)	0.25 (.24)	1.61 (.25)	1.61 (.24)
News coverage (range 0.6–1.9)	1.34 (.19)	2.59 (.69)	0.86 (.26)	1.48 (.31)
Seniority (log of years in office)	0.42 (.16)	2.02 (.51)	–	–
Last victory margin (log point difference)	0.13 (.12)	−.13 (.27)	–	–
Days since election (range 1–75)	−0.0024 (.0027)	0.004 (.006)	−0.006 (.005)	−0.008 (.005)
Acceptance function				
Intercept	1.60	−2.26	0.07	−0.54
Awareness (standardized)	−1.43 (.32)	−0.25 (.30)	−0.89 (.39)	−0.04 (.55)
Loquacity (Count of party remarks)	0.32 (.08)	0.11 (.03)	0.15 (.07)	0.21 (.09)
Party attachment (range −2 to +2)	−0.45 (.13)	0.20 (.06)	0.19 (.12)	−0.14 (.12)
Partisan inertia (Net party likes and dislikes)	−0.00 (.07)	0.07 (.04)	0.27 (.11)	0.20 (.10)
Issue distance from incumbent	−0.47 (.16)	0.52 (.07)	–	–
Issue scale (standardized)	–	–	0.13 (.12)	−0.47 (.19)

Note: Dependent variables are sum of all remarks of given type, recoded to 0–1 range. Up to four remarks were counted in connection with each probe, except the challenger-dislike probe, for which only two remarks were counted, since no one made four remarks of this type and less than .5 percent made three. The model is Equation 10.1, estimated by nonlinear least squares. Approximate standard errors appear in parentheses. Number of cases, which include all cases in which an incumbent sought reelection in a contested race, is 1545.

Source: 1978 NES survey.

Note, first of all, that seniority has significant coefficients in both the incumbent-likes and the incumbent-dislikes models, thereby indicating quite unequivocally that seniority does, as suggested earlier, generate cross-cutting effects.

One's first suspicion is that these cross-cutting effects might be mutually canceling. But this is not generally the case. Because the intercept in the reception function of the incumbent-dislikes model is low, seniority has sizable effects only at high values of the other reception variables. Thus, the negative effects of seniority come into play only in high-intensity campaigns. Meanwhile, the intercept in the incumbent-likes model is higher – the highest, in fact, of the four cases; this means that the positive effects of seniority can come into play even at low values of the other reception variables, which is to say, even in low-intensity campaigns. (See Chapter 7 at Figure 7.3 for an explanation of why the variables in a logistic function automatically interact with one another.)

Thus, a careful reading of Table 10.4 indicates that seniority has cross-cutting effects that tend to be net positive for the incumbent in low-intensity races and net negative in higher spending races. This conclusion, which is readily confirmed by graphical analysis (not shown), confirms my earlier analysis of voter defection rates, which also found seniority to be helpful in low-intensity races and harmful in high-intensity ones (see Table 10.1).

Senator Edward Kennedy of Massachusetts may exemplify the kind of politician for whom seniority has cross-cutting effects. In a low-intensity race, his glamour and family background are immediate selling points, helping him to roll up large vote margins. But in a high-intensity race, a skilled challenger might, even without raising issues from Kennedy's personal life, find much useful ammunition in the senator's long record as an unabashed liberal. Thus, the potentially negative effects of Kennedy's long record might become important only in the presence of a potent challenge.

The present analysis of the cross-cutting effects of seniority is more solidly founded than the earlier one in these respects: It derives from coefficients that are highly statistically significant and it is based on a sample that includes all respondents rather than only outpartisan voters.[11] The present analysis is also more theoretically informative, since, by decomposing the political campaign into its parts and noting their differential intensities, it has been able to show why seniority has the cross-cutting effects that it does.

The other point to notice about the variables in the reception function is that, although there are three individual-level measures of political attentiveness in each model of candidate considerations, they obtain correctly signed coefficients in all cases and achieve statistically significant effects in 10 of 12 trials. This, in combination with the usually large magnitudes of the coefficients, in-

---

11 It is possible that there is an endogenous interaction here, such that senior incumbents do not normally encounter serious challenges unless there is a serious weakness in their record. An analysis along the lines of Westlye (1991; ch. 8) would be needed to deal with this possibility.

dicates that individual-level differences in attentiveness are a major determinant of the acquisition of candidate information.

I turn now to coefficients from the acceptance function. The inertia variable, first of all, performs weakly. Its four coefficients range from moderately large in the expected direction to moderately large in the unexpected direction, with the remaining two cases close to zero.[12] These results are a further indication of the limits of preexisting considerations, which is what the inertia variable is intended to capture, as a source of resistance to incoming information from dominant political campaigns. Inertia, as we saw in Tables 10.1 and 10.3, is important as a counterweight to fresh campaign information at the point of making vote decisions; however, it seems to have no consistent impact on the acceptance of new candidate information as positive or negative considerations.

The party attachment and the issue distance variables, on the other hand, perform well, obtaining correctly signed coefficients in all equations in which they appear and achieving statistical significance in five of eight cases. This pattern indicates the existence of a partisan bias in citizens' processing of the candidate information to which they are exposed: Given reception of a range of campaign messages, people tend to accept what is congenial to their partisan values and to reject what is not. Although it is not apparent from simple inspection of these coefficients, their net impact on the formation of candidate considerations, as will be revealed shortly in graphical analysis, is large.

This brings us to the final important acceptance variable, political awareness. Here the evidence is mixed. Awareness appears to play a role in promoting partisan resistance to positive candidate information – incumbent and challenger likes – at the point of encountering it, but does not induce resistance to negative information about the candidates.

Unsure what to make of this mixed outcome, I conducted parallel investigations of the effect of awareness in inducing resistance to candidate considerations in Senate elections and in the 1984 presidential election. What I found is that awareness is *not* importantly associated with resistance to likes/dislikes information for either incumbents or challengers in either of these types of election.[13]

Taking the three types of elections together, then, the evidence suggests that awareness has relatively little effect in enhancing partisan resistance to persuasion at the level of incoming candidate information – even though, as we have seen in Figure 10.1, political awareness is strongly associated with resistance to

12 The one correctly signed and statistically significant coefficient involves the challenger-likes model, where, as suggested a moment ago, my ability to measure ideological distance from the challenger is marginal. It is a good bet, therefore, that inertia is functioning here more as a proxy for ideological distance than as a measure of inertial resistance.

13 In particular, I have not found any cases in which awareness picks up a statistically significant coefficient in the acceptance function of a reception-acceptance model of candidate likes or dislikes, except the two cases in Table 10.4.

incumbent campaigns at the level of summary vote decisions in House elections. (For comparable evidence on Senate and presidential elections, see Figure 10.6.)

These seemingly contradictory findings are possible because awareness-enhanced partisan resistance to communication at the point of encountering it is only one of three ways in which awareness can induce resistance to a dominant campaign message. The other two awareness-mediated resistance mechanisms, inertial and especially countervalent resistance, have large effects even though the first does not.

Still, however, it is natural to ask why, in contrast to what occurs in other domains, there is little or no resistance effect from awareness in the formation of considerations about candidates in partisan elections. Recall, in particular, that political awareness was associated with resistance to ideologically inconsistent considerations involving controversial issues (job guarantees, government services, aid to blacks, and presidential performance; see Tables 8.2 and 8.3 and Figure 8.7).

Although the answer to this question cannot be demonstrated from the available data, it is easy to infer what is going on. Note, first of all, that there is no absence of partisan resistance in the formation of candidate considerations. Democrats and liberals differ sharply from Republicans and conservatives in the considerations they form (Table 10.4). What is different for candidate considerations, in comparison with issue-relevant considerations, is that the least politically aware people exhibit nearly as much partisan discrimination as the most aware. If the RAS model is correct, this can only be because the cueing information necessary to achieve partisan resistance is much more widely available in election campaigns, especially in Senate and presidential campaigns, than in other political contexts – so widely available that even the least politically aware people manage to acquire it.

It is quite plausible that this is the case. Contested elections are organized as competitions between opposing partisan groups. Reflecting this, news reports routinely identify the partisan affiliations of the contending candidates, as do political advertisements, the other principal source of candidate information. As a result, anyone encountering candidate information can very easily recognize its partisan implications. The same cannot be said for nonelectoral political communication. Although I am aware of no study of the subject, my observation is that news reports on political issues only rarely carry clear partisan cueing information.

If this impression is correct, and if, as the RAS model contends, political awareness induces partisan resistance precisely by virtue of its association with cueing information that is obscure or esoteric, then it would follow that its association with partisan resistance would be markedly weaker in partisan election campaigns than in other contexts.

Altogether, then, political attentiveness, as measured by awareness, interest, and vote turnout, has consistently large and usually significant effects on reception of campaign information, but awareness has only inconsistent effects on the acceptance process. Insofar as attentiveness affects the acquisition of campaign information, it appears therefore to be mainly via its effect on reception.

Simulating the effects of campaign intensity

The coefficients in Table 10.4, in conjunction with the equations that generated them, imply a comprehensive account of attitude formation in House campaigns. By using the coefficients in graphical simulations, we can gain further insight into the dynamics of resistance to persuasion.

Let me first use simulations to make a methodological point. In introducing the likes/dislikes questions as measures of the candidate information that has reached voters, I noted a suspicion that may still linger in some readers' minds: that these questions mainly measure individual differences in motivation to discuss politics. The coefficients in Table 10.4 enable us to test this possibility. Let us consider low-intensity and high-intensity races, as defined earlier. Let us also assume that the first has a two-year incumbent running for reelection and the second a ten-year incumbent.

Campaign intensity, operationalized in this way, has a large impact on what citizens are able to learn about their House members. The average number of considerations expected from a modal outpartisan in low-intensity races is 0.27; in high-intensity races, it is 2.51. This average difference is entirely attributable to differences in campaign intensity. Moreover, the simulated number of remarks in a hypothetical race in which there is no campaign – no spending by either candidate, the lowest level of press coverage, and no incumbent seniority as a source of information – is 0.20. Almost all of these remarks come from moderately aware and especially highly aware persons who give reasons for liking the incumbent, a result that is, if anything, a bit low in light of House members' continuous efforts to build constituency support during the periods between elections.

These findings should resolve any doubts that the volume of likes/dislikes remarks reflects to any important degree simple individual differences in willingness to talk. There are, as there ought to be, large individual differences in sensitivity to political campaigns, but people's ability to make remarks about candidates depends very heavily on the intensity of the campaigns.

I turn now to more substantive concerns. We saw in Figure 10.2 that increases in seniority and in campaign intensity produce distinctive changes in the pattern of defections to incumbent House members, as measured against a baseline involving a two-year incumbent in a low-intensity race. Figure 10.5 depicts the same seniority and campaign effects that were shown earlier, except at the level of considerations. Thus, on the left of Figure 10.5, we see that an increase in incumbent seniority from two years to ten years produces a slight increase in net proincumbent considerations, where the increase is measured against the same type of baseline race as in the earlier analysis. The effect is concentrated

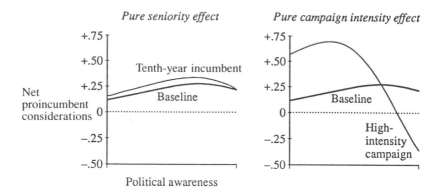

Figure 10.5. Effect of information flow on the formation of considerations among out-partisans in 1978 House elections. Estimates are derived from coefficients in Table 10.4. Baseline is a race in which the incumbent has two years of seniority and is involved in a very low-intensity reelection campaign. Plots give estimates for modal outparty voters. *Source:* 1978 NES survey.

mainly among outpartisans scoring middle to low on political awareness, which is roughly the same group that was most affected by seniority in the earlier analysis of vote defections. On the right of Figure 10.5, we see that an increase in campaign intensity from low to high produces higher than baseline support for the incumbent among less aware outpartisans, and lower than baseline support among the highly aware outpartisans. These results also match the effects of campaign intensity on outpartisan defections, as shown in Figure 10.2.[14]

Given the differences in the methods used to produce Figures 10.2 and 10.5 – the former involving the *votes* of 277 outpartisans, the latter the net *likes* and *dislikes* of the two candidates by some 1,500 respondents – the substantive correspondence between the two sets of estimates seems quite impressive. And yet, as can be seen, the magnitude of the effect of seniority on considerations seems quite small in relation to the magnitude of the effect of defections, as shown earlier. What is going on?

An explanation is suggested by an important analysis by Mann and Wolfinger (1980). They note that the rise of a personal vote for incumbent House members has not been associated with any detectable increase over time in the ability of

14 In these and subsequent simulations of candidate considerations, the effect of political awareness is simulated by simultaneously manipulating scores on the three awareness measures: knowledge, interest, and voting. Knowledge runs from -1.8 SD to 1.5 SD, with the asymmetry reflecting the skew in the measure. In Figure 10.2, interest was included in the awareness scale; in the present analysis, it is entered as a separate variable in the reception function and, for purposes of simulation, is manipulated over the range of 1.0 to 2.6 on the original three-point scale, with an adjustment for purging. Vote turnout is manipulated over a range of 0 to 1, with an adjustment for purging. The loquacity variable, the sum of party likes and dislikes, was set to 2.0 in all cases, thereby eliminating its correlation with political awareness.

voters to recall the incumbent's name. But, they maintain, incumbency advantage does not require recall ability; it requires only that the voter be able to recognize the incumbent's name when encountering it in the voting booth. Hence the rise of the personal vote may rest on little more than an increase in the ability of voters to recognize incumbents' names.

The nub of this argument is that incumbency advantage, which is large at the level of the ballot box, depends on cognitive underpinnings that are exceedingly slight. And this is exactly the pattern I have found: The effect of seniority – which, I reiterate, is merely a proxy for the things that incumbents do to build a personal vote – is large at the level of vote defections in Figure 10.2 but small at the level of candidate considerations in Figure 10.5.[15]

My conclusion, therefore, is that the modest magnitude of the seniority effect in Figure 10.5 is probably an accurate indication that the effect really is small, but not so small that it cannot make a big difference in the voting booth when the incumbent is competing against a challenger who is all but invisible.

Before leaving Figure 10.5, I want to return to the question of why exactly high campaign intensity has the cross-cutting effects that it does. Since Figure 10.5 has been produced by computer simulation, it is possible to say exactly what has generated the cross-cutting effects.

The cause of these cross-cutting effects, as I suggested earlier, is differential information flow. Scores on net candidate considerations in the baseline race have been produced by a dominant but not very intense proincumbent communication flow, and a countervalent prochallenger message that is extremely faint. As campaign intensity increases, the dominant proincumbent message gains sufficient power to reach low awareness voters who could not pick it up in a baseline race. Hence support for the incumbent among the least aware outpartisans increases as campaign intensity increases. The countervalent challenger message also gains in intensity, but only enough to reach the most politically aware people, who, if they are outpartisans, then become less favorable toward the incumbent.

These points are made clear in Table 10.5, which shows the simulated number of dominant considerations (incumbent likes plus challenger dislikes) and countervalent considerations (incumbent dislikes plus challenger likes) in both a low-intensity and a high-intensity race. The effects are shown separately for a high-awareness outpartisan voter and a low-awareness one.

In the first row of the table, which depicts a low-intensity race, neither high-awareness nor low-awareness outpartisans volunteer many considerations, and most of what they do express involves information from the dominant campaign. The challenger's campaign, thus, is almost invisible even to highly aware outpartisans.

15 The effects are small in the sense that the *net* of positive and negative considerations that seniority can explain is small; the coefficients responsible for the separate positive and negative effects, as shown in Table 10.4, are not small.

Table 10.5. *Effect of campaign intensity on formation of considerations among outpartisans*

| | High awareness outpartisan | | Low awareness outpartisan | |
	Proincumbent considerations	Prochallenger considerations	Proincumbent considerations	Prochallenger considerations
Low-intensity campaign	0.24	0.07	0.16	0.01
High-intensity campaign	1.09	1.43	0.92	0.26
Gain from campaign	+0.85	+1.36	+0.76	+0.25
Net gain/loss to incumbent	−0.41		+0.51	

Note: Cell entries are simulated mean number of considerations in each category for modal outpartisan voters, where simulations are based on coefficients in Table 10.4.
Source: 1978 NES survey.

In a high-intensity race, as shown in the second row of the table, highly aware voters acquire additional considerations, but more countervalent considerations than dominant ones. (These respondents were heavily exposed to both campaigns, but, as outpartisans, they accept mainly countervalent considerations.) As a result, their net evaluation of the incumbent falls below the baseline.

Meanwhile, the effect of an intense campaign on less aware outpartisans is quite different. They are, as we have seen in Table 10.4, predisposed to accept countervalent information, but most of what reaches them is information from the dominant campaign. Hence, in contrast to high-awareness outpartisans, they acquire more dominant considerations than countervalent ones, which leads them to raise their net evaluations of the incumbent above baseline levels.

These data on the effects of differential information flow offer a striking parallel to the notable case of changes in public attitudes toward the Vietnam War between 1964 and 1966, when less aware liberals became more supportive of the war while more aware liberals became less so. The only difference is that, in the case of House elections, we have been able to capture the effects of a two-sided information flow both at the level of summary statements of preference (that is, vote choices, as in Figure 10.2) and at the more basic level of the considerations underlying summary decisions.

Summary on House elections

The analysis of House elections has given us our best opportunity to pick apart the dynamics of resistance to persuasion by a dominant political message, and especially the role of political awareness in such resistance. What have we learned?

Converse, in his study of information flow in partisan elections, proposed one mechanism by which awareness induces resistance to persuasion. More aware people, he argued, develop larger stores of long-term partisan information, and this internalized ballast enables them to withstand the campaign messages they encounter. The House data produced support for this view. People who are generally attentive to politics do have larger stores of preexisting partisan considerations (Table 10.2), and preexisting considerations are associated with resistance to incumbent-dominated campaigns (Tables 10.1 and 10.3, and Figure 10.1). This type of resistance is what I have termed *inertial resistance*.

But political awareness remains associated with resistance even after controlling for its intervening effect as a proxy for inertial considerations. One reason for this is that awareness also enhances *partisan resistance* to political communications at the point of encountering and deciding whether to accept them, as shown in Table 10.4.

Yet the effects of awareness-induced resistance to persuasion were neither large nor consistent. They played a role in resistance to incumbent-dominated campaigns, but not a large one.

This brings us to the third form of resistance to dominant political campaigns, *countervalent resistance*. Countervalent resistance involves sensitivity to sources of information other than the dominant campaign, which, in the present case, means sensitivity to the prochallenger and antiincumbent information from the challenger campaign.

The major finding in this area has been that, as shown most clearly in Figure 10.4, highly aware persons, but not most other people, receive significant amounts of information from the countervailing challenger campaign. As a result, highly aware outpartisans, but not most others, develop reasons for opposing the incumbent and supporting the challenger. This, in turn, enables highly aware outpartisans to resist the dominant incumbent campaign in the elementary sense that, although they may internalize some proincumbent messages, they do not end up supporting the incumbent.

It is worth emphasizing that what drives the countervalent resistance of the politically aware is not resistance per se, but the ability to pick up low-intensity communications from the political environment. Countervalent resistance appears to be the most important source of resistance to dominant political campaigns.

It might be objected that what I am calling countervalent resistance to a dominant message is not really resistance at all, but merely susceptibility to alternative sources of persuasion. This objection may perhaps be reasonable in cases in which the countervalent message is nearly as intense as the dominant one. But it should not be forgotten that countervalent resistance involves, most fundamentally, being exposed to two streams of influence and picking out the one that is more congenial with one's values rather than simply the one that is louder. As long as this sort of autonomous choice is being made, it makes sense to say that one message has been chosen and the other resisted.

HOUSE ELECTIONS IN COMPARATIVE PERSPECTIVE

Most analysis of electoral choice, as I indicated in Chapter 1, focuses on a single type of election. Because the present analysis of House elections has been cast in terms of the general RAS model, however, there is every reason to try to extend it to more cases. This is what I undertake to do in this section.

One would not, of course, expect identical patterns of electoral choice in widely dissimilar cases. One would, however, expect the basic *processes* of information diffusion and influence to be the same. If so, voting behavior across types of elections should appear fundamentally similar, once systematic differences in the flow of information are taken account of. Since House elections provide less information to voters than any other type of national election, and in this sense mark a sort of limiting case, the obvious question becomes: What happens to electoral choice as campaign intensity increases, thereby providing voters with larger amounts of candidate information?

To answer this question, I brought together data on voter defection to the incumbent from three other types of races: low- and high-intensity Senate campaigns, and the 1984 presidential race. These data are shown in Figure 10.6. Let me briefly describe the procedures used to generate these data.

House elections. Defection patterns in low- and high-intensity House races are the same as in the right-hand panel of Figure 10.2. These patterns, as may be recalled, depict the effects of campaign intensity, net of the effect of seniority, which is held at its minimum value.

Senate elections. Defection patterns in Senate elections have been estimated from the 1990 wave of the NES Senate election study. These data involve the twenty-five races in which an incumbent sought reelection under challenge from the opposition party. The model and procedures used in estimating defection patterns are exactly the same as in the case of House elections. The defection patterns shown in the figure are estimates for modal partisans, as described in Appendix A to this chapter. As in the case of the House data, low-intensity races have been defined by scores on the three campaign-intensity variables and correspond to roughly the 10th percentile of overall campaign intensity; high-intensity races have been defined by scores at about the 90th percentile.[16] Also as in the case of House elections, the incumbent is assumed to have just completed a first term. Details of variable construction are found in Appendix A.

16 To control for differences in state population, I divided campaign spending by the number of congressional districts in the state. Low-intensity races were ones in which the total of the incumbent's spending, including party and other sources, was $1.5 million per district, the total of the challenger's spending was $500,000 per district, and the aggregate media intensity score was near the bottom of its range at 0.05. High-intensity races were ones in which incumbent and challenger spending were $10 million, and media intensity was .75.

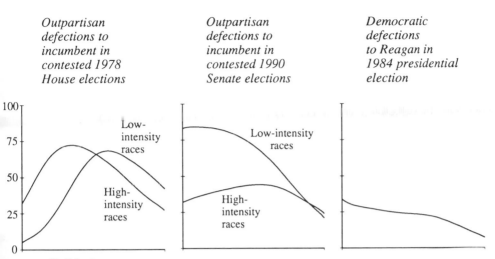

Figure 10.6. Defections to incumbent party in U.S. national elections. House estimates are based on coefficients in Table 10.1; Senate estimates are based on coefficients in Table 10.6; presidential data are based on a polynomial regression. *Source:* National Election Study surveys.

Presidential elections. Estimation of defection rates to the incumbent's party in 1984 was sufficiently straightforward that it could be accomplished by a simple polynomial regression.

In examining Figure 10.6, it is immediately apparent that the nonmonotonicity often associated with the reception-acceptance model shows up strongly in House elections but is essentially absent from the other cases. As explained in Chapter 8, this is neither a problem nor even a surprise for the RAS model, since nonmonotonicity is only one of the possible outcomes of the reception-acceptance process. If the change-inducing message is sufficiently intense to reach the least politically aware stratum of the electorate, politically unaware persons can be expected to be more susceptible to influence than anyone else. Thus, Dryer (1971) found that the nonmonotonicity that Converse discovered in the 1952 presidential election did not show up in any subsequent presidential contest. Instead, there has been a monotonically negative relationship between awareness and probability of vote defection. "The flow of short-term stimuli," as Dryer explained, "has effectively penetrated all segments of the electorate," thereby ironing out the nonmonotonicity and producing attitude change even in the least politically active stratum of the electorate (Dryer, 1971: p. 533).

What Figure 10.6 adds to Dryer's account is that even Senate campaigns now achieve sufficient intensity to penetrate to the least aware stratum of the electorate, but that most House elections do not.

There is, however, a prominent feature of Figure 10.6 that cannot be readily accommodated within a one-message framework. It is the fact that peak levels of defection occur in House elections and in low-intensity Senate elections, which have relatively low levels of campaign intensity, while the lowest defection rates occur in a presidential election, which has the highest intensity.[17] Nothing in my typology of attitude change, as presented in Figure 8.2, or any other manipulation of the logic of the one-message model, can explain this occurrence. The cross-cutting effects of campaign intensity in the case of House elections likewise defy the logic of a one-message model. In order to explain the patterns of vote defection in Figure 10.6, which should be understood most generally as patterns of attitude change, it is necessary to take account of both sides of the communication flow to which citizens have been exposed.

With respect to House elections, this task has already been accomplished by my discussion of the effect of differential information flow on the formation of candidate considerations. Figure 10.7 gives us the evidence necessary to extend this discussion to Senate and presidential elections.

Figure 10.7 displays summary measures of candidate evaluations for all three types of elections, based on administration of the same likes/dislikes questions in each case. The data on House elections in the figure are derived from the coefficients presented in Table 10.4; the data for Senate elections have been simulated by the same procedures as used for House elections (see Appendix A to this chapter); and the data for the 1984 presidential election are simply plots of the raw means for Democrats and Republicans by levels of political awareness.

The immediately evident pattern in these data is that more intense campaigns, both across types of elections and within them, lead inpartisans and outpartisans to develop overall candidate evaluations – measured as the net of the four candidate consideration measures – that are more polarized along partisan lines. Given that, as we saw in Table 10.3, candidate considerations powerfully affect vote decisions, the effect of this polarization of considerations along party lines is to generate more party-line voting in the more intense races and hence lower defection rates.

Since it has been produced by simulation, the greater polarization of net candidate considerations in high-intensity races is fully explainable. Two main factors are at work: More intense races entail, in the construction of these figures as well as in actual practice, both more evenly balanced communication flows and a larger overall volume of communication. It is no mystery that a balanced communication flow contributes to party polarization, since it gives each side the informational basis of a partisan evaluation of the candidates, but sheer volume of communication is also extremely important. Let us see why.

We have already seen that Democrats tend to accept more of the pro-Democratic messages they encounter than they do of the pro-Republican ones,

---

17 The 1984 presidential election, of course, produced higher levels of defection to the inparty than in most presidential elections, but is otherwise typical of other cases. Even among House elections, higher-intensity races produce lower overall levels of defection than low-intensity races (mean 41 percent vs. 59 percent, $t = 2.87$, $p < .01$).

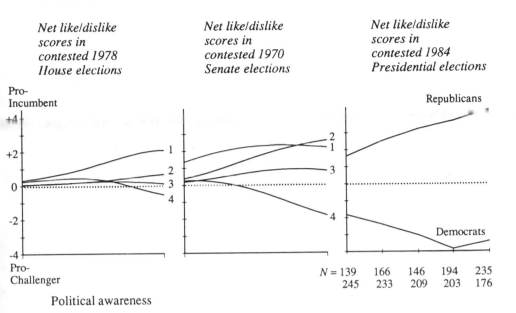

Figure 10.7. Candidate evaluations in U.S. national elections. House estimates are based on Equation 10.1 and the coefficients in Table 10.4; Senate estimates are based on coefficients in Table 10.7; presidential data depict raw data. *Sources*: National Election Study surveys.

and that Republicans exhibit the reverse tendency. Let us assume, for the sake of argument, that the acceptance rate is 67 percent for congenial messages, but 33 percent for uncongenial ones. This amounts to partisan bias in information processing that is roughly in line with the rates implied for median respondents by the coefficients in Table 10.4. If, then, a Democrat is exposed to three pro-Democratic messages and three pro-Republican ones, his expected net score will be +1 in the Democratic direction (he will accept two of the first type and one of the second, for a net score of +1). But if he is exposed to six messages of each type, his expected net score will increase to +2 (he will accept four congenial messages and two uncongenial ones). In general, the larger the number of messages on which this or any consistent Democratic bias operates, the larger the expected net score in the Democratic direction. The same process, of course, drives Republicans to a higher net score in the Republican direction.

This argument explains why, all else equal, there is more party polarization in high-intensity (high-information) races. Since highly aware partisans ingest more campaign information than less aware partisans, it also explains why highly aware Democrats and Republicans are more polarized in their net considerations scores than are less aware partisans of each stripe.

It is worth emphasizing, then, that the main reason for the greater partisan polarization of more aware voters – especially in presidential elections, where the flow of candidate information is essentially evenly balanced – is *not* that the more aware voters are more selective in deciding which communications to accept (though there may be some tendency for them to be). It is, rather, that more aware partisans, owing to the effect of awareness on reception, ingest much more information than less aware partisans, and processing this *greater volume* of information with (almost) the *same partisan bias* as everyone else leads them to form net evaluations that are more highly polarized.

This argument explains why there is more party-line voting in elections in which information flow is more intense, and why, within both presidential and Senate elections, there tends to be more party loyalty among more aware voters. In House elections there is a nonmonotonic relationship between awareness and defection, but the reason for the exceptional pattern is clear. The amount of information about the candidates reaching less aware voters in House elections is lower than in any other type of race, an amount that is fairly close to nil.[18] Voters who are undisturbed by *any* new information do not defect to the opposition.

A modified form of Converse's original information flow argument would, in light of all this, explain the cross-election pattern of defections in Figure 10.6 as follows: Voters at the lowest awareness levels *and* in the lowest intensity elections remain loyal to their party because, as Converse originally argued, they get almost no new information. As the information reaching voters rises from nearly nil to some, partisan instability shoots to its highest levels; these are the cases of middle-awareness voters in low-intensity House races, and low-awareness voters in low-intensity Senate races. The reason for the marked instability of these voters is that most of the information they get is proincumbent information, which they have little inertial capacity to resist. As campaign information reaching outpartisan voters continues to rise, instability falls from its peak levels, reaching a limit of almost no partisan defection among highly aware voters in presidential elections. Inertial resistance is only a small part of the explanation for the decline in instability from peak levels. The main reason is that *more attentive voters* are receiving *higher volumes* of *more balanced* candidate information, all of which conduce toward greater party polarization of candidate evaluations and hence higher levels of partisan loyalty.

This analysis leads to an observation of some theoretical significance: Although resistance to dominant political campaigns depends heavily on factors that are internal to individuals – notably stored considerations, political values and attachments, and political awareness – intraindividual predispositions to-

18 The simulated mean number of remarks across both candidates for voters in the lowest awareness
    category in a low-intensity, low-seniority House race is 0.13.

ward resistance cannot, by themselves, explain very much. In order to have real effect, they must be nourished by exposure to a countervalent information flow. When people are exposed to two competing sets of electoral information, they are generally able to choose among them on the basis of their partisanship and values even when they do not score especially well on tests of political awareness. But when individuals are exposed to a one-sided communication flow, as in low-key House and Senate elections, their capacity for critical resistance appears quite limited.

The conclusion I draw from this is that the most important source of resistance to dominant campaigns – certainly in elections and, as evidence from the mainstream model indicates, perhaps in other contexts as well – is countervalent information carried within the overall stream of political information.

Before I conclude this argument, let us examine one final case of attitude formation and change.

THE DYNAMICS OF PRESIDENTIAL PRIMARIES

One difficulty in studying attitude change in the context of partisan elections is that most vote decisions are so strongly moored to stable party identifications that there is little opportunity to observe change. In examining rates of defection of voters in House elections, for example, it was necessary to set aside most voters on the grounds that, as partisans of the inparty, they produced almost no cases of defection from party voting. This difficulty obviously does not arise in presidential primary elections. Indeed, the problem is more nearly the opposite: Preferences sometimes shift so rapidly that it is impossible to get a good fix on them. It is therefore interesting to see whether the understanding of electoral dynamics that works so well in the relatively stable context of partisan elections applies to a more free-wheeling election as well.

Background

In the first weeks of the 1984 Democratic nomination contest, it appeared that a serious race might never develop. John Glenn was mounting an inept and faltering campaign, and this left Walter Mondale almost unopposed in a Democratic pack consisting, except for him, of unknowns. Shortly before the New Hampshire primary, the *New York Times* released a national poll showing that Mondale was further ahead than any candidate had ever been at that point in the nomination contest.

But big things were stirring in Iowa. In the week prior to that state's caucuses, Gary Hart was moving up fast, and this began to be reflected in national newsweeklies. If *Time* or *Newsweek* included a picture of any candidate other than Mondale or Glenn, it was likely to be Hart. Hart went on to place well in Iowa, finishing second to Mondale. Then, more unexpectedly, Hart trounced Mondale in New Hampshire and, on the massive tide of publicity that followed, seemed on the verge of knocking Mondale out of the race. Hart's picture, of course, graced the covers of the newsweeklies and, overnight, his name became a house-hold word. But although performing very strongly in the Super Tuesday prima-ries that followed two weeks after New Hampshire, Hart couldn't quite force Mondale from the race. Instead, he suddenly found himself the butt of jokes about his name and his age, and trying to answer the question "Where's the beef?" Through late March, April, and May, Hart and Mondale engaged in trench warfare, with Mondale finally prevailing.

These events, as complex a stimulus to mass opinion as any encountered in this book, provide a final opportunity to observe the effects of information flow on the evolution of the public's political preferences.

Data and model

During the primary period, the NES conducted a continuous survey of attitudes toward the contending candidates. Although these surveys contacted only about forty-five Democrats a week, they provide an extremely valuable, if slightly fuzzy, series of snapshots of the race.

In analyzing these data, I have broken the primary season into periods that coincide with the major swings in public attitudes. The first, covering January and early February, is the time when Mondale seemed to have the race locked up and when Hart was a mere blip in the national polls. The second, covering the last two weeks of February, was the period when Mondale was widely considered unstoppable but Hart was beginning to build momentum in the Iowa and New Hampshire campaigns. The third is the three-week period from immediately after New Hampshire to just before the Illinois primary, the race in which Hart suf-fered his first serious defeat; this was the period in which Hart enjoyed his amaz-ing surge in the polls, but also the period in which he began to encounter the first questions about his character and his supposedly "new issues." The fourth pe-riod runs from late March through the end of the primary season, a period of many minor ups and downs from which Mondale eventually emerged the victor.

Figure 10.8 provides a breakdown of mean support for each candidate among Democrats in each time period. Even from visual inspection, these data tell an obvious story of differential information flow – that is, a story of the differential penetration of candidate messages of differing intensities. In the period before the Iowa primaries, higher levels of political awareness are associated with steadily greater support for Mondale, the candidate who, at that point, had no debilitating warts and was, according to the media, the Democrat with the best chance of winning the nomination (Brady and Johnston, 1987; Tables 7 and 8). Gary Hart had minimal support, but what little he had was concentrated among the most politically aware members of the Democratic party, who were the only people sufficiently attentive to politics to have become aware of such a "second tier" candidate.[19]

---

19 Thus, as Sam Popkin has noted, the politically aware are often "leading indicators" of future change (oral remarks, Southern California Running Dog Seminar, San Diego, February 1988).

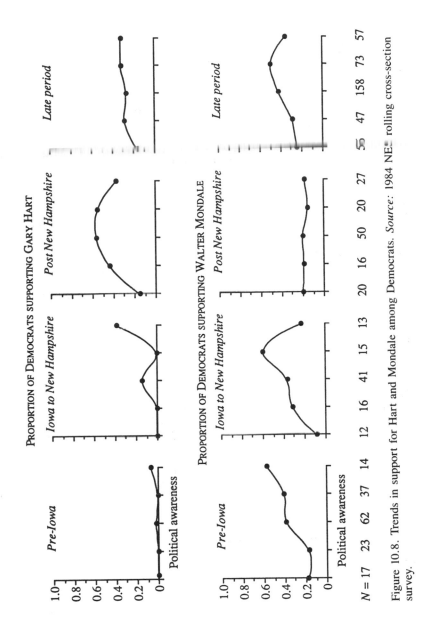

Figure 10.8. Trends in support for Hart and Mondale among Democrats. *Source*: 1984 NE₅ rolling cross-section survey.

The finding that the most aware Democrats were most susceptible to influence by the dominant Mondale campaign of this period may seem surprising. But it shouldn't. If, as has been argued, awareness is associated with resistance to persuasion because it proxies for reception of alternative information sources – notably, the stored mass of previously formed considerations, cueing messages, and countervalent information flows – there is no reason to expect awareness-induced resistance effects in this period. Democrats had no memory of bad experiences with Mondale; national elites largely supported his candidacy, or at any rate provided no opinion leadership against him; and the Hart campaign was too weak to be an effective source of countervalent information. In such circumstances, there would be no informational basis for resistance to persuasion and no cueing messages that would impede the internalization of pro-Mondale messages, so that influence should depend wholly on levels of reception of the dominant campaign message.

In the two-week period preceding the New Hampshire primary, Hart began his rise. But at this early point, the esoteric Hart message was still able to reach only the most aware quartile of the Democratic rank-and-file. There was no resistance to this message, because Hart, like Mondale, was getting one-sidedly positive coverage in the press and because Democrats had no prior information about Hart that would give them a basis for resistance. Meanwhile, the Mondale message, which was still more intense than that of Hart before the New Hampshire primary, was making converts among the ranks of the moderately aware, who had not been paying sufficient attention to receive the Mondale message in the precampaign period and were now just tuning in. But the Mondale message could make no more converts among the most aware Democrats because, within this segment of the Democratic community, it was in direct competition with the Hart campaign.

So in this period, there was still no evidence of resistance to persuasion. The most aware were clearly the most influenceable, and by a very wide margin. (The sharp nonmonotonicity in net support for Mondale in the second period was not evidence of resistance to change; it was evidence that the most aware Democrats were deserting Mondale in order to follow Hart, and that less aware ones had not yet gotten the news about Hart's rising star.)

Trends were markedly different in the third time period. Although Hart was enjoying his post–New Hampshire publicity surge, he was unable to gain any more support among highly aware Democrats. Nor did Mondale lose any support in this group. Thus, highly aware persons had begun to exhibit resistance to the dominant campaign message. The reason, presumably, was that they had now acquired enough information about the two candidates that they could no longer be blown about by every new turn in the campaign. Meanwhile, Hart's post–New Hampshire publicity binge was strong enough finally to reach moderately aware Democrats, who rapidly deserted Mondale and swung to Hart in large numbers. The largest attitude swings in this period were clearly concentrated among persons of moderate political awareness. The magnitude of this

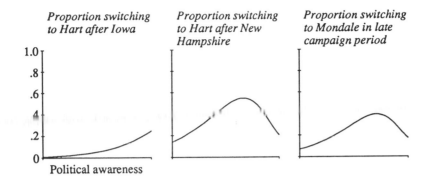

Figure 10.9. Estimated rates of preference change in Mondale vs. Hart contest. *Note:* Estimates are derived from coefficients in Table 10.8 and model in Appendix B to Chapter 10. Estimates involve Democrats only.

popular surge – to which the most aware and least aware Democrats contributed little – was what nearly drove Mondale from the race.

In the final period, moderately aware Democrats, following the news of Mondale's increasing success in the later primaries, swung back to Mondale while the most politically aware Democrats continued largely to hold their ground. Again, then, political awareness was associated with resistance to change, presumably because highly aware persons had, by this time, been able to firmly anchor their evaluations in an inertial mass of stored information about the two candidates. The least aware Democrats were also fairly stable, with most of them unable even to form a preference in the primary contest. This left moderately aware persons most susceptible to the currents of the time.[20]

Unfortunately, there are no data at the level of candidate likes and dislikes with which to check this account of the microdynamics of attitude change. It is, however, possible to fit the reception-acceptance model to the data shown in Figure 10.8 in order to see whether the story I have just told can, in a statistical sense, hold together. This modeling exercise is relegated to Appendix B of this chapter. The only point that needs to be made here is that the model fits the data extremely well and confirms my basic account in every important respect. For example, Figure 10.9 gives the rates of attitude change toward Hart and then toward Mondale in the final phases of the campaign, as estimated from coefficients in the model.

Summary on primary elections

These findings, especially those from the early phases of the campaign, underscore a critical theoretical point: Awareness-induced resistance to dominant political campaigns is not automatic. It depends on access to alternative com-

---

20 From different perspectives, Bartels (1988) and Brady and Johnston (1987) also stress that voter learning takes place over the course of the primary campaign.

munications – either in the form of stored considerations and information from past campaigns or in the form of current reception of countervalent communications or cues. Hence when, as in the early stages of the 1984 primaries, the most aware persons have no informational basis for resistance, they exhibit no hint of resistance. To the contrary, they are more reactive to campaigns of the moment than any other segment of the public. Only in the later stages of the campaign, by which time there was a two-sided information flow and some development of inertial considerations, do we find that the most aware Democrats are most resistant to change.

CONCLUDING REMARKS

This chapter has been only incidentally concerned with elections. Its real aim has been to show how people's summary political decisions, whether vote choices or responses to closed-ended survey items, are based on considerations that form from the competing influences to which they have been exposed.

The advantage of this chapter over preceding ones is that it has had, for the first time, abundant, measurable variability in the intensities of the opposing messages to which individuals have been exposed, along with measures of the considerations that underlie summary expressions of political preferences. This has made it possible to directly observe the effects of inertial resistance (in the form of party likes and dislikes) and, more important in the context of elections, the effects of countervalent resistance (in the form of prochallenger and antiincumbent communication flows). But the theoretical machinery underlying these observations has been exactly the same as in earlier analyses of attitude formation and change.

APPENDIX A: DEFECTIONS IN SENATE ELECTIONS

The model used in estimating defection to the incumbent in Senate elections was the same as for House defections. The variables used in the model are as follows:

Political awareness. Although the Senate election study contained an unusually weak selection of awareness items, I built the best measure I could, as described in the Measures Appendix.

Campaign intensity. The 1990 Senate study asked all respondents:

How many stories did you read, see or hear regarding the campaign in this state for the U.S. Senate? Would you say that you read, saw, or heard a good many, just one or two, or none?

As described in the case of the House data, I converted responses to this question to a state-level measure of the intensity of media coverage.[21] The variable runs from 0 to 0.74 scale units, as denominated by the original two-unit scale.

21 There may be some heteroskedasticity in measurement of the aggregate media variable, but it is likely to be small since N's of the state-level means are approximately the same.

Table 10.6. *Coefficients predicting vote*
for Senate incumbent among outpartisans

Reception function	
Intercept	0.19
Awareness	0.40
(standardized)	(.39)
Incumbent spending	0.015
(in $10 thousands per cong. district)	(.008)
Challenger spending	−.012
(in $10 thousands per cong. district)	(.008)
Media coverage	−2.65
(range 0 − .74)	(1.42)
Seniority	1.14
(logged)	(1.41)
Seniority x Challenger spending	−0.0035
	(.0031)
Acceptance function	
Intercept	4.05
Awareness	−1.31
(standardized)	(.50)
Partisan strength	−1.18
(range 1–2)	(.57)
Policy distance	−0.70
(see text)	(.31)
Challenger spending	0.001
	(.001)
N	450

Note: Model is Equation 10.1, estimated by
maximum likelihood. Standard errors are in
parentheses. Dependent variable is whether
outpartisan voted for the incumbent.
Source: 1990 NES Senate survey.

Political values. The Senate study carried the traditional party identification
measure, scored in the usual way. It was also possible to measure ideological or
policy distance from the incumbent. The distance measure was constructed by
summing incumbents' scores on the Americans for Democratic Action and
American Conservative Union rating scales from the year prior to the election,
standardizing the scores, and subtracting from a standardized measure of respondents' ideological self-description. The variable has been coded so that, if
the Democratic candidate is to the left of the Republican candidate, higher
scores indicate greater policy affinity to the challenger.

The coefficients for the Senate defection model are shown in Table 10.6. One
point of interest in these coefficients is that, although the seniority effects in
Senate elections are smaller than in House elections (as shown in Table 10.1)

Table 10.7. *Coefficients for diffusion of likes and dislikes in contested 1990 Senate races*

	Incumbent likes	Incumbent dislikes	Challenger likes	Challenger dislikes
Reception function				
Intercept	−1.60	−2.96	−3.10	−2.20
Awareness	1.00	0.82	0.62	0.94
(standardized)	(.18)	(.14)	(.12)	(.16)
Voted in 1978	1.20	0.35	0.71	0.94
(range 0–1)	(.24)	(.15)	(.18)	(.23)
Incumbent spending	5.11	5.37	2.91	−1.77
(log $10,000s per cong. dist.)	(2.23)	(1.57)	(1.51)	(2.20)
Challenger spending	−3.80	−4.99	−2.73	1.18
	(2.02)	(1.45)	(1.37)	(1.99)
News coverage	−0.89	1.70	2.51	5.45
(range 0 − .75)	(.53)	(.42)	(.52)	(.89)
Seniority	1.02	0.03	–	–
(log of years in office)	(.36)	(.20)		
Prior elective office	–	–	0.12	0.27
(0 or 1)			(.07)	(.09)
Acceptance function				
Intercept	−0.50	−1.32	−0.79	−1.32
Party attachment	−0.21	0.30	0.43	−0.12
(range −2 to +2)	(.03)	(.06)	(.09)	(.04)
Issue distance from	−0.12	0.38	–	–
Incumbent	(.05)	(.09)		
Ideological identification	–	–	0.03	−0.29
(standardized)			(.07)	(.05)
Domestic spending attitudes	−0.06	0.06	0.21	−0.13
(standardized)	(.04)	(.06)	(.08)	(.05)

Note: Dependent variables are sums of all remarks of given type, recoded to 0–1 range. Up to five remarks were counted in conection with each probe. The model is Equation 10.1. Approximate standard errors are in parentheses. N of cases, which involve all states in which an incumbent sought reelection in a contested race in 1990, is 1866.
Source: 1990 NES Senate survey.

and do not approach statistical significance, they follow the same pattern as in the House case: a positive main effect for seniority and a negative interaction with challenger spending.

The x-axis for Senate elections in Figure 10.6 manipulates political awareness over a range of −1.9 SD to +1.86, which, as usual, represents 98 percent of the total range of the scale. The idealized outpartisans used in the analysis in Figure 10.6 are people having a party identification score of 1.3 and a policy distance score of +2.

I might add that the effects of the predispositions variables, which are not displayed in Figure 10.6 because it shows trends only for modal outpartisans, are substantial. Among voters ideologically closest to the incumbent, defection patterns actually increase with political awareness; among those most ideologically distant, the decline in defection associated with awareness is steeper than shown in Figure 10.6. Thus, the pattern of defection for different types of partisans somewhat resembles the voter defection curves in Figure 10.1, except for a more intense message.

My estimates of net candidate consideration scores for Senate elections in Figure 10.7 were produced by the same general method used in creating the House estimates, as reported in Table 10.4. In the reception function, I used political awareness, voter turnout (purged of the effects of campaign intensity), logged spending by the incumbent, logged spending by the challenger, logged seniority, and media coverage; in the models for challenger likes and dislikes, I also used a variable measuring the previous electoral experience of the challenger. In the acceptance function, I used party attachment and policy distance. I specified the distance variable in the acceptance equation as the absolute value of policy distance (note, I assume that left–right policy distance affects vote choice, as described a moment ago, but that absolute policy difference affects liking and disliking, so that, for example, a conservative voter to the right of a conservative Senator will not be led to vote against the incumbent but may be led to dislike him or her). The survey also carried a series of questions on budget priorities. I combined these items into a scale, standardized the scale, and adjusted the scoring so that low scores indicate affinity with the incumbent. To measure issue distance from the challenger, I used respondents' ideological self-identification, standardizing and coding it to fit the party affiliation of the challenger.

Note that I did not use political awareness in the acceptance function of the estimates of likes and dislikes for the Senate candidates. This is because, when it was included, it behaved oddly, picking up large positive coefficients (indicating less resistance among the highly aware), while causing the awareness variable in the reception function also to pick up negative coefficients (indicating less reception among the more aware). I do not understand why Equation 10.1 behaved nonsensically in this case after it had worked well in so many others, but elimination of awareness from the acceptance function restored sense to the estimates, as shown in Table 10.7.[22]

The values used to create the idealized outpartisans in Figure 10.7 were the same as those used in the House analysis of likes/dislikes: party distance scores of 1.3 and −1.3, absolute policy distance scores of 2 and 0, budget attitude

---

22 There was a similar tendency in estimates of the House likes/dislikes data when the loquacity measure (a count of all party likes and dislikes, regardless of direction) was left out of the House model. The loquacity measure, which is, of course, positively correlated with awareness, was not available in the Senate data. A possible explanation for this difficulty is that the model, which contains some of the same variables in both a reception and an acceptance function, is not identified if the true value of the awareness coefficient in the acceptance function is zero.

scores of 1 and -1, and ideological distances from the challenger of 1 and -1 for outpartisans and inpartisans, respectively.

APPENDIX B: MODELING THE MONDALE–HART PRIMARY CONTEST

To model trends in candidate support in the 1984 Democratic primaries, we specify an initial support equation for Hart and Mondale, as follows:

$$H_1 = P_{HC_1} \qquad (10.4a)$$

$$M_1 = P_{MC_1} \qquad (10.4b)$$

Here H_1 and M_1 are levels of support for Hart and Mondale at time 1, and P_{HC_1} and P_{MC_1} are functions that specify this support, "Hart change" and "Mondale change," in relation to levels of political awareness. Each subsequent time period is then conceived as a "campaign" that either adds to Mondale's support by subtracting from Hart's or vice versa.

During the second time period, a certain proportion of Democrats convert to Hart, as given by P_{HC_2} which is also a function of political awareness. Then, following Equation 7.7, we may write

$$H_2 = H_1 + P_{HC_2} * (1 - H_1) \qquad (10.4c)$$

$$M_2 = M_1 - P_{HC_2} * M_1 \qquad (10.4d)$$

That is, Hart support at time 2 is equal to initial Hart support plus the proportion of initial nonsupporters who convert to Hart. Mondale support at time 2 is equal to initial Mondale support minus the proportion of initial support lost to Hart. The remaining equations are then

$$H_3 = H_2 + P_{HC_3} * (1 - H_2) \qquad (10.4e)$$

$$M_3 = M_2 - P_{HC_3} * M_2 \qquad (10.4f)$$

$$H_4 = H_3 - P_{MC_4} * H_3 \qquad (10.4g)$$

$$M_4 = M_3 + P_{MC_4} * (1 - M_3) \qquad (10.4h)$$

where P_{HC_3} and P_{MC_4} are the proportions converting to Hart in period 3 and to Mondale in period 4. These P_{C_t} terms model the effect of the dominant message of each period, and each is a form of the usual reception-acceptance process, as in Equation 7.5 in the text.

Equations 10.4a–h represent a series of nested equations, such that terms from each earlier equation appear in later ones as well. After appropriate substitutions, for example, the four Hart equations become

$$H_1 = P_{HC_1}$$
$$H_2 = [P_{HC_1} + P_{HC_2} * (1 - P_{HC_1})]$$
$$H_3 = [[P_{HC_1} + P_{HC_2} * (1 - P_{HC_1})]$$
$$+ P_{HC_3} * (1 - [P_{HC_1} + P_{HC_2} * (1 - P_{HC_1})])]$$

Table 10.8. *Coefficients for presidential primaries model*

	Reception function	Acceptance function
Hart$_1$ intercept	−4.92 (2.12)	a
Mondale$_1$ intercepts	1.17 (.64)	−0.02 (.27)
Hart$_2$ intercept	−2.59 (.50)	a
Hart$_3$ intercepts	0.32 (.40)	2.44 (1.46)
Mondale$_4$ intercepts	−0.44 (.41)	2.41 (1.62)
Awareness (standardized)	1.17 (0.80)	−2.87[b] (1.43)

Note: The data for this model are the 40 aggregate means in Figure 10.8. Standard errors appear in parentheses.
[a] Acceptance function eliminated to conserve degrees of freedom; see text.
[b] Coefficient applies to acceptance function only in third and fourth time periods.
Source: 1984 NES primary election survey.

$$H_4 = [[P_{HC_1} + P_{HC_2} * (1 - P_{HC_1})]$$
$$+ P_{HC_3} * (1 - [P_{HC_1} + P_{HC_2} * (1 - P_{HC_1})])]$$
$$- P_{MC_4} * [[P_{HC_1} + P_{HC_2} * (1 - P_{HC_1})]$$
$$+ P_{HC_3} * (1 - [P_{HC_1} + P_{HC_2} * (1 - P_{HC_{11}})])]]$$

where each of the P_{HC} terms represents a reception-acceptance process having the form of Equation 7.5. The four Mondale equations have a comparable form.

Each of the five P_{C_i} terms in these equations has four parameters – an intercept for the reception and acceptance functions, and a coefficient on attentiveness in both functions – which add up to a total of twenty parameters to be simultaneously estimated.

In estimating this cumbersome model, I used the aggregate data shown in Figure 10.8 – some 40 data points (4 periods × 2 candidates × 5 awareness groups). To preserve degrees of freedom, I simplified the model by constraining or eliminating as many parameters as possible. First, I constrained awareness to have the same effect in the reception functions of all P_{C_i} terms, leaving the intercept terms, a_0, to pick up differences in the intensities of the various messages. This is a strong but not unreasonable constraint: After controlling for message intensity via intercept shifts, awareness *ought* to have the same strength of relationship with reception in each campaign in each time period. Second, since visual examination of the data and initial estimates indicated that the acceptance function made no contribution to the estimation of Equations 10.4*a–d*, it was eliminated, which saved several parameters.[23] The awareness variable was eliminated as an acceptance factor in Equation 10.4*b* on the same grounds. Finally, I constrained awareness to have the same effect in the acceptance functions of Equations 10.4*e–h*; separate awareness coefficients would have been preferable here, but none of the coefficients could have approached statistical significance if estimated separately. The imposition of these constraints left ten coefficients for the forty data points. Equations 10.4*a–h* were simultaneously estimated with a nonlinear regression program.

The coefficient estimates are shown in Table 10.8. Because most of the terms represent intercept shifts in the reception or acceptance functions and hence involve only five or ten data points, it is not worrisome that some fall short of statistical significance in this highly interactive model. What is important is that coefficients denoting the effects of awareness on reception and on acceptance both achieve some degree of statistical significance.[24] As a further indication of goodness of fit, it may be noted that the correlation between the $\hat{y}$-estimates from the model and the raw data is .92 ($r^2 = .84$). Given the sampling error in the raw data and the constraints on the model, this would seem to be as much accuracy as could be hoped for.

23 Coefficient estimates for b_0 tended toward $+\infty$, indicating no resistance.
24 Because the model has been estimated from data aggregates derived from different cell sizes, significance tests should be regarded as being only roughly suggestive.

11

Evaluating the model and
looking toward future research

"If the public had an opinion and there was no pollster around to measure it, would public opinion exist?" Like the old conundrum about the tree falling in the forest with no one to hear it, this question is not completely vacuous. The answer depends on what one means by public opinion. If by public opinion one means the hopes, fears, feelings, and reactions to events of ordinary citizens as they go about their private lives, then certainly there is public opinion whether or not there is a pollster to measure it. But if by public opinion one means ordinary citizens walking around saying to themselves things like "I strongly approve of the way George Bush is doing his job as president" or "I think we should take a stronger stand, even if it means invading North Vietnam," then most of what gets measured as public opinion does not exist except in the presence of a pollster.

The RAS model has been about both kinds of public opinion, the "considerations" that people form in response to the flow of political communications, and the process by which they translate typically disorganized considerations into the survey responses that virtually everyone now takes as constituting public opinion.[1]

To the extent one evaluates the RAS model on the conventional criteria of empirical breadth and theoretical parsimony, it looks quite good. Its four axioms can be used to explain a wide variety of phenomena, including some concerning attitude change, that would be difficult to explain except by essentially similar ideas.

The most important feature of the model is its marriage of a theory of information diffusion through a population that is differentially attentive to politics (axioms A1 and A2), with a theory of how people transform this information into survey responses (A3 and A4). It is the union of these two processes that gives the model its breadth of coverage, and that creates the potential for further extensions and applications of the model.

However, the model has the vice of its virtues: Breadth and parsimony have been achieved at the expense of significant simplification and omission. Hence,

---

1 An exception is Ginsberg, 1986. For an analysis of differing conceptions of public opinion, see Price, 1992.

one can argue with some justice that each of the four axioms misses much of what actually occurs.

In this concluding chapter, I will try to give a fair assessment of both the strengths and shortcomings of the RAS model. Since some parts of the argument may no longer be fresh in the reader's mind, I begin with a quick recapitulation. Then, in succeeding sections, I enumerate what I see as the major weaknesses of the model, suggest possible improvements and extensions, and, finally, assess the value of the model to the public opinion field.

THE BASIC ARGUMENT RESTATED

The public forms considerations in response to political campaigns that consist of multiple, frequently conflicting streams of persuasive messages. In general, the greater a person's level of habitual political awareness, the more likely she is to receive these messages. Also, the greater a person's level of awareness, the more likely she is to be able, under certain circumstances, to resist information that is inconsistent with her basic values or partisanship.

Political communications, if internalized, become considerations in a person's mind, which is to say, they become reasons for taking one side rather than another on a political issue. When asked their opinions in surveys, people respond on the basis of whatever considerations are most immediately salient in their minds. The reason that their survey responses are unstable from one interview to the next is that what is at the top of a person's head varies stochastically over time.

This is not to say, as I have stressed, that individuals reply entirely randomly to survey questions. The balance of messages to which individuals are exposed, and their own selectivity in internalizing some while rejecting others, systematically determine the mix of considerations in their heads, and this, in turn, affects the likelihood that one rather than another survey response is made. Thus, individuals vacillate in their responses, but only within a certain, systematically determined range. Further, which of several competing ideas is at the top of a person's head at a particular moment is more than pure accident; it depends on such things as what happened to be in the news that day, the way questions are phrased or ordered on the questionnaire, and recent personal experiences.

Attitude change, understood as a change in people's long-term response probabilities, results from change in the mix of ideas to which individuals are exposed. Changes in the flow of political communication cause attitude change not by producing a sudden conversion experience but by producing gradual changes in the balance of considerations that are present in people's minds and available for answering survey questions.

The effect of any persuasive communication depends on the other ideas already present in a person's mind and on the opposing ideas to which the individual may be concurrently exposed. This makes resistance to a political campaign, where a campaign normally consists of a *dominant* campaign (or message) and a *countervalent* campaign, a rather complicated phenomenon. If a person has a large *inertial* mass of stored information, or exposure to countervalent information sources, no single piece of information from a dominant campaign is likely to have much effect. But if a person has little prior information and little access to alternative communication flows, information reaching him from a dominant campaign will have a large effect.

Resistance to attitude change also depends on a person's political predispositions, especially values. Values regulate the acquisition of countervalent and inertial considerations, as well as the internalization of messages from the dominant campaign. Thus, Democrats and Republicans tend to reject messages from the opposing party, and liberals and conservatives reject persuasive communications that are inconsistent with their ideologies. This form of resistance, called *partisan* resistance, tends to be more pronounced among highly aware persons, since, in many situations, they are more likely to possess the contextual information (the cueing messages) necessary to perceive the implications of a given issue for their values.

The effects of political campaigns can be quite different, depending on the relative intensity of the opposing messages and individuals' prior stores of partisan information. Sometimes the least aware persons are most susceptible to influence (in situations in which the information flow is very intense, as in presidential elections), sometimes moderately aware persons are most susceptible (in situations in which messages are moderately intense and partisan orientations are activated, as in contested House elections, presidential popularity, the later stages of the Vietnam War), and sometimes the most aware are most open to influence (in situations in which there is little partisan or ideological basis for resistance to persuasion, as in the early stages of the 1984 presidential primaries, or little access to countervalent information, as in the early stages of the Vietnam War). These differences across types of persuasion situations depend on differences in what people have been and are being exposed to – most importantly, whether they are being exposed to two-sided information flows and, if they are, the relative intensity of the opposing messages – and not on differences in individual psychology in different political contexts.

Throughout the second part of the study, I have been especially concerned to uncover the dynamics of resistance to dominant persuasive communications. One conclusion that emerged from this investigation was that resistance to persuasion depends very heavily on the availability of countervalent communications, either in the form of opposing information or of cueing messages from oppositional elites. Inertial resistance, the one form of resistance that does not depend on exposure to current communications and relies instead on individuals' internal resources, seemed the least important of the three resistance mechanisms in the one case in which it was possible to examine the effects of all three mechanisms, namely, the case of electoral attitudes.

The argument now restated, let me critique it.

WHO LEADS WHOM?

According to an oft told tale, a nineteenth-century revolutionary was sipping wine in a café one afternoon when a mob suddenly rushed past in the street. "Mon Diéu!" he cried, "the people are on the move, I am their leader, I must follow them." He then raced out into the street and to the head of the crowd.

Although the story is perhaps apocryphal, the problem it raises is real. One regularly observes "leaders" at the head of mass movements, but one cannot, on this evidence alone, be certain that elites are actually leading. They might, of course, be leading, but they might also be following.

With one exception,[2] this is not a problem I have been able to deal with systematically in this study. I have taken the intensities of opposing political communications to be exogenous variables and have limited my analysis to the supposed effects of these communications on public opinion. My working assumption, thus, has been that elite communications shape mass opinion rather than vice versa.

I justify this working assumption on two grounds. First, in several of the cases examined, it is clear from the nature of the particular cases that the elite stimulus to mass attitude change really was either mainly or wholly exogenous. It is perhaps most clear in the case of the Iran–Contra scandal, which produced change in public attitudes toward presidential performance and Central America policy, as discussed in Chapters 7 and 8. At the time the scandal broke, President Reagan's popularity was high and he had no serious problems on the horizon. The congressional attacks on Reagan's role in the Iran–Contra events, thus, must have occurred in spite of his initial standing with the public rather than because his popularity was already low.

Similar arguments can be made for four other cases:

1. It is hard to argue that the Supreme Court's decision in *Brown v. Board of Education* was a response to popular pressure for an end to Southern school segregation. Inside accounts indicate that, on the contrary, the Court perceived the public as largely hostile to federal intervention on this issue. The Court did indeed have a problem with public opinion, but the problem was not how far it would be forced to go in opposing discrimination but how far it could go without provoking a political backlash (Kluger, 1975). To be sure, the National Association for the Advancement of Colored People was pressuring for a desegregation ruling, but it had, at that point, minimal political clout. Thus, the Brown decision appears to have been motivated primarily by the moral convictions of the justices. How these convictions formed, and why they took the form they did in the mid-1950s, is obviously a deep and important question, but it is not one that

2 In the analysis of campaign effects in House elections, I controlled for incumbents' prior victory margins in order to find out whether the most intense campaigns were directed against incumbents who were already weak. The evidence indicated essentially no reason for concern in this particular case. See footnote 10 in Chapter 10.

creates problems for my assumption that the court was predominantly leading rather than following mass opinion in the Brown case.

2. The nuclear freeze movement of the early 1980s involved a great deal of grassroots public activity. Almost certainly, many politicians got on the freeze bandwagon only because they perceived it to be an extremely popular issue. The impetus for the freeze movement, however, can be clearly traced to people who would have to be considered elites, namely members of the professional arms control community who had been losing internal debates and calculated that politicians would not pay any attention to them until they mobilized public support for their cause (Pringle, 1982). The impetus to the mass movement that led many politicians to climb on the freeze bandwagon was thus itself the product of other elites who were quite self-consciously attempting to lead opinion.

3. The bullish news reports that led to optimistic assessments of the U.S. economy in late 1982 among some members of the public were no doubt some combination of hopeful prognostications by President Reagan and the business community, and technical economic reports. In neither case, and especially the latter, could one say that these reports were a response to what the public already believed.

4. The Bush administration's mobilization of public support for the Persian Gulf War is one of the most striking cases of elite opinion leadership examined in this book. When Iraq invaded Kuwait in August, 1990, only a small fraction of Americans was aware that Kuwait existed (Lang, Lang, and Larson, 1991). Yet within two weeks, public support for the use of American troops to prevent further Iraqi aggression was topping 80 percent in the polls, and this support eventually carried over into solid backing for a war to liberate Kuwait (Mueller, 1992). What makes this mobilization of mass opinion impressive is that it was accomplished in the absence of any communist threat, which for 40 years had been the standard justification for the use of American troops abroad, and despite the fact that, before the war began, most people expected it to be costly in American lives. Since no polls were apparently taken in the period between the initial Iraqi invasion and President Bush's declaration that the aggression would not be allowed to stand, there is no empirical basis for ruling out the possibility that Bush was simply responding to a groundswell of public demand for a firm American response. However, few informed observers of these events are likely to take this possibility seriously. The Persian Gulf War was, by all appearances, a case in which a politically skilled president, with the support of the press and most other elites, handily shaped mass opinion.

The general point here is that, however difficult it may be to resolve the direction of elite–mass influence in the abstract, it is often possible to make plausible judgments in particular cases.

Second, even when politicians pursue a certain policy because of perceived public pressure to do so, it is often the anticipation of that pressure, rather than actual pressure, that is critical. This is a point that V. O. Key (1961) has emphasized. The public opinion to which elites try to be responsive is not the public opinion that is reflected in polls at the point of making decisions, but the public opinion that an opponent might be able to call into existence at the next election. Politicians who slavishly follow existing opinion are, as Key argues, likely to fare poorly in the long run.

Let me take a simple case of such anticipatory influence, followed by a more complicated one. President Nixon's surprise announcement of wage and price controls in summer 1971, as described at the beginning of Chapter 6, was surely an act calculated to obviate criticism of his record on handling the economy in the upcoming presidential election. In this sense Nixon was responding to public opinion. Yet he was also leading it, since, as we saw, his speech had a definite impact in moving public opinion further in the direction of support for controls.

Now consider the infinitely more complicated case of the Vietnam War. From Gelb's account (Gelb with Betts, 1979), we know that President Johnson was well advised on the difficulties of trying to use American military force to stabilize a noncommunist government in South Vietnam. Johnson was also well aware that there was no groundswell of popular support for sending troops to Vietnam. Yet Johnson feared that if he permitted South Vietnam to fall to the North Vietnamese, he would open himself to the charge of being "soft on communism" and having "lost Vietnam" in the same way that President Truman had supposedly "lost China." Quite likely, Johnson feared, this would doom his Great Society domestic agenda and set off a new round of McCarthyist recriminations in which he would be the loser.

In this situation, Johnson led as well as followed the public into a war that neither he nor it was eager to prosecute. He was following public opinion in the sense that he anticipated a harsh retrospective judgment if he allowed a communist takeover, but leading public opinion in the sense that, in order to avoid this judgment, he had to mobilize public support for policies that were by no means immediately popular.

If, then, Johnson was, in a sense, genuinely leading public opinion on the war, perhaps a case can be made that antiwar politicians were the ones who were following public opinion more than leading it. Though more plausible, this, too, is a hard case to make. For it was at the high tide of popular *support* for the war in 1966 that mainstream politicians began to oppose the war. Further, the earliest mainstream opponents of the war were from constituencies that could not be described as hotbeds of antiwar feeling. Take the case of Senator J. William Fulbright of Arkansas, the earliest important political figure to turn against the war. Fulbright must have made a calculation that an antiwar position would not lead to insurmountable problems with his constituents. Yet it is implausible to think that Fulbright was in any more direct way responding to antiwar pressures back home in Arkansas. In fact, the evidence indicates that he took his antiwar position in spite of the best advice of his political staff (but because of advice he was getting from his foreign policy advisory staff).[3] Another early mainstream opponent of the war, Representative Tip O'Neill of Massachusetts, likewise relates that his early opposition was a response to what military authorities privately told him about the futility of the war, and in spite of his belief that opposition to the war was political suicide (O'Neill, 1987: p. 195).

The media were, of course, another important source of antiwar communications. To a very considerable extent, however, media reporting reflected, as it always does, what the media's sources were saying. For example, Charles Mohr, a correspondent for *Time* and later for the *New York Times*, has written of the antiwar reporting that originated among reporters in South Vietnam:

The debate was not essentially, as some seem to believe, a quarrel between the press and the U.S. officials in Vietnam. It was, rather, a quarrel between factions within the U.S. Mission. For the most part, field advisers closest to the action and to the Vietnamese took the pessimistic view. Some of the more senior officials in Saigon, who were reporting to Washington on the progress of the programs they themselves were administering, were publicly and persistently optimistic. The reporters quickly became aware of this dispute, because brilliant young field officers, as exemplified by the late John Paul Vann, increasingly turned to the journalists. The reporters did not invent the somber information that sometimes appeared in their stories. (1983: p. 56)

Since these sources were mostly in the military, the CIA, and the State Department (Hallin, 1986; Mohr 1983; Halberstam, 1979), it seems unlikely that their leaks of antiwar information were in any simple sense a response to changes in public opinion.[4]

Perhaps the most important exception to the claim that press reporting tends to reflect press sources occurred during the Tet offensive in early 1968, when the press depicted what was apparently a decisive American military victory as, instead, a serious defeat (Braestrup, 1979). This apparent misreporting of the news in an antiwar direction does not, however, appear to have been a response to public opinion in the United States, which still largely supported the war at the time of Tet. Rather, reporting appears to have reflected the press corps' surprise that the Viet Cong were able to mount an apparently credible nationwide military offensive after American officials had been saying that the Viet Cong were all but defeated. (It is conventional wisdom in American electoral politics that any competitor who does "better than expected" by the press finds him- or herself the beneficiary of an excited overreaction by the press; see Polsby, 1983.)

None of this is to deny a significant degree of elite responsiveness to mass opinion, particularly in the later phases of the Vietnam War. Most likely, though it is difficult to imagine how anyone could really be sure, marginal reductions in public support for the war made it incrementally safer for those politicians

---

3 Halberstam, 1972: p. 420.
4 For an account of the disdain with which the foreign policy elite regard public opinion, see Cohen, 1973.

predisposed against the war to go public with their antiwar sentiments. Presumably a similar interaction occurred between press and public, though it is again important to note that the press, especially the elite press, was carrying significant amounts of antiwar information in 1965 and 1966, well before there was any indication that declining public support for the war was making it safe to do so. Each increment of additional elite opposition made safe by changes in public opinion may then have produced an additional increment of change in mass opinion, which may have further emboldened the potential elite opposition, and so forth. The late entry of Robert Kennedy as an antiwar candidate in the 1968 Democratic presidential primaries may be an example of a politician who acted only after preliminary soundings of public opinion – in the form of Eugene McCarthy's success in the New Hampshire primary – signaled that an antiwar position was politically promising.

Such elite–mass dynamics are by no means inconsistent with an assumption of elite opinion leadership. One argument might be that weakening public support for the Vietnam War created discretion for elites to move in a similar direction. The elites who took advantage of this discretion would have been those predisposed by ideology or analysis to do so. Thus, elites act autonomously to shape opinion, but only after they calculate that it is safe to do so. An alternative argument for elite leadership would posit a differentially autonomous elite, some parts of which, primarily including upwardly mobile politicians, are somewhat responsive to mass opinion, and other parts of which, including most foreign policy experts, military officers, and government officials critical of the war, are largely independent of public opinion. The more autonomous segments of the elite, by this argument, use the media to generate public pressure to which other, more responsive elites, the politicians, then accede. A weak form of the argument for elite opinion leadership – and one that seems to me much too weak – would be that antiwar elites were *simply* responding to mass opinion, but that their responses took the form of antiwar messages, which diffused through the media in a manner specified by the reception-acceptance process, thereby producing further mass change, which in turn further pressured elites toward change. By this weak argument, it would be a nonautonomous elite that was influencing mass opinion.

It is important to recognize that, strictly speaking, one cannot use the results of my modeling to support even a weak argument for elite influence. The reason is that the RAS model, as formulated, is entirely agnostic about the sources of the political communications that move public opinion. Thus, it is consistent with the model that elites, including even the media, have no influence whatsoever on public opinion, and that all political communications diffuse through the population by personal contact, like germs. So long as political awareness is positively associated with reception of political communications and negatively associated with acceptance – as it would be in either a germ or elite-driven scenario – the model applies. This may be part of the reason the model performs so well: Because the diffusion process has the same formal properties whether it proceeds via an elite-dominated media or by humble word-of-mouth, the reception-acceptance model can capture the joint effects of both modes of diffusion.[5]

The allusion to germs, incidentally, is not fanciful. The reception-acceptance model, as formalized in this book, is a generic diffusion model. Given appropriate measures of exposure and resistance, it might be used to describe the diffusion of new fashions, religious beliefs, or even diseases. Within an adult population, for example, susceptibility to a socially transmitted disease might be nonmonotonic with respect to age: Young adults might be high on the social interactions associated with exposure to the disease but also healthy enough to resist it; the old might be vulnerable but socially reclusive; and so the middle-aged might be hardest hit. The incidence of AIDS may present an example of this sort of interaction, since raw data published by the U.S. Centers for Disease Control suggests that the incidence of AIDS was, at least for a time, nonmonotonic with respect to age ("Federal Planning," 1987).

What all this indicates is that a close fit between the reception-acceptance model and data on mass attitude change does not, by itself, indicate anything about the extent of elite influence. The model is simply a means for specifying the process of diffusion of elite influence, where the reasons for believing that it is elite influence, rather than something else, that is diffusing must be supplied independently of the model. (See the discussion on pp. 43–4.)

There is, as I have been arguing (and argued earlier in Chapter 2), an ample supply of such reasons. And yet, a fully adequate account of elite opinion leadership is not one that sees a public that responds to elite initiatives in a completely mechanical fashion, though a positive response by the public to well-crafted initiatives can usually be counted upon. Rather, it is an account in which elites – always having some ideas that are autonomously their own, always potentially split among themselves along partisan lines and maneuvering for partisan advantage, and always looking over their shoulders to see what the public is thinking and might think in the future – attempt to lead and to follow at the same time. Or, to put the point somewhat differently, the question is not whether elites lead or follow, but *how much* and *which elites* lead rather than follow mass opinion, and *under what circumstances* they do so. A full analysis

---

5 It should be noted, however, that the classic studies of personal influence provide no mechanism for explaining how interpersonal communications could bring about systematic changes in the distribution of mass opinion independently of elite influence. Rather, these studies have emphasized the role of personal discussion either as a conservatizing force that buttresses the individual against external influence, as in the Berelson, Lazarsfeld, and McPhee (1954) study titled *Voting*, or as a mediating force, as in the Katz and Lazarsfeld (1955) study titled *Personal Influence*, which shows how local opinion leaders pick up ideas in the media and pass them on to friends. In the first case, no attitude change occurs, while in the second, opinion leaders may be said merely to aid in the diffusion of elite-generated information. With respect to the second point, MacKuen and Brown (1987) conclude that political discussion is basically another "information channel" (p. 485): "[T]he social circle is not an active independent force in politics but instead shapes the information that comes from outside. Thus it is proper to think of the social environment not as a source of influence but as an intervening mechanism in a larger communication system" (p. 483).

of these problems is well beyond the scope of this book. My only aim in this brief discussion has been, first, to make clear what exactly my formal models of attitude diffusion do and do not prove about elite opinion leadership, and second, to make it appear plausible that, in a broad range of circumstances, the amount of autonomous leadership exercised by elites is substantial. (I return to this problem in Chapter 12.)

<h2>CRITICAL REVIEW OF BASIC AXIOMS</h2>

Critical evaluation of the RAS model may be organized around its defining axioms, beginning with A1, the Reception Axiom. The assertion in A1 is that greater attention to an issue is associated with greater reception of messages concerning that issue. This claim would seem initially unexceptionable.

Yet what exactly is it that people receive? Almost certainly, different people can be *exposed* to the same message and yet *receive* quite different messages, or even no intelligible message, depending on their prior knowledge about the issue. There are at least two ways in which this can happen. First, as noted in Chapter 8, people may better comprehend stories on subjects about which they have more initial familiarity. Thus, for example, more people learned about the sentencing of the colorful Marine, Oliver North, for his conviction in the Iran–Contra controversy than learned the reason for the resignation of the comparatively bland House Speaker Jim Wright, even though the latter story played out over a period of several months and received far more extensive coverage. (In fact, one poll suggested that almost as many people knew the name of Oliver North's striking secretary, Fawn Hall, as knew why Wright resigned the speakership.) Second, and more speculatively, individuals who are exposed to the same message may, if they take notice of it, perceive it differently. For example, the air force may stage an elaborate spectacle for the maiden flight of the B2, its new flying wing bomber, to show that the plane really works. Some members of the public may receive this as a pro-B2 message, but others may "see" in the flight "an obviously useless batmobile." In both of these cases, differences in reception (given equal attentiveness to the same message) will depend on people's previously existing ideas (or schemata) which may differ both in content and degree of development across individuals (Fiske and Kinder, 1981). The RAS model, as presently constituted, makes no allowance for these ways in which prior opinion may affect reception or partisan perception of the communications one encounters.

Consider next the Resistance Axiom, A2, which claims that people can resist persuasion only to the extent that they have acquired an appropriate cueing message, where cueing messages are assumed to have an origin that is, at least in principle, separate from the persuasive message itself.

This specification of the Resistance Axiom is intended to follow Converse's (1964) notion that people need to acquire contextual knowledge of "what goes with what" in order to develop conventionally left–right belief systems. With the inference (from A1) that more aware persons are more likely to possess cueing information, this axiom played a crucial role in explaining attitude change. All else equal, more aware persons are more likely to resist messages, given reception of them, that are inconsistent with their basic values – that is, to exhibit partisan resistance.

But how can we be certain that it is possession of relevant contextual information, rather than something else, that explains the greater critical resistance of more aware persons? As the reader may have noticed, I have been unable to produce any *direct* evidence on this point, that is, any data that credibly measure possession or nonpossession of a particular cueing message and link it to the acceptance or nonacceptance of a new consideration.

I have, however, pointed to abundant evidence of the importance of contextual information about message sources in mass communications – evidence that information or cues about the person providing a message greatly affects how people respond to it. So my emphasis on cueing messages rests on a solid foundation of past research. I have, moreover, been able to produce a fair amount of indirect evidence of the importance of cueing information.

An important piece of this evidence comes from the Vietnam War. When a mainstream elite consensus existed, exposure to the elite consensus, as measured by individuals' levels of political awareness, was associated with greater support for the war, with no resistance among the most politically aware. With the appearance of elite ideological disagreements in 1966, however, politically sophisticated liberals began to resist prowar messages and to accept antiwar ones. Thus, elite cues functioned to activate ideological predispositions among the politically aware.

The examination of the mainstream and polarization models in Chapter 6 provided several other cases in which political awareness either was or was not associated with political polarization, depending on the configuration of elite cues. Perhaps the most striking of these cases involved attitudes on recognition of Communist China in 1972. Political awareness was not associated with resistance to this policy, even though it is easy to imagine that some politically sophisticated conservatives would have eagerly resisted it if appropriate ideological cues had been given.[6]

Thus, most of my evidence for the importance of cueing messages derives from examination of the attitudes of the politically aware, who are extremely responsive to what ideologically congenial elites urge them to believe. In one type of case, however, the entire mass public – and not just the most politically attentive segment – relies heavily on partisan cues. This is the case of contested elections, where all citizens are about equally partisan in their tendency to accept the information supplied by their own party's candidate and to reject that of the opposition party's candidate.

6 *Congressional Quarterly* reports "a rising chorus of praise" for establishing relations with China, but also some criticism. Among the critics were John Ashbrook, an aspirant for the Republican presidential nomination, and columnist William F. Buckley (March 4, 1972: 472–3).

It is thus clear that awareness is associated with resistance to persuasion in some cases but not others. If one rejects my explanation – that cueing messages are subtle in some cases (typical partisan issues, such as job guarantees), completely obvious in others (partisan elections), and nonexistent in still others (mainstream issues), so as to make highly aware persons more capable of partisan resistance in the first type of situation but not in the second or third – then it becomes necessary to propose some other explanation for why awareness has this pattern of resistance effects. Since, for the moment, no alternative explanation is apparent, it is reasonable to accept the idea that, in many but not all situations, awareness brings with it esoteric knowledge of "what goes with what," and that this contextual knowledge is an important element of resistance to persuasion.

A more serious criticism of the Resistance Axiom can be made on conceptual grounds. Let us assume, as I suggested earlier, that some people see in the maiden flight of the B2 a comical batmobile – and see this, I should add, precisely because they have earlier received and, as doves, accepted stories about poor performance by high-technology weapons – while others see in the flight a magnificent flying machine. People whose preconceptions so influence what they perceive do not then need to engage in a separate evaluation to see whether the message should be accepted as a pro-B2 consideration. Perception and evaluation constitute for them a single, schema-driven step. Hence, it may reasonably be objected that the RAS model, in sharply distinguishing the reception step from the acceptance step, is creating a purely theoretical distinction.

The alternative would be to design a theory in which the internalization of prior, ideologically cued communications affects both the likelihood of receiving a message and the form in which the message will be perceived. Thus, if someone hears from a trusted source that the B2 is a costly and useless colossus, the person may be more likely to notice future news about the B2 and to interpret that news in ways consistent with this initial information bias.

There is much research on mental organization in social psychology indicating that perception is theory-laden in this way. It would therefore be valuable to graft a theory of perception onto the RAS model. The lack of such a theory is, in my opinion, one of the greatest deficiencies of the present model.

The Accessibility Axiom, A3, is perhaps the most defensible of the four axioms. The notion that ideas that have been used recently or frequently are more readily recalled from memory is extremely well supported both by experimental psychology (as in Wyer and Srull, 1989) and by research on political attitudes (Iyengar and Kinder, 1987; Iyengar, 1991), and the RAS model simply capitalizes on this evidence.

There must, however, be more to accessibility than recency of activation. For example, the studies of Wilson et al. (for reviews see Wilson, Kraft, and Dunn, 1989; Wilson et al., 1989) and Millar and Tesser (1986) clearly indicate that people call to mind different considerations when asked to articulate the reasons for their attitudes than when asked to think about their feelings on a subject. This would seem to indicate, unsurprisingly, that memory search depends on subtle features of the task in whose service it is being performed. It seems likely that memory search is also affected by such matters as mood, social context, and other recent activities, even if unrelated to the task at hand.

I have finessed these potential complications by assuming a large degree of simple randomness in the memory search process – or, as I have expressed it, randomness in "the ideas that happen to be at the top of one's head at a given moment." Although this seems to me acceptable as an initial strategy, future model builders might profitably pay more attention to how memory search occurs. The expected payoff would be the ability to explain more of the instability over time that is associated with people's survey responses.

Another shortcoming of the Accessibility Axiom is that, since it permits the activation of one idea to increase the accessibility of related or similar ideas, it is natural to wonder what exactly it is that determines when ideas are related or similar. This is something that the RAS model does not currently address but might, with greater attention to the representation of ideas in the mind, eventually be able to address. It might well turn out that, for example, which ideas are related to one another is less a function of logic or linguistic similarity than of elite cues and other features of the external environment.

But since, notwithstanding these limitations, A3 seems to accomplish its role in the model quite adequately, there would seem less need to tamper with it than with some of the other axioms.

The Response Axiom, which claims that individuals answer survey questions by averaging across the considerations that are most immediately accessible in memory, is the most contestable of the four axioms. One important shortcoming is that it provides no means of taking into account either the "strength" or the "extremity" of the attitude statements people are willing to make. That is, it allows people to favor one or the other side of an issue, but not to take positions that are more or less strong, or more or less extreme.

There is nothing inherently wrong with this binary approach. Much of the time when public opinion enters into elite politics, it enters as a single number, the percentage who approve of the president's handling of his job, or who support busing to achieve racial integration, or who want an immediate pullout from Vietnam. Elections, as conducted in the United States, are likewise aggregations of 0–1 choices.

Nonetheless, it would be valuable to take account of attitude strength and extremity within the RAS model. One approach would be to assume that the extremity or strength of an individual's attitude report varies with the net directional thrust of her considerations and the total number of salient considerations. "A preponderance of mutually consistent considerations" would thus be the cause of extreme or strong attitude reports.

I am aware of no data for testing this idea in connection with political issues, but it is readily tested in connection with evaluations of politicians. In the 1984 NES election study, for example, respondents were asked their likes and dislikes

Table 11.1. *The relationship between evaluational extremity and underlying considerations*

	Rating of Reagan on 100-point scale						
	0–25	26–35	36–45	46–55	56–65	66–75	75–100
Average *Net* of likes and dislikes	−2.75	−2.09	−1.78	−0.91	−0.52	0.39	1.90
Average *Sum* of likes and dislikes	3.02	2.97	2.68	1.76	2.69	2.98	3.14
N	287	123	146	234	245	419	757

Source: 1984 NES survey.

about Ronald Reagan and then immediately afterward were asked to evaluate him on a 100-point feeling thermometer. Responses to the former question can be taken as a measure of the number and thrust of considerations relating to Reagan that were immediately salient in the respondent's mind, while responses to the latter can be used to measure attitude extremity.

Table 11.1 presents the relevant data. As can be seen in the top panel, there is a strong positive relationship between net Reagan likes/dislikes and the overall warmth of feelings toward him. As the bottom panel further shows, the relationship between total number of Reagan considerations and feelings scores is strongly nonmonotonic. Thus, people with the largest average number of Reagan likes and dislikes evaluated him most extremely.

This little analysis raises the possibility that attitude extremity might be a relatively simple function of the number and direction of accessible considerations.

Another difficulty with my simple top-of-the-head response rule is that it is openly at odds with a considerable research literature which argues that, instead of making "memory-based" judgments from accessible ideas, as in A4, people's judgments are normally made "on-line" at the point of initial processing of incoming information (Hastie and Park, 1986; Lichtenstein and Srull, 1987; Lodge, McGraw, and Stroh, 1989; McGraw and Pinney, 1990). When asked to express an attitude, people simply retrieve their current evaluation and report it, rather than, as I have claimed, construct their attitude reports on the basis of the ideas most immediately salient to them.

The on-line model is obviously a plausible one, but not necessarily equally plausible for every type of problem. It is notable, first of all, that most of the evidence Hastie and Park cite involves nonpolitical subjects, especially personality evaluation. As they point out, it is extremely difficult to prevent people from forming integrated evaluations of other personalities as information comes in. Apparently this is something that people do naturally and effortlessly.

It is by no means obvious, however, that the same is true of political controversies. In fact, the opposite may be nearer the truth. Indirect evidence from a variety of sources indicates that it is difficult under the best of circumstances to induce citizens to form coherent impressions about political subjects (see, for example, Lane, 1962; Converse, 1964; Hochschild, 1981: ch. 9).

Park and Hastie do specify special conditions in which people make evaluations on the basis of ideas immediately available in memory, namely, when people encounter information that is so unimportant to them that they don't bother to keep updated evaluations but are then unexpectedly asked to state an opinion. When this happens, people are forced to rely on ideas recalled from memory as the basis of attitude reports. I suggest that these conditions are the norm in political information processing. In fact, the issues on which survey respondents are invited to offer opinions are simply too numerous, too multidimensional, and, taken as a group, too obscure for it to be feasible for them to engage in on-line processing of relevant information (see McGraw and Pinney, 1990).

The strongest evidence that the on-line model is inappropriate in the domain of political attitudes is that people's attitude reports exhibit so much *purely chance* variation over time and are systematically affected by things, such as question order, that ought, by the logic of the on-line model, to be irrelevant. Even attitude reports concerning well-known politicians, as an experiment by Wilson, Kraft, and Dunn (1989) has shown, appear to depend on the ideas at the top of the head at the moment of response rather than any deeper true attitude. It thus appears that the on-line model suffers from the same weaknesses as the conventional "true attitude" models discussed earlier. In fact, the on-line model is essentially just a variant of the old notion that survey responses represent *revelations* of preexisting states of opinion, a notion that, as I have argued at length, fails to work very well.

Having now, I believe, strongly defended the Response Axiom from criticism motivated by the on-line model, I would like to back off a bit. For although the memory-based judgment process embodied in A4 is defensible, it should be regarded only as a rough first approximation of what must actually occur. It seems to me likely that people do engage in what might be called *bounded on-line processing* of political information. That is, they may make on-line evaluations of particular subjects but then fail to integrate each newly updated evaluation into a fresh global evaluation. So if, for example, people encounter information about third-generation welfare families, they make an on-line update of their judgment of the value of social spending for the alleviation of poverty. If, sometime later, they encounter information about the needs of homeless persons, they update their judgment on the unmet welfare needs of the nation. But what they do *not* do, unless called to do so by an unusual event such as a public opinion survey, is to make an update of their global attitude toward the welfare system. Thus, if asked on a survey to make a global statement on the proper level of welfare spending, they will have no up-to-date global evaluation to retrieve but will instead have to make an on-the-spot judgment from whatever (updated) considerations, whether involving homeless persons or something else, come most readily to mind. By this account, A4 is not so much wrong as underspecified: Memory-based decision making occurs, but so, at another level, does on-line processing.

This limitation points to a more general weakness of the entire RAS framework, namely its failure to provide any mechanism for integration of information that has been acquired. By its axioms, people screen information at the point of first encountering it, but once internalized, each bit of information becomes just another consideration in a mental "bin" full of such atomized cognitions.

This is obviously a drastic simplification. Although total disconnectedness may, as Luskin (1987) skillfully argues, occur within certain segments of the public, it cannot be the whole story. Some people, and probably most, surely do build up complexly differentiated cognitions that cannot be adequately captured by my simple notion of a consideration. Contrary to the RAS model, these mental structures undoubtedly grow in size and subtlety as new information is encountered and integrated, thus perhaps increasing their chronic accessibility and hence relative "importance" as determinants of attitude reports. Integrated information structures might also play a major role in both the perception and critical scrutiny of incoming communications.

Another shortcoming in this same vein is that the model makes no provision for multiple reception of the same message. Does a message that has been accepted two or more times then become two or more considerations? Or, more in the spirit of the RAS model, might re-reception of an idea increase its salience and hence its likelihood of use? Or finally, does re-reception make it more likely that an idea will be integrated within some larger, more complex mental structure? Probably the answer to all of these questions, each of which challenges the basic structure of the RAS model, is yes.

The reason that I have left so much that I believe to be true out of the RAS model is, quite simply, that there has been no pressing need to include it. The machinery of the current model has been able to explain a large part of the variance in the existing survey evidence that seems presently amenable to systematic explanation, and I have been loathe to make the RAS model any more elaborate than necessary to do this.

In the longer run, however, greater elaboration of the model will become appropriate. Perhaps a fifth axiom could specify that the effect of thought about a subject – perhaps even thought that is independent of any elite influence (see Tesser, 1978) – is to build up integrated cognitive structures, presumably schemata. As these structures grow, they might colonize or neutralize opposing, less developed considerations, thereby reducing response instability. They might also influence the interpretation and processing of new communications, thereby preventing the future formation of opposing considerations.

It would be easy, however, to take the notion of integrated cognitive structures too far. One should, in particular, never take this idea so far as to overlook the substantial extent to which most people's political ideas are *not* integrated into coherent mental structures, the extent to which opposing ideas and feelings regularly coexist comfortably within the same brain, and the large element of chance in the process by which one rather than another idea comes to the top of the head and exerts momentary control over a behavior or attitude statement.

What would be most desirable, then, is not the RAS model I have proposed, but a Receive-Accept-*Integrate*-Sample Model, in which the outcome of initial information processing affects reception, acceptance, and integration of subsequent information.

I doubt, however, that theoretical elaboration of the RAS model along these lines will become fruitful to analysts of public opinion until we learn how to measure more than the simple "likes" and "dislikes" that have been featured in my analysis. This, in turn, will require some way of measuring, among other things, the volume and complexity of discrete cognitions, and where, in a stream of verbal statements from a survey respondent, thoughts organized by one cognitive structure leave off and those associated with another begin. These sorts of improvements in measurement capacity in mass surveys are not, so far as I am aware, immediately in prospect.

So, although I readily acknowledge phenomena that the axioms of the RAS framework cannot presently accommodate, and can make fairly specific suggestions about how the framework might be parsimoniously elaborated in order to better accommodate them, I do not see any reason for opinion researchers to make these elaborations until the data necessary for their testing become available.

MODELS OF THE RECEPTION-ACCEPTANCE PROCESS

If the most general achievement of the RAS model is its integration of a wide range of empirical regularities within a compact model, its most particular success centers on its treatment of attitude change. The core idea here has been that reception of persuasive communications increases with attentiveness to politics, and that capacity for resistance to uncongenial communications also increases with attentiveness. This dual claim, which originated in work by Philip Converse and William McGuire in the 1960s, has both motivated the discovery of some interesting patterns of attitude change and provided a basis for organizing them, as in the typology proposed in Chapter 8.

Even if, as will doubtless occur, future research turns up cases of attitude change that are not immediately explicable within this typology, researchers should be reluctant to discard either the reception-acceptance dynamic or the role of political attentiveness in mediating it. As I have attempted to show, individual differences in propensity to receive political communications are so great and so consequential under a wide range of conditions that it is virtually never safe to ignore them. The effects of attentiveness on acceptance or nonacceptance of persuasive messages, given reception, are less universal – in particular, they seem to wash out in high-intensity partisan elections – but they are nonetheless extremely important in many types of situations, and therefore also dangerous to ignore.

But despite the general importance of the reception-acceptance dynamic, there are a number of questions that may be raised about my development of particular reception-acceptance models. I group these questions under two rubrics: general theoretical issues and methodological issues.

Theoretical issues

In my opening discussion of attitude change in Chapter 7, I said that attitude change cannot be understood within the RAS model as a conversion experience – the replacement of one crystallized belief by another. It must instead be understood as a change in the balance of positive and negative considerations relating to a given issue. Owing to the lack of appropriate data, I have been unable to do full justice to this theoretical position. That is, I have been unable to show how changes over time in the balance of considerations in people's heads lead to graduated changes in closed-ended attitude reports, such as a movement from ''strong agreement'' with a particular policy to ''not so strong'' agreement. Rather, all of my analyses have dealt with the dichotomous case: Either people change their initial position to the opposite position or they remain unchanged.

Dichotomous scoring of attitude change measures does have technical advantages: The 0–1 scoring metric, which distinguishes those who support a given position from all others, including those who say ''Don't know,'' is the only one-dimensional metric that avoids treating ''Don't know'' responses as missing data. Since people who respond ''Don't know'' are less politically aware than counterparts who do answer survey questions, their loss as missing data would introduce significant distortion into estimates of the effect of awareness on opinion formation and change. For example, most of the attitude change in the early stages of the Vietnam War consisted of the conversion of respondents without opinions into supporters of the war.

Notwithstanding all this, attitude scales that measure strength or extremity of attitude reports are conveying real information about people's opinions. Changes in the degree of strength or extremity of an attitude, even if they do not involve crossing the threshold to support a policy that was previously opposed, likewise convey information. The problem is how to use it.

Two possibilities are suggested in Table 11.2. The issue is U.S. involvement in Central America, on which attitudes were measured on a seven-point scale at two time points. In the top half of Table 11.2, I simply took the mean difference over time in scores on the seven-point scale, omitting ''Don't know'' respondents. As can be seen, these patterns of change are radically different from those found in the earlier analysis.

However, there is an obvious difficulty with this method of measuring attitude change: Many highly aware hawks were at points 5 or 6 on the seven-point scale at the first interview, so that little proinvolvement change was possible for them; some were even at point 7, where no movement to the right was possible. In general, the greater a respondent's propensity to change in the direction of a particular message, the more limited the room for change was likely to be. Mean-

Table 11.2. *Two measures of opinion change on U.S. policy in Central America*

	Level of political awareness			
	Low			High
Method one: Attitude change as difference of means				
Hawks				
1986 mean	3.67[a]	3.65	4.23	5.26
1987 mean	4.28	4.15	4.59	5.60
Mean difference	0.61	0.50	0.36	0.34
N	(18)	(40)	(44)	(15)
Centrists				
1986 mean	3.47	2.76	3.53	3.71
1987 mean	4.07	3.95	4.05	3.71
Mean difference	0.60	1.19	0.52	0.00
	(30)	(37)	(40)	(14)
Doves				
1986 mean	3.87	2.97	2.60	2.27
1987 mean	4.07	3.16	3.00	3.19
Mean difference	0.20	0.19	0.40	0.92
	(15)	(31)	(50)	(26)
Method two: Attitude change as proportionate change				
Hawks				
	0.18[b]	0.03	0.09	0.18
	(17)	(37)	(41)	(13)
Centrists				
	−0.01	0.23	0.14	−0.19
	(29)	(37)	(37)	(14)
Doves				
	−0.09	0.03	0.05	0.16
	(14)	(30)	(49)	(26)

[a] Cell entry is mean score on 7-point scale.
[b] Cell entry is proportionate change between surveys, as described in text.
Source: 1986 and 1987 NES surveys.

while, highly aware doves were concentrated at points 1 and 2, where there was much room for rightward movement, including movement that did not require them to cross the threshold into actual support for greater involvement in Central America.

As a way of taking into account these floor and ceiling factors, I calculated change scores for each respondent, as follows,

$$\text{Change} = \frac{\text{Time}_2 - \text{Time}_1}{7 - \text{Time}_1}$$

This measure, calculated from panel data, scores each respondent's change as a proportion of his opportunity for change. Since division by zero is impossible, this approach requires the elimination of respondents who were at point 7 at the first interview, a plausible requirement in view of the impossibility of further rightward movement by such persons.

The results of this maneuver, as shown in the lower half of Table 11.2, are somewhat closer to the results of my earlier analysis, which also implicitly controls for floors and ceilings.[7] However, except for taking into account ceiling effects, this set of results has no more theoretical warrant than the first. For like the simple subtraction approach, it fails to link probability of switching sides on an issue with graduated change in the mix of considerations in people's heads.

To see what linkage might look like, consider an issue in which communications so strongly favor one side – say, the liberal side – that even conservatives take the liberal side of a dichotomous item. But such conservative support would presumably be ambivalent. Hence any intensification of conservative communications would tip the balance of considerations for many conservatives, producing heavy switching to the conservative side of the dichotomy. Liberals, because initially less ambivalent, would be less likely to cross the threshold. Thus, even if both groups formed exactly the same new considerations – and in this sense exhibited equal change – conservatives would be more apt to switch sides, with the most aware most likely to do so owing to heavier exposure to new ideas and (most likely) greater initial ambivalence resulting from prior reception of countervalent communication. This sort of argument could, I believe, make a useful starting point for future research in this area.[8]

---

7 The pattern in Table 11.2 would be perfect, except for high-awareness doves, who show much larger than expected change. I was naturally curious about this problem and so investigated it. Virtually all of the difficulty is with two individuals (in a cell of 26) who shifted from 1 on the seven-point Central America scale in 1986 to 7 in 1987, a maximal change in the wrong direction. Immediately following this question in the 1987 survey was a question about whether aid to the Contra guerrillas should be increased, decreased, or kept the same. Both of the problematic doves responded by *volunteering* that aid to the Contras should be entirely cut off! Apparently, then, their stated support for "much greater U.S. involvement in Central America" is misleading. One possibility is that they wanted the United States to be more involved in development projects or humanitarian relief. More likely, however, is that they simply made an error in using the seven-point scale. This would have been easy since the 1987 survey was conducted by telephone. In this mode, interviewers describe a seven-point scale to respondents rather than, as in a regular NES survey, give respondents a show-card with a labeled seven-point scale. I monitored many of the 1987 telephone interviewers and heard one case in which I was certain that a respondent picked the wrong number to describe her self-described position on Central America and another in which I felt it was likely that an error had been made. The SRC interviewing staff is generally reluctant to use seven-point scales over the telephone, and this case may illustrate why.

8 Because it is difficult to anticipate issues on which attitudes will change in the real world, it might be necessary to pursue the relationship between considerations and susceptibility to change in a laboratory setting. A type of opinion that is particularly suitable for use in examining attitude change in a natural setting is presidential approval, which can be counted upon to exhibit relatively large amounts of variation over time.

Another important question about the reception-acceptance process is why exactly critical resistance to persuasion often increases with levels of political awareness. I have offered a three-part explanation for this resistance, centering on the mechanisms of inertial resistance, countervalent resistance, and partisan resistance.

Of the three, countervalent resistance – the claim that better informed people are more resistant to dominant persuasive messages because they are more likely to become aware of low-intensity countervalent information flows – seems to have the strongest empirical support. It is hard to imagine how one might explain the peculiar patterns of change that arose during the Vietnam War and in voting in congressional elections without reference to the effects of countervalent communications.

Partisan resistance, the claim that people reject ideas that they are able to recognize as being inconsistent with their values, likewise seems to be on a firm foundation, as just indicated.

This brings us to inertial resistance, which is the idea that people having a large store of initial considerations on an issue are more resistant to subsequent change. This resistance mechanism, although dating to Converse's (1962) introduction of the reception-acceptance dynamic, is open to question. The problems are both theoretical and empirical. On the theoretical side, suppose that C_1 and D_1 are countervalent and dominant considerations in a person's mind at an initial point in time, and that C_2 and D_2 are countervalent and dominant considerations acquired over a subsequent time period. The expected response change over time is then given by:

$$\text{Change in response probability} = \frac{(C_1 + C_2)}{(C_1 + C_2) + (D_1 + D_2)} - \frac{C_1}{C_1 + D_1} \tag{11.1}$$

The claim of inertial resistance is that the larger C_1, the greater the person's resistance to the effects of the dominant message. If so, the derivative of Equation 7.1 with respect to C_1 ought to be positive, which would indicate that higher initial numbers of countervalent considerations are, all else equal, associated with higher levels of continued support for the countervalent position. However, this derivative turns out not to be positive; it is a complicated function that indicates no clear relationship between C_1 and resistance to a dominant message.[9]

Despite this, the notion of inertial resistance remains an intuitively plausible one. There was, moreover, some clear empirical support for it in the analysis of voting in House elections. One might, in addition, count the steadfast loyalty of

9 Numerical analysis of the derivative with plausible values for the key terms indicates that C_1 is, as expected, often associated with resistance to a dominant message, but never very strongly.
  Derivatives of Equation 7.1 testing for the effects of C_2 and D_2, which are associated with countervalent and partisan resistance, do have the expected signs.

sophisticated older partisans to established ideas concerning Korea and Vietnam, as discussed in Chapter 8, as evidence for inertial resistance. The idea here would be that old partisans have longer experience with these ideas and hence a greater store of inertial considerations making them resistant to change.

But there are also some empirical problems. A particularly troubling one involved the public's response to President Nixon's initiatives toward the communist government of mainland China, as discussed in Chapter 6. This was an issue that had exercised conservatives for two decades, and so I expected that sophisticated conservatives, especially older ones, would exhibit some inertial resistance to admission of "Red China," as the country was then called, to the United Nations. But I searched diligently for evidence of such inertial resistance – which should have taken the form of a nonmonotonic relationship between awareness and support for recognition of China – and could find none. The relationship to the new mainstream norm was, as reported in Chapter 6, as monotonically positive among conservatives as among other types of people.

Another disappointment, from the point of view of inertial resistance, was the breathtakingly swift movement of Republican activists, individuals who would undoubtedly score at the top of measures of both partisanship and political awareness, toward wage and price controls once Nixon announced his support of them in 1971, as also discussed in Chapter 6. This policy was as antithetical to traditional Republican conservatism as any that one can imagine, but it provoked scarcely any resistance.

These two cases, in combination with the moderate magnitudes of the effect of inertial resistance in congressional elections, feed the impression that inertial resistance is less important than either partisan or countervalent resistance as a source of resistance to dominant political messages. The notion of inertial resistance should certainly be kept alive, but it should also be treated with reserve until a reformulated theory or better data can provide it with a stronger warrant.

One possibility is that inertial resistance, like the other two forms of resistance, depends on nourishment from current communications. I suggest this because in the two cases in which there was something like inertial resistance to a new idea – the contrasting cases of sophisticated older conservatives resisting the Korean War and of sophisticated older liberals resisting anti–Vietnam War ideas – there was ample reinforcement for preexisting attitudes in elite discourse. In the case in which, as it seemed to me, inertial resistance should have been present but apparently was not – Nixon's reversal of U.S. policy toward communist China – there was virtually no elite opposition to Nixon's new policy and also no resistance among sophisticated conservatives.

Hence what I am calling inertial resistance may work something like this: People with large stores of preexisting considerations with respect to an issue may exhibit unusual resistance to new ideas but only so long as elite discourse gives some indication of the continued relevance of their old feelings. Absent minimal elite validation, old feelings may be swamped by ideas of the moment, as in Nixon's policy reversal on China. Elite validation, on this view, might be insufficient to implant a new idea in anyone's head, but adequate to awaken and invigorate preexisting ideas.

It is useful to recall at this point that two of my three resistance mechanisms, partisan and countervalent resistance, depend on nourishment from elite discourse (cueing messages in the first case, countervalent communications in the second). Now it turns out that even inertial resistance, already the least important of the three mechanisms, may also depend on elite communication. The implication of all this is painfully clear: The capacity of citizens for autonomous resistance to dominant elite communications is very distinctly limited.

I turn, finally, to a large but almost invisible simplification in the reception-acceptance model, namely the implicit assumption that individuals never think for themselves, but instead rely exclusively on the reception of communications reaching them from the external environment. Technically, this presupposition may be stated as follows:

$$\text{Prob(Attitude change)} = \text{Prob(Reception)} \times \text{Prob(Acceptance} \mid \text{Reception)} \\ + \text{Prob(Acceptance} \mid \text{No reception)}$$

where Prob(Acceptance | No reception) is constrained always to be zero.

It is difficult to say how large a simplification is involved here. But before discussing that question, I want to put the model's constraint concerning independent thought in perspective by noting what the model *does* allow. It does allow people to vary in their political predispositions, so that citizens may be more or less strongly predisposed toward equality, hawkish military policies, tolerance of dissent, and so forth. Whether these predispositions are products of socialization, adult experience, self-interest, inborn personality, or reasoned choice, they represent critical, internally motivated influences on opinion and, as such, afford citizens an important degree of autonomy from elite information flows.

To put the matter more strongly: The model does not claim, as a reader of an early draft of this book complained, that individuals are the passive receptacles of whatever elites want them to believe; the claim, rather, is that citizens pick and choose, *on the basis of their predispositions*, from the menu of elite-sponsored alternatives to which they have been exposed.

This is still a strong claim, but a less outrageous one. The argument is that most citizens, to the extent they are attentive to politics, align themselves with leaders or groups that share their predispositions and have more information than they do. In this way, they avoid the necessity – and perhaps the practical impossibility – of really thinking about issues. (The normative and research implications of this claim are considered in Chapter 12.)

Let me play out this logic as it applies to a concrete case that has been extensively examined in this book, the Vietnam War. This is an issue that is often said to have been agonizingly difficult for many persons, especially educated liberals. These were people who tended to be strong supporters of the war in its initial phase but found the war increasingly difficult to support and eventually turned, amid much discomfort, overwhelmingly against it.

The model, of course, explains both the initial support and subsequent opposition of educated liberals as a response to the cues of liberal elites. If, as was the case, it proved difficult for many educated liberals to turn against the war as liberal elite opinion leaders became increasingly antiwar, this might simply be a case of ambivalence between opposing considerations, where the ambivalence has been brought about by "inertial resistance" to the new antiwar message. Such inertial resistance was, as the model would expect, much stronger among older liberals, who, in contrast to younger ones, had built up large stores of anti-communism and other Cold War–type considerations. Although few educated liberals may have consciously experienced themselves as suffering the effects of inertial resistance to a new elite norm, it does not seem to me that the model does an obvious injustice in claiming that this is what occurred.

I am less confident that the argument of this book can capture the processes by which the attitude reports of less attentive people are formed. The reason is that, being less politically attentive, they are less influenced by the flow of political communications that is at the heart of the book's argument.

How less attentive persons respond to political issues in the absence of attention to or information about many of them is a difficult question. Part of the answer, as we have seen, is that their attitude reports tend to be unreliable, in that they lack temporal stability and are poorly correlated with their political predispositions. Another part of the answer is that politically inattentive people may often give "mistaken" attitude reports, in the sense that they respond on the basis of an incorrect guess about the meaning of the questions they have been asked. I was able to report one clear case of this in Chapter 5, where it was shown that inattentive persons responded to a sparely worded question about U.S. spending on aid to the Contra rebels as if they were being asked about government spending in general. The result was that social welfare liberals were most supportive of aid to the Contras and social welfare conservatives most opposed. This wrong-way correlation with ideology disappeared, however, when a more elaborate question conveyed the information that the Contras were opponents of communism.

These observations accentuate the negative, in that they stress what is missing from the attitude reports of the politically inattentive. This is not inappropriate, but there must be a positive side, as well, to indicate what does occur.

It seems likely that the same predispositions that animate the attitude reports of the politically aware are present and influential among the less aware. It is just that they may operate more directly on opinion – or at least operate independently of any mediation via the information and leadership cues carried in elite political discourse. Thus, for example, Sniderman, Brody, and Tetlock (1991) report that, among poorly educated persons, feelings or affect toward various political and social groups are a potent influence on attitude reports, whereas, among better educated persons, indicators of ideology are the dominant influence.

However, the dynamics of a "public opinion based on intergroup feelings" need not fundamentally differ from the dynamics of a public opinion based on elite discourse, as proposed in this book. People who pay little attention to elite discourse would still need to acquire information about the world and to evaluate it in light of some understanding of what the information means; they would also still formulate attitude reports on the basis of top-of-the-head information (or feelings), with all that follows from this. Only the sources of the leadership cues and information flows need be different: They might originate in informal or neighborhood subcultures rather than in a mainstream elite, and might diffuse by word of mouth rather than via the media. Such communication flows may be as likely to contradict as to corroborate information from the elite communication channels, as an example from the former Soviet Union will shortly illustrate, but they need not contradict any principles of the reception-acceptance model. As I observed earlier, communications transmitted by face-to-face interaction in the manner of germs may obey the principles of the model to the same extent as elite communications that diffuse through the mass media.

But might not the ideas that originate among the public and diffuse by word of mouth be different from those that originate among elites? Indeed, they might. Taxpayer revolts and backlashes of various types, including white backlashes against federal efforts to promote racial equality, are probably one type of attitude that tends to originate more often among the public than among elites – though, even here, there are cases in which politicians stir up backlashes and voter revolts because they expect to profit politically by them.

All this brings us back to the question discussed earlier: How often do elites autonomously lead opinion and how often do they simply go along with a public that operates on its own internal dynamic? And as in my earlier discussion, I have no general answer to this question. I can only observe that in the particular cases examined in this book, there is reason to believe that elites predominately led rather than followed.

Methodological issues

The central effort of the latter half of this book has been to show how public opinion is formed from an interaction between aggregate-level variation in the intensity of political communications and individual-level differences in political awareness and political values. Additional issues arise in the statistical modeling of this interaction.

I have taken two general approaches, one that assumes the diffusion of a single message through the public, and another that assumes two competing messages. The first approach, though based on a simplification, yields surprisingly accurate predictions about what should be expected under a range of particular conditions. But, as Chapters 9 and 10 have made clear, there are important features of mass opinion that cannot be explained by a one-message model. In particular, the cross-cutting movements of liberal opinion early in the Vietnam War, and the inverse association between campaign intensity and aggregate-level defection to the opposition party in elections, require the explicit modeling of a two-message information flow.

I suspect that some readers will experience the progression of my argument from one-message to two-message models with a degree of frustration. Two-message models are statistically cumbersome, impose data requirements that can rarely be met, and fail to yield clear predictions about what will happen in a given situation. And if the predictions of the one-message model – which are not only clear but aesthetically attractive – have only limited applicability, these readers will wonder what, after all, a reception-acceptance model is really worth.

I think, however, that any disparagement of two-message variants of the reception-acceptance model is unwarranted. For although two-message models cannot readily be used deductively, they can certainly be used, as in the Vietnam case and the presidential primaries case, as the basis for rigorous statistical modeling. Moreover, two-message models perform the important service of explaining why the simpler one-message model breaks down in the cases in which it does break down, and of doing so in a way that vindicates the essential principles of the reception-acceptance process.

If criticism is due the reception-acceptance models I have developed, it is that there is too little connection between the one-message and two-message versions of them. It would be preferable to have a single statistical model that would, by means of explicit simplifying assumptions, reduce to various simpler forms. But I have been unable to formulate such a master reception-acceptance model.

Another concern is statistical robustness. Some of my results, as has been apparent, are quite fragile. The fragility manifests itself in large standard errors for coefficients and the need to constrain parameters in models in order to obtain conventionally significant estimates. This statistical imprecision has sometimes involved the two most theoretically important effects in the RAS model, the effects of awareness on reception and on resistance to persuasion, given reception.

Two remarks are in order here. First, contemporary statistical theory, though not most public opinion research, tends to downplay the importance of statistical significance as estimated from a single test of a model on a single dataset. It instead emphasizes the stability of results obtained across related problems and datasets, and emphasizes, as well, the substantive magnitude of particular effects and the theoretical pattern into which they fit (Achen, 1983). Evaluated in light of these criteria, the results reported in Chapters 7 through 10 of this book are strong. Political awareness, in particular, has proven itself extremely important, producing large, theoretically intelligible and occasionally nonintuitive effects. When the magnitudes of these awareness effects have varied, the variation has often been in conformity with theory (as in the lack of an awareness effect on resistance in certain situations). The collective weight of this evidence, including the background theory and research on which the RAS model is founded, makes it seem bootless to worry about the standard errors of particular coefficients.

And yet, the information conveyed by the frequently large standard errors and loose statistical fits is real. Even with the constraints I have imposed on the RAS model, it has often been unable to obtain statistically precise fits.

There appear to be three sources of the problem. One is the highly interactive nature of my one-message and two-message models. Theory requires political awareness to be entered into these models several different times. Thus, in the one-message model in Equation 7.7, awareness must be entered in the reception functions of both the baseline and change models, and in the acceptance functions of both models. In the two-message model proposed in Chapter 9, awareness appears in the reception function for both the liberal and conservative messages, in the acceptance function for both messages, and in the recall function. The predispositional variables are entered twice. The net effect of all this, even after some constraints have been imposed, is to create a large amount of multicollinearity, and thereby a loose statistical fit to the data.

Another source of statistical imprecision is that much of what the model is trying to capture involves the behavior of small subgroups of the overall sample. In particular, the model's estimate of the effect of awareness on resistance depends heavily on the handful of persons who are both heavily exposed to a message and predisposed to resist it. Such people may constitute about half of the upper 10 percent of the sample on political awareness, which is to say, about five percent of the sample – a sample that, in several of my cases of attitude change, was quite small to begin with. Multicollinearity in the presence of small case numbers in critical subgroups can knock the statistical precision out of any model, no matter how well crafted it might be.

In consequence of all this, the difference between a fit in which political awareness affects resistance to persuasion and one in which it has no such effect may be small. This is apparent in Figure 11.1, which shows what small difference is made in estimated patterns of opinion change on U.S. involvement in Central America if awareness is deleted from the acceptance function.[10] (Note that I have altered the scale of the *y*-axis in Figure 11.1 from the usual 0–1 range in order to make it easier to see what is happening.) Little wonder, in light of this figure, that the effect of awareness on resistance is difficult to reliably detect.

Even the effect of awareness on reception, which appears by my estimates to be a highly reliable effect, may be difficult to detect in particular cases. Look back, for example, at the patterns of voter defections to the Republican presidential candidate, as shown in Figure 10.6. Greater awareness is associated with greater resistance to the presidential campaign, with no hint that political awareness may have any positive effect on reception. There is similarly little evidence, either visual or statistical, of strong reception effects from political awareness apparent in the data on vote defection in Senate elections, as also shown in Figure 10.6. Yet the mass of data presented in the second half of this book, as well

---

10 In estimating the model on which Figure 11.1 is based, I fixed the coefficients in the baseline function to be the same as in Table 7.4, thereby allowing only the coefficients in the change function to freely vary.

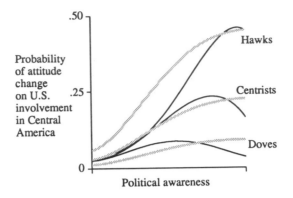

Figure 11.1. When awareness-induced resistance is set to zero. Solid black lines show estimated probabilities of opinion change from standard model; gray lines show estimated change when political awareness is omitted from the acceptance function. *Source:* 1986 and 1987 NES surveys.

as particular data involving these elections (as in Figure 10.7), make it clear that awareness is associated with large individual-level differences in reception in these cases as in the others we have examined.

In the face of these difficulties – multicollinearity, the dependence of results on relatively small subgroups of the overall sample, and effects that may be either subtle or invisible in particular contexts – what can be done?

It is important, first of all, to be clear that none of these difficulties is a difficulty of the RAS model itself. It is not, that is, a difficulty of the model that political awareness has both reception and acceptance effects, and that these effects may, under certain conditions, interact in ways that produce gentle nonmonotonic curves that are hard to distinguish from negatively sloped straight lines or almost flat lines. The difficulty, rather, is in finding ways to test the model that give its expected effects a fair chance to show up in typically noisy survey data.

The precautions necessary to conduct reliable tests of statistical models are generally well-known, but let me add a few remarks relating to peculiarities of the RAS model.

Reliable measures. Inasmuch as results often depend on the behavior of relatively small subgroups at the extremes of high and low awareness, it is essential to have measures of political awareness that can reliably distinguish those subgroups.

As explained in Chapter 2 and in the Measures Appendix, simple tests of political knowledge seem to discharge this measurement function better than alternative measures. In every case in which I had an opportunity to make comparisons, other types of measures did worse in the sense that they showed weaker effects than measures of political knowledge were able to detect. Thus, if I had used variables other than political knowledge in my tests of the reception-acceptance model, I would have obtained significantly weaker results than I did – and in some cases, nothing of interest at all.

It is an interesting oddity that different disciplines prefer different types of items to measure what I have been calling political awareness. Political scientists are partial to interest in politics, especially self-report measures of interest in election campaigns.[11] Communication specialists prefer self-reports of media exposure (though see Price and Zaller, 1990). Sociologists like to use education, which they see as a measure of social stratification. Only psychologists, for reasons no less rooted in disciplinary prejudice, make widespread use of political knowledge, which they take as a measure of "expertise," on which they have a large literature.

It is, as always, also important to use statistically reliable measures. Three- or four-item knowledge scales, in which all of the items have roughly middling levels of difficulty, will normally fail to provide good discrimination in the critical extremes of high and low political awareness. If a researcher can use only three or four items, they should at least be knowledge tests that vary in difficulty from easy to hard.[12]

The RAS model is no less sensitive to reliable measurement of political predispositions. For example, my findings on attitude change on U.S. involvement in Central America are entirely dependent on the availability of an eight-item militarism scale, which, by pure luck, happened to be undergoing testing in a study that spanned the Iran–Contra controversy.

Survey size. It seems likely that the two-wave survey of 360 persons, as used in the estimation of attitude change on Central America, is near the minimum number of cases necessary to adequately test the reception-acceptance model. I say this because the amount and pattern of attitude change, as apparent in the raw data, conform well to theoretical expectations, and the measures necessary to capture this change were about as good as they could reasonably have been, including, as they did, both a 22-item awareness scale with an alpha reliability of .87 and the Peffley–Hurwitz militarism items to which I just referred. Despite all this, the RAS model produced coefficient estimates that, although having good magnitudes, were barely able to achieve conventional levels of statistical significance, even after constraining the model.

It will, of course, be quite difficult to achieve large sample sizes in surveys designed to capture attitude change, since it is rarely possible to anticipate in advance when attitude change will occur and what questions will be necessary to capture it.

11 See pp. 235–6 in Chapter 10 for a discussion of the particular pitfalls of this measure.
12 Knowledge items that pose easy or hard tests tend, because of their limited variance, to produce misleadingly low item-to-total correlations (see Zaller, 1985, for examples). Thus, researchers wanting to build powerful measures of awareness need either to ignore the item-to-total correlations of their easy and hard items, or use suitable nonlinear and nonstandardized measures of statistical association (for example, item-to-total logit or probit coefficients).

Variance in information flow. Large datasets and reliable measures, despite their importance, may bring only minor gains in testing of the RAS model. What is most essential is good variance on the principal independent variable in the model, namely, the aggregate-level flow of change-inducing persuasive communications. To get this variance, it is necessary to move away from simple cases like those examined in Chapters 7 and 8, where the whole public has been exposed to the same flow of persuasive communications between a single pair of survey observations, and to try instead to locate cases in which there is usable aggregate-level variation in information flow. Chapter 9, which analyzed attitude change on the Vietnam War over a six-year period, and Chapter 10, which examined the effect of 77 different House campaigns on voter attitudes, showed what can be learned from such cases. The fine analyses of Erbring, Goldenberg, and Miller (1980), MacKuen (1984), and Bartels (1988) provide further examples of the testing of sophisticated individual-level models of attitude formation and change by capitalizing on variance in the flow of political information.

Modeling technology. Nothing in the four axioms of the RAS model requires that it be operationalized and tested by means of the complicated nonlinear models I have used in this book. But given the inevitable limitations of the data available for testing the model, it is essential to squeeze as much meaning as possible from the available evidence. At least in the case of the RAS model, this will mean frequent resort to complicated nonlinear models. My analysis of attitude change would have been much less successful if it had relied on standard linear regression models, including interactive variants of these models, instead of taking the path it has.

I certainly do not claim that the operational forms into which I have cast the RAS model are ideal. But they do have the virtue of taking central account of the complex interaction that exists among political awareness, political predispositions, and the flow of political information, and some type of nonlinear model that can efficiently do this is essential for testing the RAS model.

Modeling technology is the one factor in testing the RAS model that is fully under the control of opinion researchers. They should not fail to make the most of it.

A final methodological issue is my measurement of aggregate-level information flow. Although the flow of elite communications in the media is a prime independent variable in my analysis, I have made no attempt to measure it precisely. This is true even in my analysis of attitudes toward Vietnam, where I commissioned counts of stories for and against the war in several newsmagazines.

The difficulty is that, as explained a few pages ago, message intensity involves more than just the number and salience of stories that are carried in the media. It also involves characteristics of a mass audience that does or does not find a story interesting. In the long run, it will be desirable to distinguish sharply the separate contributions of media attention and mass receptivity to the penetrating power of a given message, which is how I defined message intensity. Progress on this problem will involve more than better story-counting techniques. It will likely involve the union of a more refined theory of the "message receiver" with a closely allied theory of media content analysis.

In the meantime, researchers comparing particular cases of mass attitude change will have to depend on their *judgments* of the intensities of the communication flows that have brought about change, even when they have made precise counts of media reportage. And to this extent, their tests of the model will be somewhat ad hoc.

Having now done my best to evaluate my formulation and testing of the RAS model, I wish to consider possible extensions.

PARSIMONY AS A VALUE

The centrifugal urge in academic research, by which I mean the tendency to develop new concepts and new theoretical machinery for each new substantive problem, is very strong in the political behavior field. It appears, moreover, that the most gifted researchers experience the urge most strongly. The result, as I lamented in the opening of this book, is that opinion research has become deeply and needlessly fragmented, almost completely lacking in theoretical coherence as each new survey question emerges as the object of its own specialized research literature.

This book has been written in self-conscious opposition to this centrifugal urge. The aim has been to identify a compact set of core ideas and to tie as many phenomena as possible to this core. Although this effort might be unflatteringly characterized as imperialistic, the animating spirit has been that of parsimonious understanding. For, all else equal, the more concepts and distinctions used to account for a given set of phenomena, the less well those phenomena are understood.

In the spirit of parsimony rather than imperialism, then, I would like to suggest some additional phenomena that currently exist as separate research topics but that, I believe, can be fruitfully analyzed within the framework of the RAS model. The issues are evaluation of presidential character, trust in government, and popular support for authoritarian regimes.

Evaluation of presidential character

In a classic of the voting literature, Stokes (1966) argued that fluctuations in the public's assessments of the personal qualities of presidential candidates are the most important factor in explaining interelection swings in the vote. Recent research has tried to specify more precisely the nature of these character assessments. Two streams of analysis have emerged. One is concerned with emotional reactions to the candidates – feelings of fear, hope, pride, and so forth. The other focuses on the public's evaluations of presidential character, especially the extent to which the candidates seem to possess the traits of personal integrity and competence.

Both streams of research have tended to focus on the factor structure of popular reactions to presidential character – that is, the dimensions of judgment that underlie people's assessments (see, for example, Kinder, 1986). It has not devoted much attention to how, and whether, people form their assessments of presidential character. The implicit assumption in this area of opinion research, as in most of the public opinion field, has been that all citizens pay enough attention to politics to develop structured reactions to the nation's leading political figures.

The approach taken here, in contrast, is to consider "information" about a president's character a "campaign message" like other persuasive messages, and to use the reception-acceptance model to capture the diffusion patterns of this message. The idea is that people who pay more attention to politics receive more information relating to presidential character and that they respond to this information on the basis of their general levels of political awareness, their ideological values, and their partisanship. Less attentive citizens encounter less evidence of presidential character and are less able to make partisan and ideological evaluations of the evidence they do come across.

Such an approach seems at least initially plausible. Presidential candidates always try in a general way to project sterling personal qualities and to keep their warts hidden from view. Occasionally, their efforts may become conspicuous, as in Jimmy Carter's attempt to demonstrate trustworthiness in the 1976 campaign or Ronald Reagan's determination to demonstrate levelheadedness in the 1980 contest. But however subtle or obvious these campaign messages, citizens may still vary in both their attentiveness to and their disposition to accept them.

Let us, then, turn to analysis of evaluations of Reagan in the 1984 election campaign. Reagan was by this point as well known as most presidential candidates are likely to get. With a strong economy and a record unblemished by personal scandal, one would expect him to have at least moderately high ratings on competence and, given his ability to project sincerity, perhaps even higher ratings on personal integrity. To measure assessments of Reagan on these two dimensions, which fall on the two major dimensions on which Americans are said to assess presidential character (Kinder, 1986), I rely on the following items from the NES battery:

> Now I'd like to know your impressions of Ronald Reagan. I am going to read a list of words and phrases people use to describe political figures. After each one I would like you to tell me how much the word or phrase fits your impression of Ronald Reagan.

> Moral
> Knowledgeable

According to popular lore, one of Reagan's principal achievements as president was to make America feel good about itself again. The idea that under Reagan the United States was "standing tall" in world affairs was a continuing refrain of his years in office. At the same time, many liberals confessed to apprehension; there was something about Reagan that seemed to scare them. The NES study of the 1984 election included questions measuring voters' emotional reactions to Reagan on both these dimensions:

Now we would like to know something about the feelings you have toward the candidates for President. I am going to name a candidate, and I want you to tell me whether something about the person, or something he has done, has made you have certain feelings like anger or pride.

Think about Ronald Reagan. Now, has Reagan – because of the kind of person he is, or because of something he has done – ever made your feel:

Angry
Proud

To gauge public responses to these items I used the basic reception-acceptance model as embodied in Equation 7.5. The resulting estimates, shown in Table 11.3, are depicted graphically in Figure 11.2.[13] (The raw data closely resemble the estimates in Figure 11.2 and so are not shown.)

These results are notable in several respects. The first is that Americans are highly partisan in their assessments of presidential character. This, of course, is no longer news at this point (Campbell et al., 1960; Converse and DePeux, 1962). What is news, at least to the scholarly literature of this subject, is how strongly individual differences in political awareness interact with partisanship and ideology in the assessment of presidential character. Among less aware citizens, partisanship has less effect; among the highly informed, the effect of partisanship is more pronounced.

The third salient feature of these results is how differently the public reacted to Reagan's knowledgeability than to his other characteristics. By these data, Reagan was less successful in projecting competence than in projecting morality, instilling pride, and, in certain groups, provoking fear. Highly aware Republican conservatives, the group that most strongly supports Reagan on other matters, failed to rally behind him on this aspect of presidential performance. Rather, it is moderately aware Republican conservatives who were most likely to assert that Reagan was extremely knowledgeable about politics. Thus we have, in this case but no others, a strong nonmonotonic relationship among Republicans between political awareness and belief in Reagan's good qualities.

This pattern is, I believe, best explained in terms of the differential intensities of a dominant and countervailing message. The dominant message is the carefully crafted image of presidential media advisors who, by skilled scripting of Reagan's public appearances, effectively project the idea that Reagan is the commanding leader of the national government. This is the message that most people encountered most of the time they received information about Reagan in

---

13 Although Figure 11.2 is based on Reagan evaluations in the postelection NES survey, highly similar patterns appear in data in the preelection survey. In particular, awareness has a resistance effect for knowledge but not for the other three ratings.

Table 11.3. *Coefficients for presidential evaluation*

	Traits		Emotional reaction	
	Knowledgeable	Moral	Pride	Fear
Reception function				
Intercept	1.18	2.95	2.94	0.90
Awareness	0.74	1.59	1.52	0.96
	(.28)	(.75)	(.36)	(.35)
Acceptance function				
Intercept	0.48	0.32	1.27	-0.72
Awareness	−1.25	−0.17	−0.21	0.20
	(.24)	(.17)	(.13)	(.21)
Party	−0.56	−0.52	−0.88	0.66
(range −2 to +2)	(.11)	(.08)	(.11)	(.12)
Ideology self-id	−0.37	−0.20	−0.34	0.30
(range −3 to +3)	(.10)	(.07)	(.07)	(.09)
Race (1 if black, else 0)	0.11	−1.09	−1.47	0.05
	(.35)	(.28)	(.26)	(.28)
N	1921	1923	1932	1987

Note: Model is equation 7.5, estimated by maximum likelihood. Trait items coded 1 for "extremely," 0 otherwise; emotional reaction items coded 1 for "yes," 0 otherwise. Other political variables coded liberal high. Dependent variables are from postelection survey. "No opinion" respondents on ideology (V369 and V370) were coded to middle position. Standard errors appear in parentheses.
Source: 1984 NES survey.

the media. But there was also a countervailing message which appeared, though much less prominently, in "op-ed" and "news analysis" pieces, and which depicted Reagan as uninformed and uninterested in the details of governance. This message, because less intense, reached only the most politically aware segments of the public. But within this group of people, it counteracted the effects of the dominant pro-Reagan message, thereby producing the nonmonotonicity that is apparent in Figure 11.2.

Note that political awareness has an important effect in the acceptance function of the knowledgeability model in Table 11.3, but in none of the other models. This is consistent with my argument, developed in Chapter 7, that one reason that awareness is often associated with resistance to a dominant message is that it is a proxy for exposure to countervalent communications that are insufficiently intense to reach the whole public.

Unfortunately, there is no easy way to make direct measurements of the intensity of the actual pro-Reagan and anti-Reagan messages on each of the characteristics examined in Figure 11.2, and hence no way to check the validity of this argument beyond an appeal to the reader's intuition. My argument does

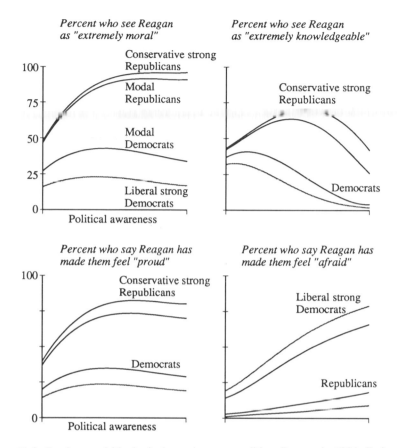

Figure 11.2. Partisan and ideological reactions to candidate Reagan in 1984. Estimates are derived from coefficients in Table 11.3. Awareness runs from −1.97 SD to +2.02 SD. Modal partisans have scores of ±1.3 on the party measure and ±1 on a 7-point measure of ideological self-location. Strong partisans have scores of ±2 on each of these measures. *Source:* 1984 NES survey.

nonetheless provide a new and, I hope, interesting slant on the public's judgment of presidential character. This argument, quite simply, is that the dynamics of public opinion on this matter are much the same as on others: Political communications emanate from the elite centers of society, in this case political campaigns, media advisors, and the president's record in office; the mass response to these messages depends on individual differences in value orientations and attention to politics, and on the relative intensities of the various messages.

TRUST IN GOVERNMENT

In the mid-1960s, as the United States was about to enter the war in Vietnam, popular trust in government appeared impressively high (Lane, 1965). But then, beginning about 1965, confidence began to erode, a trend that soon affected attitudes not only toward government but toward virtually the full range of American institutions, including even the clergy (Miller, 1974; Citrin, 1974; Lipset and Schneider, 1982).

The reason for the decline has never been entirely clear, but it has been widely argued that the tumultuous events of the 1960s, especially the unpopular war in Vietnam, the protest against it, and the black urban riots, were at the root of the phenomenon.

Should the wave of cynicism that swept over the country in this period conform to the dynamics of the reception-acceptance model?

If one conceives of the decline in trust as a sort of mood change, a humor reflecting the generally bad times on which the country had fallen, the answer would probably be no. The reception-acceptance model is designed to capture the diffusion of particular ideas and messages, not the spread of amorphous moods and humors.

But if, on the other hand, one conceives of the decline in trust as the public's response to attacks on national integrity by alienated protesters and leftist intellectuals, then the answer would be yes. The message of "liberal alienation" should follow the same diffusion path as any other type of message.

Since I could never decide which of these conceptualizations was more valid, and since I feel obligated to report both the successes of the model and its failures, I was reluctant to subject the model to a test in this domain. Recently, however, Jack Citrin, who specializes in analysis of trust in government, concluded that the reception-acceptance model might plausibly be applied to the problem, and asked for my advice in building political awareness scales. I sent him copies of these scales for all NES surveys and waited for the results of his analysis.

Some of his results are shown in Figure 11.3. As can be seen, the increase in governmental distrust over the period of the Vietnam War appears to have followed the pattern associated with the diffusion of liberal messages. Among liberals, there is a roughly linear and positive relationship between awareness and change in the direction of a liberal message; among conservatives, this relationship is sharply nonmonotonic. (Centrists, not shown, follow an indistinct middle pattern.) Citrin, in examining patterns of change in trust in government over several other time periods, found little additional support for the reception-acceptance model.[14] One reason for this, no doubt, is that fairly large amounts of attitude change are necessary before the *patterns* of change begin to stand out against background levels of measurement error, and most changes in trust levels since 1972 have been of modest magnitude. Another, more substantive reason may be that none of the change-inducing information flows had a clear ideological valence. It has not, in other words, always been clear whether liberals or conservatives or perhaps even centrists should be most susceptible to the presumed change-inducing message.

14 Citrin's results are part of a book manuscript in progress: "Governing the Disenchanted," Department of Political Science, University of California, Berkeley.

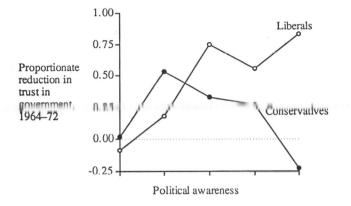

Figure 11.3. Decline in trust in government. Data are from 1964 and 1972 CPS surveys, as provided by Jack Citrin, University of California, Berkeley. Trust is measured by a two-item index, whether government can be counted to do what is right, and whether government is run by a few big interests.

Citrin's investigation of the performance of the reception-acceptance model in the domain of government trust underscores a key theoretical point: The model applies only to cases in which one can demonstrate or plausibly assume the existence of particular change-inducing messages having distinct ideological colorations. When one cannot do this, the reception-acceptance model does not perform, and should not be expected to perform, in the manner suggested by my analysis.

POPULAR SUPPORT FOR AUTHORITARIAN REGIMES

The RAS model originated in studies of American public opinion and American political psychology. There is, however, no reason to believe that it applies only in the United States. It is an entirely general model and, as such, ought to apply in any situation in which public opinion forms and changes in response to the diffusion of political communications. In an effort to show this, I collaborated with Barbara Geddes, a specialist in comparative politics, in an application of the model to a less developed nation.[15]

The problem that Geddes and I examined was popular support for authoritarian regimes. Every authoritarian government attempts to control the flow of news and information to the public – but with what effect? The RAS model, with its emphasis on the diffusion of elite communication, is ideally suited to answering this question. Presumably the most politically aware members of the public receive the largest amounts of government propaganda, and are also most

15 The joint paper was proposed by Geddes, who, upon becoming familiar with the reception-acceptance model, asserted that if it was as general as I claimed, it ought to be capable of explaining patterns of popular support for, and resistance to, the authoritarian regime then in power in Brazil. This was the beginning of an extremely fruitful collaboration.

capable of resisting it. Hence we should expect that people in the broad middle ranges of political awareness are most likely to exhibit support for the policies of authoritarian regimes.

Without going into technical detail that is readily available elsewhere (Geddes and Zaller, 1989), this is exactly what we found. Using opinion data collected in Brazil at the height of its authoritarian period in the early 1970s, Geddes and I show that support for the government's authoritarian policies was greatest among citizens exhibiting moderate levels of political awareness. Support for authoritarian policies rises steadily with increases in political awareness (which is measured, as in this book, by simple tests of factual knowledge about politics) until about the 90th percentile on awareness. At that point, the trend flattens and then reverses as support for government policies begins to decline.

This nonmonotonic pattern was not obtained for all policy items, however. For policies in which the authoritarian government simply carried forward the mainstream policies of the previous democratic regime, there was no nonmonotonicity: The most aware persons were most likely to support the government's mainstream line. Hence in Brazil as in the United States, mainstream communications encountered no resistance. Nonmonotonic patterns were obtained only in policy areas, such as censorship of the press, in which the military government departed from policies of the previous regime.

The Brazilian data were not strong enough to show why exactly more aware persons were less willing to accept authoritarian policies and, in particular, whether their unwillingness was rooted in inertial, countervalent, or partisan resistance. The Brazilian survey did, however, contain an abbreviated version of the classic F-scale, and this enabled us to extend the model in another direction.

The F-scale, as readers may recall, was proposed by the authors of *The Authoritarian Personality* (Adorno et al., 1950) as a measure of predispositions toward fascist ideologies. The items in the scale involve such matters as obedience to parents, respect for elders, and contempt for weakness. Although none of the items contains manifestly political content, they are nonetheless intended to measure deeply rooted personality predispositions toward authoritarian political policies and ideologies.

Unfortunately, the effectiveness of this scale has never been fully tested in a setting in which the masses of ordinary citizens were being heavily exposed to a dominant authoritarian message. The Brazilian dataset therefore afforded a valuable opportunity to see whether the scale performs as expected.

As can be seen in Figure 11.4, both the F-scale and political awareness are associated with support for authoritarian policies, but not in a straightforward way.[16] Persons who pay little attention to politics do not reliably support the policies of the military government even when their personality dispositions, as

---

16 Both relationships are highly statistically significant in a fully specified model ($p < .01$) (see Geddes and Zaller, 1989: table 3).

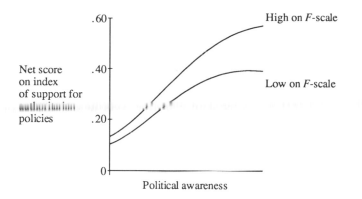

Figure 11.4. The *F*-scale and support for the authoritarian regime in Brazil. Dependent variable is an 8-item scale indicating support for authoritarian policies, such as press censorship and suppression of unions. The *F*-scale consists of five items, purged of the effects of education, sex, race, and residential location. General procedures used in constructing the figure are the same as reported in figure 3 of Geddes and Zaller (1989). Authoritarians and nonauthoritarians in the figure have been constructed from scores of approximately ±1.25 SDs on the *F*-scale; other background variables have been set to their modal values. *Source:* 1972–73 survey by researchers at the Instituto Universitario de Pesquisas do Rio de Janeiro and the University of Michigan.

measured by the *F*-scale, indicate they ought to do so. This is presumably because they pay too little attention to politics to know what policies the authoritarian government stands for. (Note that persons scoring low on awareness in Brazil were, by U.S. standards, extremely uninformed about politics; many were illiterates who did not even know the name of the country's president.) Moderately aware persons exhibit more support for authoritarian policies, but not much more evidence of ideological acumen. Like the partisan defectors in House elections, they are simply responding uncritically to the dominant political message in the environment. Only among highly aware persons is there an important relationship between authoritarian predispositions and support for authoritarian policies. This is because, in Brazil as in the United States, highly aware persons are the only ones capable of responding in a consistently ideological fashion to the political communications they encounter.

These results represent an important qualification of the theory of the authoritarian personality. They suggest, first of all, that exposure to authoritarian propaganda may be at least as important in accounting for support for authoritarian regimes as are authoritarian personality orientations. They further suggest that personality predispositions are just that: predispositions. Whether, or to what extent, authoritarian predispositions manifest themselves in the form of support for authoritarian policies depends, as always, on a critical interaction with political awareness.

Dispositions toward authoritarianism are not, of course, the only factor influencing support for authoritarian policies. Education is also important. Better educated Brazilians, perhaps because greater literacy increased their reception of countervalent communications that were largely uncensored by the military, were significantly more resistant to authoritarian policies, given reception of them, than were poorly educated ones. The result was a pattern much like that shown in Figure 11.4, except with education substituted for scores on the F-scale.

One surprise in our analysis involved chronological age. We expected older, politically aware Brazilians, because of their experience with the democratic norms of the previous regime, to be more resistant than their young counterparts to the policies of the authoritarian government. Age, however, turned out to have no discernible effect, perhaps because it was associated with two mutually canceling effects, commitment to the democratic norms of the previous regime and a preference for the order and stability of authoritarian government.

One should not place too much emphasis on the particular patterns of regime support found in Brazil. The reception-acceptance model would lead one to expect significant variation in these patterns from one country to another. These expectations are set out in Figure 11.5, a typology claiming that variations in regime support depend on how vigorously governments seek to indoctrinate their citizens, and how much access citizens have to countervalent communication.

In countries in which the government makes energetic efforts to indoctrinate its citizens – the governments of Nazi Germany and the now defunct Soviet Union[17] are examples – even the least politically informed members of society may (in comparison with the least informed Brazilians) exhibit moderately high levels of support for regime norms (compare the cases in the left-hand column of Figure 11.5 to those in the right-hand column). A second source of variation in popular support for authoritarian regimes is the access of citizens in different countries to countervalent sources of values. Many citizens in authoritarian Brazil retained access to books and other small circulation publications that carried alternative values; some also remembered the democratic norms of the previous regime. In other authoritarian countries, however – North Korea comes to mind – scarcely any segment of the population has either personal memory of, or access to, sources of antiregime values. In consequence, the decline in support for regime policies that we found among the most aware Brazilians should show up more weakly, or perhaps not at all, among the most aware citizens of countries such as North Korea (compare cases in the top row of Figure 11.5 to those in the bottom row).

17 In developing this typology, we assume that authoritarian regimes espouse authoritarian policies. The Gorbachev government in the Soviet Union, however, was a partial exception. Its *glasnost* and *perestroika* policies must be viewed, in the context of Soviet history, as nonauthoritarian. One would therefore expect patterns of support for these policies to differ from those forecast for other cases.

REGIME EFFORT TO MOBILIZE OPINION
High effort   Low effort

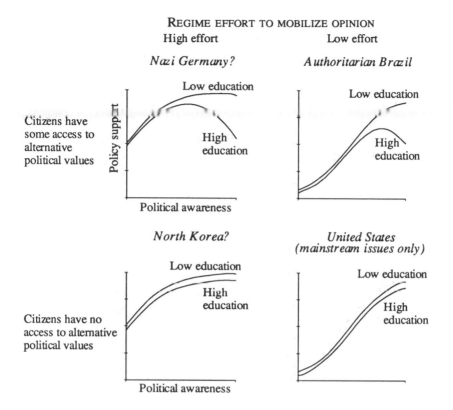

Figure 11.5. A typology of support for government policies.

It is difficult to think of modern authoritarian countries that fall clearly into the lower right cell of Figure 11.5. However, one might reasonably consider the United States an example of a nonmobilizing regime whose elites have achieved high levels of voluntary agreement on certain norms relating to capitalism, democracy, and, at times, foreign policy. The analysis of Chapter 6 indicates that when such elite consensus exists, American public opinion indeed conforms to the pattern in the lower right cell. (See Figure 6.5.)

In proposing this typology, Geddes and I had in mind cases in which the government maintains at least the appearance of competence and effectiveness. Certainly this was true of the Brazilian regime at the time of our survey. For cases in which governments are markedly less effective (or less lucky with the economy), one would expect more resistance to government policies. The model readily accommodates the effects of such heightened resistance. Returning to Figures 8.2 and 8.3, we see that as resistance increases, patterns of policy support become nonmonotonic and perhaps negative. Hence for the case of an ineffective government, we would expect, ceteris paribus, a gently nonmonotonic pattern of support among the moderate to poorly educated, and a nearly flat or negative relationship with awareness among the better educated. (It is straightforward to redraw Figure 11.5 to illustrate such cases.)[18]

The reception-acceptance model thus specifies the ways in which a variety of factors – a nation's prior experience with alternative ideologies, the intensity of the regime's efforts at public mobilization, the access of citizens to alternative sources of ideas, and the regime's performance – interact to affect overall patterns of regime support.

A smattering of evidence from what used to be known as Eastern bloc communist countries in the pre–Gorbachev era provides additional support for the RAS model. A 1984 study by Polish researchers at the University of Warsaw found that support for martial law and opposition to the union Solidarity were greatest among people at low-to-middle levels of education. In 1985, when the government had begun to promote a return to normalcy, many poorly educated respondents had lapsed into no opinion, so that support for martial law was then greatest among people at middle levels of education (Ryszka, 1987: p. 253).[19] These findings are readily intelligible if, as seems reasonable, one is willing to assume that education is positively associated with reception of proregime communications and negatively associated with a disposition toward uncritical acceptance of these communications.

Similar, though somewhat sketchier evidence is available from the former Soviet Union. Philip Roeder (1985, 1989) reviews studies showing that, although opposition to the Soviet regime was greatest within the best educated segments of society, education was positively associated with individual susceptibility to indoctrination programs in factory settings. In other words, support for the regime seemed to increase with education – except at the very highest levels of education, where support declined somewhat. On the basis of this and other evidence, Roeder suggests that ''the relationship between dissent and social mobilization is curvilinear, declining with early social mobilization under Party tutelage, but rising as education and urbanization become still more advanced.'' The inverse of Roeder's dissent curve is, of course, a pattern in which support for the regime increases as education increases, but then declines at the highest levels of education.

By far the most provocative evidence from a former Eastern block nation involves changing patterns of support for the Afghan War among the Soviet public. It seems that after an initial period in the early 1980s in which the Soviet media gave relatively little publicity to the war, the government became concerned about signs of public disquietude. Consequently, it made a ''decision to develop 'information' – particularly on television – about the war.''[20] The

18 It is interesting to note that when the Brazilian economy faltered, support for the regime collapsed first in just those quarters in which our analysis would lead one to expect it: among the most highly educated and politically involved segments of the population (Alves, 1984; Lamounier, 1980).

19 I thank Stanislaw Gebethner for bringing these data to my attention.

20 *Foreign Opinions* (June 1987), Centre d'Analyse et de Prévision, Ministère des Affairs Etrangers, Number 4, Paris. I thank Chris Achen for bringing these data to my attention.

result, according to a Radio Free Europe survey of Soviet citizens traveling in the west, was that between 1984 and 1986

approval increased among those who had so far proved hesitant, in particular young people, uneducated, [and] central Asian citizens. On the other hand, opposition has developed in key sectors such as Moscow, Leningrad, among graduates and party members. (Roeder, 1985)

In addition, no-opinion rates, which had been high in 1984, fell during this period of intensified progovernment communications, and fell most of all in provincial areas. In Siberia, the most peripheral region of the Soviet Union, "Don't know" rates declined from 59% to 31% between 1984 and 1986, while support for the war rose from 24% to 51% and opposition rates remained unchanged. But in Moscow and Leningrad, the least peripheral regions, the biggest change was an increase in opposition from 20% to 35%.

These Soviet results present a striking parallel to changing patterns of support for the Vietnam War in the United States between 1964 and 1966. It will be recalled that, in this period, support for the war rose in the least aware stratum in response to an intensified prowar campaign by the government, but that, at the same time, it fell among the mostly highly aware doves, who were the only ones likely both to receive and to accept the antiwar message.

One wonders about the source of the anti–Afghan War message in the Soviet Union. Our only evidence about it is that antiwar Soviets were most likely to mention "word of mouth" as their main source of information about the war. This no doubt represents a genuine and important difference from the United States. Where the media are controlled by the government, countervalent communications must diffuse through informal channels. But aside from this, the effects of dominant and countervalent messages are, as far as one can tell from the available data, surprisingly similar in these two cases of unpopular foreign wars.

There is, however, an important caveat to all this. Much evidence suggests that popular support that is built up by means of one-sided communications can collapse virtually overnight when two-sided communications are allowed. A demonstration of this occurred in authoritarian Brazil shortly after our data were collected. In a highly controlled "election campaign" in which only government approved candidates were allowed access to the mass media, the government candidates were so far ahead of the opposition in the public opinion polls that the government felt it safe to permit the opposition candidates limited access to the media a few weeks before the 1974 election. When it did so, support for the official candidates plummeted. Many found themselves in suddenly close races, and a number were actually defeated (Lamounier, 1980).

That mass opinion may prove highly changeable is by no means evidence of its insignificance. Weakly held or superficial opinions that conduce toward acquiescence in authoritarianism or are the basis for choices between radically different candidates in elections can be immensely consequential in spite of their superficiality. Mass opinion may be, in many cases, an inherently superficial force, but it is directly attached to the levers of government, and this can make it extremely powerful.

It should also be noted that, in some authoritarian countries, opposition activists develop unofficial networks to challenge regime domination of political ideas. This happened in the Philippines during the Marcos regime and recently in South Korea.[21] More strikingly, as events in Romania showed in 1989, it is possible for a citizenry to stage a spontaneous rebellion even in the absence of such communications networks.[22] It is obviously important to understand how such events occur. The dynamics of the RAS model, however, offer no clear insight to such problems.

CONCLUDING REMARKS

The common framework developed in this book involves the interactive effects of four types of variables: at the aggregate level, variation in the *intensity* of political communications; at the individual-level, variation in citizens' *attention to politics* and in their *political predispositions* (especially values); and, again at the aggregate level, in the *accidental factors that make considerations momentarily salient* to people, such as news reports or questionnaire construction.

These variables interact in a four-axiom model that specifies how individuals acquire political considerations from the political environment and use them to formulate answers to questions about their political preferences. The general model seems to work approximately equally well in a wide range of political contexts, from elections to support for foreign wars to evaluation of presidential character.

The four-axiom RAS model actually reduces to two main ideas. The first is that individuals do not possess "true attitudes," in the usual technical sense of the term, on most political issues, but a series of considerations that are typically rather poorly integrated. The crude model I have proposed does not begin to do justice to the process by which competing considerations are formed, interact with one another, and stochastically determine people's responses to particular survey questions. But the core claim of the RAS model that people do not typically have "just one attitude" on issues is, as I have sought to show, essentially correct and deserves, in one form or another, a central place in our understanding of the nature of mass opinion.

The other main idea in the RAS model is that an interaction between political awareness and political predispositions is fundamental to the process by which citizens use information from the political environment to form opinions. This interaction was almost completely neglected in studies of political behavior in the 1960s and 1970s but seems to be getting more attention from attitude re-

21 In the latter case, the government, although authoritarian, allowed the mass media a fair amount of latitude for criticizing its policies.

22 A report on National Public Radio, however, contended that the Romanian revolution began in peripheral areas of the country because that was where access to alternative communications, in the form of news reports from neighboring countries, was greatest.

searchers – though not yet from many voting behavior specialists – in recent years (see Erbring, Goldenberg, and Miller, 1980; MacKuen, 1984; Franklin and Kosaki, 1989; Krosnick and Kinder, 1990; Stoker, 1990; Jacoby, 1991; Pollock, Lisle, and Vittes, 1991; Sniderman, Brody, and Tetlock, 1991; Franklin, 1992; and Hurwitz and Peffley, in press). But even so, standard procedure in the majority of political behavior studies is still to assume that citizens react to the stimuli they encounter – whether political campaigns, presidential performance, the state of the economy, issues of war, peace, or domestic policy – solely on the basis of their values and interests. The idea that, owing to differences in political awareness, citizens may vary substantially in their ability to act on their values and interests is typically not recognized.

The model I have proposed is certainly not without weaknesses. In view of them, especially the inability of the model in its present form to accommodate either the integration of discrete information into larger mental structures, or the process by which political perception is influenced by past experience, the model must be considered approximate and provisional.

It is, I should also note, very much an open question whether the particular operational models by which I have sought to accommodate the interactive effects of political awareness and political predispositions, especially as embodied in Equations 7.7 and 9.8, are ideal. I certainly do not claim that they are. My claim is only that researchers need to find some way of taking these interactions into central account in their own model building, because these interactions are both very common and substantively important.

Despite its various limitations, the general RAS model has the virtue of pulling together within one theoretical system a wide variety of empirical phenomena, many of which are analyzed by specialists who rarely or never communicate with one another. The specialized division of labor is a strength of scientific activity, but when the vast majority of work concentrates on issues of topical importance – even great topical importance, such as racial attitudes, or support for U.S. intervention in foreign wars, or elections – with little regard for anything besides the inherent importance of the topic, specialization has great costs. My feeling, as I have indicated, is that these costs have become too great, and that it is time to start incurring a few costs on the other side of the ledger. The RAS model, in accepting the costs of nonspecialization, has been able to make clear the great, presently largely untapped potential for synthesis within the public opinion field.

The RAS model also swims determinedly against the current of much political behavior research, which cheerfully emphasizes the diversity of individuals' responses to politics. In so doing, the model reflects my conviction that the appropriate scientific response to the diversity of nature is not to rejoice, but to redouble the effort to find strong models and broad generalizations that will fruitfully simplify the realities that we experience in daily life.

12

Epilogue: The question of
elite domination of public opinion

The voice of the people is but an echo. The output of an echo chamber bears an inevitable and invariable relation to the input. As candidates and parties clamor for attention and vie for popular support, the people's verdict can be no more than a selective reflection from the alternatives and outlooks presented to them (p. 2).
                                    —V. O. Key, Jr., *The Responsible Electorate*

In the 1930s and 1940s, many observers feared that the rise of the modern mass media would bring a new era of totalitarian domination. Mass circulation newspapers, the newly invented radio, and motion pictures seemed ideal tools for playing upon the fears of the new mass societies, and the great though temporary success of Hitler in Germany, Mussolini in Italy, and Stalin in the Soviet Union seemed to confirm everyone's worst fears.

George Orwell's famous novel *1984* is perhaps the best-known expression of this foreboding over the dark potential of the mass media, but many social scientists shared Orwell's apprehension. As a result, attempts to measure the effects of the mass media on public opinion were a staple of early opinion research.

This early research turned out to be reassuring, however. Compared to what many feared the media might be able to accomplish, surveys found media effects to be relatively small (Klapper, 1960). The media most often served to reinforce and activate existing opinion rather than to create it, and much of the impact the media did have was mediated by community leaders in a kind of "two-step flow" (Lazarsfeld, Berelson, and Gaudet, 1944; Berelson, Lazarsfeld, and McPhee, 1954).

If media effects were, as almost all research indicated, "minimal," then the danger from political elites who might exploit the media to manipulate mass opinion must be minimal as well – or so it seemed to the majority of mainstream communication researchers who, notwithstanding the importunings of a handful of identifiably leftist academics (for example, Miliband, 1969), were content to ignore the possibility of elite domination of mass opinion by means of the mass media.

Recently, however, the standard belief in "minimal" effects has come under severe attack. Using widely different methodologies but converging on the same conclusion, several research groups have found evidence of substantial media effects (Patterson and McClure, 1974; Patterson, 1980; Iyengar, Peters, and Kinder, 1982; Iyengar and Kinder, 1987; Bartels, 1988; Fan, 1988; Brody, 1991; Page, Shapiro, and Dempsey, 1987; Page and Shapiro, in press). No single news story or broadcast may have great effect, but the cumulative effect of many stories over a period of months or years may nonetheless be large (Iyengar, 1991). Thus, although the old model of the media as a "hypodermic needle" that could inject ideas into the body politic on command has not been revived, mainstream communication research has now developed a healthy respect for what the media, and the politicians who use it, can accomplish.

If the theory of minimal media effects has lost its academic warrant, then so has complaisance over the potential for elite manipulation of mass opinion through use of the media. In this concluding section, I therefore turn to this issue. My discussion will be heavily structured by the categories of my earlier, empirical analyses.

DEFINING ELITE DOMINATION

The argument of this book is, on first inspection, scarcely encouraging with respect to domination of mass opinion by elites. Many citizens, as was argued, pay too little attention to public affairs to be able to respond critically to the political communications they encounter; rather, they are blown about by whatever current of information manages to develop the greatest intensity. The minority of citizens who are highly attentive to public affairs are scarcely more critical: They respond to new issues mainly on the basis of the partisanship and ideology of the elite sources of the messages.

If many citizens are largely uncritical in their response to political communications as carried in the mass media, and if most of the rest respond mechanically on the basis of partisan cues, how can one deny the existence of a substantial degree of elite domination of public opinion?

It all depends on how one defines elite domination. If one takes it to mean any situation in which the public changes its opinion in the direction of the "information" and leadership cues supplied to it by elites, indeed, there is not much to argue about. Not only the present study, but several others provide abundant evidence of this sort of elite domination (Iyengar and Kinder, 1987; Page, Shapiro, and Dempsey, 1987; Fan, 1988).

Yet the matter cannot be decided so easily. Of course the public responds to elite-supplied information and leadership cues. How could it be otherwise in a world in which events are ambiguous and in which the public must regularly have opinions about matters that are, to use Lippmann's phrase again, "out of reach, out of sight, out of mind" (1922, 1946: p. 21)?

Page and Shapiro (in press), recognizing an unavoidable dependency of public opinion on elite discourse, frame the problem in terms of the *"quality of information and interpretation* [that] is conveyed to the public." They continue,

To the extent that the public receives useful interpretations and correct and helpful information – information and interpretations that help it arrive at the policy choices it would make if fully informed – the policy preferences it expresses can be considered "authentic." . . . Individuals or institutions that influence public opinion by providing correct, helpful political information can be said to *educate* the public.

On the other hand, to the extent that the public is given erroneous interpretations or false, misleading, or biased information, people may make mistaken evaluations of policy alternatives and may express support for policies harmful to their own interests and to values they cherish. An extreme result of such mistaken evaluations could be the systematic "false consciousness" or "hegemony" of which some Marxists and other theorists speak. . . .

Those who influence public opinion by providing incorrect, biased, or selective information may be said to *mislead* the public. If they do so consciously, and deliberately, by means of lies, falsehoods, deception, or concealment, they *manipulate* public opinion. (ch. 9; emphasis in original)

The difficulty in this way of framing the problem, as Page and Shapiro acknowledge, is that it requires independent knowledge of (or assumptions about) which interpretations and information are correct, and such independent knowledge is largely unavailable. Despite this, however, Page and Shapiro attempt to identify cases of elite manipulation. For example, they write that President Reagan

misled or manipulated the public on a variety of foreign policy matters. Calling the Soviet Union an "evil empire," with leaders willing to "lie, cheat, and steal" for their ends, he made exaggerated charges that the Soviets had broken the SALT arms control treaties, and he portrayed the U.S. as advocating arms control while he in fact resisted reaching agreement. (ch. 9)

Though not wishing to defend either the Reagan administration's policies or its use of rhetoric in these instances, I would also be reluctant to cite them as cases of manipulation of public opinion. Who, after all, can say that the Soviet Union was not, in some sense, an evil empire, or that it was truly the United States rather than the Soviet government that was dragging its feet on arms control? Judgments on such matters are inherently political – which often means ideological – and it is a mistake, in my view, to undertake an evaluation of elite–mass relations on the assumption that one's own judgments can, in general, rise above partisanship.

Yet Page and Shapiro's notion of "information and interpretations that help [the public] arrive at the policy choices it would make if fully informed" is, I believe, a conceptually useful one. For one thing, "fully informed" judgments, if they refer to all *available* information rather than to all possible information, need not always be correct judgments. One can make one's best decision on the basis of available information and still be dead wrong. Further, people who are "fully informed" may nonetheless disagree, as experience regularly shows. On these two counts, then, there is latitude for opposing groups to disagree radically without each of them risking a charge from the other that it is seeking to manipulate – or in my terms, to dominate – public opinion.

With this in mind, I define elite domination as a situation in which *elites induce citizens to hold opinions that they would not hold if aware of the best available information and analysis.* This conception is still problematic in that it depends on an assessment of what the public would believe *if* it were fully informed. But this difficulty is not, I believe, an insurmountable one, as the following parable will suggest.

THE PARABLE OF PURPLE LAND

Once there was a country that was inhabited by two kinds of people, blues and reds. Blues and reds shared many values, but they evaluated public policies differently. Blue people preferred short, round policies expressed in strong colors, whereas the reds preferred tall, rectangular policies articulated in pastel colors.

In consequence of their ideological differences, which might or might not have been rooted in differences of material interest, reds and blues were in constant political disagreement. But both sides valued reason and evidence, and so each commissioned experts to advise them. Of course, blues hired blue persons as experts and reds hired red persons as experts, but they charged their expert advisors to argue, discuss, and debate with one another in an effort to achieve, if at all possible, the best resolutions to policy problems. To encourage experts to get the best answers to policy dilemmas, they offered very large prizes – consisting of status, research support, and, in a handful of cases, public recognition – to those experts who were able to make convincing arguments to other experts.

Like all free countries, Purple Land had professional politicians and political activists to take the lead in public affairs. But the politicians and activists of Purple Land were pragmatic and people-oriented sorts who rarely came up with ideas on their own. Rather, they looked to experts of their own coloration for ideas, and when a congenial expert group proposed something new, the politicians and activists didn't ask many hard questions. Their main concerns were the readiness of the public to receive the idea, advantageous framing of the idea in partisan debate, and other matters of effective marketing. Hence, the politicians rarely ventured beyond the parameters of expert discourse.

Neither red nor blue citizens were especially interested in politics. They preferred to devote their time to their jobs, their families, and to baseball, the national pastime. So they didn't take the trouble to follow political debate very carefully; rather, they commissioned communication specialists to keep them informed, in general and easily comprehensible terms, of what each political group thought.

Citizens were so apolitical that few paid attention to which experts or politicians endorsed which particular policies, but those who did notice would mechanically adopt the opinions of their own type of elite, as reported by communication specialists in the press. The remainder simply spouted whatever idea was at the top of their heads, without attaching much significance to what they said. The one thing no citizen ever did was to think for himself or herself. All simply selected from the menu of elite-supplied options.

If elite domination consists of elites inducing the public to hold attitudes that it would not hold if fully informed, it may be said that the citizens of Purple Land entirely avoided elite domination. When, despite differences in outlook, blue and red experts agreed with one another and got most politicians and citizens to go along with them, citizens could feel assured that, even if they devoted their whole lives to investigating the given policy problem, they would not reach conclusions much different from the ones advocated by the experts. For the expert community included persons having the same values as the community at large, and reached its conclusions after extensive analysis of the best available information.

Even in cases of elite disagreement, in which each type of citizen mechanically followed the advice of his or her own type of politician or expert, there was no elite domination. For citizens could still be confident that, the more closely they looked into a subject, the more likely they would be to reach the same conclusion reached by the expert subcommunity sharing their own values.

This parable shows that it is possible at least to imagine conditions in which the dependence of mass opinion on the information and analyses carried in elite discourse is great, and yet in which elite domination of public opinion, by a plausible construction of the term, is unlikely to occur. These conditions are

1. predispositional differences among the experts paralleling those within the general public, such that experts are motivated to examine issues from all viewpoints;
2. institutional incentives for experts to develop effective solutions to pressing problems;
3. a press that, whatever else it also does, provides ample coverage of all expert viewpoints, where the term "expert" is broadly construed to include anyone having specialized knowledge of a problematic subject;
4. politicians and activists that keep within the parameters of expert opinion;
5. a citizenry that is capable, in cases of elite disagreement, of aligning itself with the elite faction that shares its own predispositions.

Although one may be able to imagine better or stronger safeguards against elite domination, the ones proposed here would be reasonably effective, and they have the virtue of being researchable by standard empirical techniques. The researcher need have no special or suprapolitical insight into the "correctness" of the leadership provided by elites. It is only necessary to examine the processes by which leadership cues are generated and diffused.

The remainder of the chapter will use these conditions as the basis for examining the degree of elite domination that exists in the United States. The aim will not be to settle the question, which is obviously impossible in the few pages that remain in this study, but to show the kinds of issues that need to be discussed and the kinds of additional evidence necessary to reach a convincing conclusion.

THE POLITICAL COMMUNICATIONS SYSTEM
OF THE UNITED STATES

The press

Scholars interested in the quality of information and analyses available to the public have tended to focus on the press as the most proximate source of that information. Hence, a great deal of information about it is available.

One of the clearest findings to emerge from the scholarly literature on the press is that reporters will regard as newsworthy that which their "legitimate" sources say is newsworthy (Cohen, 1963). As Leon Sigal (1973) writes,

Even when the journalist is in a position to observe an event directly, he remains reluctant to offer interpretations of his own, preferring instead to rely on his news sources. For the reporter, in short, most news is not what has happened, but what someone says has happened. (p. 69)

As one journalist put it: "We don't deal in facts, but in attributed opinions" (cited in Gans, 1980: p. 130). One reason for the well-established reliance of reporters on their sources is that journalists have a tendency to "go native," identifying with the sources and wanting to promote the source's world view. As Russell Baker has written,

The State Department reporter quickly learns to talk like a fuddy-duddy and to look grave, important, and inscrutable. The Pentagon man always looks like he has just come in from maneuvers. The Capital Hill reporter . . . affects the hooded expression of a man privy to many deals. Like the politicians he covers, he tends to garrulity, coarse jokes, and bourbon and to hate reform. (cited in Sigal, 1973: p. 49)

A more fundamental reason that reporters rely so heavily on sources is that they have no real choice. Reporters have neither the time nor the training nor, in most cases, the inclination to do primary investigations. As David Halberstam has written in *The Powers That Be* (1979) of the journalists who cover foreign affairs,

they had come to journalism through the traditional routes, they had written the requisite police stories and chased fire engines and they had done all that a bit better than their peers, moving ahead in their profession, and they had finally come to Washington. If after their arrival in Washington they wrote stories about foreign policy, they did not dare inject their own viewpoints, of which they had none, or their own expertise, of which they also had none. Rather they relied almost exclusively on what some American or possibly British official told them at a briefing or at lunch. The closer journalists came to great issues, the more vulnerable they felt. (pp. 517–18)

Journalists have reputations as swashbuckling characters who are never afraid to say what they think is true. It would be more accurate to say that journalists are never afraid to say what other people think is true. Yet in a world in which there are enormous pressures – some political, some economic, and some arising from the prejudices of the populace – to suppress what is true, an intense commitment to publicizing the views of a wide range of sources can be an extremely valuable service.

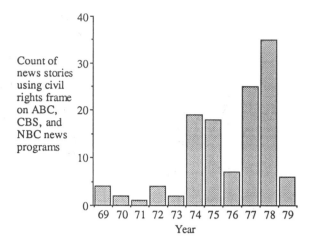

Figure 12.1. Number of stories using civil rights frame on network television news. *Source:* Vanderbilt Television News Archives.

It is, however, a mistake to think of the relationship between the press and its sources in mechanistic terms. The sources responsible for a given story may not be quoted in it, consulted for it, or even personally familiar to the reporter. This is because, most generally, what the press attempts to do is to cover the news from "all legitimate points of view," where legitimacy is conferred not only by government authorities and interest group leaders, but also by subject matter specialists who have been, in effect, accredited by mainstream institutions such as the government, universities, research institutes, or major book publishers. Hence, if there is a significant fraction of mainstream expert opinion that holds a particular view, the press will look for ways to use that view as the basis of news reports. When, for example, CBS television news correspondent Morely Safer filed his famous story of a U.S. marine using his cigarette lighter to burn a Vietnamese peasant's thatched roof hut (Halberstam, 1979), a story that was obviously antiwar in its implications, it is doubtful that Safer checked with any particular source on how to frame the story. However, he was nonetheless reflecting a view of the war that was held by a significant fraction of foreign policy experts.

In asserting such a broad dependence of media reporting on expert opinion, I am going beyond the existing literature on the press, which has formulated press dependency in terms of dependence on particular sources, most often government officials dealing with a foreign policy issue. However, there is no reason to believe that a press which is congenitally dependent on government sources for a type of story that is dominated by the government will shed that dependence in other types of situations. The broader dependence may be more difficult to document, but it is likely to be present nonetheless.

Consider the treatment of homosexuality in the media. In the period in which the American Psychiatric Association (APA), as the most authoritative source of secular understanding of this subject, regarded homosexuality as a disease, press coverage of the issue was dominated by antihomosexual stereotypes. Thus, if one looks up homosexuality in the *New York Times Index* of 1950, one finds a request to see the perversion and scandal listings. But when the APA declared, by a poll of its membership in 1974, that homosexuality was no longer to be considered a disease, the press began to employ a "civil rights' frame of reference alongside the old "vice" frame, thus offering the public an alternative way of conceptualizing the issue of homosexuality.

The change in network television news coverage of homosexuality, in particular, occurred quite suddenly at the time of the APA vote. In the five years prior to the APA vote in 1974, TV network news devoted 14 minutes to stories that, implicitly or explicitly, referred to homosexuals as a minority group seeking its rights. In the next five years, the networks devoted 135 minutes to stories of this kind, a nearly tenfold increase.[1] The same data, arrayed in terms of story counts, are shown in Figure 12.1.

My examination of this new civil rights coverage, which was generally but not always sympathetic to gays,[2] indicates that most fell into one of three categories:

1. Coverage of a lawsuit by Air Force Lieutenant Leonard Matlovich, who was attempting to reverse the decision of the military to dismiss him for being homosexual. Over several days, all three networks devoted significant attention to this story.
2. Coverage of state and local referenda on gay rights. Following the APA vote, the media regarded these referenda, beginning with one in Dade Country, Florida, as having national political significance.
3. Human interest stories on gay and lesbian organizations, especially those forming on college campuses. These stories examined the loneliness of homosexual students, and their efforts to form support organizations, hold social events such as gay dances, and oppose discriminatory rules.

It might be objected that none of these stories had any direct connection with the APA vote, and that what really changed was the behavior of homosexuals, who were becoming increasingly militant and increasingly effective in demanding their rights.

Certainly the increased militancy and visibility of homosexuals contributed to the change in press coverage. But it was hardly the whole explanation. For example, nothing in the gay rights movement compelled the spate of largely sympathetic stories about campus gay rights organizations. In one of these stories, NBC reporter Betty Rollins noted:

The question is, do homosexual organizations encourage homosexuality? Psychiatrists we spoke to think not. They point out that in this society, no one wants to be a homosexual who isn't one and that if a kid goes as far as joining a homosexual club, he is a homosexual. All the club does is to make him feel less alone and less terrible about the sexual feelings he has and can't help having.[3]

1 Calculated from the *Television News Archive* of Vanderbilt University.
2 Some of news under the civil rights rubric included persons arguing against civil rights for gays, as in the case of the well-publicized opposition of singer Anita Bryant to a Dade County, Florida ordinance that outlawed discrimination on the basis of sexual preference.
3 NBC Evening News, April 13, 1973.

The explicit reference to expert opinion in this story is not, however, typical of the new coverage of homosexuality. To the extent that expert opinion was important in most stories, it was as deep background. For what changed in the 1970s was that the press was no longer seeing homosexuals as social deviants, but as ordinary citizens suffering the effects of homophobic prejudice. Given this change of view, which as I show later on, clearly originated among psychiatric experts, much else followed more or less automatically.

Consider the contrast between the last story dealing with gay rights on CBS news prior to the APA vote, and the first such story following the vote. In the earlier story, gays had won a court victory permitting them to demonstrate at the Democratic national convention in Miami in 1972. Walter Cronkite, in a slot often used for light news at the end of his program, reported the victory this way:

Miami Beach had laws against female impersonation. Today a federal judge in Miami struck them down, saying they were too vague, and besides, discriminated against men.

The suit was brought by the Civil Liberties Union on complaint of gay activists who plan to demonstrate at the Democratic convention next month. They'll apparently give the fashion reporters something to contemplate. And that's the way it is.[4]

Thus, gays were still fair target for mild ridicule on the national news in 1972. The next gay rights story on CBS occurred shortly after the APA vote and involved the attempts of gay activists in New York City to win passage of an anti-discrimination law, an effort that had been under way for several years. Cronkite introduced the story as follows:

Part of the new morality of the 1960s and 70s is a new attitude toward homosexuals. The homosexual men and women have organized to fight for acceptance and respectability. They have succeeded in winning equal rights under the law in many communities, but in the nation's biggest city, the fight goes on.[5]

Coverage of the Matlovich case represents an equally significant change in press behavior. Matlovich was far from being the first homosexual to protest being dismissed from a government job because of his sexual orientation. He was, however, the first to get extensive, respectful coverage on the evening TV news for doing so. That this coverage came very soon after the APA's declaration on homosexuality seems more than coincidence.

The point, then, is that homosexuals had been seeking equal rights for some years when, in the aftermath of the APA vote, the mainstream press began to take a different view of their efforts. The change in media reporting cannot be linked in a mechanical way to the APA vote but is nonetheless best understood as reflecting the press's general sensitivity to expert authority.

It was not, incidentally, only the press, but also many mainstream politicians whose behavior changed in the aftermath of the APA vote. Thus, when voters in California were asked in 1978 to decide on a ballot initiative that would make it easier to fire homosexual schoolteachers, three nationally prominent politicians

4 June 22, 1972.   5 May 6, 1974.

came out in opposition to the measure: California governor Jerry Brown, former governor and presidential aspirant Ronald Reagan, and President Jimmy Carter. It is hard to imagine such behavior on the part of ambitious politicians in an era when experts were in unanimous agreement that homosexuality was a form of mental illness and in which the press routinely categorized news about homosexuality under the rubric of perversion.

There is, in sum, reason to believe that the press is to a considerable degree dependent on subject matter specialists, including government officials among many others, in framing and reporting the news. I have attempted to summarize the nature of this dependence by asserting that the press undertakes, in general, to cover the news from all legitimate points of view, where legitimacy is determined by what mainstream experts take seriously.[6]

Experts

The argument of the preceding section, if correct, places the real responsibility for selecting the ideas that reach the public with the press's sources. As V. O. Key, Jr. (1961), concluded in this regard, "The picture of the press collectively as the wielder of great power on its own initiative does not fit the facts" (p. 394). The managers of the mass media, he continues,

should no more be held accountable for the materials that flow through their channels than should the managers of transportation concerns be blamed for the quality of the printed matter they transport from place to place. The tone and quality of the content of the media tend to be mightily influenced, if not fixed, by those who manufacture news. (p. 395)

This in turn suggests that if we are interested in the quality of the information reaching the public, we must understand how it is manufactured, which is to say, we must understand the politics of expert communities as they relate to the generation and diffusion of knowledge claims, policy recommendations, and general frames of reference. We especially need to know the extent to which these communities are ideologically diverse, open to challenge, and institutionally supportive of serious-minded attempts to discover feasible solutions to pressing problems.

There has been, as far as I can tell, little scholarly attention to these questions. There are, to be sure, numerous accounts of how particular groups of individuals have attempted to resolve particular policy dilemmas. But attempts to generalize from these accounts, or to answer systematically questions of the type just posed, appear to be almost entirely lacking in the literature of political science and communication studies.

Let me, then, offer an anecdotal glimpse of the workings of the subcommunity of persons specializing in questions of nuclear strategy. It involves types of personal interactions that, as far as I have been able to tell, are outside existing

6 This argument is similar to Bennett's (1990) indexing hypothesis, except that it refers to a broader range of sources than Bennett considers to be influential.

studies of communication, but that are, I believe, of the utmost importance for understanding the forces that ultimately shape public opinion.

A few years ago, it was proposed by a group of scientists that any significant use of nuclear weapons by either the United States or the former Soviet Union would result in an environmental disaster of monumental proportions. The idea was that the explosion of large numbers of nuclear bombs, possibly only a few dozen, would throw up enormous amounts of dust, debris, and smoke into the atmosphere, blocking out the sun and creating a decades long "nuclear winter" of near-total darkness and freezing temperatures. As a result, the use of nuclear weapons, even in self-defense, would be suicidal not only for one's nation, but for one's race and for all of the earth's creatures (Schell, 1982).

The idea of nuclear winter was, as would be expected, most popular among liberals, who used it as an argument for restricting production of nuclear weapons.

At the time when these ideas were being debated in the media, I was put in charge of organizing a speaker program at my university on the subject of the morality of nuclear war. One of the people I invited was a well-known conservative expert who had written extensively on nuclear war, including strategies for fighting nuclear wars on a limited but, according to the theory of nuclear winter, potentially catastrophic scale. When I asked a liberal nuclear war policy expert to introduce this person and to serve as moderator for the ensuing discussion, he flatly and firmly refused. The ideas of the conservative war expert were deeply immoral, the liberal expert said, and it would hardly be possible for him to attend the talk, let alone serve as moderator for it. However, after much coaxing – including my insistence that, as moderator, he would be in a better position to oppose the baleful influence of the conservative expert – he agreed to serve as moderator.

On the day of the talk, I was chatting with the conservative expert when the liberal dropped in. After standard introductions were made, the liberal calmly asked his fellow expert, "Well, what are you working on these days?"[7]

"Nuclear winter," replied the conservative.

"That's interesting," said the liberal. "What are you finding?"

"That it's basically a nonstarter," replied the conservative.

I stepped back and looked around for shelter, fearing a nuclear explosion was about to occur. But the worry was unfounded.

"Yeah, that's pretty much the way I see it, too," said the liberal, who was a physicist by training. "I've done an awful lot of calculations and I can't come up with any that make nuclear winter seem like a real possibility."

With that, the two men launched into a discussion of exactly what the incineration rates of various substances were, how much of what kinds of combustible materials are found in typical cities, and other technical parameters of the process by which nuclear winter might or might not be created. They appeared to agree on almost everything.

---

7 Quotations are approximate.

Shortly after these events, discussion of nuclear winter disappeared from the popular media and the issue was seemingly forgotten.

This anecdote, which is straight out of Purple Land, suggests several important points. First, despite agreement on nuclear winter, there is clear evidence of ideological diversity of a sort that doubtless manifests itself in other situations. Second, strong ideological differences are not an insuperable barrier to rational discussion and to the achievement of agreement on particular issues. The key to bridging ideological differences appears to be the existence of a body of conventional scientific knowledge, in this case the laws of physics and chemistry, which both experts accepted. This knowledge is apparently sufficiently well developed and routinized that it can lead its users to accept conclusions they are predisposed against. Third, the press apparently lost interest in the issue after relevant experts on both sides concluded that it was a nonstarter, and did so despite a consumer market for stories on nuclear winter that was presumably as strong as it had ever been.

How often these things are true of other issues and expert communities is impossible to say. Certainly one can readily imagine expert communities that enforce ideological homogeneity on their members, or that, if they do permit diversity, are so deeply polarized that no rational discussion can occur, or that have no conventional knowledge that is sufficiently strong to compel acceptance among differently predisposed users.

These issues, I maintain, are important ones. They go to the heart of the functioning of the political communications system in the United States, affecting not only public opinion but government action. Yet, as I emphasize, they seem to be outside the scope of current investigation.

By way of making a preliminary but, I hope, suggestive examination of these issues, let me return to the issue of homosexuality. I have already sketched an argument about the effect of expert opinion on media treatment of this issue. I will now look briefly at how expert opinion on this issue developed.

At mid–twentieth century, there had been a lengthy history of homosexual rights groups seeking acceptance by society. But the groups had been small, short-lived, and ineffective. Although some of the early rights groups had believed that "the period of passing over the matter [of homosexuality] and disregarding it is past, for good,"[8] Lauritsen and Thorstad (1974) observed that

The early homosexual rights movement was cut short, in the 1930s, after 70 years of existence, having achieved virtually no lasting breakthroughs. The small, isolated groups that came into existence here and there during the next two decades could not even be called holding actions, since there was little left to hold onto. (p. 71)

It seems that homosexuals faced two problems. As a minority group almost universally considered deviant, they were not able to make headway without having at least a few allies inside the system, and they had none. Also, far from wanting to challenge mainstream society's characterization of their plight, many

8 Cited in Lauritsen and Thorstad, 1974: p. 22.

homosexuals accepted and internalized it. As a homosexual rights activist wrote in the 1960s:

The homosexual, whether born or bred (and the psychiatric argument is still raging) has been conditioned to think of himself as . . . something to be despised. The minute he discovers he's "different" he avidly reads anything he can on the subject. And what does he find? More ammunition for his self-contempt. He's told by psychiatric "authorities" that he's "sick." So he begins to tell himself *not* that "The psychiatrists say I'm sick," *but* "I'm sick." He programs himself into perpetual feelings of unworthiness." (emphasis in the original)[9]

In the late 1940s, however, a handful of professional psychiatrists and psychologists undertook research that placed homosexuality in a new light. There had, to be sure, been prior research and theorizing on the subject, but the new research was, in a small but important way, more rigorous than earlier efforts: Rather than study homosexuals who were either imprisoned for some crime, often a sex crime, or actively seeking psychiatric help, the new studies found ways of examining homosexuals who were leading ordinary lives (Bayer, 1981). The results were a surprise to almost everyone. Alfred Kinsey, in his interview-based studies of male sexuality, turned up evidence that, he said, indicated that a large fraction of males would have a homosexual experience ending in orgasm at some point in their lives. As he further argued:

The opinion that homosexual activity in itself provides evidence of a psychopathic personality is materially challenged by these incidence and frequency data. Of the 40 or 50 percent of the male population which has had a homosexual experience, certainly a high proportion would not be considered psychopathic personalities on the basis of anything else in their histories. (1948: 659)

Another researcher, Evelyn Hooker of UCLA, administered personality assessment tests to matched samples of homosexual and nonhomosexual men in the early 1950s and found no differences in their overall levels of personal adjustment. Other researchers followed suit, and soon there was a considerable body of psychiatric evidence that raised serious question about whether homosexuality was a form of mental illness.

It is notable that Hooker, whose research proved the most influential, used standard social scientific research techniques. That is, she administered standard tests of personal adjustment and interpreted their results in conventionally established ways. These tests, Rorschach inkblot tests interpreted by judges blind to which had been provided by homosexuals, may not inspire great confidence among nonpsychiatrists, but, with respect to the issue of homosexuality, they constituted an application of neutral scientific knowledge.

No doubt because of this, the initial response of a significant fraction of the psychiatric community was immediately favorable. Her work was quickly accepted for publication in an important journal, and Hooker herself went on to a distinguished career. She was even asked by the Nixon administration to head a 1969 federal task force on homosexuality, and by the *International Encyclopedia*

9 Leo Martello, cited in Marotta, 1981: p. 103.

of the Social Sciences to write its section on homosexuality. Thus, far from pe-nalizing Hooker for her ideas, the psychiatric and political communities re-warded her.

Hooker's research and follow-up studies gave homosexuality, for perhaps the first time in American history, a solid foundation of sympathetic opinion in a mainstream institution. The new view was by no means universally held within psychiatry; Traditional psychotherapists continued to argue that homosexuality was a disease and to treat it as such. But psychiatry was no longer monolithic in its view of homosexuality, and if my general view of efforts by the media to report the news from "all legitimate points of view" is correct, this was enough to bring about an important degree of change in public discussion of the issue.

The earliest and most attentive audience for this new research consisted of homosexuals. Their response was not only interesting – for it suggests that the authority of expertise is accepted by groups other than the media – but part of the story of how further change occurred within the psychiatric commu-nity. The initial response, according to Bayer (1981), was one of keen but cau-tious interest. Homosexuals wanted to know more about the new research but didn't leap to any conclusions about it. Their meetings and publications gave roughly equal play to the new research and to representatives of the traditional school. "Where medical men, psychoanalysts, and social scientists fail to agree," one contributor to a homosexual publication wrote, "laymen can only cower in silence."[10]

Yet it was probably inevitable that homosexuals, having been offered a choice between seeing themselves as mentally ill and seeing themselves as normal and healthy, would eventually gravitate toward the latter view. As this occurred, the newer psychiatric view of homosexuality took on great importance in efforts by homosexuals both to organize themselves and to instigate social change.

Frank Kameny, the leader of a group of Washington, D.C., gays, was a key figure in both respects. "The entire homophile movement," he said, "is going to rise or fall upon the question of whether homosexuality is a sickness."[11] Ka-meny personally rejected the authority of psychiatry over the status of homo-sexuality but nonetheless invoked scientific values and the new psychiatric evidence to persuade members of his organization to proclaim publicly that their sexual preferences were normal and healthy. However, it was not until 1965 that Kameny was able to win approval for such a statement, and even then, it was carefully hedged: "in the absence of valid evidence to the contrary," read the resolution of the Washington D.C. Mattachine Society, "homosexuality is not a sickness . . . but is merely a preference."[12]

In a still later phase of its response to the new psychiatric evidence, homo-sexuals began to publicly reject psychiatric authority. Even as this occurred, however, friendly psychiatric experts remained welcome allies. These experts, Bayer (1981) comments,

10 Cited in Bayer, 1981: p. 74.   11 Cited ibid.: p. 82.
12 Cited in D'Emillio, 1983: p. 164.

provided homosexuals with evidence and with a vocabulary of criticism that were invaluable in the effort to tear the mantle of authority from those who claimed that science itself had discovered the psychopathology inherent in homosexuality. The role of the expert at homophile meetings shifted from that of providing homosexuals with insight into the etiology of their sexual preferences to that of providing insight into the illegitimate power of psychiatry. (p. 86)

It is interesting to note that the behavior of homosexuals in this period conforms to the basic notions of the mainstream and polarization models. When homosexuality was considered by virtually all specialists and the press to be a disease, homosexuals largely accepted this mainstream norm by staying, as the phrase goes, "in the closet." This orientation was obviously sustained in part by realistic fears of what would happen if they were discovered; but it is clear that in many cases, the mainstream norm against homosexuality was to a significant degree internalized. But then, offered by some psychiatric authorities a choice of considering themselves sick or merely to have an alternative sexual preference, homosexuals naturally allied themselves with the friendlier view.

Part of the effort to overcome society's prejudice against homosexuality was a years' long series of confrontations between militant gays and the American Psychiatric Association, which continued in its official publications to classify homosexuality as disease. Thus when the APA met in Washington in 1970, Frank Kameny helped to lead the protest:

The planned disruption occurred on May 3, when gay and anti-war activists stormed the prestigious Convocation of Fellows. During the ensuing uproar, Kameny grabbed a microphone and denounced the right of psychiatrists to discuss the question of homosexuality. Borrowing from the anti-war movement, he declared, "Psychiatry is the enemy incarnate. Psychiatry has waged a relentless war of extermination against us. You may take this as a declaration of war against you." Fist-shaking psychiatrists, infuriated by the invaders, compared their tactics to that of Nazi storm troopers. (Bayer, 1981: p. 105)

Such disruptions no doubt impelled the leaders of the APA to think more carefully about the issue of homosexuality than they would otherwise have done. As a result, when the trustees of the APA, and later a majority of the APA membership in a referendum, voted to delete homosexuality from its official list of mental disorders, both those who won the vote and those who lost felt that the action had involved a large political component – as obviously it had.

But equally obviously, there was more to the politics of this expert community than 1960s-style pressure tactics. As Bayer observed, some of the trustees voting for the change were genuinely convinced that homosexuality was not necessarily a disease, while others "felt privately that homosexuality was indeed a disorder . . . [but] nevertheless acknowledged that the evidence required to substantiate their position was lacking" (p. 136). In short, standard psychiatric evidence, whatever its intrinsic merit, appeared to count.

If this seems a naive view, consider the significance of the psychiatric evidence in coldly political terms. Once the findings of Hooker and others began to accumulate, the psychiatric profession faced a genuine dilemma, one that had eventually to be faced whether gay militants demanded it or not. Either psychiatrists could remove homosexuality from the list of mental disorders on the grounds that the standard assessment techniques had failed to uncover evidence of psychic problems among homosexuals, or they could devalue the standard assessment techniques – the basis for psychiatry's authority in other domains – on the grounds that they had failed to uncover the pathology inherent in homosexuality. This must, in the end, have been an easy choice.

The reader should notice that nowhere in this account have I evaluated the correctness of the view of homosexuality taken by psychiatrists. This is because the correctness of elite views is, from the perspective I am proposing, irrelevant. What matters is, in effect, procedural correctness: whether the relevant expert communities are ideologically diverse and whether they have institutionalized incentive structures that impel members to make their best efforts to resolve pressing problems.

With respect to these questions, the psychiatric profession appears to deserve a favorable evaluation. A researcher of no initial standing in her field, an untenured research associate at what was then a minor state university, was able to open the first important crack in a previously impregnable power structure, and to do so in the mid-1950s, a time not obviously propitious for such an undertaking. This is an impressive achievement not only for the individual, but for the institutional arrangements that made it possible. The most important of these institutional arrangements, I have suggested, was the existence within the psychiatric community of standard personality assessment techniques, which I have referred to as conventional scientific knowledge.

The last few pages have used a case study in order to examine the politics of an expert community. I do not believe, however, that the understanding of the dynamics of expert communities should be too heavily dependent on case studies. Rather, an attempt should be made to develop a general account of how expert communities generate ideas and how these ideas diffuse. The key issues in such a general account, I believe, should be possible bias in recruitment to the expert communities, professional incentive structures within the communities, and the development of a body of conventional knowledge strong enough to compel agreement among differently predisposed users.

There exists some solid literature on the first question. It indicates that persons of different ideological orientations are attracted to different academic disciplines (Lipset and Ladd, 1970) and, one assumes, to different occupational groupings as well. Whether this results in ideological homogeneity within groups, or pressures that make it difficult for the minority to do its work, is an important but presently unanswered question. To the extent that recruitment to expert communities, whether by means of voluntary self-selection or purposive enforcement of ideological standards, limits the types of persons who can become experts, the range of elite discourse is restricted and the specter of elite domination is raised.

With respect to the second question, the existing literature is, if anything, even more lacking. From my previous discussions, it nonetheless seems plausible to maintain that at least some experts, professionals, and other types of subject matter specialists do often have incentive structures that strongly emphasize the advancement of knowledge for the solution of pressing societal problems. A conspicuous example of them may be found in the medical research community, within which status, research support, and salary all depend on the practical or theoretical value of the research one has done, as judged by peers in the field. Similar incentive structures are in place in most academic disciplines – or at least the individuals who serve on recruitment and promotion committees within universities devote a great deal of energy to trying to make sure that they are. Thus, one need not posit experts and professionals who are altruistic in order to believe that many of them are genuinely interested in the discovery of knowledge of good public policy. One need only posit incentive structures that encourage them to have such interests. Such incentive structures obviously cannot eliminate bias or guarantee correct conclusions. But they may nonetheless serve as effective inducements to try to reach these goals.

The incentive structures prevalent in expert communities, especially if internalized, may provide a strong influence on a person's behavior. I once spoke to a sociologist doing research in association with medical scientists who, in the early stages of the AIDS epidemic, were trying to isolate the AIDS virus and determine its mode of transmission. Many of these researchers, the sociologist told me, were either gay or sympathetic to gays, and so had a strong desire to find that AIDS was not as readily transmissible as many viruses. For a short initial period, he said, this preconception seemed to affect research plans. But very quickly, he said, all researchers, gay and nongay alike, began to focus on winning "the big prize" – that is, being the first to discover the true nature of AIDS, regardless of their personal interests or wishes concerning its nature.

It is, I reiterate, an open empirical question how strongly such incentives are felt across what range of expert and professional occupation groups to which reporters and politicians go for information – but an empirical question well worth investigating.

My notion of professional and expert communities obviously draws heavily on the idealized conception of a scientific community (see Merton, 1982; Hagstrom, 1965). This should not, however, obscure the critically important fact that, for much of the subject matter that is relevant to politics, the personal and political predispositions of experts and professionals can and regularly do influence the conclusions they reach (or at least try to reach). I am aware of no research on this point, but I doubt that many will dispute it. Certainly within any subfield of social science, all of us know studies which reflect the ideological tendencies of researchers who can, on other grounds, be identified as more or less liberal or conservative. It seems quite likely that this is true of other professional and expert communities as well. Thus, to return to the AIDS example, it seems likely that, if there were some medical researchers who wanted, for reason of their predispositions or perceived interests, to be able to show that AIDS could not be casually transmitted, there were other researchers whose predispositions or perceived interests motivated the opposite conclusion.

I see no conflict in comparing professional and expert communities to scientific communities, while also giving very wide scope to the operation of ideologically motivated preconceptions. As my UCLA colleague Richard Sklar has observed, social science theories are often conceived in ideological sin rather than scientific virtue. But, although people may be motivated by various preconceptions, they must, in order to maintain high standing in their specialized communities, justify their eventual conclusions in terms of arguments that everyone can accept, including persons who do not share their predispositions or preconceptions.

Moreover, a case can be made that ideological bias, so long as it is operating within pluralistic professional and expert communities, has salutary effects. It would tend to assure that every potentially controversial issue is scrutinized by persons having a range of motivated preconceptions. To the extent that such differently motivated persons can agree on a common answer, as very often they do, the rest of society who are not specialists can have some confidence that the answer proposed by the experts is sound – or if not sound, the best that anyone can do for the moment. And to the extent that differently motivated persons cannot agree, they would, as sources for reporters and staff advisors to politicians, air their disagreements in public, thereby alerting ordinary citizens to the existence of uncertainty.

This brings us back to our main concern about elite domination. When, despite their divergent predispositions, all relevant specialists agree on a policy, any source whom journalists consult will say roughly the same thing, with the result that society will have "elite consensus" and a "mainstream norm" that will be most strongly supported by the most politically attentive members of society. But when predispositions induce relevant specialists to disagree, journalists will publicize the disagreement, often in starkly ideological terms that invoke images of good and evil. Politicians and publicists, who maintain lines of communications to like-minded specialists, will also disagree.[13] The result will be a polarization of the general public along lines that mirror the elite ideological conflict, with the most attentive members of the public most ideologically polarized.

Ideology, in this view, *is a mechanism by which ordinary citizens make contact with specialists who are knowledgeable on controversial issues and who share the citizens' predispositions.* As such, ideology can make a valuable contribution to democratic politics in a society in which people are expected not only to have opinions about a range of impossibly difficult issues, but to use those opinions as the basis for choosing leaders and holding them accountable.

Note that ideology, as the term is being used here, is not, as it is often taken by opinion researchers to be, the unified product of an individual creative genius, such as Karl Marx or Edmund Burke or John Locke. Rather, it is an

13 Congressional committee and personal staffs, policy institutes and think tanks, and overlapping parts of the federal bureaucracy often have distinct political colorations, thereby tying politicians to members of specialist communities who share their values.

agglomeration of views of different specialists sharing a common predispositional bent.[14] Thus, for example, what passes for conservative economics or conservative foreign policy will be what most conservative economists and conservative foreign policy experts agree needs to be done. When the experts change their views, as liberal experts changed their opinion about Vietnam, mass belief systems will, with the sorts of lags I have documented in earlier chapters, tend to follow the elite view. There is no particular need for members of the general public to know technical details of the expert debate on these issues, or to know why a given set of policies is conservative or liberal, in order to take positions on them that are consistent with their ideological predispositions; they need only be able to recognize which elites share their predispositions and take cues from them.

I have now sketched an idealized system of public information in which political ideas and perspectives develop among various kinds of policy specialists and diffuse downward to the public via politicians and the mass media. This idealized system is obviously not the whole picture, for it neglects the extremely important role of political institutions, partisan competition, and political censorship in regulating the flow of information through society. But even so, my account of this system makes two useful points. It sets out, first of all, a set of idealized conditions that, if met, would greatly mitigate the normatively objectionable effects of a heavy dependence of mass opinion on elite discourse. It further shows that, as an empirical matter, some of these conditions – expert communities operating at least some of the time within salutary incentive structures, and a press that is attentive to these communities – are at least partially met in the current information system of the United States.

I turn now to some brief remarks about the effect of political factors on the operation of my idealized information system.

POLITICS AND INFORMATION

In leaving until now any discussion of the effects of "politics" on the flow of information, I imply that the generation of information is primary and that political factors that regulate its dissemination, including the activities of government officials, other politicians, and interest groups, among others, are secondary.

The reason for this emphasis is, quite simply, that political information precedes political action. All political actors, including the government, must form some view of what is happening in the world before undertaking any action, including action to censor or manipulate the flow of information to the public, and this view is invariably a product of various kinds of policy and information

---

14 This common bent presumably involves non–issue specific predispositions toward order, stability, and social control, among other things (for some empirically grounded conjectures, see McClosky and Zaller, 1985, ch. 7; Costantini and Craik, 1980).

specialists. Moreover, since much of the information system exists outside of the government, the ability of politicians to suppress or control information is, though important, limited. For any given issue, there are expert communities in place, each at least potentially divided along ideological lines, and each with established lines of communication to government decision makers, political oppositions and, via the press, to the public.

This perspective on the flow of information in the United States is unorthodox. Most accounts, which are based on studies of the "sources" that give information to the press, emphasize the role of government in the generation of information and its role in manipulating or censoring that information (Cohen, 1963; Sigal, 1973, Hallin, 1986; Bennett, 1990).

These accounts, to the extent that they aspire to answer general questions about the sources of the information that reaches the public, focus too narrowly on what is comparatively easy to observe and study. Government officials may be the proximate source of much of the information that reaches the public, but they are not necessarily the creators of the information, nor can they always control how information is framed by the press or what the press is interested in, nor are they equally important on all types of issues.

An illuminating case of how members of the nongovernmental information system can exert influence independently of government was described by *Washington Post* reporter David Broder some twenty years after it occurred. Early in the Vietnam War, when U.S. involvement still had the support of almost all mainstream politicians and when the government was providing little antiwar information, Senator Frank Church, a young Senator from Idaho with a strong interest in foreign policy, arranged a "dinner seminar" for some reporters on the subject of Vietnam. As Broder relates:

Church's guest at the dinner was Hans J. Morgenthau of the University of Chicago, an authority on foreign policy. The two men tried their best to make a largely skeptical group of reporters reexamine the prevailing assumptions about Vietnam. The struggle taking place there, they asserted, was not aggression by proxy from China or Moscow but an indigenous revolution, led by a man Ho Chi Minh – who appeared to be the only authentic Vietnamese leader on the scene. . . .

If Americans . . . went down the path the French had followed, Church and Morgenthau said, then we would pay a terrible price.

I went home thoroughly unconvinced that night, but had many occasions in the next dozen years to recollect the warning. (Broder, 1984)

The details of the discussion, even though anticipating the line antiwar liberals would eventually take, are unimportant. What is important is Church's – or perhaps Morganthau's – apparently self-conscious effort to influence the reporting of leading journalists by exposing them to academic viewpoints.

Informal discussions like these, which are by no means rare in journalism, are one route by which the ideas of leading policy specialists reach and inform the work of practicing journalists. Books are probably at least as important. Bright young reporters arriving on a beat about which they know little routinely seek out the leading books on their new subjects and use them for intellectual orientation. In the case of Vietnam, these books were the books of Bernard Fall, a historian who was apparently read by most of the journalists in Vietnam (Halberstam, 1979) and whose theme was that the Vietnam War should be understood in light of antiimperialism and Vietnamese nationalism rather than, as most U.S. government policymakers thought, as a struggle between democracy and communism.[15] If, after absorbing such ideas, reporters found it difficult to be as staunchly anticommunist as many of their official sources, if they actively sought out dissenting voices within the government, if by the questions they asked at press conferences they constantly and impatiently pressured high officials to give evidence of "results," and if they often took the opportunity to play up embarrassments to U.S. policy (such as corruption within the South Vietnamese government or mistreatment of Vietnamese peasants by the military), at least part of the explanation should be laid to the influence of the extragovernmental experts who created the intellectual framework that helped motivate such actions.

In stressing the nongovernmental origins of much official information, I by no means deny that government regularly uses what influence it can muster to color or to censor what reaches the public. It is also certainly true that "politics" – the tendency of partisan elites to disagree with one another no matter what experts might say, the tendency of politicians to pander to whatever interests can help them stay in office, and the tendency of government officials to suppress and manipulate the flow of information – can easily override the influence of policy specialists and academic experts in the short run, where the short run may be sufficiently long to commit the nation to an ill-advised course of action.

But the corrupting influence of partisan politics should not be exaggerated. For example, fear of the AIDS virus and of the homosexuals and drug users who were initially its principal carriers was surely one of the most potentially explosive backlash issues of the 1980s. Yet a backlash political issue never emerged. A national strategy of public education and intensive scientific research came to be accepted by both political parties and virtually the entire political elite as the best way of dealing with the problem. Such disagreement as occurred centered almost exclusively on speed of the research response and levels of public funding rather than on the strategy itself. Thus AIDS has remained a medical and public health issue – that is, an expert-dominated one – despite having great potential as a partisan political controversy (Colby and Cook, 1991). Yet can anyone doubt that, if medical experts had disagreed on this fundamental strategy – if, for example, a significant number had favored a quarantine policy – the issue would have become instantly and bitterly partisan and ideological?

A similar argument can be made with respect to race. No issue in American society is more deeply political than race, and yet, a variety of experts, most

15 It is not, I imagine, uncommon for politicians to look to expert opinion for orientation when they take on a new subject. Thus, Fall's books were reputed also to have been a major influence on Senator William Fulbright, an early critic of the Vietnam War.

notably psychologists concerned with human intelligence and with the harmful effects of racial segregation, have been active and seemingly influential on this issue throughout the twentieth century. Early in the century, the thrust of expert opinion was predominantly racist, as discussed in Chapter 2. However, during the 1920s, a period that was, incidentally, widely regarded as a time of cultural conservatism in the country as a whole, expert opinion on group differences in intelligence underwent a virtual revolution. By 1930 a new scholarly consensus, minimizing the existence and especially the significance of any possible group differences in intelligence, had become dominant. It is at least arguable that this new expert consensus, which soon came to be reflected in the opinions of educated white persons, is the reason that the white power structure of the country, after centuries of suppressing the efforts of blacks to gain equality, began at last to see their point (Myrdal, 1944).

There are, without question, myriad ways in which political authorities and other interests can short-circuit the idealized system I have sketched and distort the flow of information to the public. Expert communities are themselves prey to myriad internally caused dysfunctions. The existing literature on the press and mass communications has, to some extent, focused on the breakdowns. An unintended consequence of this emphasis is that we sometimes get a better idea of how the system fails to work than of how it works at all. In view of this, my aim in this chapter has been to direct attention toward a broader range of factors than is normally examined, especially the existence of policy specialists who are relatively independent of political authority and other interests, who play a major role in raising and framing issues, and who are linked to public opinion, via the press and politicians, by shared ideological predispositions.

CONCLUDING REMARKS

In any complex society, as in Purple Land, there must be a division of labor in the conduct of politically relevant debate. This necessity suggests an objection to my general argument. If, as I have implied, only specialists are competent to conduct political debate, why bring the public into it at all? Why not let government policy reflect the preponderant weight of expert opinion?

There are several answers. One is that, quite simply, it is the people's right to settle any debate they feel moved to settle. Another is that, as J. S. Mill and others have argued, political participation is a value in itself, ennobling and self-fulfilling to all who partake of it. I, however, would not find either of these arguments very attractive if I believed that the public, in exercising its undoubted rights and seeking its self-fulfillment, regularly made decisions that I regarded as morally abhorrent or technically stupid. I therefore offer a third reason for involving the public in political debate: That government, in the absence of checks, invariably goes astray and becomes overbearing or worse.

A few specialists do not constitute a viable check on political authority. It is too easy to ignore, jail, kill, or otherwise silence them. Their only hope of being effective is to publicize and politicize whatever disagreements arise, so that the masses of ordinary citizens can weigh into the debate. I do not see any obvious reason to believe that the whole citizenry will be, in general, wiser than specialists, so long as the specialists are broadly recruited and given freedom to operate within a salutary system of incentives. It is the collective ability of citizens in a democracy to pressure leaders in useful directions and, when necessary, to remove the leaders, more than the collective wisdom of the people, that seems to me critical.

All of this assumes, of course, that an independent public opinion can actually check political authorities. Given the continued existence of competition among partisan elites for public support in the current American political system, I do not see this assumption as particularly problematic. The real problem is guaranteeing the existence of an equally vigorous competition among opposing ideas.

Measures appendix

POLITICAL KNOWLEDGE

Since political awareness is the key independent variable in this study, I have extensively investigated how it may be most effectively measured (Zaller, 1985, 1986, 1990; Price and Zaller, 1990). Although some of this work has involved conceptual clarification, most of it has been mundanely empirical, as I have painstakingly tested alternative measures across a variety of datasets and issues. The routine empirical work, however, has paid a useful dividend: It has shown that the effects one attributes to political awareness can depend greatly on how one goes about measuring it.

How to measure political awareness

The surveys of the National Election Studies (NES), which provide the data for almost all of the new analyses reported in this book, contain numerous measures that would seem suitable as measures of political awareness. These include level of political participation (such as engaging in political discussions with friends, giving money to candidates), level of political interest, level of media use, educational attainment, and neutral factual knowledge about politics.

There is no agreement in the existing scholarly literature about which of these measures is best.[1] Even Converse has given mixed signals on this question. In

1 Some scholars use a single-item control, most commonly education or information, or, less commonly, interest (e.g., Dean and Moran, 1977; Sniderman, Brody, and Tetlock, 1991; Judd and Milburn, 1980); sometimes they use up to five or six controls either simultaneously (Achen, 1975) or combined into an index (Erikson, 1979); and sometimes they introduce a series of single-item controls in bivariate form (Fiorina, 1981). In general, researchers seem simply to use whatever measure of awareness is handy and permits them to get on with their main analysis.

These measures, all compounds of the same family of variables, are given a variety of names: political interest and involvement (Converse, 1964, 1980); cognitive ability (Stimson, 1975); political sophistication (Chong, McClosky, and Zaller, 1984; Erikson, 1979; Neuman, 1986; Sidanius, 1988; Luskin, 1990); political expertise (Fiske and Kinder, 1981; Fiske, Lau, and Smith, 1990); ideological sophistication (Knight, 1985); and indicators of rational civic man (Fiorina, 1981; Key with Cummings, 1966). Judd, Krosnick, and Milburn (1981), having been criticized by Converse (1980) for relying on education as their measure of awareness, show that their results hold whether they use education, interest, or political activity; Luskin (1987) and Fiorina (1981) also test several different measures across a limited range of criterion variables.

his classic 1964 study of mass belief systems, he made clear that there is a cluster of variables – information, activity, sophistication, education, status as a member of the political elite, and political interest – that are associated with constrained belief systems; of these, the latter two, and especially the last, seem most central to his argument. Yet in a paper written around the same time, Converse (1962) employs media usage, a variable given little play in his belief systems paper, as the measure of the extent to which individuals are both exposed to partisan election campaigns and endowed with the capacity to resist their appeals. In his 1975 article in the *Handbook of Political Science,* Converse further reports that "after a long and rather unrewarding search" he found that a measure of "partisan political involvement" functions as the most important determinant of attitude stability, though not necessarily of other properties of well-developed belief systems (p. 104). He reiterates this position in 1980 in commenting on a paper that had used education as its control variable, here referring to the key variable more simply as "political involvement."

Even in the absence of empirical evidence on comparative performance of the various possible measures of awareness, one would find some operational measures more attractive than others. For example, people who develop the abstract learning skills that are supposedly imparted by formal schooling would seem likely, by that account, to be more adept at the comprehension of political ideas. Yet education is only moderately correlated with political interest and media exposure. This suggests that many educated people, although having the cognitive skill necessary to develop political awareness, nonetheless lack the interest or motivation to keep abreast of political events (Luskin, 1990).

Standard measures of media exposure would appear, at first glance, excellent candidates for measuring awareness of political ideas. They have, however, important weaknesses. One is that, as Price and I have argued (1990), it is probably necessary to distinguish between exposure to "low-brow" political media – Action News on TV, *People* magazine, talk show radio, local weekly newspapers – and exposure to "high-brow" media, such as the TV network news, National Public Radio, and the *Wall Street Journal.* Only the latter carry the rich diet of national and international news necessary to create political awareness. Yet the measures of media exposure on most existing surveys do not permit one to distinguish between low-brow and high-brow media. Second, even if separate measures were available, it would be difficult to know how to calibrate them; intermittent attention to National Public Radio might, for example, contribute more to political awareness than avid attention to local TV news. Third, measures of self-reported media exposure suffer from subjective differences in self-rating standards, and also social-desirability–induced exaggeration. For example, Price and I (1990) found that, according to survey self-reports, 40 percent of the American public listens to National Public Radio several times a week, a level that is both implausibly high and above NPR's own internal estimates by a factor of about 10. In another example, some respondents, having claimed to read the *Wall Street Journal,* responded to a follow-up that they normally read the paper seven days a week. This sort of misreporting, even if it occurs fairly infrequently, can wreak havoc with models that depend on the ability to discriminate accurately at the top levels of political awareness. And finally, media exposure, even if well measured, is still only a measure of exposure to politics rather than, as required by the model, propensity for actual reception of information.

Political participation also has serious weaknesses as a measure of awareness. For example, a city maintenance worker who must contribute work or money to the party machine in order to keep his job would be indistinguishable on most political participation measures from an activist in an issue-oriented political club, even though their differences in political awareness (as defined here) could be very great. It is, moreover, easily possible for a person to achieve very high levels of political awareness without ever giving money to candidates, working for parties, or otherwise participating in politics.

This brings us to neutral factual knowledge about politics, a type of measure that, to a greater extent than any of the others, captures political learning that has actually occurred – political ideas that the individual has encountered, understood, and stored in his head. This is exactly what we want to be measuring.

Factual knowledge is preferable on other theoretical grounds. Alone among the possible measures of awareness, tests of political knowledge are relatively immune to a social desirability response set; that is, individuals cannot overstate their levels of information holding because they perceive that it is socially desirable to appear politically aware.[2] Tests of factual knowledge are also relatively immune to response effects, such as Bishop et al.'s (1984) demonstration that expressed levels of political interest are readily affected by the context in which interest questions are asked. Finally, unlike media exposure and political interest, tests of knowledge do not require respondents to estimate subjective behaviors or inner states; they either pass or fail particular tests.

In an attempt to settle the measurement problem empirically, I tested the performance of several alternative measures of political awareness in predicting a variety of relevant criterion variables (Zaller, 1986, 1990). The awareness measures were education, media exposure, participation in politics (donating money, attending speeches, etc.), interest in politics, and political knowledge. The criterion variables included levels of observed attitude stability, attitude consistency, and degree of correlation between vote choice and party attachment. Price and I (1990) also examined the comparative ability of political knowledge, education, and media exposure to specify individual-level reception probabilities for prominent news stories; we also tested the comparative performance of knowledge and media use in a reception-acceptance model of attitude change. The results of these tests were unambiguous: In each individual test, neutral factual information was always a respectable competitor and almost

---

2 Individuals can attempt to guess correct answers, but a guessing penalty can be introduced to correct for this. I have experimented with guessing penalties and found that they do not improve the performance of information scales.

always the leading performer. No other measure gave an overall performance that was nearly as good. These results also agree with the somewhat narrower range of tests conducted by Luskin (1987).

Accordingly, neutral factual information is, on both theoretical and empirical grounds, the preferred measure of political awareness and is used as such throughout this book. In the cases in which an insufficient number of knowledge items is available, they are supplemented by measures of interest and education, as described below.

Issues in the measurement of political information

Granting that political knowledge is the best available measure of political awareness, there remain several questions about how knowledge itself should best be measured. One that has attracted interest is whether information is best measured globally by means of general tests of political knowledge, or whether measures must be specific to the particular domain in which information effects are expected (Iyengar, 1990).

From a theoretical perspective, awareness clearly should, to the extent possible, be measured separately within each domain for which effects are expected. This follows from axiom A1, which claims that reception depends not on global awareness, but on attention to particular issues. Therefore, we should expect to find stronger awareness effects for domain-specific measures of information than for global measures.

The evidence supports this expectation (Iyengar, 1990; Zaller, 1986; McGraw and Pinney, 1990). There is, however, a serious difficulty in producing domain-specific effects. The difficulty is that, as a practical matter, people who pay attention to one facet of politics tend to pay attention to other facets as well. As a result, it is difficult to build domain-specific scales that exhibit a satisfactory degree of discriminant validity. Iyengar (1990) manages to obtain such validity, but only at the cost of eliminating many face valid items that were too highly correlated with one another across domains; these exclusions significantly reduce the reliability of his scales. Using the same dataset, I built domain-specific scales that included all face-valid items that were available (Zaller, 1986); when I did so, I found that domain-specific knowledge scales concerning economics, foreign policy, and minority relations were intercorrelated in the range of .70 (without correcting for scale unreliabilities). These domain-specific knowledge scales outperformed a general knowledge scale in predicting relevant criterion variables (such as attitude stability), but never by margins that approached statistical or substantive significance. I therefore concluded

It is clear that the effects of political information on public opinion are, to some extent, domain specific. . . . At the same time, the superiority of domain specific measures of information is both modest and uneven. . . . Together, these results suggest that political information is a relatively general trait that can be effectively measured with a general-purpose information scale. (Zaller, 1986)

A subsequent inquiry coauthored with Vincent Price (Price and Zaller, 1990) reached a similar conclusion.

From necessity, this book relies almost exclusively on general-purpose rather than domain-specific measures of political awareness. Although domain-specific measures would be preferable, the loss from not having them is apparently slight.

Types of information tests

The items available as measures of political information vary greatly in number, quality, and format over the twenty-four ICPSR datasets that have been used in this book. In a handful of cases, notably the NES studies of 1986 and 1988 and the Brazilian public opinion survey, there is a good selection of items which had been consciously designed as tests of factual knowledge. In a few other cases, most seriously the 1978 NES congressional study and the 1984 "rolling thunder" survey of presidential primaries and the 1990 NES Senate study, there were few or no such items.[3] And in the majority of cases, there was a handful of good information tests, but too few to produce highly reliable awareness scales, by which I mean scales with alpha reliabilities of 0.85 or higher.[4] Hence it was necessary to locate items that, though not direct measures of political awareness, could be converted to this use. In the course of this book, I have made extensive use of the following three types of information tests:

1. The ability to make "correct" comparative placements of groups and candidates on issue dimensions, which I call "location tests." Since 1968, CPS/NES surveys have regularly asked respondents to place themselves on an issue dimension and also to place certain political objects – such as the presidential nominees, the parties, and liberals and conservatives – on these same scales. Thus, for example, a respondent might have been asked to place herself on a seven-point defense-spending scale (where 1 is the most antispending position and 7 is the most pro-spending position), and then asked to place 1988 presidential candidates George Bush and Michael Dukakis on the same scale. It is very difficult to say exactly where Bush's "true" position on this scale might be, but it can be confidently asserted that Bush should be located to the pro-

---

3 The 1984 survey contains measures of citizen awareness of various presidential contenders, but these are not well suited to my purposes. The difficulty is that such measures, as Bartels (1988) has shown, register higher levels of awareness over the course of the primary campaign as people learned more about the candidates. This is a difficulty because my theory holds that people who are high on habitual awareness will react differently to the fresh information they encounter than will people who are low on habitual awareness. Hence it is necessary to measure people's habitual awareness, and measures that are reactive to the current campaign cannot do this.

4 A three- or four-item scale of the type used in many opinion studies will normally have a reliability in the range of .65. Such a scale can easily fail to detect mild nonmonotonicity of the type shown in Figure 8.2 or subtle features of attitude change curves, as depicted in Figure 8.5. For the purposes of this book, much lengthier scales are needed.

spending side of Dukakis. Hence a respondent who locates Bush to the right of Dukakis on this scale can be counted as having "correctly" answered a test of political knowledge.

The analyst must use judgment in converting location items into knowledge tests since, for some items, it is impossible to say that one candidate or party differs from the other. For example, it is not at all obvious whether Jimmy Carter or Gerald Ford was farther to the left on women's rights, which makes this issue unsuitable for use in measuring political knowledge. But in many cases, correct relative placements are obvious to any informed observer of American politics.[5]

2. Willingness to rate certain political figures on "feeling thermometers," which may be referred to as "recognition items." NES surveys regularly ask respondents to rate various political figures – including presidents, senators, and political notables (such as Ralph Nader) – on 100-point "feeling thermometers." Respondents are, however, offered the option of saying they are unfamiliar with the given political figure, and those taking this option may be counted as having failed a knowledge test.

It is common for researchers to use these items as knowledge tests (Bartels, 1988; Mann and Wolfinger, 1980). Nonetheless, because this type of knowledge test is highly susceptible to a social desirability response set, I use it only sparingly and only when better alternatives are unavailable.

3. Many CPS/NES surveys require interviewers, upon completing each interview, to rate each respondent's apparent level of political information on a five-point scale. I have extensively analyzed the performance of these rating scales and concluded that, at least in surveys involving face-to-face interviews and considerable political content,[6] they perform extremely well (Zaller, 1985). In particular, a single five-point interviewer rating scale performs about as well as a scale constructed from 10 to 15 direct knowledge tests, where the measure of performance is the ability to predict relevant criteria.

A fear in relying upon such interviewer ratings is that they might be systematically biased in favor of higher-status persons, notably whites and males. However, I checked carefully for evidence of such bias and was able to find none (Zaller, 1985).

5 Prior to 1970, CPS surveys sometimes directly asked respondents which party was more likely to favor a certain policy (e.g., Medicare for the elderly). I found that, in all years in which this type of item was asked, it performed poorly as a knowledge test in the sense that item reliabilities were relatively low. I suspect this is because these items are one-shot items, whereas the comparative location items depend on three responses (self-rating, and ratings of each of two objects). The multiple-step measures provide more opportunities to screen out guessers. In general, I discarded items with low reliability, no matter their face validity, unless the low reliability was due to a strong skew.

6 This qualification is important. One would not expect interviewer ratings of respondent awareness to work unless the interviewer had ample opportunity to observe the respondent deal with political matters.

Most of the awareness scales used in this book have been constructed from these three types of items – especially the comparative location tests – and from more standard, direct tests of knowledge (such as, Which party controls the House of Representatives? What is the term of office of a U.S. senator?).

It is natural to wonder whether "catch-all" scales of the type I use perform as well as scales constructed from more conventional knowledge tests. The 1985 NES pilot study affords an opportunity to investigate this question. It carries some twenty-seven direct knowledge tests, that is, questions which directly asked respondents to supply the answer to a factual question about politics. When a scale constructed from these twenty-seven items was pitted against one of my catch-all scales, there was essentially no difference in their ability to predict three criteria: attitude stability, attitude consistency, and issue salience (Zaller, 1986).[7]

Coding conventions

In converting a variety of items to tests of political information, I have, with exceptions explicitly noted below, adhered to the following coding conventions:

1. Each discrete test of information has been given equal weight. In cases in which a single item could capture multiple bits of information, each bit was counted separately. In 1966, for example, respondents were asked to name as many Supreme Court justices as they could; I awarded one point for each justice they could name (up to four names). For another example, the interviewer rating scale has five points; I awarded respondents one point for each level above the lowest level.
2. In keeping with the previous point, I created simple additive scales, except in a few cases as noted.[8]
3. Persons who failed to give a correct answer because they responded "Don't know" were counted as having given an incorrect response. This includes cases in which respondents were not asked the comparative location of candidates on an issue scale because they had no opinion on the issue itself.[9]
4. Persons with missing data were not eliminated unless more than two-thirds of their responses were missing. Instead, these persons were assigned the average score for the items for which data were available.

All of the awareness scales I use, except the 1951 scale, the 1978 House elections scale, and the 1990 Senate elections scale, have alpha reliabilities in the

7 The catch-all scale in this case was based on items culled from the 1984 NES study. It had twenty-two items and an alpha reliability of .87. The twenty-seven-item scale had a reliability of .89.
8 I experimented with use of principal components analysis to extract the most important common factor from a set of items. Although this made little difference for the results I obtained, I was reluctant to use the technique because it gave small weights to items which, although strongly skewed, had high discriminating power. Technically, the problem is that principal components assume a linear relationship between items and the underlying awareness factor, and this assumption is egregiously false for skewed items, as shown in Zaller, 1985. I regarded skewed items as strong items, because they isolated respondents at the extremes of the awareness continuum; but principal components regarded them as weak items, because they appeared to explain little variance in the underlying construct.
9 In the 1968 survey, respondents were asked to rate candidates even on issues on which they had no opinion. It turned out that scarcely any people who had no opinion on an issue were willing to estimate the positions of others on that issue.

range from about .80 to .90, with most having alpha reliabilities around .85. The three exceptions have reliabilities in the range of .60 to .70. Since, however, the assumptions underlying the use of the alpha statistic, especially the assumption of equal item difficulty, are not met in the data I use, and since other measures of reliability are not readily available, there seems no point in providing reliabilities for each scale. Other detailed information about the measures of awareness I have used is given below.

Scale construction

Variable numbers refer to the relevant ICPSR codebook. (The SPSSx code for building these scales is available via bitnet to any scholar wishing to use it.)

1951 CPS "minor election study." Awareness is measured by a three-point interviewer rating of the respondent's apparent understanding of world affairs (col. 65), plus a one-point measure indicating whether the person specifically mentioned Dean Acheson in the course of the interview (col. 67).

1956 CPS election study. There were an insufficient number of items to build an information scale from the 1956 study alone. Hence I used twelve tests scattered across all three waves of the 1956–58–60 panel, as follows: V142, V145, V317, V318, V394 (two items), V395, V608, V609, V611, V612, V613, V615, V798. The unstandardized measure has a mean of 7.8 and a standard deviation of 3.08.

1964 CPS election study. A sixteen-point scale, as follows: L.B.J.'s and Goldwater's home state and religion (V294 to V297); which party is more conservative (V302); majority in Congress (V305, V306); congressional candidates' names, incumbency status (three items, V309, V312); which party favors government utilities (V346); China's form of government and U.N. status (two items, V352); form of Cuba's government (V354); knowledge of 1964 Civil Rights Act (V406, V407). The unstandardized measure has a mean of 10.4 and a standard deviation of 4.13.

1966 CPS election study. A fifteen-point scale, as follows: congressional candidates' names and incumbency status (three items, V90, V92); majority in Congress (V100, V101); names of U.S. Supreme Court justices (up to four points, V167); interviewer rating of respondent's information level (up to four points, V242). Since this scale was used to measure exposure to news about Vietnam, I awarded up to two points for expression of interest in foreign affairs (V65). The unstandardized measure has a mean of 7.48 and a standard deviation of 4.7.

1968 CPS election study. A seventeen-point scale, as follows: China's form of government and U.N. status (two items, V107); form of Cuba's government

(V109); which party is conservative (V361); congressional candidates' names and incumbency status (three items, V386, V387); majority in Congress (V305, V306); up to two points for expression of interest in foreign affairs (V102). Also two interviewer rating scales, V269 on preelection and V531 on postelection, which were averaged to yield a maximum of four points; and two tests of ability to make proper comparative placements of politicians on issue scales, as follows: Johnson and Wallace on Vietnam (V466 and V469); Humphrey and Wallace on urban unrest (V461 and V463). The unstandardized measure has a mean of 11.39 and a standard deviation of 4.41.

1970 CPS Awareness scale. An eighteen-point scale, as follows: Attention to Vietnam (V40); which party is more conservative (V177); congressional candidate (V203); percentage of tax dollar to defense (V256); who can change law (V258); number of allowable terms as president (V259); term of U.S. senator (V260); term of congressional representative (V261); interviewer rating of respondent's information (up to four points, V396). There were four comparative location tests, as follows: Democrats and Republicans on Vietnam (V93 and V94); Muskie and Wallace on aid to minorities (V110 and V111); Democrats and Nixon on inflation (V114 and V116); and Muskie and Wallace on criminal rights (V124 and V125); also two 1-item location tests, Wallace on urban unrest and Vietnam (V90, V97). The unstandardized measure has a mean of 9.54 and a standard deviation of 4.44.

1972–74–76 NES panel awareness scale. This scale is described in Zaller, 1990.

1978 NES election awareness scale. An unusually diverse scale, as follows: Meaning of liberalism (V410), meaning of conservativism (V413), party control of House of Representatives before and after election (V500, V501). Three recognition items, Ronald Reagan (V139), Jerry Brown (V141), and Ralph Nader (V144). Four comparative location items: Democrats and Republicans on job guarantees (V359, V360), on rights of the accused (V375, V376), on government medical insurance (V383, V384), and on liberalism and conservativism (V401, V402). Political interest, V43; and interviewer rated information, V636. Because I was unsure whether these items deserved equal weighting, I combined them into a scale by means of weights obtained from a principal components analysis. Because the political interest variable is correlated with the intensity of particular House races, as measured by the media-intensity variable (see text of Chapter 10), I purged it of this influence before adding it to the awareness scale. The unstandardized measure has a mean of 7.4 and a standard deviation of 3.3. (In the analysis of likes/dislikes in Chapter 10, the interest item is used as a separate variable.)

1980 NES election awareness scale. A twenty-five-point scale, as follows: ten comparative location items: Carter and Reagan on ideology (V268 and V269);

Kennedy and Connally on ideology (V270 and V271); two parties on ideology (V278 and V279); Carter and Reagan on defense spending (V282 and V283); parties on government services (V296 and V297); parties on jobs and inflation trade-off (V306 and V307); Carter and Reagan on abortion (V312 and V313); Carter and Reagan on cooperation with Russia (V1079 and V1080); parties on job guarantees (V1121 and V1122); Reagan and Kennedy on aid to minorities (V1064 and V1066). These additional items: heard poll results (V219), expresses opinion on tax cut proposal (V322), name and party of congressional candidates (four items, V826, V829), names of Senate candidates (four items, where relevant, V837 and V840; respondents were not penalized for living in a state without a Senate race), party that supports stronger federal government (V1131). There were two interviewer rating scales, V726 on preelection and V1186 on postelection, which were averaged to yield a maximum of four points. The unstandardized measure has a mean of 9.6 and a standard deviation of 5.7.

1982 NES election awareness scale. A twenty-five-point scale, as follows: Three recognition items: John Anderson, Bush, and Mondale (V125, V134, V135). Five comparative location items: Democrats and Republicans on ideology scale (V404, V405), on defense spending scale (V409, V410), on job guarantees (V427, V428), and on government services (V445, V446); liberals and conservatives on aid to minorities (V422 and V423). Also two single object-location tests: Ronald Reagan located right of center on ideology (V394) and defense spending (V408). Name and party of congressional candidates (four items, V102, V106), name and party of Senate candidates (four items, where relevant, V115, V118). Party control of House and Senate, party that elected most new members to House (V523 to V525). Interviewer rating of respondent information (up to four points, V768). The unstandardized measure has a mean of 11.7 and a standard deviation of 6.3.

1984 NES Continuous Monitoring Study awareness scale. A twenty-four-point scale, as follows: V136 (three items), V407 (four items), V614, V622, V626, 805 (two items), V876. Eleven recognition items, V220, V222 to V231. Because I was unsure whether these items deserved equal weighting, I combined them into a scale by means of weights obtained from a principal components analysis.

1984 NES election awareness scale. A twenty-four-point scale, as follows: There were eleven comparative location items, several of which required respondents to place objects two or three points apart: Reagan and Mondale on ideology (V371 and V372, at least two points apart), government services (V376 and V377, at least two points apart), aid to minorities (V383 and V384), U.S. involvement in Central America (V389 and V390), defense spending (V396 and V397), cooperation with Russia (V409 and V410), job guarantees (V415 and V416), Reagan and Mondale on ideology (distance of three points required for correct answer, V1017 and V1018); liberals and conservatives on government services (V1034 and V1035, three points apart), involvement in Central America (V1045 and V1046, three points apart), job guarantees (V1054 and V1055, three points apart). In addition: name and party of congressional candidates (four items, V741, V745), which party is more conservative (V875), which party has more members in House and Senate before and after election (V1006 to V1009), recognition of Bush and Ferraro (V292 and V304). There were two interviewer rating scales, V713 on preelection and V1112 on postelection, which were averaged to yield a maximum of four points. The unstandardized measure has a mean of 9.8 and a standard deviation of 5.9.

1986 NES election and 1987 pilot awareness scale. A nineteen-point scale, as follows: ability to name political offices held by Bush, Weinberger, Rehnquist, Volker, O'Neill, Dole (V635 to V642), names of House candidates (V202, V206), two recognition tests, Hart and Jackson (V242, V244). Four location items: Democrats and Republicans on ideology (V730 and V731), on defense spending (V749 and V750), on involvement in Central America (V811 and V812), and on government services (V831 and V832); comparative rankings on ideology, defense, and services had to be at least two points apart to get credit for a correct answer. An additional point was awarded for placing Reagan on the conservative side of the ideology scale, which is a noncomparative location test (V723). The unstandardized measure, as used in the analysis of attitude change on Central America, has a mean of 7.9 and a standard deviation of 4.2.

1989 NES pilot awareness scale. A twenty-two-point scale, as follows: budget knowledge (V835), which party is more conservative (V5656), the political offices held by Kennedy, Schultz, Rehnquist, Gorbachev, Thatcher, and Arafat (V5827 to V5833), party control of Congress (V834, V835), and names of congressional candidates (V5106). Seven location items: comparative placements of the Democrats and Republicans on ideology (V421 and V422), government services (V606 and V607), defense spending (V610 and V611), medical insurance (V620 and V621), job guarantees (V627 and V628), and cooperation with Russia (V712 and V713); in addition, a point was given for ranking Dukakis two or more points to the left of Bush on ideology (V417 and V418). Respondents could also get up to four points from the interviewer rating of respondent information (V1241). The unstandardized measure has a mean of 10.5 and a standard deviation of 5.7.

1990 NES awareness scale. A fourteen-point scale consisting of tests of the ability to give the political office held by Quayle, Mitchell, Rehnquist, Gorbachev, Thatcher, Mandella, and Foley (V835 to V841); plus party control of Congress (V842, V843) and interviewer rating of respondent knowledge (V1231). The unstandardized measure has a mean of 4.95 and a standard deviation of 2.74.

1990 NES Senate study awareness scale. The 1990 Senate study contained only five political knowledge items – tests of respondent's ability to locate George

Bush, the Democratic Party, and the Republican Party on a seven-point liberal–conservative scale (V517, V533, V534), and the names of the candidates in House elections (V41, V45). I combined these with tests of willingness to evaluate Bush's job performance (V36) and to state an opinion on aid to minorities (V537). This scale had a mean of 3.04 and a standard deviation of 1.53. The purged interest item (see 1978 awareness scale) and the scale were standardized, combined, and restandardized, thereby giving equal weight to each component in the final awareness scale.

POLITICAL PREDISPOSITIONS

With the exception of the 1951 and 1956 studies, my measures of political awareness are quite strong and essentially comparable in all years. Measurement of political predispositions is much more uneven and, on the whole, much less adequate. Except in two studies – notably the 1987 NES pilot study, which contains the Hurwitz–Peffley (1988) measure of foreign policy predispositions, and the 1989 pilot study, which contains an excellent selection of Conover–Feldman equality items – I was always dealing with measures that I felt were more or less inadequate to the tasks to which I put them. Although many of the surveys contained reasonably good value measures, they did not contain value measures *of the particular dimension* on which public opinion was undergoing change. Chapter 2 provides the theoretical justification for opportunistically using whatever measures are available.

The least adequate studies were the 1951 and 1956 studies. The only measure of general partisan orientation in the 1951 study was recalled vote in the 1948 election. Although this measure served as the basis for the original statement of the Michigan theory of party identification (Belknap and Campbell, 1951–2), the measure leaves much to be desired. The 1956 study contains a number of good preference questions, but none that seem well suited for capturing the predispositions that underlie racial attitudes. Since 1984, NES surveys have carried a generally excellent selection of value measures.

Coding conventions

In building value scales, I made full use of whatever information was contained in an item (that is, I did not recode to a smaller number of categories). The items were combined into scales by means of weights obtained from principal components analysis, unless all items had the same range, in which case simple additive indices were created.

Scale construction

1956 CPS election study. There were two main sets of items, one concerning domestic politics and the other foreign politics. The items in each cluster were separately scaled by means of principal components analysis. The items in the domestic policy cluster were V32, V38, V53, V59; the items in the foreign policy cluster were V35, V50, V68, V71.

1964, 1966, 1968, 1970 CPS election studies. See appendix to Chapter 9.

1978 NES election study. The items used to measure respondent attitudes are V357, V365, V373, V399, V443. See footnote 8 in Chapter 10 for further information.

1982 NES election study. For use in diffusion of economic news, three economic policy items: job guarantees (V425), government services (V443), regulation of business (V459). For use with nuclear freeze issue, two defense spending items (V317 and V407).

1984 NES election study. Four items: liberal–conservative self-identification (V369), government services (V375), minority aid (V382), and job guarantees (V414).

1987 NES pilot study. Items from Hurwitz–Peffley foreign affairs battery combined into hawk–dove scale, as follows: V2245, V5233, V5249, V5251, V5252, V5253, plus two additional items (Russia and Defense spending), V742 and V907.

The social welfare ideology scale consists of fourteen Conover–Feldman items plus two measures of ideological self-designation, as follows: V620 to V622, V624, V626, V701 to V706, V2176, V2178, V2179, plus V722 and V1010.

The government spending scale consisted of V716–V725.

References

Abramowitz, Alan I. 1980. "A comparison of voting for U.S. senator and representative." *American Political Science Review*, 74, 633–40.

Abramson, Paul. 1983. *Political Attitudes in America*. New York: Freeman.

Achen, Christopher H. 1975. "Mass political attitudes and the survey response." *American Political Science Review*, 69, 1218–31.

    1983. "Toward theories of data: The state of political methodology." Paper given at the annual meeting of the American Political Science Association, Washington, D.C.

Adorno, Theodore W., Else Frenkel-Brunswik, Daniel Levinson, and R. N. Sanford. 1950. *The Authoritarian Personality*. New York: Harper.

Allport, Gordon. 1954. *The Nature of Prejudice*. New York: Doubleday.

Altemeyer, Bob. 1981. *Right-Wing Authoritarianism*. Winnipeg: University of Manitoba Press.

Alves, Maria Helena Moreira. 1984. *Estado e Oposição no Brasil* [State and Opposition in Brazil]. Petrópolis, Brazil: Vozes.

Anderson, Barbara, Brian Silver, and Paul Abramson. 1988. "Interviewer race and attitudes of blacks." *Public Opinion Quarterly*, 52, 289–324.

Anderson, Norman. 1974. "Information integration theory: A brief survey." In David Krantz, Richard Atkinson, R. Duncan Luce, and Patrick Suppes (eds.), *Measurement, Psychophysics, and Neural Information Processing* (pp. 236–305). San Francisco: W. H. Freeman.

Arnold, Douglas. 1990. *The Logic of Congressional Action*. New Haven, Conn.: Yale University Press.

Atkinson, Richard, Gordon Bower, and Richard Crothers. 1965. *An Introduction to Mathematical Learning Theory*. New York: Wiley.

Bachrach, Peter, and Morton Baratz. 1962. "The two faces of power." *American Political Science Review*, 56, 947–52.

Bartels, Larry. 1988. *The Dynamics of Presidential Primaries*. Princeton, N.J.: Princeton University Press.

Barton, Alan H. 1974–5. "Consensus and conflict among American leaders." *Public Opinion Quarterly*, 38, 507–30.

Bayer, Ronald. 1981. *Homosexuality and American Psychiatry: The Politics of Diagnosis*. New York: Basic.

Belknap, George, and Angus Campbell. 1951–2. "Party identification and attitudes toward foreign policy." *Public Opinion Quarterly*, 15, 601–23.

Bennett, Stephen. 1989. " 'Know-nothings' revisited: The meaning of political ignorance today." *Social Science Quarterly*, 69, 476–90.

Bennett, W. Lance. 1980. *Public Opinion in American Politics*. New York: Harcourt, Brace, Jovanovich.

1990. "Toward a theory of press–state relations in the U.S." *Journal of Communication*, 40, 103–25.

Berelson, Bernard, Paul Lazarsfeld, and William McPhee. 1954. *Voting*. Chicago: University of Chicago Press.

Bishop, George F., Robert Oldendick, and Alfred Tuchfarber. 1984. "What must my interest in politics be if I just told you 'I don't know'?" *Public Opinion Quarterly*, 48, 210–19.

Bobo, Larry, and F. C. Licari. 1989. "Education and tolerance: Testing the effects of cognitive sophistication and target group affect." *Public Opinion Quarterly*, 53, 285–318.

Bowen, Gordon. 1989. "Presidential action and public opinion about U.S.–Nicaraguan policy." *PS*, 22, 793–9.

Brady, Henry, and Richard Johnston. 1987. "What's the primary message: Horse race or issue journalism?" In Gary Orren and Nelson W. Polsby (eds.), *Media and Momentum* (pp. 127–86). New York: Chatham.

Braestrup, Peter. 1979. *The Big Story*. New Haven, Conn: Yale University Press.

Brigham, Carl. 1923. *A Study of American Intelligence*. Princeton, N.J.: Princeton University Press.

1930. "Intelligence tests of immigrant groups." *Psychological Review*, 37, 138 –65.

Broder, David. 1984. "Frank Church's challenge." *Washington Post*, January 22.

Brody, Richard. 1991. *Assessing Presidential Character: The Media, Elite Opinion, and Public Support*. Stanford, Calif.: Stanford University Press.

Cain, Bruce, John Ferejohn, and Morris Fiorina. 1987. *The Personal Vote*. Cambridge, Mass.: Harvard University Press.

Campbell, Angus, Philip Converse, Warren Miller, and Donald Stokes. 1960. *The American Voter*. New York: Wiley.

Cantril, Hadley. 1944. *Gauging Public Opinion*. Princeton, N.J.: Princeton University Press.

Carmines, Edward, and James Stimson. 1982. "Racial issues and the structure of mass belief systems." *Journal of Politics*, 44, 2–20.

1989. *Issue Evolution: Race and the Transformation of American Politics*. Princeton, N.J.: Princeton University Press.

Chaiken, Shelly. 1980. "Heuristic versus systematic information processing and the use of source versus message cues in persuasion." *Journal of Personality and Social Psychology*, 37, 1387–97.

Charters, W. W., Jr., and Theodore Newcomb. 1958. "Some attitudinal effects of experimentally increased salience of group membership." In E. Macoby, T. Newcomb, and E. Hartley (eds.), *Readings in Social Psychology*, 3d ed. New York: Holt, Rinehart.

Chong, Dennis, Herbert McClosky, and John Zaller. 1984. "Social learning and the acquisition of political norms." In Herbert McClosky and John Zaller (eds.), *The American Ethos* (ch. 8). Cambridge, Mass.: Harvard University Press.

Citrin, Jack. 1974. "Comment: The political relevance of trust in government." *American Political Science Review*, 68, 973–88.

Cohen, Bernard. 1963. *The Press and Foreign Policy*. Princeton, N.J.: Princeton University Press.

1973. *The Public's Impact on Foreign Policy*. Boston: Little, Brown.

Colby, David, and Tim Cook. 1991. "The mass-mediated epidemic: AIDS on the nightly news, 1981–1987." In Elizabeth Fee and Daniel Fox (eds.), *AIDS Contemporary History*. Berkeley: University of California Press.

Converse, Philip. 1962. "Information flow and the stability of partisan attitudes." *Public Opinion Quarterly*, 26, 578–99.

1964. "The nature of belief systems in mass publics." In David Apter (ed.), *Ideology and Discontent* (pp. 206–61). New York: Free Press.

1975. "Public opinion and voting behavior." In Fred Greenstein and Nelson Polsby (eds.), *Handbook of Political Science*, 4, 75–169. Reading, Mass.: Addison-Wesley.

1980. "Comment: Rejoinder to Judd and Milburn." *American Sociological Review*, 45, 644–6.

Converse, Philip, and George DePeux. 1962. "Politicization of the electorate in the U.S. and France." *Public Opinion Quarterly*, 26, 1–23.

Converse, Philip, and Greg Markus. 1979. *Plus ça change...* The new CPS panel study." *American Political Science Review*, 73, 32–49.

Costantini, Edmond, and Kenneth Craik. 1980. "Personality and politicians: California party leaders, 1960–1976." *Journal of Personality and Social Psychology*, 38, 640–66.

Cotton, John L. 1985. "Cognitive dissonance and selective exposure." In Dolf Zillmann and Jennings Bryant (eds), *Selective Exposure to Communication*. Hillsdale, N.J.: Erlbaum.

Dawson, Michael C., Ronald E. Brown, and Cathy Cohen. n.d. "Racial differences in presidential approval." Unpublished paper, Department of Political Science, University of Michigan, Ann Arbor.

D'Emillio, John. 1983. *Sexual Politics, Sexual Communities*. Chicago: University of Chicago Press.

Dean, Gillian, and Thomas Moran. 1977. "Measuring mass political attitudes: Change and uncertainty." *Political Methodology*, 4, 383–424.

Degler, Carl. 1991. *In Search of Human Nature*. New York: Oxford University Press.

Delli Carpini, Michael X., and Scott Keeter. 1990. "The structure of political knowledge: Issues of conceptualization and measurement." Paper given at annual meetings of American Political Science Association, San Francisco.

In Press. "Stability and change in the U.S. public's knowledge of politics." *Public Opinion Quarterly*.

Downs, Anthony. 1957. *An Economic Theory of Democracy*. New York: Harper.

Dryer, Edward C. 1971. "Media use and electoral choices: Some political consequences of information exposure." *Public Opinion Quarterly*, 35, 544–53.

Duch, Raymond, and James Gibson. n.d. "Cultural barriers to European integration? A cross-national analysis of democratic tolerance." Unpublished paper, Department of Political Science, University of Houston.

Edelman, Murray. 1964. *The Symbolic Uses of Politics*. Urbana: University of Illinois Press.

Erbring, Lutz, Edie Goldenberg, and Arthur Miller. 1980. "Frontpage news and real world cues: A new look at agenda setting by the media." *American Journal of Political Science*, 24, 16–49.

Erikson, Robert. 1971. "The advantage of incumbency in congressional elections." *Policy*, 3, 395–405.

1979. "The SRC panel data and mass political attitudes." *British Journal of Political Science*, 9, 89–114.

Fan, David. 1988. *Predictions of Public Opinion from the Mass Media*. New York: Greenwood.

"Federal planning assumptions: Prevalence of AIDS virus infection." 1987. *The New York Times*, February 27, p. 11.

Feldman, Stanley. 1989. "Reliability and stability of policy positions: Evidence from a five-wave panel." *Political Analysis*, 1, 25–60.

Feldman, Stanley, and John Zaller. 1992. "Political culture of ambivalence: Ideological responses to the welfare state." *American Journal of Political Science*, 36, 268–307.

Fenno, Richard. 1978. *Homestyle: House Members in Their Districts*. Boston: Little, Brown.

Fiorina, Morris 1977. *Congress: Keystone of the Washington Establishment*. New Haven, Conn.: Yale University Press.

1981. *Retrospective Voting*. New Haven, Conn.: Yale University Press.

Fiske, Susan T., and Donald Kinder. 1981. "Involvement, expertise, and schema use: Evidence from political cognition." In N. Cantor and J. Kihlstrom (eds.), *Personality, Social Cognition, and Social Interaction*, Hillsdale, N.J.: Erlbaum.

Fiske, Susan, Richard Lau, and Richard Smith. 1990. "On the varieties and utilities of political expertise." *Social Cognition*, 8, 31–48.

Franklin, Charles H. 1989. "Estimation across data sets: Two-stage auxiliary instrumental variables estimation (2SAIV)." *Political Analysis*, 1, 1–24.

1992. "Learning the consequences of actions: Public opinion and the Persian Gulf War." Paper presented at Conference on the Consequences of War, Brookings Institution, Washington, D.C.

Franklin, Charles H., and Liane C. Kosaki. 1989. "Republican schoolmaster: The U.S. Supreme Court, public opinion, and abortion." *American Political Science Review*, 83, 751–72.

Fredrickson, George M. 1971. *The Black Image in the White Mind*. New York: Harper.

Gamson, William, and Andre Modigliani. 1966. "Knowledge and foreign policy opinions: Some models for consideration." *Public Opinion Quarterly*, 30, 187–99.

1987. "The changing culture of affirmative action." In R. D. Braungart (ed.), *Research in Political Sociology* (vol. 3, 137–76). Greenwich, Conn.: JAI Press.

Gans, Herbert. 1980. *Deciding What's News*. New York: Vintage.

Geddes, Barbara, and John Zaller. 1989. "Sources of popular support for authoritarian regimes." *American Journal of Political Science*, 33, 319–47.

Gelb, Leslie, with Richard Betts. 1979. *The Irony of Vietnam: The System Worked*. Washington, D.C.: Brookings.

Gerber, Elisabeth, and John Jackson. 1990. "Endogenous preferences and the study of institutions." Paper presented at the annual meeting of the American Political Science Association, San Francisco.

Ginsberg, Benjamin. 1986. *The Captive Public*. New York: Basic.

Glenn, Norval D. 1977. *Cohort Analysis*. Beverly Hills, Calif.: Sage.

Graber, Doris. 1984. *Processing the News: How People Tame the Information Tide*. White Plains, N.Y.: Longman.

Grossman, Michael, and Martha Kumar. 1981. *Portraying the President*. Baltimore: Johns Hopkins University Press.

Hagstrom, W. O. 1965. *The Scientific Community*. New York: Basic.

Hahn, Harlan. 1970. "Correlates of public support for war: Local referenda on the Vietnam issue." *American Political Science Review*, 64, 1186–98.

Halberstam, David. 1972. *The Best and the Brightest*. New York: Random House.

1979. *The Powers That Be*. New York: Dell.

Hallin, Daniel. 1984. "Vietnam and the myth of the oppositional media." *Journal of Politics*, 46, 1–24.

1986. *The Uncensored War*. Cambridge: Cambridge University Press.

Hamilton, R. F. 1968. "A research note on public support for 'tough-minded' military policies." *American Sociological Review*, 33, 439–49.

Hanushek, Eric, and John Jackson. 1977. *Statistical Methods for Social Scientists*. New York: Wiley.

Hastie, Reid, and Bernadette Park. 1986. "The relationship between memory and judgment depends whether the task is memory-based or on-line." *Psychological Review*, 93, 258–68.

Hibbing, John. 1991. "Contours of the modern congressional career." *American Political Science Review*, 85, 405–28.

Higgins, E. Tory, and G. King. 1981. "Accessibility of social constructs: Information-processing consequences of individual and contextual variation." In N. Cantor and J. F. Kihlstrom (eds.), *Personality, Cognition, and Social Interaction* (pp. 69–121). Hillsdale, N.J.: Erlbaum.

Hochschild, Jennifer. 1981. *What's Fair?* Princeton, N.J.: Princeton University Press.

Hollis, Michael. 1991. "The Public's Social Policy Preferences: Structure and Antecedents. Unpublished dissertation, University of California, Los Angeles.

Hurwitz, Jon, and Mark Peffley. 1987. "How are foreign policy attitudes structured? A hierarchical model." *American Political Science Review*, 81, 1099–130.

1988. Report to the NES Board of Overseers on new militarism items from the 1987 pilot. National Election Studies, Ann Arbor, Mich.

In Press. "America assesses the U.S.S.R.: An analysis of belief revision." *American Journal of Political Science*.

Iyengar, Shanto. 1990. "Shortcuts to political knowledge: Selective attention and the accessibility bias." In John Ferejohn and James Kuklinski (eds.), *Information and the Democratic Process* (pp. 160–85). Urbana: University of Illinois Press.

1991. *Is Anyone Responsible?* Chicago: University of Chicago Press.

Iyengar, Shanto, and Donald Kinder. 1987. *News That Matters*. Chicago: University of Chicago Press.

Iyengar, Shanto, Donald Kinder, Mark Peters, and Jon Krosnick. 1984. "The evening news and presidential evaluations." *Journal of Personality and Social Psychology*, 46, 778–87.

Iyengar, Shanto, Mark Peters, and Donald Kinder. 1982. "Experimental demonstrations of the 'not-so-minimal' consequences of television news programs." *American Political Science Review*, 76, 848–58.

Jackman, Mary. 1978. "General and applied tolerance: Does education increase commitment to racial integration?" *American Journal of Political Science*, 22, 302–24.

Jacobson, Gary. 1980. *Money in Congressional Elections*. New Haven, Conn.: Yale University Press.

1991. *The Politics of Congressional Elections*. 3d ed. Boston: Harper, Collins.

Jacobson, Gary, and Sam Kernell. 1981. *Strategy and Choice in Congressional Elections*. New Haven, Conn.: Yale University Press.

Jacoby, William. 1991. "Ideological identification and ideological issue attitudes." *American Journal of Political Science*, 35, 178–205.

Johannes, John R., and John C. McAdams. 1987. "Determinants of spending by House challengers, 1974–1984." *American Journal of Political Science*, 31, 457–83.

Judd, Charles, Roger Drake, James W. Downing, and Jon Krosnick. 1991. "Some dynamic properties of attitude structures: Context-induced response facilitation and polarization." *Journal of Personality and Social Psychology*, 60, 193–202.

Judd, Charles, and Jon Krosnick. 1989. "The structural bases of consistency among political attitudes: Effects of political expertise and attitude importance." In A. R. Pratkanis, S. J. Beckler, and A. G. Greenwald (eds.), *Attitude Structure and Function* (pp. 99–128). Hillsdale, NJ: Erlbaum.

Judd, Charles, and Michael Milburn. 1980. "The structure of attitude systems in the general public: Comparison of a structural equation model." *American Sociological Review*, 45, 627–43.

Judd, Charles, Michael Milburn, and Jon Krosnick. 1981. "Political involvement and attitude structure in the general public." *American Sociological Review*, 46, 660–9.

Just, Marion, W. Russell Neuman, and Ann Crigler. 1989. "Who learns what from the news: Attentive publics versus a cognitive elite." Paper given at the annual meeting of the American Political Science Association, Atlanta.

Katz, Elihu, and Paul Lazarsfeld. 1955. *Personal Influence.* Glencoe, Ill.: Free Press.

Kelley, Stanley, Jr. 1983. *Interpreting Elections.* Princeton, N.J.: Princeton University Press.

Key V. O., Jr. 1961. *Public Opinion and American Democracy,* New York: Knopf.

Key, V. O., Jr. (with Milton Cummings). 1966. *The Responsible Electorate.* Cambridge, Mass.: Harvard University Press.

Kinder, Donald. 1986. "Presidential character revisited." In Richard Lau and David Sears (eds.), *Political Cognition* (pp. 233–56). Hillsdale N.J.: Erlbaum.

Kinder, Donald, and Lynn Sanders. 1990. "Mimicking political debate with survey questions: The case of white opinion on affirmative action for blacks." *Social Cognition,* 8, 73–103.

Kinder, Donald, and David Sears. 1985. "Public opinion and political action." In G. Lindzey and E. Aronson (eds.), *Handbook of Social Psychology,* 4th ed. (pp. 659–741). New York: Random House.

Kinsey, Alfred, et al. 1948. *Sexual Behavior in the Human Male.* Philadelphia: Saunders.

Klapper, Joseph T. 1960. *The Effects of Mass Communications.* Glencoe, Ill.: Free Press.

Kluger, Richard. 1975. *Simple Justice.* New York: Vintage.

Knight, Kathleen. 1985. "Ideology in the 1980 election: Ideological sophistication does matter." *Journal of Politics,* 47, 828–53.

Krosnick, Jon. 1988. "Attitude importance and attitude change." *Journal of Experimental Social Psychology,* 24, 240–55.

(ed.). 1990. Thinking about Politics: Comparisons of Experts and Novices. Special issue of *Social Cognition,* 8, 1.

Krosnick, Jon, and Matthew Berent. 1992. "Comparisons of party identification and policy preferences." Unpublished manuscript, Department of Psychology, Ohio State University, Columbus.

Krosnick, Jon, David Boninger, Yao-chia Chuang, and Catherine Carnot. 1992. "Attitude strength: One construct or many related constructs?" Unpublished manuscript, Department of Psychology, Ohio State University, Columbus.

Krosnick, Jon, and Donald Kinder. 1990. "Altering the foundations of support for the president through priming." *American Political Science Review,* 83, 497–512.

Krosnick, Jon, and Michael Milburn. 1990. "Psychological determinants of political opinionation." *Social Cognition,* 8, 49–72.

Krosnick, Jon, and Howard Schuman. 1988. "Attitude intensity, importance, and certainty and susceptibility to response effects." *Journal of Personality and Social Psychology,* 54, 940–52.

Lamounier, Bolívar (ed.). 1980. *Voto de Desconfiança* [No Confidence Vote]. São Paulo: Vozes/Cebrap.

Lane, Robert. 1962. *Political Ideology.* New York: Basic.

1965. "Politics of consensus in an age of affluence." *American Political Science Review,* 38, 874–94.

1973. "Patterns of political belief." In Jeanne Knutson (ed.), *Handbook of Political Psychology* (pp. 83–116). San Francisco: Jossey-Bass.

Lang, Gladys, Kurt Lang, and James Larson. 1991. "Press as prologue: Saddam's Iraq in Britain, Germany, and the U.S.A." Paper given at the SSRC workshop on the Media and Foreign Policy, University of Washington, Seattle, September 27.

Lauritsen, John, and David Thorstad. 1974. *The Early Homosexual Rights Movement (1864–1935).* New York: Times Change Press.

Lazarsfeld, Paul, Bernard Berelson, and Helen Gaudet. 1944. *The People's Choice.* New York: Duell, Sloane, and Pearce.

Lichtenstein Meryl, and Thomas Srull. 1987. "Processing objectives as a determinant of the relationship between memory and recall." *Journal of Experimental Psychology,* 23, 93–118.

Lippmann, Walter. 1946. *Public Opinion.* New York: Penguin. Originally published in 1922 by Macmillan.

Lipset, S. M., and Carl Ladd. 1970. *The Divided Academy.* New York: Basic.

Lipset, S. M., and William Schneider. 1982. *The Confidence Gap.* New York: Free Press.

Lodge, Milton, Kathleen McGraw, and Pat Stroh. 1989. "An impression-driven model of candidate formation." *American Political Science Review,* 83, 399–420.

Lord, Charles, Lee Ross, and Mark Lepper. 1979. "Biased assimilation and attitude polarization: The effects of prior theories on subsequently considered evidence." *Journal of Personality and Social Psychology,* 37, 2098–109.

Lord, Frederick, and M. Novick. 1968. *Statistical Theories of Mental Test Scores.* Reading, Mass.: Addison-Wesley.

Luker, Kristin. 1984. *Abortion and the Politics of Motherhood.* Berkeley: University of California Press.

Lusk, Cynthia, and Charles Judd. 1988. "Political expertise and structural mediators of candidate evaluations." *Journal of Experimental Social Psychology,* 24, 105–26.

Luskin, Robert. 1987. "Measuring political sophistication." *American Journal of Political Science,* 31, 856–99.

1990. "Explaining political sophistication." *Political Behavior,* 12, 331–61.

McClosky, Herbert. 1958. "Personality and conservativism." *American Political Science Review,* 52, 27–45.

McClosky, Herbert, and Alida Brill. 1983. *Dimensions of Tolerance.* New York: Basic.

McClosky, Herbert, and John Zaller. 1984. *The American Ethos: Public Attitudes toward Capitalism and Democracy.* Cambridge, Mass.: Harvard University Press.

McGraw, Kathleen, Milton Lodge, and Pat Stroh. 1990. "On-line processing in candidate evaluation: The effects of issue order, issue salience, and sophistication." *Political Behavior,* 12, 41–58.

McGraw, Kathleen, and Neil Pinney 1990. "The effects of general and domain-specific expertise on political memory and judgment." *Social Cognition,* 8, 9–30.

McGuire, William J. 1968. "Personality and susceptibility to social influence." In E. F. Borgatta and W. W. Lambert (eds.), *Handbook of Personality Theory and Research* (pp. 1130–87). Chicago: Rand-McNally.

1969. "The nature of attitudes and attitude change." In G. Lindzey and E. Aronson (eds.), *Handbook of Social Psychology,* 2d ed. (pp. 136–314). Reading, Mass.: Addison-Wesley.

McWethy, Jack. 1972. *The Power of the Pentagon,* Washington, D.C.: CQ Press.

MacKuen, Michael. 1984. "Exposure to information, belief integration, and individual responsiveness to agenda change." *American Political Science Review,* 78, 372–91.

MacKuen, Michael, and Courtney Brown. 1987. "Political context and attitude change." *American Political Science Review,* 83, 471–90.

Mann, Thomas 1978. *Unsafe at Any Margin: Interpreting Congressional Elections.* Washington D.C.: Brookings Institution.

Mann, Thomas, and Raymond Wolfinger. 1980. "Candidates and parties in congressional elections," *American Political Science Review,* 74, 617–32.

Mansbridge, Jane. 1986. *Why We Lost the ERA.* Chicago: University of Chicago Press.

Marcus, George, D. Tabb, and John Sullivan. 1974. "The application of individual differences scaling to the measurement of political ideologies." *American Journal of Political Science,* 18, 405–20.

Markus, Hazel, and Robert Zajonc. 1985. "The cognitive perspective in social psychology." In G. Lindzey and E. Aronson (eds.), *Handbook of Political Psychology,* 4th ed. (pp. 137–230). New York: Random House.

Marotta, Toby. 1981. *The Politics of Homosexuality.* Boston: Houghton, Mifflin.

Mayhew, David. 1974. *Congress: The Electoral Connection*. New Haven, Conn.: Yale University Press.

Merton, Robert. 1982. *Social Research and the Practicing Professions*. Cambridge, Mass.: Abt.

Milburn, Michael. 1987. "Ideological self-schemata and schematically induced attitude consistency." *Journal of Experimental Social Psychology*, 23, 383–98.

Miliband, Ralph. 1969. *The State and Capitalist Society*. New York: Basic.

Millar, Murray, and Abraham Tesser. 1986. "Effects of affective and cognitive focus on the attitude–behavior relation." *Journal of Personality and Social Psychology*, 51, 270–6.

Miller, Arthur. 1974. "Political issues and trust in government." *American Political Science Review*, 68, 951–72.

Miller, Warren E., and Theresa Levitan. 1976. *Leadership and Change*. Cambridge, Mass.: Winthrop.

Mohr, Charles. 1983. "Once again – Did the press lose Vietnam?" *Columbia Journalism Review*, 22, 51–6.

Monroe, J. P. 1990. "Political values and the structure of mass attitudes." Unpublished manuscript, Department of Political Science, University of California, Los Angeles.

Mueller, John. 1973. *War, Presidents, and Public Opinion*. New York: Wiley.
    1992. "American public opinion and the Gulf War: Trends and historical comparisons." Paper given at Conference on the Consequences of War, Brookings Institution, Washington, D.C., February 28.

Myrdal, Gunnar. 1944. *An American Dilemma*. New York: Harper & Row.

Nelson, Candace. 1978–9. "The effects of incumbency on voting in congressional elections." *Political Science Quarterly*, 93, 665–78.

Neuman, W. Russell. 1986. *The Paradox of Mass Politics*. Cambridge, Mass.: Harvard University Press.
    1990. "The threshold of public opinion." *Public Opinion Quarterly*, 54, 159–76.

Nie, Norman, Sidney Verba, and John Petrocik. 1976. *The Changing American Voter*. Cambridge, Mass.: Harvard University Press.

Niemi, Richard, and Anders Westholm. 1984. "Issues, parties, and attitudinal stability: A comparative study of Sweden and the United States." *Electoral Studies*, 3, 65–83.

O'Neill, Thomas P., with William Novak 1987. *Man of the House*. New York: Random House.

Page, Benjamin, and Robert Shapiro. In press. *The Rational Public*. Chicago: University of Chicago.

Page, Benjamin, Robert Y. Shapiro, and Glenn R. Dempsey. 1987. "Television news and changes in Americans' policy preferences." *American Political Science Review*, 83, 23–44.

Patterson, Thomas. 1980. *The Mass Media Election*. New York: Praeger.

Patterson, Thomas, and Robert McClure. 1976. *The Unseeing Eye*. New York: Putnam.

Petrocik, John. 1989. "Issues and agendas: Electoral coalitions and the 1988 election." Paper given at the annual meeting of the American Political Science Association, Atlanta.

Petty, Richard T., and John E. Cacioppo. 1986. *Communication and Persuasion*. New York: Springer-Verlag.

Pierce, John, Kathleen Beatty, and Paul Hagner. 1982. *The Dynamics of American Public Opinion*. Glenview, Ill.: Scott, Foresman.

Pollock III, Philip H., Stuart Lisle, and M. Elliot Vittes. 1991. "Hard issues, core values, and vertical constraint." Unpublished paper, Department of Political Science, The University of Central Florida.

Polsby, Nelson. 1983. *Consequences of Reform*. New York: Oxford.

Popkin, Sam. 1991. *The Reasoning Voter*. Chicago: University of Chicago Press.

Price, D. J. 1961. *Science since Babylon.* New Haven, Conn.: Yale University Press.
Price, Vincent. 1989. "Social identification and public opinion." *Public Opinion Quarterly,* 53, 197–224.
    1991. "Priming ideological leanings: The impact of salience and commitment." Report to the National Election Studies Board of Overseers, Ann Arbor, Mich.
    1992. *Communications Concept IV: Public Opinion.* Newbury Park, Calif.: Sage Publications.
Price, Vincent, and John Zaller. 1990. "Measuring individual differences in like fluwui ui newb reception." Paper given at the annual meeting of the American Political Science Association, San Francisco.
Pringle, Peter. 1982. "Disarming proposals." *New Republic,* April 21, pp. 15–17.
Rao, R., and R. Miller. 1971. *Applied Econometrics.* Belmont, Calif.: Wadsworth.
Rasinski, Kenneth. 1989. "The effect of question wording on support for government spending." *Public Opinion Quarterly,* 53, 388–94.
Rhine, R., and L. Severance. 1970. "Ego-involvement, discrepancy, source credibility, and attitude change." *Journal of Personality and Social Psychology,* 16, 175–90.
Rivers, Douglas. 1988. "Heterogeneity in models of electoral choice." *American Journal of Political Science,* 32, 737–57.
Roeder, Philip. 1985. "Dissent and electoral avoidance in the Soviet Union." Presented at the annual meeting of American Political Science Association, New Orleans.
    1989. "Modernization and participation in the Leninist developmental strategy." *American Political Science Review,* 83, 859–4.
Rokeach, Milton. 1973. *The Nature of Human Values.* New York: Free Press.
Ryszka, Franisek (ed.). 1987. *Kultura Polityczna Spoleczenstwa Polskiego (1983–1985)* [The Political Culture of Polish Society]. Warsaw: University of Warsaw.
Schell, Jonathon. 1982. *The Fate of the Earth.* New York: Avon.
Schuman, Howard, and Stanley Presser. 1981. *Questions and Answers in Attitude Surveys,* New York: Wiley.
Schuman, Howard, and Jacqueline Scott. 1987. "Problems in the use of survey questions to measure public opinion." *Science,* 236, 957–9.
Schuman, Howard, Charlotte Steeh, and Larry Bobo. 1985. *Racial Attitudes in America.* Cambridge, Mass.: Harvard University Press.
Sears, David, and J. Freedman. 1967. "Selective exposure to information: A critical review." *Public Opinion Quarterly,* 23: 194–213.
Seligman, Clive, Russell Fazio, and Mark Zanna. 1980. "Effects of salience and extrinsic rewards on liking and loving." *Journal of Personality and Social Psychology,* 38, 453–60.
Sheatsley, Paul. 1966. "White attitudes toward the Negro." *Daedalus,* 95, 217–38.
Shipler, David. 1986. "Poll shows confusion on aid to the Contras." *New York Times,* April 15, p. A6.
Sidanius, James 1988. "Political sophistication and political deviance." *Journal of Personality and Social Psychology,* 55, 37–51.
Sigal, Leon. 1973. *Reporters and Officials.* Lexington, Mass.: D.C. Health.
Sigelman, Lee, and Pamela Conover. 1981. "Knowledge and opinions about the Iranian crisis: A reconsideration of three models." *Public Opinion Quarterly,* 45, 477–91.
Smith, Eric R. A. N. 1989. *The Unchanging American Voter.* Berkeley: University of California Press.
Smith, M. B., J. Bruner, and R. W. White. 1956. *Opinions and Personality.* New York: Wiley.
Smith, Tom W. 1984. "Non-attitudes: A review and evaluation." In Charles Turner and Elizabeth Martin (eds.), *Surveying Subjective Phenomena,* 2 (pp. 215–55). New York: Russell Sage Foundation.

Sniderman, Paul. 1975. *Personality and Democratic Politics.* Berkeley: University of California Press.

Sniderman, Paul, Richard Brody, and James Kuklinski. 1991. "The principle–policy puzzle: The paradox of American racial attitudes." In Sniderman, Brody, and Tetlock, *Reasoning and Choice* (ch. 4). Cambridge: Cambridge University Press.

Sniderman, Paul, Richard Brody, and Philip Tetlock. 1991. *Reasoning and Choice.* Cambridge: Cambridge University Press.

Sobel, Richard. 1989. "The Polls: U.S. intervention in El Salvador and Nicaragua." *Public Opinion Quarterly,* 53, 114–28.

Stimson, James. 1975. "Belief systems, constraint and the 1972 election." *American Journal of Political Science,* 19, 393–417.

Stoker, Laura. 1990. "Judging presidential character: The demise of Gary Hart." Paper given at the annual meeting of the American Political Science Association, San Francisco.

Stokes, Donald. 1966. "Some dynamic elements of contests for the president." *American Political Science Review,* 60, 19–28.

Stouffer, Samuel. 1954. *Communism, Conformity, and Civil Liberties.* New York: Wiley.

Sullivan, John, James Pierson, and George Marcus. 1981. *Political Tolerance and American Democracy.* Chicago: University of Chicago Press.

Sussman, Barry. 1986. "Do Blacks approve of Reagan? It depends on who's asking." *Washington Post,* weekly edition. February 10.

Taylor, Shelly E., and Susan Fiske. 1978. "Salience, attention, and attribution: Top of the head phenomena." In L. Berkowitz (ed.), *Advances in Social Psychology* (pp. 249–88). New York: Academic Press.

Tesser, Abraham. 1978. "Self-generated attitude change." In L. Berkowitz (ed.), *Advances in Social Psychology* (pp. 289–338). New York: Academic Press.

Tichenor, P. J., G. A. Donohue, and C. N. Olien. 1970. "Mass media flow and differential growth in knowledge." *Public Opinion Quarterly,* 34, 159–70.

Torgerson, Warren. 1958. *Theory and Methods of Scaling.* New York: Wiley.

Tourangeau, Roger, and Kenneth Rasinski. 1988. "Cognitive processes underlying context effects in attitude measurement." *Psychological Bulletin,* 103: 299–314.

Tourangeau, Roger, Kenneth Rasinski, Norman Bradburn, and Roy D'Andrade. 1989. "Carryover effects in attitude surveys." *Public Opinion Quarterly,* 53: 495–524.

Tversky, Amos, and Daniel Kahneman. 1982. "The framing of decisions and the psychology of choice." In Robin Hogarth (ed.), *Question Framing and Response Consistency.* San Francisco: Jossey-Bass.

Westlye, Mark. 1991. *Senate Elections and Campaign Intensity.* Baltimore: Johns Hopkins University Press.

White, G. E. 1976. *The American Judicial Tradition.* New York: Oxford University Press.

Wicklund, Robert A., and Jack Brehm. 1976. *Perspectives on Cognitive Dissonance.* Hillsdale, N.J.: Erlbaum.

Wiley, David, and James Wiley. 1970. "The estimation of measurement error in panel data." *American Sociological Review,* 35, 1122–7.

Wilson, Glenn D. 1983. *The Psychology of Conservatism.* New York: Academic Press.

Wilson, Timothy, Dana S. Dunn, Dolores Kraft, and Douglas Lisle. 1989. "Introspection, attitude change, and attitude-behavior consistency: The disruptive effects of explaining why we feel the way we do." In L. Berkowitz (ed.), *Advances in Social Psychology,* 19: 123–205, Orlando, Fla.: Academic Press.

Wilson, Timothy D., and Sara D. Hodges. 1991. "Attitudes as temporary constructions," In A. Tesser and L. Martin (eds.), *The Construction of Social Judgment.* Hillsdale, N.J.: Erlbaum.

Wilson, Timothy, Dolores Kraft, and Dana S. Dunn. 1989. ''The disruptive effects of explaining attitudes: The moderating effect of knowledge about an attitude object.'' *Journal of Experimental Social Psychology,* 25, 379–400.

Wyckoff, Michael. 1987. ''Measures of attitudinal consistency as indicators of ideological sophistication.'' *Journal of Politics.* 49, 148–68.

Wyer, Robert, and Thomas Srull. 1989. *Memory and Cognition in Their Social Context.* Hillsdale, N.J.: Erlbaum.

Zaller, John. 1984a. ''The Role of Elites in Shaping Public Opinion.'' Unpublished Ph.D. dissertation, University of California, Berkeley.

1984b. ''Toward a theory of the survey response.'' Paper presented at annual meeting of the American Political Science Association, Washington, D.C.

1985. ''Proposal for the measurement of political information.'' Report to the NES Board of Overseers. Center for Political Studies, University of Michigan.

1986. ''Analysis of information items in the 1985 pilot study.'' Report to the NES Board of Overseers. Center for Political Studies, University of Michigan.

1987. ''The diffusion of political attitudes.'' *Journal of Personality and Social Psychology,* 53, 821–33.

1988. ''Vague questions vs. vague minds: Experimental attempts to reduce measurement error.'' Paper given at the annual meeting of the American Political Science Association, Washington, D.C.

1989. ''Bringing Converse back in: Information flow in political campaigns.'' *Political Analysis,* 1, 181–234.

1990. ''Political awareness, elite opinion leadership, and the mass survey response.'' *Social Cognition,* 8, 125–53.

1991. ''Information, values and opinion.'' *American Political Science Review,* 85, 1215–38.

1992. ''Political awareness and susceptibility to elite opinion leadership on foreign policy issues.'' Paper given at the annual meeting of the American Political Science Association, Chicago, Illinois.

Zaller, John, and Stanley Feldman. In press. ''A simple model of the survey response: Answering questions versus revealing preferences.'' *American Journal of Political Science.*

Zaller, John, and Vincent Price. 1990. ''A study in everyday memory: Learning and forgetting the news.'' Paper given at the annual meeting of the Midwestern Political Science Association, Chicago.

Index

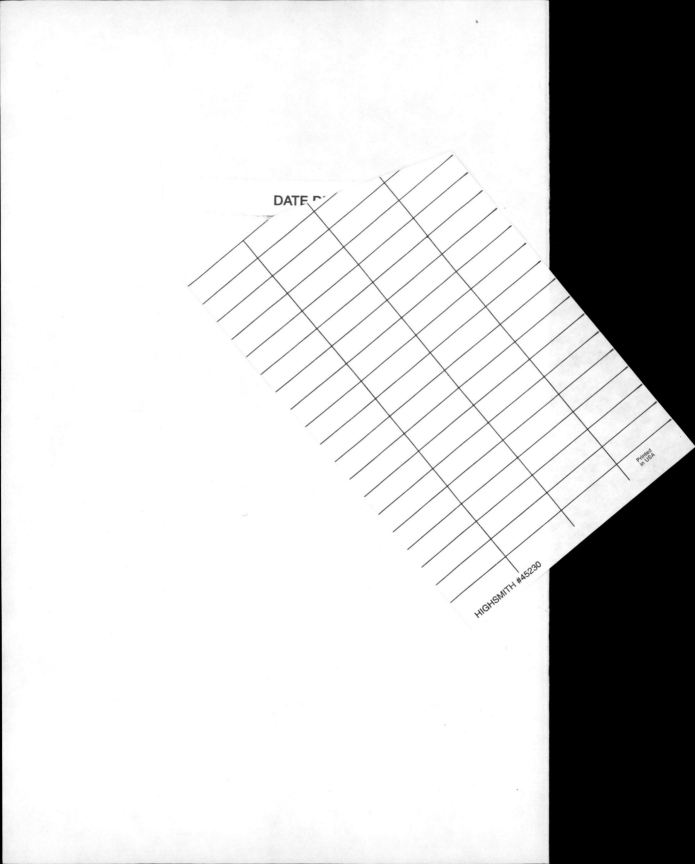

DATE D

HIGHSMITH #45230

Printed
in USA